JUNG`S RED BOOK FOR OUR TIME

Searching for Soul under Postmodern Conditions

Murray Stein
and
Thomas Arzt
Editors

Volume 2

CHIRON PUBLICATIONS • ASHEVILLE, NORTH CAROLINA

© 2018 by Chiron Publications. All rights reserved. No part of this publication may be reproduced, stored in a retrieval system, or transmitted, in any form by any means, electronic, mechanical, photocopying, recording, or otherwise, without the prior written permission of the publisher, Chiron Publications, P.O. Box 19690, Asheville, N.C. 28815-1690.

www.ChironPublications.com

Interior and cover design by Danijela Mijailovic
Printed primarily in the United States of America.

ISBN 978-1-63051-578-2 paperback
ISBN 978-1-63051-579-9 hardcover
ISBN 978-1-63051-580-5 electronic
ISBN 978-1-63051-581-2 limited edition paperback

Library of Congress Cataloging-in-Publication Data Pending

TABLE OF CONTENTS

INTRODUCTION   5
by Murray Stein and Thomas Arzt

CHAPTER 1   13
The Quest for Meaning after God's Death in an Era of Chaos
by Romano Màdera

CHAPTER 2   33
The Return of the Sacred in an Age of Terror
by David Tacey

CHAPTER 3   53
The Red Book as a Religious Text
by Lionel Corbett

CHAPTER 4   71
Blundering into the Work of Redemption
by Ann Belford Ulanov

CHAPTER 5   87
Jung, the Nothing and the All
by John Dourley

CHAPTER 6   109
Abraxas: Then and Now
by J. Gary Sparks

CHAPTER 7   129
The Metamorphosis of the Gods: Archetypal Astrology and
the Transformation of the God-Image in *The Red Book*
by Keiron Le Grice

CHAPTER 8   153
The Way Cultural Attitudes are Developed in Jung's
Red Book – An "Interview"
by John Beebe

CHAPTER 9   171
Integrating Horizontal and Vertical Dimensions of Experience
under Postmodern Conditions
by Gražina Gudaitė

CHAPTER 10   189
On Salome and the Emancipation of Woman in *The Red Book*
    by Joerg Rasche
CHAPTER 11   215
Soul's Desire to become New: Jung's Journey, Our Initiation
    by Kate Burns
CHAPTER 12   231
Aging with *The Red Book*
    by QiRe Ching
CHAPTER 13   247
The Receptive and the Creative: Jung's *Red Book* for
Our Time in Light of Daoist Alchemy
    by Ann Chia-Yi Li
CHAPTER 14   269
The Red Book of C.G. Jung and Russian Thought
    by Lev Khegai
CHAPTER 15   297
India in *The Red Book*: Overtones and Undertones
    by Noa Schwartz Feuerstein
CHAPTER 16   323
A Lesson in Peacemaking: The Mystery of Self-Sacrifice in
The Red Book
    by Günter Langwieler
CHAPTER 17   341
Trickster, His Apocalyptic Brother, and a World's Unmaking:
An Archetypal Reading of Donald Trump
    by Randy Fertel
CHAPTER 18   365
Dreaming *The Red Book* Onward: What Do the Dead Seek Today?
    by Al Collins

BIBLIOGRAPHY   389
ABOUT THE CONTRIBUTORS   407

Introduction

Murray Stein and Thomas Arzt

Lest readers find themselves somewhat confused by the terms in the title of this series, *Jung's Red Book for Our Time: Searching for Soul under Postmodern Conditions*, the editors would like to offer some clarification. The work that was published in 2009 titled *The Red Book: Liber Novus* is actually much more than the work that Jung created and titled *Liber Novus*. As the editor of *The Red Book* explains, in the creation of this work Jung "first recorded [his] fantasies in his *Black Books*. He then revised these texts, added reflections on them, and copied them in a calligraphic script into a book titled *Liber Novus* bound in red leather, accompanied by his own paintings. It has always been known as the *Red Book*."[1] The volume that we now have, which was edited and published with an extensive introduction by Sonu Shamdasani in 2009, includes a facsimile of Jung's own *Liber Novus* plus additional material. Jung left *Liber Novus* unfinished. A considerable amount of material of the edited and reworked text from the *Black Books* was not entered, and this material has been added to the transcribed (and translated) text in the published work. This includes the last chapters of "Liber Secundus" and the section titled "Scrutinies" in the English translation ("Prüfungen" in the original German). To make it clear to readers and to avoid misunderstandings, the editors have chosen to italicize *Red Book*, but not the article preceding, when the author is referring to the book Jung himself created, and to italicize *The Red Book*, with the article, when the author is referring to or quoting from the published work. *Liber Novus* refers to the whole of the work Jung intended but did not finished copying into his *Red Book*.

The other terms in the title that require some explanation and clarification are "our time" and "postmodern conditions." These refer to the same historical period, the time we live in now in the 21st century. In his opening essay in Volume 1, Thomas Arzt offers a thorough discussion of the current understanding of the term "postmodernity" and its meanings in culture studies. The time in which Jung wrote *Liber Novus* is usually referred to as "modernity." The "spirit of the times" that Jung leaves behind when he follows the call of the "spirit of the depths" was the spirit of modernity—rational, scientific, positivistic, irreligious. The "spirit of the times" that we live in today is the spirit of postmodernity—disruptive, confused due to an unbearable acceleration in all venues of life, high-tech, internet-connected and –driven, an *interim* of "ceaseless flux and irresolvable complexity … [and] metaphysical disorientation," as Richard Tarnas has pointed out in his work *Cosmos and Psyche*.[2] Our present "spirit of the times" is arguably even more seductive, persuasive, and all-pervading in the contemporary psyche than was the "spirit of the times" in Jung's age of modernity. On a global level we are more tightly wired together today than people have been collectively at any time previously in human history.

When we asked the authors for this series to reflect on the topic, *Jung's Red Book for Our Time: Searching for Soul under Postmodern Conditions*, we were asking them to bring to our attention how "the spirit of the depths," which called Jung to his journey into and through the inner world and to the incubation and initiation processes that brought him into contact with his soul and transformed him decisively, might be made accessible to us in our times through a deep reading of *Liber Novus*. The concept of "Jung's Red Book for Our Time" is to bring this work and its meaning into our time, into the postmodern time frame. What does Jung's *Liber Novus* have to say to our times? Composed a hundred years ago, it nevertheless has a perennial message. Why? We would argue that it is because it speaks with the voice of "the spirit of the depths."

This brings us to the intriguing question: Who wrote *Liber Novus*? Was it Carl Gustav Jung, resident of Küsnacht/Zurich, psychiatrist in private practice, father of five children and husband of Emma Rauschenbach? Or was it someone else, another personality? Jung speaks famously of Personality No. 1 and Personality No. 2 in *Memories, Dreams, Reflections*,[3] with No. 1 speaking for ego consciousness in all its ages and stages of life and No. 2 for the self.

Toward the end of *Liber Novus*, Jung confesses: "... I knew that Philemon had intoxicated me and given me a language that was foreign to me and of a different sensitivity. ... Probably the most part of what I have written in the earlier part of this book was given to me by Philemon. Consequently I was as if intoxicated."[4] The editor adds an intriguing footnote: "The handwritten manuscript of "Scrutinies" continues: 'and spoken through me.'"[5] It's like the question: Who wrote the Bible? Is it simply the work of many human hands, authors, and redactors from various historical periods, or is the Holy Spirit the hidden author behind the scenes? It makes a difference how you answer this question, for with the answer comes the ability to hear the deeper message of the Bible or not. The same is true in the case of *Liber Novus*. Is this work a reflection of "the spirit of the times" (Jung's modernity), or is it a message from "the spirit of the depths" (timeless and eternal)?

It is significant that the real title of this work is not *The Red Book*. This casual moniker is merely given to the book because of the color of its cover. The actual title, *Liber Novus*—from the ancient Latin and meaning "The New Book"—deliberately plays on the title of the biblical New Testament, as I argued in "How to read *The Red Book*, and why."[6] And as that canonical work did for its time, *Liber Novus* brings a new message from "the spirit of the depths" for the present times, and like its predecessor, it offers a new god-image.

An aura of sacrality hovers over the essays in this second volume in the series *Jung's Red Book for Our Time*. The Italian Jungian psychoanalyst Romano Màdera picks up on the archetypal image of "the quest" in his essay, the quest for meaning in this time of chaos that characterizes the postmodern world we live in. It is a quest not lightly undertaken, as *Liber Novus* so amply illustrates, and the problems in advance of even venturing out on a journey like this are nearly insurmountable. Given the turbulence of the times and the intense seductiveness of the spirit of these times, only the clear-minded and the brave will venture beyond the confines of this culture. But the stakes are high! Meaning itself is the issue, and this is an archetypal need embedded at the base of the psyche. Thus, as David Tacey argues in the essay that follows, "The Return of the Sacred in an Age of Terror," the undeniable hunger for spirituality is also a remarkable feature of our times. New forms of the spiritual quest and the pathways that search for the sacred are explored. The amazing architectural constructions in all parts of the world testify to this drive for transcendence, whether in airports, museums, or shopping centers. Jung's *Liber Novus* is a harbinger of the New Age rendition of the archetypal search for meaning and spiritual awakening.

Lionel Corbett, the well-known author of many books and articles on psychology and spirituality, takes up the challenge of arguing that *Liber Novus* is a religious text and should be considered and studied as such. The thrust of his argument derives from Jung's definitions of "the religious" and his regard for the importance of numinous experiences in one's life. In *Liber Novus*, one can read Jung's testimony to religious experience and the mysteries of the numinous. This theme is picked up in Ann Ulanov's essay, "Blundering into the Work of Redemption," where this author of nearly countless works on psychology and religion over the course of her career as professor at Union Theological Seminary in New York follows Jung's path through *Liber Novus* as he finds his way to his personal myth. There are many lessons for us as we trace Jung's path, and Professor Ulanov is an expert guide through this territory.

John Dourley, noted Canadian Jungian psychoanalyst and professor of theology, ponders some of the deeper theological implications of Jung's thinking as expressed in the stories, images, and reflections of *Liber Novus*. His essay, "Jung, the Nothing and the All," brings into focus the deeply mystical nature of Jung's experiences as recorded in this work. A close reader of *Liber Novus* will be drawn into this depth with the author, Dourley demonstrates, and experiences the dissolution of fixed mental constructs and gains a vision of totality. Following up on Dourley's contribution, J. Gary Sparks, American Jungian psychoanalyst and teacher, throws a bright light on the meaning of the Gnostic figure Abraxas as a symbol of wholeness. In the cosmology of *Liber Novus*, Abraxas is a god who emerges out of the All, the Pleroma, and antedates divisions between the opposites that afflict our culture and cause fierce conflicts to flare up among peoples who project and attack the recipients of their split-off parts. *Liber Novus* helps us to understand this dynamic in ourselves individually and collectively, and perhaps offers a way to hold the opposites together and thus avoid the dread consequences of the splitting apart and identification with only one side of the whole.

Liber Novus has a lot to do with the emergence of a new god-image for our postmodern times. Keiron Le Grice discusses the astrological background and foundations of this emergence of the new god-image that we witness in *The Red Book*. His essay places Jung's work in the big picture of the evolution of human culture and consciousness. John Beebe, eminent Jungian psychoanalyst resident in San Francisco, in turn finds that he can identify the emergence of a religious attitude in Jung in *Liber Novus*, which parallels the birth of a new god-image for Jung personally and for his and our cultures. Beebe's expert analysis of cultural attitudes in *The Red Book* and his exquisite reflections on psychological typology bring the reader to a new insight into how these factors may develop in all of us, also under postmodern conditions. The task at hand is not only, as Lithuanian Jungian psychoanalyst Gražina Gudaitė argues, to leave behind "the spirit of the times" and follow "the spirit of the depths," but eventually also to join them together into a unity. Her practical essay suggests that the goal of our struggles for soul under postmodern conditions must result in action, in offering benefits to the world of the present and the future. This is a call to integration of the two dimensions and with appropriate action following.

In his essay on "On Salome and the Emancipation of Woman in *The Red Book*," noted German Jungian psychoanalyst Joerg Rasche explores the sources of Jung's anima concept. While conceding that the images of the collective unconscious are autonomous and have a life and personality of their own apart from the will and intention of ego consciousness, Rasche argues that Jung's experiences with real women in his life played an important role in shaping his thinking about the anima archetype. Kate Burns, who practices as a Jungian psychoanalyst in Houston, Texas, continues this type of biographical exploration in her essay on initiation themes in *Liber Novus*. In her work, she highlights the element of suffering necessarily woven into the fabric of initiation processes and illustrates this with passages from *Liber Novus*. QiRe Ching, Jungian psychoanalyst and teacher in San Francisco, offers a personal statement about struggles with aging as he has experienced this inevitable process in his life, and he reveals how *Liber Novus* has been a resource for coming to terms with human limitations and finitude.

An essential feature of this series of essays on "Jung's Red Book for Our Time" is its international scope. We asked authors from many different parts of the world to relate *The Red Book* to their cultures. Ann Chia-Yi Li, Taiwanese by birth and currently living and practicing Jungian psychoanalysis in Zurich while also teaching in her native Taiwan and in Singapore, takes up the challenge to look at parallels to Chinese Daoist alchemy and philosophy. This is followed by Lev Khegai's essay on *The Red Book*'s reception in Russia and its resonances with important cultural movements in Russia at the time Jung was composing *Liber Novus*. Noa Schwartz Feuerstein, an Israeli Jungian psychoanalyst, investigates the many threads that tie *The Red Book* to India thematically and spiritually. The reader will be astonished at what she has discovered.

The remaining three essays in this volume consider public, political, and cultural matters of our times and relate them to *Liber Novus*. The German Jungian psychoanalyst Günter Langwieler reflects on how Jung's work provides a lesson in peace-making in the work's prominent themes of self-sacrifice. Randy Fertel, the noted scholar, teacher, and author, brings *Liber Novus* into the fray of American politics by comparing and contrasting Donald Trump and Jung as "tricksters," both of them engaged in improvisation, the theme of Fertel's brilliant study, *A Taste of Chaos*.[7] His conclusions are highly instructive as lessons in how to relate to this important archetypal figure. Finally, Al Collins, a Jungian scholar and clinical psychologist who practices in Anchorage, Alaska, picks up on a crucial theme in *Liber Novus* by asking: What do the Dead seek today? His essay offers a spiritual challenge for our postmodern times.

It is with great pleasure and immense gratitude to the authors of the essays contained in this work that we offer the second volume in this series, *Jung's Red Book for Our Time*, to the public.

Endnotes

[1] Sonu Shamdasani, "Preface," in C.G. Jung, *The Red Book: Liber Novus. A Reader's Edition*, ed. Sonu Shamdasani, trans. John Peck, Mark Kyburz, and Sonu Shamdasani (New York, NY: W. W. Norton, 2012), xi.

[2] Richard Tarnas, *Cosmos and Psyche: Intimations of a New World View* (New York, NY: Viking, 2006), 483.

[3] C.G. Jung, *Memories, Dreams, Reflections*, ed. Aniela Jaffé (New York, NY: Vintage Books, 1963), 33ff.

[4] Jung, *The Red Book*, 483.

[5] Ibid., n42.

[6] Murray Stein, "How to read *The Red Book* and why," *Journal of Analytical Psychology*, 57:3, 2012, 280-298.

[7] Randy Fertel, *A Taste for Chaos: The Art of Literary Improvisation* (New Orleans, LA: Spring Journal Books, 2015).

The Quest for Meaning after God's Death in an Era of Chaos

Romano Màdera

In an exceptionally pregnant passage in his Terry Lectures, Jung presents his diagnosis of our era:

> ... perhaps, we could say with Nietzsche, 'God is dead.' Yet it would be truer to say, 'He has put off our image, and where shall we find him again?' The interregnum is full of danger, for the natural facts will raise their claim in the form of various -isms, which are productive of nothing but anarchy and destruction because inflation and man's hubris between them have elected to make the ego, in all its ridiculous paltriness, lord of universe. That was the case with Nietzsche, the uncomprehended portent of a whole epoch.
>
> The individual ego is much too small, its brain is much too feeble, to incorporate all the projections withdrawn from the world. Ego and brain burst asunder in the effort; the psychiatrist calls it schizophrenia. When Nietzsche said 'God is dead,' he uttered a truth which is valid for the greater part of Europe. People were influenced by it not because he said so, but because it stated a widespread psychological fact. The consequences were not long delayed: after the fog of -isms, the catastrophe. Nobody thought of drawing the slightest conclusions from Nietzsche's pronouncement.[1]

Jung was speaking of the First World War when he referred to the chaos produced by "various -isms," but he gave his Terry Lectures at Yale in 1937, and the augmented edition was published in 1940 during the Second World War!

The tremendous importance of Nietzsche's announcement of God's death demands that we return precisely to his wording in *The Gay Science*. The chapter's title, "The Madman," is itself revealing:

> Have you ever heard of the madman who on a bright morning lighted a lantern and ran to the market-place calling out unceasingly: 'I seek God! I seek God! ... Where is God gone?' he called out. 'I mean to tell you! We have killed him you and I! We are all his murderers! But how have we done it? How were we able to drink up the sea? Who gave us the sponge to wipe away the whole horizon? What did we do when we loosened this earth from its sun? Whither does it now move? Whither do we move? Away from all suns? Do we not dash on unceasingly? Backwards, sideways, forwards, in all directions? Is there still an above and below? Do we not stray, as through infinite nothingness? ... God is dead! God remains dead! And we have killed him! ... Is not the magnitude of this deed too great for us? Shall we not ourselves have to become Gods, merely to seem worthy of it? There never was a greater event and on account of it, all who are born after us belong to a higher history than any history so far!'[2]

Jung's answer in *Psychology and Religion* is clear: We can find in the Christian archetype, as in many other religious traditions, the image of the dying and self-transforming God, and "Christ himself is the typical dying and self-transforming God."[3] The drama of God's death announced by Nietzsche "is anticipated in perfect form"[4] in the life of Christ. Jung continues:

> The psychological situation from which we started is tantamount to 'why seek ye the living among the dead? He is not here' (Luke 24:5f.). But where shall we find the risen Christ?
> ... I am not, however, addressing myself to the happy possessors of faith, but to those many people for whom the light has gone out, the mystery has faded, and God is dead.

… To gain an understanding of religious matters, probably all that is left us today is the psychological approach. That is the way I take these thought-forms that have become historically fixed, try to melt them down again and pour them into moulds of immediate experience …

God's death, or his disappearance, is by no means only a Christian symbol. … Such a wide distribution argues in favour of the universal occurrence of this typical psychic process: the highest value, which gives life and meaning, has got lost. This is a typical experience that has been repeated many times. … The death or loss must always repeat itself: Christ always dies, and always is born; for the psychic life of the archetype is timeless in comparison with our individual time-boundness. According to what laws now one and now another aspect of the archetype enters into active manifestation, I do not know. I only know— and here I am expressing what countless other people know—that the present is a time of God's death and disappearance. The myth says he was not to be found where is body was laid. 'Body' means the outward, the erstwhile but ephemeral setting for the highest value. The myth further says that the value rose again in a miraculous manner, transformed. It looks like a miracle, for, when a value disappears, it always seems to be lost irretrievably. So it is quite unexpected that it should come back. The three days' descent into hell during death describes the sinking of the vanished value into the unconscious, where, by conquering the power of darkness, it establishes a new order, and then rises up to heaven again, that is, attains supreme clarity of consciousness. The fact that only a few people see the Risen One means that no small difficulties stand in the way of finding and recognizing the transformed value.[5]

This passage, which states the difficulty of recognizing the new form of the Risen, is a cryptic reference to the last chapter of the Gospel of Mark, where the writer says that he appeared to the disciples "in another form." This mythic process is therefore the context in which Nietzsche's dramatic narration of the death of God should be placed. *The Red Book* directly expresses the thought that the death of God signifies the loss of sense and higher value. The book itself, along with its paratext (the miniatures and the ornate Gothic script and the dimensions and the preciousness of the cover), resembles a medieval illuminated manuscript, and it is not without meaning that it opens with four biblical quotations. These are followed by a dramatization of the ventures of "sense" (*Sinn*), opposed by "countersense" (*Widersinn*) and "nonsense" (*Unsinn*), and their conjunction in "supreme meaning" (*Übersinn*).[6] Jung's terminology here is molded on and against Nietzsche's, while Nietzsche's "Superman" here becomes "supreme meaning."

My thesis is simple. It follows from the conclusion of the synthesis among *The Red Book*, Nietzsche and *Psychology and Religion*: "Sense" stands for the old dying God, "countersense" for the criticism that deposes and annihilates him, "nonsense" for the result of this conflict, and "supreme meaning" for the reappearance of God in a different form capable of containing sense and nonsense in the complexity of the relation between the opposites, united but still also distinct within the process of which they are dynamic functions.

Nietzsche proclaimed the advent of the Superman, "the sense of the earth," against Christianity and Greek philosophy from Socrates onward in his unilateral, emphatic reconstruction of these great stories irreducible to formulas. In the third chapter of *Thus Spake Zarathustra's* "Prologue" (in Thomas Common's translation, the one used by Jung in his seminars about this text),[7] Nietzsche writes: "I teach you the Superman! The Superman is the meaning of the earth. Let your will say: the Superman shall be the meaning of the earth!"[8] This passage shows how sense is the heir of the dead God, but this time it is the sense of the earth, the sense of this world and not the other, not of a world beyond, which is an image of the miserable illusion of the weak, of resentment, of "slaves." This can be seen as a necessary reaction against the widespread decay and hypocrisy dominating Christian churches as well as against the anemic intellectualization of philosophy by universities. Jung often reminds us that Nietzsche, like himself, was the son of a Protestant pastor, meaning that his reaction to a suffocating atmosphere at home and to empty formulaic doctrine was inevitable. Jung's interpretation of Nietzsche's message is aware of the reactive movement that obliges those who experience the death of their God to find a substitute: They make gods of themselves, a self-inflation through a partial identification with the god-image. From this point of view, Nietzsche's doctrine and his life, which led him to this same kind of insanity, run parallel. The exaltation of the earth is compensatory and unconscious: both in the text's images—the incongruous flight of the eagle with the serpent tied around its neck that unwillingly shows an absurd position for the serpent—and in its ideas, the sense of the earth is precisely what Nietzsche is missing, notwithstanding his prophetic proclamations. This fault is the key to Jung's criticism of Nietzsche in *The Red Book*.

The chapter titled "The Way of the Cross" is one of the more melodramatic parts of the book, and in it Nietzsche's Zarathustra is continuously evoked and recognized as having an unconscious identification with the crucified, which is dominated by a violent rage. He who aspired to be a prophet of the earth was left without earth under his feet. In this chapter we can find everything essential about the relationship of Nietzsche with the death of God:

> I saw the black serpent, as it wound itself upward around the wood of the cross. It crept into the body of the crucified and emerged again transformed from his mouth. It had become white. It wound itself around the head of the dead one like a diadem, and a light gleamed above his head, and the sun rose shining in the east. I stood and watched and was confused and a great weight burdened my soul. But the white bird that sat on my shoulder spoke to me: 'Let it rain, let the wind blow, let the waters flow and the fire burn. Let each thing have its development, let becoming have its day.'
>
> 2. Truly, the way leads through the crucified, that means through him to whom it was no small thing to live his own life, and who was therefore raised to magnificence. He did

not simply teach what was knowable and worth knowing, he lived it. It is unclear how great one's humility must be to take it upon oneself to live one's own life. The disgust of whoever wants to enter his own life can hardly be measured. Aversion will sicken him. He makes himself vomit. ... He would rather devise any trick to help him escape, since nothing matches the torment of one's own way. ...

3. He who goes to himself, climbs down. Pathetic and ridiculous forms appeared to the greatest prophet who came before this time, and these were the forms of his own essence. He did not accept them, but exorcized them before others. Ultimately, however, he was forced to celebrate a Last Supper with his own poverty and to accept these forms of his own essence out of compassion, which is precisely that acceptance of the lowest in us. But this enraged the mighty lion, who ceased down the lost and restored it to the darkness of the depths. And like all those with power, the one with the great name wanted to erupt from the womb of the mountain like the sun. But what happened to him? His way led him before the crucified and he began to rage. He raged against the man of mockery and pain because the power of his own essence forced him to follow precisely this way as Christ had done before us. Yet he loudly proclaimed his power and greatness. No one speaks louder of his power and greatness than he from whom the earth disappears under his feet. Ultimately the lowest in him got to him, his incapacity, and this crucified his spirit, so that, as he himself had predicted, his soul died before his body.[9]

The sacrifice of oneself, identifiable in theoretical form in Jung's earlier book *Wandlungen und Symbole der Libido* (*The Psychology of the Unconscious* in the 1916 translation), is effected here by means of a dialectic of renewal with the dying Christian symbol. As Shamdasani writes in his comment on the obvious structural similarities between *The Red Book* and *Thus Spake Zarathustra*: "…whereas Zarathustra proclaimed the death of God, *Liber Novus* depicts the rebirth of God in the soul."[10]

The other form of the Risen that appears to Jung contains in itself all the transformations needed to revive the Christ-Symbol.[11] The metamorphosis includes the active role of the serpent, the chthonic symbol par excellence, but the announcement is made by the white bird—this pair has a story of its own in the images of the *Liber Novus*—who is a symbol for the soul dimension and in Christian iconography for the Holy Spirit. However, and most importantly, the criticism toward Nietzsche is meant to underline the illusory nature of the overturning of his image of the divine. As shown in the final episodes of *Zarathustra*, in which ordinary life, everyday needs, and acceptance of what is common and devalued by the intelligence of the spirit aristocracy are despised, no conjunction between high and low actually happens, and the shadow is excluded from the prophetic mania. Moreover, and this will tragically and symptomatically show up in his "madness letters" sometimes signed "Dionysus the Crucified," the unconscious identification with the rejected Christ and the return of the repressed had a devastating effect on the philosopher's mental balance. Jung, on the other hand, insists on the acceptance of the lowest and the most despised as the *conditio sine qua non* of every possible answer to the death of God and hence of every possible path toward individuation and a relation with the self. A passage in *Liber Primus* reads as follows:

> The spirit of this time in me wanted to recognize the greatness and extent of the supreme meaning, but not its littleness. The spirit of the depths, however, conquered this arrogance, and I had to swallow the small as a means of healing the immortal in me. It completely burnt up my innards since it was inglorious and unheroic. It was even ridiculous and revolting. But the pliers of the spirit of the depths held me, and I had to drink the bitterest of all draughts.[12]

Unlike in Nietzsche, one could say, the supreme sense must remain aware of its ineradicable communion with the essence of the "worm." In the third paragraph of the "Prologue" of *Thus Spake Zarathustra*, the announcer of the death of God urges men to get rid of their commonality with the "worm": "Ye have made your way from the worm to man, and much within you is still worm."[13]

How far from Jung! The *Liber Novus* begins with a quotation from Isaiah announcing the prophecy of the man of sorrows: "He was despised and rejected of men; a man of sorrows, and acquainted with grief: and we hid as it were our faces from him; he was despised, and we esteemed him not."[14] In Christian interpretations of the Bible, this is a prophecy of the passion of Jesus.[15] This is very close to what Job says of himself: "And though after my skin worms destroy this body, yet in my flesh shall I see God."[16] In the final episodes of *Liber Novus*, Philemon forms a sort of syllogism: The worm and the serpent are equal, they are the devil; Christ is like the serpent; Christ and Satan are brothers.

> ... Philemon answered, 'I know only one thing, that whoever hosts the worm also needs his brother. What do you bring me, my beautiful guest? Lamentation and abomination were the gift of the worm. What will you give us?'
>
> The shade answered, 'I bring you the beauty of suffering. That is what is needed by whoever hosts the worm.'[17]

I think that is a great intuition for our times and for times to come. The dialectic of *enantiodromia* overturns the relationship between Christ and Satan: Now Christ will be the shadow of an age of culture that can no longer recognize the beauty of suffering. We deny the presence of the devil and project evil on ever different scapegoats.

In the quote above Jung says: "He who goes to himself climbs down." That is a translation of *"steigt hinunter,"* that is to say: You have to climb, but down. This phrase echoes Paul's rhetoric in the famous passage in *The Epistle to the Philippians*, which declares that Christ "emptied himself, taking the form of a servant,"[18] where "emptied himself" translates the Greek word *kenosis*. This is a movement in the opposite direction of Nietzsche's Superman, in the sense of opposing his unilateralism. Jung's response could be formulated as follows: Nietzsche has forgotten that to ascend to the Superman, he must descend below the man and recognize himself in the worm. He lacks the "extreme humility" that is needed to reach himself.[19] In other words, the way lies through the shadow and the necessary killing of the hero. Retranslated in the images of the Christian myth, after his death, the hero must go through hell. Jung writes at the beginning of the sixth chapter of *Liber Primus,* "Splitting of the Spirit": "I cried: 'To journey to Hell means to become Hell oneself.'"[20] This reminds me of another verse of Paul: "For our sake he made him to be sin."[21] The journey to Hell is for Jung above all other mythical descents to the underworld the journey of Christ: "Therefore after his death Christ had to journey to Hell, otherwise the ascent to Heaven would have become impossible for him. Christ first had to become his Antichrist, his underworldly brother."[22] The descent to Hell, the resurrection and the ascent to Heaven achieve their completeness in the Pentecost and its consequences: "The continuing, direct operation of the Holy Ghost on those who are called to be God's children implies, in fact, a broadening process of incarnation. Christ, the Son begotten by God, is the first-born who is succeeded by an ever-increasing number of younger brothers and sisters."[23] That means, as Jung writes in the last page of *Answer to Job*:

> ... the indwelling of the Holy Ghost, the third Divine Person, in man, brings about a Christification of many, and the question arises whether these many are all complete God-men. Such a transformation would lead to in-sufferable collisions between them, to say nothing of the unavoidable inflation to which the ordinary mortal, who is not freed from original sin, would instantly succumb. In these circumstances it is well to remind ourselves of St. Paul and his split consciousness: on one side he felt he was the apostle directly called and enlightened by God, and, on the other side, a sinful man who could not pluck out the 'thorn in the flesh' and rid himself of the Satanic angel who

plagued him. That is to say, even the enlightened person remains what he is, and is never more than his own limited ego before the One who dwells within him, whose form has no knowable boundaries, who encompasses him on all sides, fathomless as the abysms of the earth and vast as the sky.[24]

The "Christification of many"[25] was precisely what Jung perceived by intuition many years earlier already during his *Red Book* period, linking "the man of sorrows" of Isaiah to Christ and to the necessity of becoming Christ, realizing the Christification but at the same time avoiding the inflation subsequent to the death of God as in Nietzsche's case. In his *Red Book* he wrote:

> Your God should not be a man of mockery, rather you yourself will be the man of mockery. You should mock yourself and rise above this. If you have still not learned this from the old holy books, then go there, drink the blood and eat the flesh of him who was mocked and tormented for the sake of your sins, so that you totally become his nature, deny his being-apart-from-you; you should be he himself, not Christians but Christ, otherwise you will be of no use to the coming God.[26]

In Christian symbolism this is the equivalent of individuation already expressed in *The Red Book* with these words: "*There is only one way and that is your way.*"[27] After the era of imitation, individuation is clearly connected with the images of the Christian Pentecost:

> Imitation was a way of life when men still needed the heroic prototype. ... Human apishness has lasted a terribly long time, but the time will come when a piece of that apishness will fall away from men.
> That will be a time of salvation and the dove, and the eternal fire, and redemption will descend.[28]

A white dove appears in a dream recounted by Jung in *Memories, Dreams, Reflections* transforming into a little girl and then re-transforming herself into a dove.[29] The dream follows the famous question that Jung asked himself about the myth in which man, and he himself, lives nowadays. The answer, as we know, was that he no longer lived in the Christian myth. But around Christmas 1912, he had the dream of the girl-dove, in which possible amplifications connect to the *Tabula Smaragdina*, to Hermes Trismegistos, and to alchemy. It becomes necessary to find a new answer to the death of God—or to the 12 dead of the dream (obviously this reminds us of the *Seven Sermons to the Dead,* which he privately printed in 1916). An answer that might be announced by the dove,[30] and we know that according to Jung, the Annunciation to Mary is a good symbol of what may happen in analysis.[31] Surely, the dove of the dream announced the process that led him to the visions of the *Red Book* one year later. In "A Psychological Approach to the Dogma of the Trinity," the Holy Ghost is a *complexio oppositorum* that "gave rise to various heretical movements" and "the dual aspect of the 'Father' should reappear in the Holy Ghost, who in this way effects an apocatastasis of the Father."[32] An *apocatastasis* is a reabsorption of evil, even of Satan, into the last transformation, the apocalypse, the revelation of the complete realization of the *opus* of God in the new creation according to Origen, quoted by Jung on the same page. This was also Jung's interpretation of the prophecy of the Trinitarian stage in the works of Joachim of Fiore. This is a historical and, at the same time eschatological, realm that is for Jung a combination of Origen and Joachim and might be understood psychologically as the need to complete the Christian Trinity with the fourth element (earth, the feminine, and evil). The feminine aspect was originally present in the Holy Spirit and its symbols, including the dove, the animal also sacred to Aphrodite.

It is well-known that Jung conceived the idea of the *incarnatio continua* and that he discussed it with scholars such as Victor White, Erich Neumann, and others, but a decisive source for his intuitions was the medieval figure of the Abbot Joachim of Fiore. The god-image and the development of consciousness and responsibility in human history are deeply rooted in what the Catholic, Orthodox, and heretical tradition in different ways attribute to the reception and the action of the "Holy Spirit." To understand our present, according to Jung, we have to understand what is happening unconsciously, in an effort to reconcile and to reunite the opposites revealed by the archetypal image of the Holy Spirit and its relation to the future. In volume 11 of Jung's *Collected Works*, which is dedicated to the topic of "Psychology and Religion," we do not find any mention of Joachim of Fiore, but Jung quotes him in *Aion*[33] and in a very important letter to Victor White[34] where he assumes that Joachim glimpsed intuitively the passage from the symbol of Christ to a more complete image of God through the third state of the revelation, which is the stage of the Holy Spirit: "the *adventus diaboli* does not invalidate the Christian symbol of the self, on the contrary it complements it—it is the mysterious transformation of both."[35] Jung's interpretation of Joachim of Fiore is far from being persuasive, surely not philologically, but that is not the point for us. The point is that Jung searched for a bridge to connect the ancient and medieval Christian tradition of the Holy Spirit to our times and to our lack of transcendence, that is, psychologically translated, to our lack of meaning.[36]

According to Jung, the historical and psychological significance of these archetypal events would be to achieve a complex unification of opposites, of good and evil in human consciousness. Otherwise, projections of evil on the other will eventually lead to an era of "universal genocide."[37] In this sense, the prophecy of Joachim of Fiore of the coming age of the Holy Spirit would have been an unconscious intuition of an era of reconciliation.[38]

A member of the ecumenical group of Marburg, inspired by Rudolf Otto, was Ernst Benz, a lecturer at Eranos from 1953 until 1978. We could say that the tradition of the Holy Spirit was carried on by Benz as a disciple and successor of Buonaiuti.[39] Among his many contributions at Eranos, I have chosen *Norm und Heiliger Geist in der Geschichte des Christentums*[40] ("Norm and Holy Spirit in the History of Christianity"), because I think that it contains the summing-up of his thought about this issue and has much to say to the present as well.

> I tried to examine firstly this typical ambivalent utterance of the Holy Spirit, and I would like to summarize this ambivalence in two antithetical sentences:
> The Holy Spirit creates norm, creates rights:
> The Holy Spirit blows up existing norms, blows up existing rights.
> We could also say:
> The Holy Spirit is a Spirit of order
> The Holy Spirit is a Spirit of revolution.[41]

In these four sentences are condensed the manifold researches of this great scholar of the history of the role of the Holy Spirit in the Church, and they seem to me to correspond to the conceptual formulation of Jung's idea of the Holy Spirit as a union of opposites from the point of view of depth psychology. This could also be a historical transposition of the theological idea of the continuing incarnation (*incarnatio continua*) that Jung shared with Meister Eckhart.[42]

> The Holy Spirit creates norms because of its authority and its internal legitimacy. But where these norms are an outer shell, which threatens to encrust the life of the Spirit, then he breaks the crust and creates new forms where he can realize his life in a more suitable and free way. Creating norms and blasting them, he ultimately remains the Spiritus creator and the only certain prayer of Christians can be:
> *Veni Creator Spiritus!*
> (Come Holy Ghost, come back to us!)[43]

If this invocation could be meaningful for a Christian who is faced with the institutional sclerosis of many churches, it might seem of scarce significance for the diagnosis of the actual condition of the Western spirit. But we can argue that the Holy Spirit is the symbolical equivalent in the Christian tradition of the possible development of different and deeper discernments of the necessary changes. Today it is clear that the opposites of norms and changes, tradition and innovation, order and freedom, solidarity and individuality, etc., are at war with one another since the end of the 19th century. We could name this process the end and fall of patriarchy, understood as a long-lasting historic-cultural constellation whose slow crisis goes back to the foundations of the modern world and capitalism. It is enough to perceive the profound connection between the patriarchal structures and those of the Christian churches, especially Catholic and Orthodox. Remember the terminology: God the Father, the Holy Father, the Pope (etymologically deriving from a Greek term for "dad"), the patriarchs, the fathers in religious orders. It is hard to deny that there was a sort of identification between the culture of patriarchy and the institution of the Christian churches. At the same time, the concept of God and his image became the concept and symbol of immutability of being and of moral laws. Nietzsche's formula, "God is dead," found a great resonance exactly because of this: It summarizes the end of the trustworthiness of every idea and value depending on these traditional patriarchal assumptions. The spiritual war against the foundation of "all that is solid" was won: actually, it "has melted into air," as Marx says in the *Manifesto of the Communist Party*, a quote used by Marshall Berman for the title of his book about "the experience of modernity."[44] But no new order is in sight, no new balance between the opposites of tradition and innovation, norms and changes. A universal lack of meaning seems to be spreading epidemically in our world. As Adolf Portmann and Rudolf Ritsema, the editors of the *Eranos Jahrbuch* of 1974, wrote in their "Preface": "the word 'norm' [and] the problems it raises touch on the very foundation of contemporary social life, which, more than any before it, queries authority of the past."[45] I guess it is not a mere coincidence that the first essay of that yearbook was Gershom Scholem's, "Der Nihilismus als Religiöses Phänomen" ("Nihilism as Religious Phenomenon"). He wrote: "Nietzsche in 'The Will to Power' proclaimed that nihilism 'the most uncanny of all guests' is standing at the door, now this guest came in and has made enough space for himself at the very table that he should have overthrown."[46]

But because humankind cannot survive without any image of orientation, that is, without any meaning, I would conjecture that meaning in our time, in postmodernity, seems to be represented by the word-picture of Chaos.[47] The new norm, the new order, is living without real norms and values, in an environment of ever-changing norms, ideas, values, and tastes. The ferocious reaction against this overthrow of all traditions is the contemporary fundamentalist wave of violence. We need a new balance, and Europe might offer a decisive contribution to a new culture of equilibrium due to its experience of the two world wars on its territory. Unfortunately, the creative urge to union is now quenched by a spiritual and political atmosphere of particular interests, anachronistic nationalism, and suffocating bureaucracy. Our hopes about the European Spirit have become feeble, almost dead. On the contrary, the Roman Catholic Church, the most traditional and sclerotic patriarchal institution surviving in the modern world, after the Second Vatican Council and especially now after the election of Pope Francis, seems to be revived by the breath of the Spirit. Here I would like only to recall Pope Francis's cry: the rejection of migrants fleeing violence is "an act of war." Speaking to a youth group, he said the situation where desperate migrants were bounced from country to country seeking shelter was "an unresolved conflict … and this is war, this is violence, it's called murder."[48] This is the voice of the ancient prophet, the voice of the Spirit warning political institutions and all of us to try to stop "the universal genocide" that continues to extend itself, inch by inch, under the eyes of the blind powers of this world.[49]

Endnotes

[1] C.G. Jung, "Psychology and Religion," in *CW*, vol. 11 (Princeton, NJ: Princeton University Press, 1969), pars. 144-145.

[2] Friedrich Nietzsche, *The Gay Science*, trans. Thomas Common (New York, NY: Dover Mineola, 2006), 168.

[3] Jung, "Psychology and Religion," *CW* 11, par. 146.

[4] Ibid.

[5] Ibid., pars. 147-149.

[6] C.G. Jung, *The Red Book: Liber Novus*, ed. Sonu Shamdasani, trans. John Peck, Mark Kyburz, and Sonu Shamdasani (New York, NY: W.W. Norton, 2009), 229.

[7] C.G. Jung, *Nietzsche's Zarathustra. Notes of the Seminar Given in 1934-1939*, 2 vols. (Princeton, NJ: Princeton University Press, 1988).

[8] Friedrich Nietzsche, *Thus Spake Zarathustra*, trans. by Thomas Common (Edinburgh and London: T.N. Foulis, 1909), 6.

[9] Jung, *The Red Book*, 309-310.

[10] Ibid., 202.

[11] About the differentiation of Christianity, Christendom, Christianness and "christic epiphany" see Raimon Panikkar, "Christianity. The Christian Tradition," in *Opera Omnia*, Vol. III, part I (New York, NY: Orbis Book, 2015).

[12] Jung, *The Red Book*, 230.

[13] Nietzsche, *Thus Spake Zarathustra*, 6.

[14] *Isaiah* 53:3. King James Version of The Bible.

[15] In his outstanding guide to Jung's *Red Book*, Sanford L. Drob follows Walter Odajnyk, who interprets the first quotation of Isaiah as concerning the nature of Jung's prophetic calling, but in doing so he fails to recognize the profound resonance with the differentiation from Nietzsche's idea of Superman and with the Jungian positive transformation of the symbol of the crucified. See Sanford L. Drob, *Reading the Red Book. An Interpretative Guide to C.G. Jung's Liber Novus* (New Orleans, LA: Spring Journal Books, 2012), 2 and V. Walter Odajnyk, "Reflections on 'The Way of What is to Come,'" *Psychological Perspectives* 53:4 (October 2010): 437-454.

[16] *Job* 19:26. King James Version of The Bible.

[17] Jung, *The Red Book*, 359.

[18] *Philippians* 2:7. Revised Standard Version of The Bible.

[19] Jung, *The Red Book*, 234.

[20] Ibid., 240.

[21] *2 Corinthians* 5: 21.

[22] Jung, *The Red Book*, 243.

[23] C.G. Jung, *Answer to Job*, in *CW*, vol. 11 (Princeton, NJ: Princeton University Press, 1969), par. 658.

[24] Ibid., par. 758.

[25] This expression could remind us of the central tenet of the Orthodox faith, that is *theosis*, literally "deification," yet "Jung constantly commented on the limitations of Christianity but the Christianity he considered was the reality of Western Christian denominations. It is incredible that he ignored the entire tradition of the Christian East, the Eastern Orthodox Church." Renos K. Papadopoulos, "The other other: when the exotic other subjugates the familiar other," *Journal of Analytical Psychology* 47, 2002, 175.

[26] Jung, *The Red Book*, 234.

[27] Ibid., 231.

[28] Ibid., 245.

[29] At the beginning of the sixth chapter, "Confrontation with the Unconscious," of *Memories, Dreams, Reflections*, ed. Aniela Jaffé (New York, NY: Vintage Books, 1963), 170ff., Jung writes: "I had written a book about the hero, the myth in which man has always lived. But in what myth does man live nowadays? In the Christian myth the answer might be 'Do *you* live in it?' I asked myself. To be honest, the answer was no. ... 'Then we no longer have any myth?' 'No, evidently we no longer have any myth.' 'But then what is *your* myth—the myth in which you do live?' At this point the dialogue with myself became uncomfortable, and I stopped thinking. I had reached a dead end. Then, around Christmas of 1912, I had a dream. ... I was sitting on a gold Renaissance chair; in front of me was a table of a rare beauty. It was made of green stone like emerald. ... Suddenly a white bird descended, a small sea gull or a dove. Gracefully it came to rest on a table, ... Immediately, the dove was transformed into a little girl, about eight years of age, with golden blond hair. She ran off with the children and played with them among the colonnades of the castle. ... Then she suddenly vanished; the dove was back and spoke slowly in a human voice. 'Only in the first hours of the night can I transform

myself into a human being; while the male dove is busy with the twelve dead."

[30] See Greg Mogenson, *The Dove in the Consulting Room. Hysteria and the Anima in Bollas and Jung* (London: Routledge, 2004).

[31] In the *Seminar* given in 1925, Jung said that if he would have chosen to symbolize the analytical experience, the Annunciation seemed to him the most appropriate, see C.G. Jung, *Analytical Psychology. Notes of the Seminar given in 1925*, ed. W. McGuire (Princeton, NJ: Princeton University Press, 1991), 111.

[32] C.G. Jung, "A Psychological Approach to the Dogma of the Trinity," in *CW*, vol. 11 (Princeton, NJ: Princeton University Press, 1969), par. 279.

[33] C.G. Jung, *Aion. Researches into the Phenomenology of the Self*, in *CW*, vol. 9/II (Princeton, NJ: Princeton University Press, 1959), pars. 137-141.

[34] In a letter to Father Victor White from November 24, 1953 (Gerhard Adler, *C. G. Jung Letters*. Trans. by R. F. C. Hull. Vol. 2, 1951-1961 (Princeton, NJ: Princeton University Press, 1975)) Jung writes that the union of opposites, Christ and Satan, good and evil, will be realized in "the Oneness of the Holy Spirit," in a future age already described by Joachim of Fiore (1132-1202) as the age of the Spirit.

[35] Ibid., 136.

[36] "It seems to me that, side by side with the decline of religious life, the neuroses grow noticeably more frequent. ... of one thing I am sure, that everywhere the mental state of European man shows an alarming lack of balance. We are living undeniably in a period of the great restlessness, nervous tension, confusion, and disorientation of outlook. Among my patients from many countries, all of them educated persons, there is a considerable number who came to see me not because they are suffering from a neurosis but because they could find no meaning in their lives or were torturing themselves with questions which neither our philosophy nor our religion could answer. ... It must be a relief to every serious-minded person to hear that the psychotherapist also does not know what to say. Such a confession is often the beginning of the patient's confidence in him. I have found that modern man has an ineradicable aversion for traditional opinions and inherited truths. He is a Bolshevist for whom all the spiritual standards and forms of the past have somehow lost their validity, and

who therefore wants to experiment with his mind as the Bolshevist experiment with economics," in C.G. Jung, "Psychotherapists or the Clergy," in *CW*, vol. 11 (Princeton, NJ: Princeton University Press, 1969), pars. 514-516.

[37] "Universal genocide" is a quote of Jung (1957) in "Jung and Religious Belief," in *CW*, vol. 18 (Princeton, NJ: Princeton University Press, 1976), par. 1661. John Dourley writes: "Jung warned that humanity's failure to unite the divinely grounded opposites in itself could only lead to 'universal genocide'," (John Dourley, "The Jung-White Dialogue and why it couldn't work and won't go away," in *Journal of Analytical Psychology*, Vol. 52, issue 3 (2006): 275-95).

[38] The *Evangelium Aeternum* is not a work of Joachim; actually the title is *Liber Introductorius in Evangelium Aeternum,* and it was written by Gerardo da Borgo San Donnino, a companion of Giovanni da Parma, John from Parma, general of the Franciscan Order from 1247-1257. "This consisted of Joachim's three main works, together with a *Liber Introductorius* and gloss written by Gerard himself" (Marjorie Reeves, *Joachim of Fiore and the Prophetic Future* (London: SPCK, 1976), 33).

[39] The odd thing is that Buonaiuti and Benz belonged to the opposite sides of the political spectrum: Buonaiuti was an antifascist persecuted by the regime; Benz on the other side was a member of the SA and of the Nazi Party.

[40] Ernst Benz, "Norm und Heiliger Geist in der Geschichte des Christentums," in Rudolf Ritsema and Adolf Portmann, eds., *Norms in Changing World,* Eranos 43-1974 (Leiden: E. J. Brill, 1977), 137-182.

[41] Ibid., 139.

[42] "Since the Holy Ghost is the Third Person of the Trinity and God is present entire in each of the three Persons at any time, the indwelling of the Holy Ghost means nothing less than the approximation of the believer to the status of God's son. One can therefore understand what is meant by the remark 'you are gods' (*John* 10:34)"; see Jung, *Answer to Job*, *CW* 11, par. 656.

[43] Benz, "Norm und Heiliger Geist in der Geschichte des Christentums," 182.

[44] Marshall Berman, *All That Is Solid Melts into Air. The Experience of Modernity* (New York, NY: Verso, 1983).

[45] Portmann and Ritsema, *Norms in a Changing World*. Eranos 43-1974, Introduction.

[46] Gershom Scholem, "Der Nihilismus als Religiöses Phänomen," in Adolf Portmann and Rudolf Ritsema, eds., *Norms in a Changing World*. Eranos 43-1974, 1.

[47] About the image and concept of Chaos in *The Red Book,* see Drob, *Reading the Red Book*, 6, 13, 22-32, 46.

[48] Pope Francis, The Independent, 10 August 2015.

[49] "Why, only now, a pope named Francis?" (Bruce Chilton, in www.bibleinterp.com), this is not an odd question, because Francis of Assisi was not only the popular saint we are used to refer to, but even in his own order by the Franciscans Joachimites he was taken as an emblem of the renewal of the church and the apocalyptic world. The movements of the *"spirituali"* and *"fraticelli"* were accused of heresy. Their prophecy announcing an "angelic pope" who led the Church in the age of the Spirit was echoed at the beginning of the Society of Jesus by some Jesuits, also condemned as heretics (see Reeves, *Joachim of Fiore and the Prophetic Future*). Another curiosity is the sequence of names, from Benedict to Francis: it is a sequence typical of Joachim.

The Return of the Sacred in an Age of Terror

David Tacey

> ... when an inner situation is not made conscious, it happens outside, as fate. ... the world must perforce act out the conflict and be torn into opposing halves.[1]
>
> C.G. Jung

Jung's *Red Book* throws much light on the situation of the sacred in postmodern times. When the sacred returns, it causes disruption to social and personal order. On January 20, 1914, Jung's soul arises from the depths and asks him if he will accept war, destruction, and mayhem.[2] His soul shows him images of military weapons, human remains, sunken ships, and destroyed states. Jung struggles to integrate these images and says he "could not conceive the extent of what was to come." "I felt the burden of the most terrible work of the times ahead."[3] The soul would bring the "unleashing of chaos and its power" and "the binding of chaos." Chief among the gifts of the soul will be "the gift of religion." By *religion*, Jung does not mean membership of a church but "the attitude peculiar to a consciousness which has been changed by experience of the *numinosum*."[4] He means an encounter with the numinous in its most powerful and existential aspect. This "gift," Jung reflects, "is still to come, but it will become evident. I sat up for long nights and looked ahead at what was to come and I shuddered."[5]

We shudder, too, when we survey the landscape of the sacred today and "what is still to come." Our world has grown so far from the sacred that any approach of this reality to us is experienced as terrifying. Not only has our resistance turned the sacred into a hostile force, but the sacred shows its negative face at this time. Rudolf Otto designated the holy as a *mysterium tremendum et fascinans*.[6] It is a mystery that fascinates, but as *tremendum*, it evokes terror because it presents as an ominous, overwhelming power. In a secular age in which the only authority we acknowledge is our human will and desiring, the sacred hovers over us like a cloud. Due to our stance, it is the darkness of the sacred that eclipses its positive and creative elements, and this gives it the complexion of destructiveness.

Hence as the sacred returns, the psychological effect is that our world feels under threat, and there is indeed much that the sacred seeks to dismantle. It has been said that the divine mirrors the face that is turned toward it, and if we denounce the sacred, it will, in turn, adopt a foreboding attitude. As we run away, its pursuit of us will not be seen as loving but we will experience its anger and wrath. We live in an age of terrorism, and this is not without significance to our spiritual situation. Our inner and outer lives have a certain similitude at this time, but few have pointed to this synchronicity—because the prevailing voices are secular and do not look beyond appearances. It takes a symbolic attitude to read the signs of the times for their inward significance. Synchronicity is an acausal connecting principle; I am not saying that the spiritual climate is *causing* terrorism, only that there is a meaningful parallelism.

The sacred today is a complex field in which anger, violence, terrorism, and conflict are intermixed with redemptive possibilities of love, hope, and transformation. The sacred is linked with war and revenge, fundamentalism, moribund doctrines, an epidemic of clerical sexual abuse and loss of belief. Yet in the midst of all this chaos, the sacred is returning. According to the philosopher Jacques Derrida, this is an urgent and pressing reality, and society needs to adjust itself to the new conditions:

> Whatever side one takes in this debate about the 'return of the religious' … one still must respond. And without waiting. Without waiting too long.[7]

Like Derrida, I don't think we have time to procrastinate, as the return of the sacred demands a response, no matter what our beliefs.

When I think of the return of the sacred, images arise of floodwaters in the bed of the Todd River in Alice Springs, Australia, the town in which I grew up. Normally the river is dry, but after storms, the Todd becomes a swirling torrent, but the waters that emerge are not pristine or clear. The floodwaters are dark, muddy, turbulent, and at its head there is a wall of sludge and debris. The waters that emerge later in this desert landscape are less murky, but there is always a sense that the floodwaters remain polluted.

The rising sacred is like this river. Its waters are destined to replenish our lives, but there is an impurity at present. The sacred is a paradoxical and ambivalent reality, associated with as much bad as good. I can see why many have become atheists in the face of this turbulence of violence, wrath, and terrorism. Many don't want to be associated with the sacred, seeing it as the source of evil, as Richard Dawkins, Sam Harris, and Christopher Hitchens have argued.[8] I understand their point of view, and through a certain lens it does seem, as they claim, that the holy is what pollutes and gives a stench of decomposition to our lives.

The new atheists reverse the religious view that the sacred is the source of goodness and light, and evil derives from us and our sinful distortions. Personally, I have always held both views, strange as it may seem. I believe the sacred is the source of goodness and light, but I understand that in our distorted time the sacred is associated with the wall of sludge, debris, and darkness that comes ahead of the flood.

In *Aion*, Jung wrote: "... that the erstwhile symbols no longer express what is now welling up from the unconscious as the end-result of the development of Christian consciousness through the centuries. ... That is what the post-Christian spirit looks like," and he commented that it looks anything other than holy.[9] He said the sacred had been suppressed for so long it had become contaminated with murky contents that have washed through it during its exile in the unconscious. When it returns, it will do so as a torrent, unruly with anger and wrath:

The opening up of the unconscious always means the outbreak of intense spiritual suffering: it is as … when fertile fields are exposed by the bursting of a dam to a raging torrent.[10]

Jung wrote like a prophet when he warned of the continued defilement of the sacred and its consequences in psyche and society:

No wonder the Western world feels uneasy, for it does not know how much it plays into the hands of the uproarious underworld and what it has lost through the destruction of numinosities. It has lost its moral and spiritual values to a very dangerous degree. Its moral and spiritual tradition has collapsed, and has left a worldwide disorientation and dissociation.[11]

This is what the Hebrew prophets said: If the sacred is not nurtured, the uproarious underworld will erupt, contaminating the world with the wrong kind of spirits, leading to a perilous situation. "Our times have demonstrated what it means when the gates of the psychic underworld are thrown open."[12] Jung said that nurturing the sacred has a therapeutic effect and acts as a bulwark against the destructive forces of the unconscious. Elsewhere he personifies the numinous as a wrathful power:

Seeking revenge for the violence his reason has done to her, outraged Nature only awaits the moment when the partition falls so as to overwhelm the conscious life with destruction. Man has been aware of this danger to the psyche since the earliest times, even in the most primitive stages of culture. It was to arm himself against this threat and to heal the damage done that he developed religious and magical practices. This is why the medicine-man is also the priest; he is the saviour of the soul as well as of the body, and religions are systems of healing for psychic illness.[13]

Religions were developed to propitiate the powers that early humanity sensed could overwhelm life and cause destruction. Although Christianity had refined its understanding of the sacred to emphasize its good and gentle aspects, the Jews had a different understanding of the divine, and ferocity was part of its character. Christianity believes that its revelation superseded the Jewish story, but it may be that it lost something integral when it rejected the god-image of the "Old" Testament. In *Exodus*, Yahweh says to the Jews: "I will send my terror before you, and will throw into confusion all the people."[14] In *Proverbs*, Psalms, and the prophetic writings, we see an emphasis on divine wrath, which shocks Christians because they lost touch with this aspect of the numinous.

Centuries before Christianity, the Greeks had a stark comprehension of the destructive face of the divine. This aspect showed itself when people turned away from the sacred and saw themselves as no longer obligated to express reverence to the mystery of life. This condition, which the Greeks called *hubris*, was severely punished by the gods. Greek drama and literature are replete with the terrifying wrath that the Olympian gods delivered to those who had spurned them.[15] Perhaps it is time to reclaim these ancient heritages, Hebraism and Hellenism, which shaped Western culture. While important not to lose sight of the sacred as the source of illumination, which is the hope of Christianity, in a darkly turbulent time in which the sacred is returning after exile, we have to adjust ourselves to the paradoxical nature of divine reality.

There is, however, an alternative way to view this, which does not hinge on speculations about the nature of the divine. Perhaps it is not so much that "God" becomes evil, but that the inward figure within our being, the soul, becomes malign when we fail to connect with the divine. The soul is the "third" thing between humanity and divinity, and its job is to facilitate the connection between heaven and earth. When we neglect to attend to this relation, the soul as the organ of mediation turns awry and opposes our resistance. From where we stand, it looks as if God had taken up arms against us, but it is our soul that stares us down with wrath and terror. The soul "stands in" for the divine in this situation, and perhaps we make a mistake if we assume that this fearsome aspect is the divine itself. We ought not assume that we can behold the face of the Wholly Other or ascribe to it attributes that arise from the intermediary. The true nature of God remains an unfathomable mystery.

The soul, says Rilke, is like a towering angel that stands over against us and yet offers transformation if we surrender to it. The soul is "the beginning of terror which we are barely able to endure / and we are awed because it serenely disdains to annihilate us."[16] "Every angel is terrible, and so I hold myself back and swallow the cry of a darkened sobbing."[17] That, I suspect, is what most of us do; we retreat from the darkness of the soul, swallow our anguish, and refuse engagement. In another poem, Rilke writes that whoever is beaten by the angel emerges strengthened; winning is not what we should seek, but "being defeated decisively, by constantly greater beings" is how we develop as spiritual beings.[18] In the same years that Jung began his *Red Book* (1913-1914), an epic on the soul's eruption in modern times, Rilke was writing poetry on the annihilating and transformative forces that eclipse the ego.

There is something in the epidemic of religiously inspired terrorism that warrants close scrutiny. On the face of it, terrorism has nothing to do with the return of the sacred. In fact, it is a sign of the desacralization of the world and the misuse of religious ideas to serve ideological purposes. Secular commentators offer explanations based on economics, politics, and cultural conditions. But there is a dimension of terrorism that is not being noticed. I do not mean that the jihadists are inspired by God, as they believe, but that there is a symbolic element in their behavior that is important to understand. They are not the deliverers of divine justice or emissaries of the sacred, but carriers of a pathology that has its origins in the religious crisis of our time. There is meaning in terrorism not because of their heinous ideology, but because of what lies behind it.

Sounding like Jung, whom he did not acknowledge, Derrida wrote of the "return of the religious" and defined this as the "coming of the other,"[19] where the "other" refers to everything that is different from the ego. The "explosive force" of the religious, he said, can "interrupt history" and "tear history apart." In this interruption to "the ordinary course of history," we have to "be prepared for the best as for the worst, the one never coming without the possibility of the other."[20] Derrida said religion would return with violence because it had been suppressed with violence. He spoke of religion rising like a tumor in society, because so much had been ignored about our relation to reality. A pressure builds up in the soul, which can explode at any point:

> Religious resurgence imposes itself upon us to suggest the redoubling of a wave that appropriates even that to which, enfolding itself, it seems to be opposed. It gets carried away, sometimes in terror and terrorism. Allying itself with the enemy, hospitable to the antigens, bearing away the other with itself, this resurgence grows and swells with the power of the adversary.[21]

Originally associated with nihilistic postmodernism and still claiming to be an atheist, Derrida was driven to prophecy at the end of his life. How strange, he said, to find "the return of the religious ... not without relation to the return of radical evil." The post-9/11 celebrity atheists would argue that religion and evil are aspects of the same thing, but this is not Derrida's point. His point is that the religious impulse has been made evil by the conditions in which it has been violated. Two thousand years ago, the same point would have been framed in metaphysical terms: We have incurred God's wrath because of our betrayal of him. Many would reject this language today, and yet when we look at the terrorists, we see something of our own unknown face. Their evil expresses the darkness that has built up in the soul.

Europe's leading Lacanian, Slavoj Zizek, made this point after 9/11 and spoke of the West's need to face up to the reality of darkness:

> The American sphere of safety is now experienced by its citizens as being under threat from an Outside of terrorist attackers who are ruthlessly self-sacrificing and cowards, cunningly intelligent and primitive barbarians. Whenever we encounter such a purely evil Outside, we should gather

the courage to remember the Hegelian lesson: in this pure Outside, we should recognize the distilled version of our own essence.[22]

A century before Derrida and Zizek, Jung was making the same pronouncements. In his *Red Book*, Jung wrote of the terror of the First World War:

> But the spirit of the depths wants this struggle to be understood as a conflict in every man's own nature.[23]

Modernity encourages us to live in the confinement of the ego, said Jung, and the soul, excluded and ignored, is forced to develop an ambivalent aspect. The soul arraigns itself against us "… as something which thwarts our will, which is strange and even hostile to us, and which is incompatible with our conscious standpoint."[24] The soul "wants something different from the ego and we are at war with ourselves." He claimed that "… when an inner situation is not made conscious, it happens outside, as fate."[25] To what extent, then, is the scourge of terrorism an externalization of an internal dynamic? Jung said, "the world must perforce act out an inner conflict and be torn into opposing halves."[26] I am not claiming any *causal* connection between our spiritual situation and the world crisis. In synchronicity, "No reciprocal causal connection can be shown to obtain between parallel events. … The only recognizable and demonstrable link between them is a common meaning, or equivalence."[27]

According to Sufi texts, the notion of a "holy war" applies more to the inner than the outer realm. The true meaning of *jihad*, according to Hazrat Inayat Khan, refers to the psychological strife "to overcome the false ego."[28] When returning from battle against the infidels, the Prophet Mohammad said: "We have come back from the lesser Holy War to the Greater Holy War." His companions asked: "What is the Greater Holy War?" Mohammad replied: "The war against the ego."[29] Shahid Athar explains that in Sufi tradition, the ego is the enemy of spirit and conquering the ego's ascendancy is the best form of jihad, allowing the Sufi to be at peace with him- or herself and close to the Creator.[30] According to Thomas Cheetham, terrorists have misunderstood the symbolic nature of their quest and the call for jihad, and are externalizing this battle.[31] Wolfgang Giegerich points out that "it is so much easier to resort to resentment and to blame others for the unsatisfactory conditions one finds oneself in ... than to engage in a long-term struggle, so much easier to act out by detonating bombs than to interiorize, integrate."[32]

It would seem that the misunderstanding of jihad is called forth by the West's refusal to engage with the sacred. The West has become the "infidel" by virtue of its profane existential stance. The sacred has been forced into the role of adversary, of which Derrida and Jung speak. It is significant that the dark aspect of the holy, lost to Christianity, is being picked up by postmodern philosophy and depth psychology, as if to rescue what had been suppressed. Jung said that it is impossible to imagine that religion, which has meant so much to so many across millennia, could disappear without a trace simply because secularism has seemingly taken over. He likened the religious impulse to an instinct, and, "... like every instinct, it has its specific energy, which it does not lose even if the conscious mind ignores it."[33] This instinct would return, like everything unconscious, with considerable force as soon as conditions allow. It would not only return with explosive power, but in distorted forms, since psychic contents take on disruptive aspects when repressed.

Society has broadly accepted Freud's theory that sexuality returns in distorted forms, such as neurosis, hysteria, and criminality, when it is not made conscious in individuals. We have conceded this much to psychoanalysis, but Jung's theory is regarded as suspect because he is dealing with the less tangible reality of the religious impulse. If the "great repressed" was sexuality in Freud's time, it is religion in ours. Religion is the unlived life of modernity. Jung argues that religion will return with devastating consequences, just as sexuality returned with shocking impact in Freud's time. Postmodern philosophers have ignored Jung's work, but what they are saying is identical to his thought of a hundred years ago. Derrida's colleague Gianni Vattimo wrote:

> In spirit, something that we had thought irrevocably forgotten is made present again, a dormant trace is reawakened, a wound re-opened, the repressed returns and what we took to be an overcoming is no more than a long convalescence.[34]

Secularists imagined that spirit had died with the decline of institutional religion. Spirit for them is an obsolete idea that had been defeated by science. But as Vattimo argues, spirit was not overcome but asleep. The "secular turn" put spirit in a state of suspended animation, and the intelligentsia thought humanity had entered a new world. But this was not the case; spirit has been comatose but is now returning. The modern mind has had its spurt of progress and taste of freedom, and now it has to contend with archaic realities in the soul—which cannot be accounted for by secular materialism. As early as the 1950s, Italian philosopher Romano Guardini had made this prescient remark:

> Modern man sought for answers within his soul. Enigmatic powers awoke out of the religious spirit; the force of the numinous impinged itself directly upon the human spirit, either from within the spirit or from the world at large. Not only was the numinous beneficent but also bewildering, even destructive in its impact.[35]

This sense that the sacred can be a destructive force that has to tear apart the secular fabric is found in philosophy, psychology, and poetry. One of the most powerful accounts of this destructivity is found in the work of the Jewish philosopher Emmanuel Levinas, in *God and Philosophy*, where God is imagined as an antagonist who shreds the defensive structures of the ego.[36]

Some thought Jung odd when he announced in 1929 that "the gods have become diseases,"[37] but three generations later, Derrida felt that the "return of the religious" was welling up in the collective mind like a tsunami. Religion, said Derrida, is not something we do, but something that is done to us. It arises from a mysterious source that needs to be explored. Using the language of psychoanalysis, Derrida wrote:

> How can one account for this 'return of the religious' without bringing into play some sort of logic of the unconscious?[38]

Secularism had not taken the unconscious into account. There was unlived life that would blow secularism to smithereens. Secularists assumed that if religion could be denounced, and if science could show that its assertions were wrong, religion would disappear and never return. However, the religious urge is ineradicable, and "... to the degree that we repress it, the danger increases."[39]

Today we witness the rise of fundamentalism in all the religions—Christianity, Judaism, and Islam, and in Hinduism and even Buddhism. We live in a world in which religion and violence have become permanently associated, which is a shocking irony given that the scriptures of all religions preach love and peace.[40] But once the spirit is defiled, it emerges in distorted forms and nothing other than a change of attitude, a new reckoning or covenant, will alter its destructive course. Christopher Koch wrote, "The spirit doesn't die, of course, it turns into a monster."[41] Fragments of the sacred are found in the distorted religious forms of today, and the perpetrators of terror quote passages of scripture as they fly planes into the World Trade Center or attack railways, buses, hotels, concerts, and media outlets. This wrath is not entirely of political origin but has its source in an archetypal disposition. That is why the "war on terror" can never eradicate this violence, because we are not only talking about human carriers of evil but a predisposition to evil in the psyche itself.

But it is not as if terrorists are targeting only nonreligious or anti-religious people. An irrational process has been unleashed and lashes out in any direction, often against other Islamic traditions. There is a disturbance in the world psyche, and it will do a great deal of damage to all civilizations. The message for us is that the religious life has become pathological. Militant Islamic groups are burdened with the task of reminding the West, which they refer to as the "infidel," of the dangers of the sacred. This reality cannot be trifled with, and analyzing the post-secular condition is an urgent priority. Extremist groups or "cells of violence" are opposed to modernization and its consequences. It is not so much the "West" that these groups are opposing, but the field of modernity. Derrida reminds us that "discernment is required: Islam is not Islamism and we should never forget it, but the latter operates in the name of the former."[42] Militant groups operate in the name of religions but are to be differentiated from them. A commentator says, "When I use the phrase 'religious violence', I do not mean violence caused by religion, but violence associated with it."[43] We are witnessing a mutant religiousness that has more to do with violence than with worship.

However, the separation between Islam and terrorism can be taken too far. Some Islamic leaders deny that Islam is in any way involved in these atrocities. They claim that Islam is a peaceful religion concerned with justice and truth. In his work defending Islam, *The Secret of Islam: Love and Law in the Religion of Ethics*, Henry Bayman writes: "This drastic departure from what has been the Islamic norm for fourteen centuries can only be explained by a lack or distortion—not an excess—of Islamic sensibility." He goes on:

> Suicide attacks are not just un-Islamic, they are profoundly anti-Islamic. Historically, they had no place at all in Islamic culture. Suicide bombing was invented by other parties and began to be used by so-called 'Muslims' only during the last few decades. Its use in the Middle East is due not to a religious but to a political dispute.[44]

Other apologists blatantly deny that terrorism is an Islamic problem and say it is, instead, a human problem. I take their point but am not convinced. I don't think plain denial is helpful.

Contrary to those who wish to make a definite division between terrorism and Islam, Wolfgang Giegerich of Berlin writes:

> Many Islam scholars and many well-meaning people in the West warn against confusing the acts and ideology of the Islamic terrorists with Islam as such. True Islam, they claim, is a peaceful religion, and the 'jihad', they point out,

actually has a strictly religious meaning very different from that found in the terrorists' use of the term. As justified as this caution is academically, it is also irrelevant in the concrete situation we are in ... What the terrorists do reflects on Islam as such; maybe indeed not on 'true (authentic, original) Islam as it should be understood', but certainly on real Islam.[45]

Giegerich confronts the political correctness of our time and its inability to face facts. To offer any critique of Islam in our time is dismissed as Islamophobia.[46] My view is that militant Islamism is a traumatized version of Islam. This is a dark side of Islam that has to be integrated. Every religious culture has to admit to its shadow side and not bury it beneath espousals of goodness and piety. Psychiatrist Henry Krystal says trauma produces a regression in affect, a deficit in the capacity for symbolic representation and increase in fantasy formation.[47] There is a deficit of symbolic awareness and fantasy formation in the terrorists, many of whom are inspired by the idea of unreal rewards in heaven. The Ku Klux Klan does not represent Christianity; however it cannot be fully separated from it either; it represents the evil, demonic face of this culture. The first rule of psychology is not to disavow darkness when it appears: "This thing of darkness, I acknowledge mine."[48]

Giegerich has argued that the wave of terrorist violence is not a class struggle between rich and poor, nor is it a battle between Islam and Christianity. Rather, it is a battle between a modern and a medieval mindset.[49] The West has had a long battle with its traditional religious system, so that the natural tendency of any religion to see itself as superior to others has been fought and won. That is what makes the West "modern": a long historical and philosophical critique of its religious system, in which theological hegemony was destroyed and individual rights emerged as a powerful moral force. "An equivalent development did not take place in the Islamic world." "The critical fight with, indeed against itself and its own orthodoxy has not taken place."[50] As a result, we find premodern features still in place: the prevalence of the ancient emotions of shame and honor in a culture in which human rights are submerged. Shame and honor are more important than individual lives, which is why lives can be sacrificed so readily. The greatest sin is not to take lives but to criticize the sanctified claims of the the Islamic religious system.

This was expressed in the fatwa against novelist Salman Rushdie. In 1989, the Ayatollah Khomeini issued a fatwa ordering Muslims to kill Rushdie for supposed blasphemy in *The Satanic Verses*. Khomeini's fatwa was condemned across the Western world by governments on the grounds that it violated the rights of free speech and freedom of thought. However, human rights were not accepted as a basis for justice in Iran. The issue was said to have divided Muslims from Westerners along the fault line of culture.[51] Said the Ayatollah in 1990: "Even if Rushdie repents and becomes the most pious man of all time, it is incumbent on every Muslim to employ everything he has got, his life and wealth, to send him to hell." Here we have an example of the medieval and the modern rubbing up against each other: "The problem behind Islamic terrorism is the conflict between two different historical stages of cultural development."[52]

It is the modern experiment that is viewed as decadent by Islam, since it has radically shaken the certainties of all religious systems. The modern has made the medieval mindset indignant and angry over the relativization of values, the annihilation of traditional structures, and the arbitrariness resulting from a free and open society. By way of defense, the medieval mindset turns against the modern and tries to destroy it. It is rage against the modern that we are witnessing, including anger at elements that make the medieval world feel insecure, such as the loss of male superiority and code of honor, the decline of patriarchy, the dissolution of fixed sexual roles, and the new freedoms given to women; all of this, together with the destabilization of religious authority, makes the medieval mind see modernity as decadent and perverse. What we find in the terrorist "brotherhood" is a "masculine protest" against a new world that the old world rejects.

The West has managed to suppress its own negative response to modernity's disregard of religion. Loss of religion in the West does not register as a trauma; on the contrary, Westerners have been generally keen to give it away, seeing religion as an encumbrance they can do without. According to the script of modernity, religion is a remnant of a superstitious mindset that the West has outgrown. Only when Westerners suffer personal or collective trauma, so that their egoic encapsulation is challenged, does religion appear as something important that has been lost. In this context, it is the traumatized religion of Islamism that carries the burden that the West has been unable to accept. There is a part of us that is shaken by the modern, but this is acted out on the world stage by hostile forces. As Goya put it: "The sleep of reason produces monsters."[53] In its encounter with Islamism, the West collides with its oppositional self that wants to return to the medieval worldview. Terrorists scream "Allahu Akbar," God is Greater, as they commit atrocities, and this can be seen as the wounded religious instinct hitting back. This instinct has turned psychotic in its terrorist form.

It is hard to know how anything can be redeemed from this situation. Psychotic outbursts lead from one atrocity to another and do nothing to offer the possibility of healing, or a reintegration of the sacred. Terrorists present "God" in a form that has to be opposed by civilization. This adds to the burden of despair and confusion faced by the West. Secularists and humanists see in Islamism the image of religion they hate most of all. They see the impossibility of integrating a sacredness that has become hot with rage, furious with neglect, and anarchic with suppression. The rogue sacred is not assimilable by modernity, and no synthesis is on the horizon, if we are seeing this as a drama of the world soul. The "war on terror" reinforces the stalemate and perpetuates the outlook that may have precipitated the crisis. Thus, we are condemned to going around in circles, and so what will be the circuit breaker? It is easier to frame the question than to find an answer. But we know that there is more to this crisis than social or political factors.

The modern cannot capitulate to a premodern demand that a totalitarian expression of the sacred be worshipped. We cannot bow down before the God of terrorists, although some alienated enthusiasts are finding this an attractive proposition. Islamism presents the sacred in ways that are unassimilable by modernity. Western consciousness is faced with a great problem, how to assimilate the religious in palatable form, in such a way that consciousness is transformed? Derrida insisted that the religious impulse would not be fitted neatly into existing forms but would most likely explode them:

> The said 'return of the religious' is not a simple return, for it comports, as one of its two tendencies, a radical destruction of the religious. This makes the task all the more urgent and problematic.[54]

The return of the religious will not fill church pews or run according to any evangelical plan. What has awoken in the unconscious, Derrida felt, is more archaic than anything traditional religion would recognize *as* religious. So, there would continue to be a lack of fit between existing religious forms and atavistic urges.

Secularism is too entrenched to allow any "simple return" to religion. People will not return to traditions if it means turning away from secular freedoms, such as doubting, questioning, and dealing with religion in a critical and open atmosphere. Only a religion that respects disbelief, atheism, and agnosticism will appeal to the West. Some will be prepared to adopt various kinds of fundamentalism, but this is not in accord with the spirit of the age, which searches for a postsecular solution. This is what makes Jung's *Red Book* a seminal work for our time. It recognizes that secularism has failed us, and traditional religion has failed us as well. Only by reaching into the spirit of the depths can we find a cosmology that will be adequate for the future. Such a cosmology will draw on ancient sources, contemporary science, and personal experience. It will only be in the crucible of experience that the future religion will be formed.

Endnotes

1 C.G. Jung, *Aion. Researches into the Phenomenology of the Self*, in *CW*, vol. 9/II (Princeton, NJ: Princeton University Press, 1959), par. 126.

2 C.G. Jung, *The Red Book: Liber Novus*, ed. Sonu Shamdasani, tr. John Peck, Mark Kyburz, and Sonu Shamdasani (New York, NY: W.W. Norton, 2009), 306.

3 Ibid.

4 C.G. Jung, "Psychology and Religion," in *CW*, vol. 11 (Princeton, NJ: Princeton University Press, 1969), par. 9.

5 Jung, *The Red Book*, 306.

6 Rudolf Otto, *The Idea of the Holy*, trans. John W. Harvey (Oxford: Oxford University Press, 1950).

7 Jacques Derrida, "Faith and Knowledge: The Two Sources of 'Religion' at the Limits of Reason Alone" (1996), in Jacques Derrida and Gianni Vattimo, eds., *Religion* (Stanford, CA: Stanford University Press, 1998), 38.

8 Richard Dawkins, *The God Delusion* (London: Bantam Press, 2006); Christopher Hitchens, *God is Not Great: How Religion Poisons Everything* (New York, NY: Hatchette Book Group, 2007); Sam Harris, *The End of Faith: Religion, Terror and the Future of Reason* (New York, NY: W.W. Norton, 2004).

9 Jung, *Aion*, *CW* 9/II, par. 67.

10 C.G. Jung, "Psychotherapists or the Clergy," in *CW*, vol. 11 (Princeton, NJ: Princeton University Press, 1969), par. 531.

11 C.G. Jung, "Symbols and the Interpretation of Dreams," in *CW*, vol. 18 (Princeton, NJ: Princeton University Press, 1976), par. 581.

12 Ibid.

13 Jung, "Psychotherapists or the Clergy," *CW* 11, par. 531.

14 *Exodus* 23:27.

15 René Girard, *Violence and the Sacred* (Baltimore, MD: Johns Hopkins University Press, 1979).

16 Rainer Maria Rilke, "The First Elegy," *Duino Elegies*, trans. Stephen Mitchell (Boston, MA: Shambhala Publications, 1992), found at: http://www.homestar.org/bryannan/duino.html.

17 Ibid.

[18] Rainer Maria Rilke, "The Man Watching," in *Selected Poems of Rainer Maria Rilke*, trans. Robert Bly (New York, NY: Harper & Row, 1981); also at: http://www.poetry-chaikhana.com.

[19] Jacques Derrida, "Faith and Knowledge," 2 and 18.

[20] Ibid., 18.

[21] Jacques Derrida, in Gil Anidjar, ed., *Acts of Religion* (London and New York: Routledge, 2002), 82.

[22] Slavoj Zizek, "The Desert of the Real: Is this the end of fantasy?" located at: http://inthesetimes.com/issue/25/24/zizek2524.html.

[23] Jung, *The Red Book*, 253.

[24] C.G. Jung, "The Spiritual Problem of Modern Man," in *CW*, vol. 10 (Princeton, NJ: Princeton University Press, 1964), par. 160.

[25] Jung, *Aion*, CW 9/II, par. 126.

[26] Ibid.

[27] C.G. Jung, "On Synchronicity," in *CW*, vol. 8 (Princeton, NJ: Princeton University Press, 1969), par. 995.

[28] Hazrat Inayat Khan, *The Sufi Message*, Vol. 1 (Delhi: Motilal Banarsidass Publishers, 2011), 21.

[29] Martin Lings, *What is Sufism?* (London: George Allen & Unwin, 1975), 27.

[30] Shahid Athar, "Inner Jihad: Striving Toward Harmony," *The Sufism Journal* 10:3, 2010, available at: www.sufismjournal.org/practice/practicejihad.html.

[31] Thomas Cheetham, *The World Turned Inside Out: Henry Corbin and Islamic Mysticism* (New Orleans, LA: Spring Journal Books, 2003), 82.

[32] Wolfgang Giegerich, "Islamic Terrorism," in *Soul-Violence, Collected English Papers, Vol. 3* (New Orleans, LA: Spring Journal Books, 2008), 428.

[33] C.G. Jung, "Concerning the Archetypes, with Special Reference to the Anima Concept," in *CW*, vol. 9/I (Princeton, NJ: Princeton University Press, 1968), par. 129.

[34] Gianni Vattimo, in Derrida and Vattimo, eds., *Religion*, 79.

[35] Romano Guardini, *The End of the Modern World* (Wilmington, DE: ISI Books, 1998), 48-49.

[36] Emmanuel Levinas, "God and Philosophy," in Sean Hand, ed., *The Levinas Reader* (Oxford: Basil Blackwell, 1989).

[37] C.G. Jung, "Commentary on 'The Secret of the Golden Flower'," in *CW*, vol. 13 (Princeton, NJ: Princeton University Press, 1967), par. 54.

[38] Derrida, *Acts of Religion*, 89.

[39] C.G. Jung, "The Practical Use of Dream-Analysis," in *CW*, vol. 16 (Princeton, NJ: Princeton University Press, 1966), par. 329.

[40] Gil Bailie, *Violence Unveiled: Humanity at the Crossroads* (New York, NY: Crossroad Publishing, 1996).

[41] Christopher Koch, *The Year of Living Dangerously* (London: Michael Joseph, 1978), 236.

[42] Derrida, "Faith and Knowledge," 6.

[43] Mark Juergensmeyer, *Terror in the Mind of God: The Global Rise of Religious Violence* (Oakland, CA: University of California Press, 2017), xiv.

[44] Henry Bayman, *The Secret of Islam: Love and Law in the Religion of Ethics* (Berkeley, CA: North Atlantic Books, 2003), 56.

[45] Giegerich, "Islamic Terrorism," 418-419.

[46] Chris Allen, *Islamophobia* (Farnham, Surrey: Ashgate, 2011).

[47] Henry Krystal, *Integration and Self-Healing: Affect, Trauma and Alexithymia* (Hillsdale, NJ: Analytic Press, 1988), 28.

[48] Prospero in Shakespeare's *The Tempest*, Act 5, scene 1, lines 274-275.

[49] Giegerich, "Islamic Terrorism," 422-427.

[50] Giegerich, "Islamic Terrorism," 425.

[51] Kenan Malik, *From Fatwa to Jihad: The Rushdie Affair and its Aftermath* (New York, NY: Melville House, 2010).

[52] Giegerich, "Islamic Terrorism," 432.

[53] "The sleep of reason produces monsters," the title of a 1798 etching by Spanish artist Francisco Goya.

[54] Derrida, *Acts of Religion*, 78.

The Red Book as a Religious Text

Lionel Corbett

In his introduction to *The Red Book: Liber Novus*, Sonu Shamdasani lists several central aspects of this work, one of which is "... an attempt to grasp the future religious development of the West."[1] It is this element of Jung's text that I will pursue in what follows. I will make the case that for various reasons *The Red Book* is a religious text, not only because it deals with multiple religious themes but also in the sense of Jung's own understanding of the nature of religion. Based partly on the etymology of this word, Jung thinks of religion as careful attention to the numinous manifestations of the objective psyche.[2] In *The Red Book*, this level of the psyche appears in the form of figures such as Philemon and Salome.

The Proclamation of a New Religion

My contention that *The Red Book* is a religious text partly relies on one of Jung's dialogues with his soul, in which he is told that his calling is the proclamation of the new religion.[3] (I have discussed this in more detail elsewhere[4]). The soul tells Jung that he has received a revelation that he should not hide. This is his vocation and a priority. Jung is surprised by this and says he has no idea how to accomplish such a task, but the soul tells him he has the necessary knowledge and he should publish his material. The soul adds: "The way is symbolic"[5] rather than rational. Throughout *The Red Book*, the soul behaves like an autonomous content of the unconscious, if not a personification of the unconscious itself. Or, in Jung's words: "God and the soul are essentially the same when regarded as personifications of an unconscious content."[6] Because Jung believes that the experience of God is indistinguishable from the manifestations of the unconscious, writers such as Edward Edinger believe that Jung is proclaiming a new form of spirituality based on direct contact with the objective psyche.[7]

The Red Book often tells us that we need a new approach to old religious truths, and as Jung will later note in a letter, "present day Christianity is not the final truth."[8] Some of the seeds of this attitude are seen during Jung's conversation with the anchorite Ammonius. This sage figure tells Jung that we do not know the hidden meaning of the gospels or the meaning that is yet to come. According to Ammonius: "Every subsequent form of religion is the meaning of the antecedent."[9] The implication is that we can only know the meaning of a particular stage of religion when we are in the following stage, so that we can now look back at traditional Christianity and understand it with new eyes.

In *The Red Book*, the assimilation of the existing tradition is experienced as a ritual process, when, with a great deal of horror and resistance, Jung is asked to eat the liver of a divine child who has just been sacrificed. In traditional symbolism, the liver was considered to be a sacred organ, often used in divination. It represents the life force or sometimes the seat of the soul. By participating in this evil murder, Jung says: "… I redeemed the primordial powers and added them to my soul."[10] This act symbolizes a literal embodiment or incorporation of the spirit of the divine child into himself. Jung believed this act was redemptive in the sense that it was an act of healing analogous to the sacrifice of the Mass.

A few days later, Jung is told that the new religion only expresses itself in the "transformation of human relations," and at the visible level religion consists of "a new ordering of human affairs."[11] In a footnote, Shamdasani points out that in a seminar the following year, Jung says: "Individual relations lay the form of the invisible Church."[12] These are interesting comments, since Jung's subsequent approach to religion typically focuses on experiences of the self and the objective psyche and does not stress the religious importance of relationship.

The Prophetic Nature of the Work

By using "The Way of What Is to Come" as the title of *Liber Primus*, Jung gives the reader a sense of the prophetic nature of the work. Shamdasani notes that although the book was presented as a prophetic work, apparently this was "not to his [Jung's] taste."[13] Jung was more interested in the relationship between psychology and religion, the ways in which numinous experience is translated into doctrine and dogma, the importance of religion for the personality, and the process of making religion.

Jung begins with four prophecies about the coming of Christ, so that the work has a prophetic style whether or not the subsequent content is prophetic. Much of it proved to be so for Jung himself, although it remains to be seen how much is generalizable.[14] Certainly not everything in the book is applicable to others, and throughout the text Jung consistently insists that everyone has to find his or her own path. "My path is not your path. ... May each go his own way."[15] He rejects the notion of imitation: "The new God laughs at imitation and discipleship,"[16] and he rejects the idea of following a redeemer: "Woe betide those who live by way of examples!"[17] We must live our own life: "This life is the way, the long-sought after way to the unfathomable, which we call divine,"[18] and "I will be no savior, no lawgiver, no master teacher unto you."[19] "The time has come when each must do his own work of redemption."[20] Jung notes that Christ "imitated no one," so that "if I thus truly imitate Christ, I do not imitate anyone ... but go my own way."[21]

Jung quotes passages from Isaiah that Christian theologians believe to be a reference to the coming of Jesus. Christian theology insists that Isaiah's "suffering servant" and "man of sorrows" refer to Jesus, who, following the prophecy, "is despised and rejected." Jung seems to adhere to this interpretation because he continues with a passage that refers to the birth of Jesus (*John* 1; 14). There follows Isaiah's description of the glories of the messianic era during which the desert will blossom, the blind will see, the deaf will hear, and parched land will produce springs of water. As Shamdasani notes,[22] Jung mentions this passage elsewhere as an example of the union of the opposites of the destructive and constructive powers of the unconscious.[23] The theme of the union of opposites figures prominently in the *Red Book* and in Jung's later writing, so perhaps Jung believes that this process will be a part of the new revelation. As discussed below, the theme of the union of the opposites becomes important in Jung's discussion of the new god-image and the dark side of the self.

The New God-Image

Jung mentions God innumerable times throughout *The Red Book*, as he does throughout the *Collected Works*. In *The Red Book*, he is obviously preoccupied with the notion that a new image of God is emerging, which he mentions in several places, for example as "the coming God" in the form of the divine child.[24] After the vision of the death of Siegfried, he became aware of the birth of a new god-image, which was "… born as a child from my own human soul,"[25] although conceived with resistance. This new God could only be born when the hero had been killed, because the hero is perfection and is therefore an enemy of God because perfection has no need of God. In his 1925 seminar, commenting on this passage, Jung says that the hero referred to his intellect or the superior function.

Andreas Schweizer believes that the annunciation of the birth of God in the soul is "the most profound and central message of *The Red Book*."[26] In what way is God born in the soul? For Jung, the soul is the organ of perception that "apprehends the contents of the unconscious … and gives birth to its *dynamis* in the form of a symbol.[27] The birth of God in the soul means a new consciousness of the divine, or the development of a new image of God in the psyche. This idea is antithetical to traditional notions of an external savior or redeemer. Rather, according to Jung, "… the anointed of this time is a God who does not appear in the flesh; he is no man and yet is a son of man, but in spirit and not in flesh; hence he can be born only through the spirit of men as the conceiving womb of the God."[28] By following Eckhart's notion of the birth of the divine within the soul of the individual, which for Jung occurs during the lifelong process of individuation, Jung is clearly taking the opposite position to Nietzsche's proclamation that God is dead. Instead, for Jung a new god-image is emerging.

One of the complaints of the spirits of the dead who visit Jung at his home in 1916 is that they could not find what they sought in Jerusalem. In *Memories, Dreams, Reflections*, Jung reports that these dead represent "the voices of the Unanswered, Unresolved, and Unredeemed."[29] In other words, these are the voices of those who could not find spiritual solutions in traditional religion, adding to the urgency of the need for a new god-image. As Jung later notes in his correspondence with Victor White, religious truth is best thought of "as a thing living in the human soul and not as an abstruse and unreasonable relic of the past."[30] Religions require renewal: "The advocates of Christianity squander their energies in the mere preservation of what has come down to them, with no thought of building on to their house and making it roomier."[31] He believes that such stagnation threatens a lethal end to the tradition.

Jung insists that our gods require renewal: "If the God grows old, he becomes shadow, nonsense, and he goes down."[32] He declares that the image of the God "yet to come" appears as supreme meaning, and "… those who worship him must worship him in the image of the supreme meaning."[33] He stresses that: "It is not the coming God himself, but his image which appears in the supreme meaning."[34] Here, Jung's stress on God as an intrapsychic image presages his later insistence on the distinction between the divine itself and our images of the divine.[35] He makes two points in these passages. One is that a new god-image is going to emerge. Another seems to be that the divine appears in the form of whatever is the most meaningful to the individual, or that whatever is most meaningful to us becomes the God we worship. As he will later say more clearly, our God is whatever is of the highest value in the personality.[36] Jung stresses the importance of meaning in several places in his later work, especially in *Memories, Dreams, Reflections*, where he points out that meaning allows suffering to be bearable that would otherwise be unbearable.

During the encounter with Elijah and Salome, Jung is told that the soul brings tidings of the new god-image and the mysteries of his service.[37] In this active imagination, a black serpent winds itself around Jung's body as if he is crucified, his head becomes that of a lion (depicting the Mithraic god Aion), and his blood is squeezed out of him, in an imitation of Christ. Importantly, he notes that the serpent is the "earthly essence of man of which he is not conscious … the mystery that flows to him from the nourishing earth mother."[38] That is, this complex symbol expresses a combination of Mithraic and Christian imagery, and at the same time Jung is gripped by the earth-mother, a chthonic aspect of the divine that has been neglected by Christianity. All this means that in the process of giving birth to the new god-image, all these mysteries must be contained within it.

Elijah tells Jung that he and Salome have been "one since eternity."[39] These are important figures for Jung; he has been told to announce the new god-image, but Elijah was a fierce defender of the traditional god-image, and Salome was responsible for the death of John the Baptist, who was a herald of the new Christian god-image. Later, at the beginning of *Liber Secundus*, Jung quotes a passage from Jeremiah that warns against false prophets and warns people not to rely on dreams and personal revelations.[40] Since he puts this passage in the midst of his own revelations, it seems that Jung might be struggling with the notion that a new god-image will be born in the soul.[41]

Nevertheless, Jung describes the birth of a new symbol within himself. This symbol is the "… divine son, who is the supreme meaning, the symbol, the passing over into a new creation."[42] This is a remarkable development, and later he will note that the development of the redeeming symbol takes place where it is least expected, and from an improbable place.[43] He insists that he is not the supreme meaning himself, but "… the symbol becomes in me such that it has its substance, and I mine. Thus I stand like Peter in worship before the miracle of the transformation and the becoming real of the God in me."[44] He says that he is not the son of God himself, but he represents this son as one who was a mother to the God because he symbolically gave birth to the son of God in himself.

Therefore, he is one "to whom in the name of the God the freedom of the binding and loosing has been given. The binding and loosing takes place in me." This statement refers to *Matthew* 18:18, which says that whatever the apostles allow or disallow (loose or bind) will be ratified in heaven if it is God's will. This binding and loosing takes place in him but does not happen according to his personal will. He insists he is the servant of this transformation, like the Pope. I do not believe that this is a grandiose attempt to see himself as the Pope of a new religion, because he adds that it is "... incredible to believe such of oneself. It applies not to me, but to the symbol."[45] He realizes he is not on a par with his visions, and he is in danger of "... believing that I myself am significant since I see the significant."[46] In this context it is important that Jung told Cary Fink that he believed that Philemon was the same figure who inspired Buddha, Mani, Christ, and Mohammad, who all communed with God.[47] But Jung wanted to remain a psychologist who understood this process, rather than identify with such a figure. It is noteworthy that by the side of Jung's painting of Philemon, Jung places a quotation from the Bhagavad Gita in which Krishna says that he will incarnate whenever the world needs him.[48] The implication is that Philemon might be a divine avatar or the herald of one.

We have to wonder whether this revelatory material inspired the mandala on page 125 of *The Red Book*, which depicts a human being suspended between the human realm below and the transpersonal realm above. He seems to be holding a vase on the crown of his head into which is pouring a substance emerging from the obvious self-symbol above him. The overwhelming impression of this image is of an infusion of divine energy into the crown chakra.

In his encounter with the mythical figure Izdubar, who is dying, Jung recognizes that our god-image may be sick. He tries to heal the "pitiable" Izdubar, who has been hurt by the advent of science, which reduces our ability to believe in the gods. Jung insists that we must heal our God.[49] Reading this, we are reminded that Jung refers to mythologies of the dying and resurgent god as the representation of "a transformation of attitude" that results in "a new manifestation of life."[50] He suggests that the healing or renewal of God (for us, the god-image) takes place in "the divine sphere, i.e., in the unconscious."[51] The implication is that the renewal of the god-image is a psychological process that emerges from the unconscious, which was the process Jung experienced during the writing of his *Red Book*. To heal Izdubar, Jung decides that Izdubar is only real as a fantasy; paradoxically, by declaring him a figment of the imagination, Izdubar is saved. "So long as we leave the God outside us apparent and tangible, he is unbearable and hopeless. But if we turn the God into fantasy he is in us and is easy to bear."[52] This idea is testament both to the religious importance of the *imaginatio* as a way of giving new life to our image of God, and to Jung's insistence that the self is experienced deeply within our own subjectivity rather than as an outer, transcendent divinity. Jung believes that he can carry this idea into the West, and this is important for religious development in the West. The idea that the gods are products of the psyche makes the notion of the reality of the psyche crucial. In this context, it is noteworthy that Elijah points out that he and Salome are real. The view that the psyche is a domain in its own right contrasts with the current mainstream belief that the psyche is only an epiphenomenon of the brain, which would mean that the gods have no independent ontological reality.

One of Jung's images of the new god-image as the divine child is depicted in a painting of the god Phanes,[53] which Shamdasani describes in a long footnote based on Jung's description in the *Black Books*.[54] The name means "light bringer," or that which causes to appear. Phanes was an ancient god of procreation and new life in the Orphic tradition, where he is a dying and rising god of light and goodness who is both male and female. He is a primordial being who is said to have emerged from the world egg at the beginning of time, so he represents a new beginning.[55] Shamdasani believes that Phanes is Jung's God. Perhaps he is important to Jung not only because he gives Jung a sense of renewal but also because he embodies the cosmogonic principle of love and creative force.[56] The legend to this image says that: "This is the image of the divine child. It means the completion of a long path. ... I called him Phanes because he is the newly appearing god."[57] It is significant that Phanes is said to have been born from Aion, the solar god of the Mithraic mysteries who is the lion-headed god that appeared in Jung's vision during his encounter with Salome.

God and the Dark Side of the Self

The Red Book has a clear presentiment of Jung's later notion of an innate god-image in the psyche. Early on in the book, he says that "the depths in me was at the same time the ruler of the depths of world affairs,"[58] and later he says that "through uniting with the self we reach the God."[59] He worries that although this realization was completely unexpected and hard to believe, perhaps even sick or delusional, the experience seized him "beyond all measure" and was unshakable. Later, he describes the self as "the most immediate experience of the divine which is at all psychologically comprehensible."[60]

The notion of the dark side of the self, not fully developed by Jung until *Answer to Job*, appears early in his *Red Book*. For example: "The image of God has a shadow. ... The image of God throws a shadow that is just as great as itself"[61]; this shadow is nonsense as well as meaningful, and "the supreme meaning is great and small." Or, "meaning requires absurdity and absurdity requires meaning."[62] "The small, narrow, and banal is not nonsense, but one of both of the essences of the Godhead."[63] In these and similar passages, Jung is alluding to the notion he later develops, that our image of the divine must include all the opposites and cannot be considered to be exclusively light, as it was in traditional Christianity. The reality of the experience of the divine includes the experience of the nonsensical and chaotic. The emerging image of God will contain a mixture of positive and negative qualities; it is a paradox. Thus, the new God "approached me out of the terrible ambiguity, the hateful-beautiful, ... the inhuman-human and the ungodly-godly."[64] This God is not to be found "in absolute beauty, goodness, seriousness, elevation, humanity or even in godliness"; instead: "Ambiguity is the way of life," since an unequivocal God "... is simplicity and leads to death."[65] The new god-image is found in the relative, not only in the absolute, and in order to encompass the fullness of life, it must include that which is "beautiful and hateful, good and evil, laughable and serious, human and inhuman."[66] The absolute God cannot encompass the fullness of life, which is a mixture of opposites such as good and evil. Rather than make the traditionally radical distinction between good and evil, it is important that we accept evil, recognizing that it exists and "must have its share in life;"[67] if we accept evil, "we can deprive it of the power it has to overwhelm us." It is important that such opposites should not be thought of in purely cognitive or logical terms that can eventually be reconciled; they are lived experiences.

Jung tells us that "... we had forgotten that god is terrible. Christ taught: God is love. But you should know that love is also terrible."[68] God can even be dangerous: "If the God comes near you, then plead for your life to be spared, since the God is loving horror."[69] God "appears as our sickness. ... We must heal ourselves from the God, since he is also our heaviest wound."[70] This idea later appears in Jung's pithy phrase that "the gods have become diseases."[71]

In Philemon's third sermon to the dead, he says that Abraxas (Jung uses this name to describe the high God) draws the *summum bonum* from the sun and from the devil the *infimum malum*.[72] That is, Abraxas "produces truth and lying, good and evil, light and darkness ... therefore Abraxas is terrible" and the "cruel contra-dictoriness of nature."[73] All this is to say that evil is an aspect of the divine, and the divine must contain all polarities. Abraxas can be "known but not understood," according to Philemon.[74] Jung must free himself from the traditional god-image "... since the God I experienced is more than love; he is also hate, he is more than beauty, he is also the abomination, he is more than wisdom, he is also meaninglessness."[75]

Given all this, from the point of view of traditional Christian thinking, or from the viewpoint of the spirit of the times, it is not surprising that Jung imagines himself admitted to a "mad house," where he is pronounced to be "truly and utterly mad" by a professor of psychiatry who represents the spirit of the times. This section may represent Jung's anxiety about the sanity or validity of his experiences.

But his is a divine madness, divine intoxication, "… a madness that cannot be integrated into present-day society…"[76] As he puts it, this apparent irrationality is what happens when we enter the world of the soul, and when the spirit of the depths overpowers the spirit of the times. That is, we must overcome conventional thinking if we are to perceive authentic spiritual realities, which, like much of *The Red Book*, do not make sense in ordinary terms. Consequently: "To the extent that the Christianity of this time lacks madness, it lacks divine life."[77]

Objections to Seeing *The Red Book* as a Religious Text

In this essay, I have considered Jung's experiences in his *Red Book* to be a form of personal revelation, and I am committed to Jung's notion of the reality of the psyche, so that figures such as Philemon are ontologically real in their own right. Because these figures are so important, I would like to address some of the objections that have been raised to taking them at face value, as autochthonous products of the objective psyche. Giegerich, for example, says: "We have not become psychologists in order to listen to revelations."[78] He sees such figures only as the "*simulation* of an authentic representation of an unconscious process."[79] Giegerich objects to seeing such figures as authentic products of the objective psyche because they reflect what Jung was reading as he was writing his text. In this view, these figures are learned and not spontaneous products of the psyche. My own view is that the element of surprise and numinosity that Jung experiences in these encounters supports the idea that they do not arise from the ego. The fact that we happen to recognize an archetypal image does not make it less archetypal. Philemon, for instance, might represent receptivity to the divine realm, since this was his mythic role. The archetype often expresses itself cloaked in culturally recognizable imagery.

The Red Book has also been criticized for being a sequence of speculation and imaginings, not tethered to either argument or evidence.[80] However, the numinosity of a direct experience of the objective psyche *is* evidence, even if it is not replicable or falsifiable in the scientific sense, and in the face of such an experience, argument is not necessary. In this context, it is an interesting irony that, when they first meet, Philemon complains that Jung judges everything from the point of view of his intellect.[81] Philemon tells Jung that rationality can only comprehend the part of reality that is rational, but much of reality is nonrational, and "... our way needs not only reason but also unreason."[82] Jung eventually admits that he regards "... the fiery brilliance of the god as a higher and fuller life than the ashes of rationality."[83] For Jung, something irrational is not contrary to reason but "something beyond reason ... not grounded on reason."[84] Here he is referring to an overly rational and materialistic (I would add scientistic) view of the world, which threatens "the spiritual and psychic heritage of man with instant annihilation."[85]

The range of views that *The Red Book* has inspired is quite revealing. The book was obviously written and bound with great care and devotion. The skeptical view is that this was merely a grandiose attempt to simulate a holy book, but I believe that its impressive appearance really reflects Jung's experience of the numinosity of its contents and his attempt to capture that quality. On the other hand, David Hart sees *The Red Book* as "an essentially silly exercise ... full of the kinds of garish symbolism and pompous antinomianism one expects from more adolescent minds."[86] Hart calls the book a symptom of "the desire for transcendence without transcendence." He sees *The Red Book* as preserving "the most ungainly aspects of ancient Gnosticism"[87] because it is boringly rambling, pretentious, self-absorbed, and ethically sterile. According to Hart, the book "has the feel of an expression of arrested pubescence,"[88] and Jung was manufacturing "spiritual soporifics: therapeutic sedatives for a therapeutic age."[89] Hart goes on to say that: "The human longing for God, however, persists from age to age."[90] Tragically, he cannot see that this longing is exactly what *The Red Book* is about. *The Red Book* is a mythic or mythopoetic text with psychological and spiritual significance. It is not a piece of philosophy. It is a shamanic work, or a work of mysticism, in Jung's sense that a mystic is one who has had "a particularly vivid experience of the processes of the collective unconscious."[91]

Conclusion

I see *The Red Book* as one of the sources of Jung's myth, and like John Dourley, I see Jung's myth as undermining many of the assertions of the reigning monotheisms, a process that came into stark relief with the *Book of Job.*[92] I believe that this may be unconsciously motivating some of Jung's critics. There are several deviations from tradition in *The Red Book*, such as Jung's attempt to synthesize good and evil as components of the self, the need for a renewal of the Western god-image, the notion of the dark side of the self, and the stress on the birth of God in the soul rather than in a transcendent domain. Another aspect of Jung's myth is that everyone needs to develop his or her own myth. There is no longer one exclusive, saving truth or one road to salvation. The unconscious is infinitely creative and can produce an endless variety of numinous imagery. It is worth noting that Jung suggested that his patients should prepare their own *Red Book*, and "for you it will be your church—your cathedral ..."[93] Here he clearly implies that the material that arises from the objective psyche is sacred, consistent with his belief that contact with the objective psyche is a religious process. It is to be hoped that *The Red Book* is only the beginning of innumerable analogous books, based on individual engagement with the objective psyche.

Endnotes

Acknowledgment: I would like to thank Dr. Pat Katsky for her helpful comments on an early draft of this paper.

1 C.G. Jung, *The Red Book: Liber Novus*, ed. Sonu Shamdasani, trans. John Peck, Mark Kyburz, and Sonu Shamdasani (New York, NY: W.W. Norton, 2009), 207.

2 C.G. Jung, "Psychology and Religion," in *CW*, vol. 11 (Princeton, NJ: Princeton University Press, 1969), par. 6.

3 Jung, *The Red Book*, 211.

4 Lionel Corbett, "Jung's *The Red Book* Dialogues with the Soul: Herald of a New Religion?" in *Jung Journal Culture & Pysche*, 2011, 63-77.

5 Jung, *The Red Book*, 211.

6 C.G. Jung, *Psychological Types*, in *CW*, vol. 6 (Princeton, NJ: Princeton University Press, 1971), par. 421.

7 Edward Edinger, *Ego and Archetype* (Baltimore, MD: Penguin Books, 1973).

8 Gerhard Adler, *C. G. Jung Letters*. Trans. by R. F. C. Hull. Vol. 2, 1951-1961 (Princeton, NJ: Princeton University Press, 1975), 575.

9 Jung, *The Red Book*, 272.

10 Ibid., 291.

11 Ibid., 211.

12 Ibid. This is particularly interesting in view of the turn toward relational forms of psychotherapy.

13 Ibid., 214.

14 Sanford L. Drob, *Reading the Red Book: An Interpretive Guide to C.G. Jung's Liber Novus* (New Orleans, LA: Spring Journal Books, 2012).

15 Jung, *The Red Book*, 231.

16 Ibid., 245.

17 Ibid., 231.

18 Ibid., 232.

19 Ibid., 231.

20 Ibid., 356.

21 Ibid., 293.

22 Ibid., 229 n4.

23 C. G. Jung, *Mysterium Conjuntionis*, in *CW*, vol. 14 (Princeton, NJ: Princeton University Press, 1963), par. 258.

24 Jung, *The Red Book*, 234.

25 Ibid., 244.

26 Andreas Schweizer, "Red," in *Jung Journal Culture and Psyche*, 5, 3, 2011, 25-37.

27 Jung, *Psychological Types*, *CW* 6, par. 426.

28 Jung, *The Red Book*, 299.

29 C.G. Jung, *Memories, Dreams, Reflections*, ed. Aniela Jaffé (New York, NY: Vintage, 1963), 191.

30 Adler, *C. G. Jung Letters*, Vol. 2, 1951-1961, 387.

31 C.G. Jung, *Aion. Researches into the Phenomenology of the Self*, in *CW*, vol. 9/II (Princeton, NJ: Princeton University Press, 1959), par. 170.

32 Jung, *The Red Book*, 242.

33 Ibid., 229.

34 Ibid.

35 C.G. Jung, *Symbols of Transformation*, in *CW*, vol. 5 (Princeton, NJ: Princeton University Press, 1956), par. 95.

36 Jung, *Psychological Types*, *CW* 6, par. 47.

37 Jung, *The Red Book*, 246 n163.

38 Ibid., 247.

39 Ibid., 246.

40 Ibid., 259.

41 Ibid., 207, 354 n123.

42 Ibid., 250.

43 Jung, *Psychological Types*, *CW* 6, par. 439.

44 Jung, *The Red Book*, 250.

45 Ibid.

46 Ibid., 251.

47 Ibid., 213.

48 Ibid., 317 n281.

49 Ibid., 281.

50 Jung, *Psychological Types*, *CW* 6, par. 325.

51 Ibid., par. 300.

52 Jung, *The Red Book*, 283.

53 Ibid., 113.

54 Ibid., 301 n211.

55 Egg imagery is very common in the paintings of *The Red Book*.

[56] Jung, *Symbols of Transformation*, CW 5, par. 198.

[57] Jung, *The Red Book*, 301 n211.

[58] Ibid., 231.

[59] Ibid., 338.

[60] C.G. Jung, "Transformation Symbolism in the Mass," in *CW*, vol. 11 (Princeton, NJ: Princeton University Press, 1969), par. 396.

[61] Jung, *The Red Book*, 230.

[62] Ibid., 242.

[63] Ibid., 230.

[64] Ibid., 243.

[65] Ibid., 244.

[66] Ibid., 243.

[67] Ibid., 288.

[68] Ibid., 235.

[69] Ibid., 281.

[70] Ibid., 338.

[71] C.G. Jung, "Commentary on 'The Secret of the Golden Flower,'" in *CW*, vol. 13 (Princeton, NJ: Princeton University Press, 1967), par. 54.

[72] Jung, *The Red Book*, 350. In ibid., 349 n93, Shamdasani quotes Jung saying that Abraxas is identical with the Gnostic Demiurgos, the supreme deity or the world creator.

[73] Jung, *The Red Book*, 350.

[74] Ibid.

[75] Ibid., 339.

[76] Ibid., 295.

[77] Ibid., 238.

[78] Wolfgang Giegerich, "*Liber Novus*, That is, The New Bible: A First Analysis of C.G. Jung's *Red Book*," *Spring: A Journal of Archetype and Culture* 83 (Spring 2010), 376.

[79] Ibid., 411.

[80] Robert A. Segal, "Reply to Sanford Drob," in *International Journal of Jungian Studies* 6, 1, 2014.

[81] Jung, *The Red Book*, 313.

[82] Ibid., 314.

[83] Ibid., 339.

[84] Jung, *Psychological Types*, CW 6, par. 774.

85   C.G. Jung, "The Psychological Aspects of the Mother Archetype," in *CW*, vol. 9/I (Princeton, NJ: Princeton University Press, 1968), par. 195.

86   David B. Hart, "Jung's Therapeutic Gnosticism," *First Things* (2013), 27.

87   Ibid., 28.

88   Ibid., 29.

89   Ibid., 30.

90   Ibid., 31.

91   C.G. Jung, "The Tavistock Lectures," in *CW*, vol. 18 (Princeton, NJ: Princeton University Press, 1976), par. 218.

92   John Dourley, "Jung and the Recall of the Gods," in *Journal of Jungian Theory and Practice*, 8, 1, 2006, 43-53.

93   Jung, *The Red Book*, 216.

Blundering into the Work of Redemption

Ann Belford Ulanov

It is hard to write on *The Red Book*. You touch it in one place, and all the other places catch your paws—like tar baby! The trickster as Brer Rabbit tricking the wolf now tricks us. How to find words for the venture in *Liber Novus* without draining away its life, as well as draining the journey stirred up in us reading it—our own mystery play. We get abstracted by our interpretations or submerged by unconscious currents carrying us out to sea. Of course, Jung's critics want to say he is mad. That is the best protection against being initiated into our own task of linking the Below and the Above.

Jung is living this experience, in its midst, and is true to his vow to take seriously every wanderer he encounters.[1] He does not clean up the text but lets his complexes show in all their strife and anguish. Nor does he sum up his venture with a clear conclusion but stops abruptly, saying in the first instance he must go back to the Middle Ages to deal with the barbarian in himself, and in the second, stopping mid-sentence, he must go forward "with the help of alchemy" "to absorb the overpowering force of the original experiences."[2]

This essay focuses on three aspects of a central theme that threads through the book and on Jung's mode of addressing it: "... one blunders into the work of redemption ... neither beautiful nor pleasant ... and ... so difficult and full of torment that one should count oneself as one of the sick and not as one of the overhealthy who seek to impart their abundance to others."[3] Jung feels nauseated, empty, a beggar,[4] his path more than a thousand feet deep, indeed, "a cosmic depth" that takes him beyond what he knows to where "... the pliers of the spirits of the depths held me, and I had to drink the bitterest of all draughts."[5] Redemption means being saved, claimed, made good, recovered, regenerated, reformed, what Jung calls "smelted anew."[6] His mode of apprehending is blundering.

I. Temptation of the Good

Jung's redeeming work begins from an original angle: "Christ totally overcomes the temptation of the devil, but not the temptation of God to good and reason. Christ thus succumbs to cursing."[7] The good is what we identify with as our highest value, our hero that we must disidentify with, indeed kill, as Jung murders Siegfried with the help of a small brown man, a self-figure: "The heroic in you is the fact that you are ruled by the thought this or that is good ... indispensable ... attained in headlong striving work, this or that pleasure should be ruthlessly repressed ... you sin against incapacity. But incapacity exists. No one should deny it, find fault with it, or shout it down."[8]

This hero Jung also calls our ruling principle and identifies his as intellect, reason, logos, thinking, force, efficiency, masculine, science. God has become identified with only the good of our developed ruling principle that excludes in us and in our culture the bad, leaving it to the "mercy of decay."[9] Jung descends to his personal Hell, so boring compared to the fun and daring of everyone else's Hell. There he must deal with the rubble of everything he shoved off the table as bad, stupid, sinful that now leads him to develop his incapacity from which emerges paradoxical intelligence, knowledge of the heart, eros, feeling, feminine, and what he calls magic, which we need "to receive or invoke ... the communication of the incomprehensible."[10] Jung hears, *"You will believe you have sunk into meaninglessness, into eternal disorder. You will be right! Nothing will deliver you from disorder and meaninglessness, since this is the other half of the world."*[11] "But for him who has seen the chaos, there is no more hiding, because he knows the bottom sways ..."[12] Even Jung hard at work writing his *Red Book* the soul chides, and us too, the authors toiling over chapters for three volumes on the book: "Do you still not know that you are not writing a book to feed your vanity, but that you are speaking with me?"[13] Jung takes 25 nights in the desert to awaken his soul "to her own life, until she could approach me as a free-standing being separate from me."[14]

Jung approaches redemption from a new perspective: "Just as Christ tormented the flesh through the spirit, the God of this time will torment the spirit through the flesh"; "God does not appear in the flesh … but in spirit. … What is done to this God you do to the lowest in yourself. … Who should accept the lowest in you, if you do not?"[15] Radical acceptance of all parts of us reclaims what has been rotting in our own personal Hell. The location of transformation happens now in us in the "site of the innermost"—our psyche, soul— not outside us in gods, laws, teachings, or ideals of art, justice, reason.[16] "The beginning is always the smallest, it begins in nothing. … I see the little drop of 'something' that falls into the sea of nothingness. … where the nothingness widens itself into unrestricted freedom."[17]

Jung emphasizes the inextricable connection of personal and collective dimensions of our lives. When we serve the good to the expulsion of the bad, it lands on our neighbors; in the name of the good, we try to kill the bad, thereby destroying community. In personal relations we discover the "bloodthirsty tiger" that our neighbor denies: "… you, conscious only of your goodness, offer your human hand to me in greeting. … And suddenly I felt a smooth cord around my neck, which choked me mercilessly, and a cruel hammer blow struck a nail into my temple."[18] On the collective level, Jung learns the work of redemption includes accepting that we, too, can imagine intending and willing atrocities (and hope never to be doing them). We cannot cling to the good as protection against that awareness. I understand this to indicate our task is to hold in consciousness both our capacity to exert terrible attitudes and actions in tension with the good we love and serve. We consciously suffer this fierce stretching, neither enact nor repress the bad, and thus suffer the dissolution of a defined distinction of good and evil.[19] We thereby personally contribute to communal harmony by knowing we can harm each other. This radical knowing with the heart comes to Jung through modes of apprehension associated with the feminine, for that is what he neglected.[20]

II. Changing Gender

Jung changes gender in his *Red Book*, returning to his masculine identification enlarged and made more fluid. His mode of experiencing is to be *in* every encounter, not removed into abstract classification, but besieged by madness, up close with harangues from his soul, singing incantations mourning Izdubar's sufferings, excited to discover Izdubar's reality as a *real* fantasy, painfully strung up in his own identification with Christ's crucifixion. If a feminine mode of relating is to be in the midst, touched, immediate, Jung is visibly here, even as a lonely ignorant wanderer. Only gradually does he rescue ability simultaneously to be in the midst and reflect, previewing an expanded capacity for masculine and feminine modes at once.

Jung becomes pregnant, his soul as womb gestates and gives birth to the new god.[21] Later he becomes pregnant again with another child that might be understood as his work from which he must differentiate himself to "let everything sprout; the son grows out of himself. The myth commences, the one that need only be lived, not sung, the one that sings itself."[22] The son, his work, he contributes to collective life; Jung returns to his garden.[23] For while he is a woman gestating and birthing a child, he becomes himself a child to the god, a state he finds "humiliating and shattering" but also that reaches a presuppositionless consciousness, full of "divine astonishment," chosen over "the ashes of rationality."[24] This child consciousness that is free of constricting prejudgments is not the withering deadness of childishness, but the entry path of "what is to come." The god is a child, and Jung is a child serving this god. He sees all of us—"the spirit of man"—as a conceiving womb of God.[25]

Jung's soul is feminine and not maternal or any kind of motherly container, exclaiming in response to Jung complaining of hardship, woe, wanderings: "I am not your mother!"[26] She is another standpoint within him and a free-standing real presence in her own right, challenging his vanity, ambitiousness, self-absorption, addiction to words. In disagreements with her he often yields, but not always. She, part of primordial origins he will later call Mothers of the depths and the mother who comes back as fructive creative principle, is the birthplace in him of the new god.[27]

Jung sees a man must become a woman to be able to see the otherness of soul and avoid becoming enslaved to women. We all must go beyond the gendered but not as a hard rule, rather each person responding appropriately to her or his actual situation, hence making space for diversity of paths.[28]

Jung's identification with this feminine part of him grows from seeing how badly he mangled it and from his efforts to redeem it. Salome first appears as crazed, blind, murderous, bloodthirsty, and grows into a sane, sighted, womanly presence. She desires to give her love to Jung. He recoils! He fears intimacy with another would stifle his freedom and impose the burden of her life on him. He insists instead everyone must carry his or her own life.[29] He encouraged his wife and mistress to find their unique paths. Yet in writing and living the *Red Book* experience, Jung's actual dependence was heavy on Emma Jung, who raised their five children, sustained a steady home, presided over a big house, staff, finances, became an analyst, and helped to inaugurate the Analytical Psychology Club, allowing Jung freedom to create his new vision of psychology. For that he depended absolutely on Toni Wolff, who received and interpreted his fantasies and collaborated in creating new ideas of psyche (for which she received no official credit or footnote). Jung said of his *Red Book* experience, you need another, and probably a woman, and of his soul he said: "I found you again only through the soul of a woman."[30] Toni Wolff was his soul companion for a time (and how can that be credited on a book's title page?), became an analyst and presidential force in the Analytical Psychology Club's life. Depending on these two women simultaneously, the three of them privately and in public suffered and enjoyed the pairing, so unconventional at the time, with sadness and gain to each.

Jung presented seminar material on his *Liber Novus* ventures, depending on members to receive and validate his psychological experiences. Jung relied on some women colleagues' responses to chunks of his manuscript. He salutes the many women whose work in analysis helped him gather into theoretical articulation a feminine capacity within a man capable of enkindling relationship between conscious and unconscious.

A trenchant encounter with the feminine is Jung's discovery of a beheaded body of a small girl left in the bushes. A shrouded figure says she is the soul of the child and commands Jung to ingest a piece of the child's liver to atone for her violation and murder. Outraged, repulsed, Jung resists, then yields when recognizing he as a man partakes in the worst of human depravity and thus could have participated in the girl's desecration and killing. The shrouded figure now reveals herself as Jung's soul. Hence, his soul is feminine and is also the soul of this dead female child, and Jung atones for violation of both. He sees that by ingesting the girl's flesh, he destroys his "formation" of God that was an act of "highest creative love" and now, instead, receives within his body hot coals of the living God from whom there is no escape.[31] This God is real and wants to dwell with Jung in his everyday life. The gravity of changing the image of God and its placement within the body of the self also radically changes the image of the distinction of good and evil and of the relation of self and other.

III. Self and God

A. Good and Evil

Jung's soul is also soul of this small, violated girl, an image of his undeveloped feminine as part of his "incapacity"—the rubble he rejects as bad and leaves undeveloped in his personal Hell. Jung learns that at the bottom of our incapacity "evil that stares at you … coldly."[32] We thus blunder into redeeming our image of the distinction of good and evil. The God is not just our highest ideals of good, nor does it only dwell outside us. The coals of the living God are placed inside us, the "innermost site" of our psyche through which we have any picture of self, God, or others. If we put all our "force" (energy) into the ideal good God outside us, our human self is drained of aliveness and left mired in the bad we tried to expel.[33] God is then only of the Above and excludes the Below. We must take that energy back into our self and recognize psyche in us as bridge to the God transcending us. This God includes the Below and the Above. Our former picture of their sharp division dissolves. Good and evil unite in our growing from the Below to the Above; if we stop growing, they fall apart into hostile vying, but "... the warmth of life which contains good and evil inseparably and indistinguishably. That is the way of life. ... Yet this is not the goal, but the way and the crossing. ... beginning the recovery."[34]

B. God-Image

Jung focuses on the distinction between God and god-image. Facing the temptation to the good, Jung sees we cannot exclude the bad, and that changes our image of God. If it is true that soul is not a maternal container for us but rather that other standpoint within us, for "the God is always where you are not," for Jung that other location challenges his ambitious vanity and undeveloped feminine modality, which for him is related to feeling.[35] The point is that the Godhead is also the Other within us, in the form of god-images our soul through our psyche creates, and not some idealized distant deity unconnected to our all-too-human selves. We do not create or find God but deal always with our images of God, who also exists external to ourselves.

The new image of God manifests as *"the supreme meaning ... the bridge to what is to come. That is the God yet to come. It is not the coming God himself, but his image which appears in the supreme meaning. God is an image, and those who worship him must worship him in the images of the supreme meaning."*[36] This meaning includes images of the Below, too—nonsense, absurdity, ugliness, ambiguity— as well as images of the beautiful, good, and true.[37] We cannot put into God just the good and leave out the bad, lest we drain away energies of our aliveness and pile the bad onto our neighbor. God wants to "... sit at table with me, work with me. ... be ever-present." Jung objects: "The divine appears to me as irrational craziness" stealing into reasonable, meaningful human activity.[38] This is the real, living God.

Jung's ingesting of the murdered girl's liver, surely an image of the Below, destroys his image of God as idealized good but leads to putting the glowing coals of God into the self, a God he cannot escape from but will face in the humdrum of daily life. In taking back into the "site of the innermost" our image of God, we return all that force to the human psyche, breaking down our previous god-image domesticated in the Christianity of the "spirit of the times." We confront the temptation to the good in order to evade the divine nearness of the transcendent within our very body-self by idealizing the good in a far distant God outside us.

But Jung sees that he cannot by himself destroy his formation (image) of the highest God to which we are enthralled. Clinically, we see god-images landing on whatever we call the goods—money, political power, substances that call to us in drugs, drink, certain foods, what we see as our highest ideals of knowledge, art, science, love—whatever acts like a god in our personality around which we revolve as the ultimate value, for positive or negative effects. I understand this as a foundational image whose destruction would make us feel we will lose our mind, become disoriented, that madness will overtake us. We cannot will to destroy our god-image of the highest good by ourselves but only in shocking dependence on evil to do it for and with us.

Jung says: "You cannot dissolve good with good. You can dissolve good only with evil."[39] That dissolution leaves us with what to do in the face of evil. Our personal problem with the bad opens to the human problem of how destructiveness finds a place in living. Jung reaches his amazing response: Good and evil unite only in growth from Below to Above; when growth stops, they fall apart into violent rivalry.[40] We, too, must develop solutions to the place of devastation in existence.

C. Others and Self

The link between individual and collective life is unavoidable. Working on our personal individual problem with what to do with the bad turns out to be our contribution to the impersonal collective problem with evil. No matter how tiny our work on the bad, it is our contribution to the huge human problem to find the place for annihilation in aliveness. We are linked to each other, and the small inextricably links to the large. Evil dissolves the formation of the highest God. What we blunder to redeem, however faultily, contributes to the shared human task of seeing the distinction between and the interpenetration of our personal (individual) and shared (collective) tasks of facing the temptations of the good and of evil.

D. God and Self

The Red Book opens and closes with direct references to God and the relation of God and self. At the book's beginning, Christ is the one whom Scripture describes: "He is despised and rejected of men; a man of sorrows ..."; "... unto us a child is born ... called Wonderful, Counselor"; "the Word was made flesh." At the book's end in the garden, Christ is the shade who brings the "beauty of suffering," which I understand as the possibility that suffering, bad as it is because related to the "worm" (evil), may include creative response.[41]

Jung lost his soul connection to the god-image prevalent in the "spirit of the times." Searching for his soul, he blundered into god-images different from this conscious God but that were real, which he knew because of "the unshakeableness of the experience."[42] Dread grips him because images of "what is to come" differ radically from what is familiar. Hap designates "God's other pole," of the night, the flesh and blood spirit, of bodily juices, sperm, entrails, joints, eyes, ears, feet, sputum, excrement.[43]

Jung fights with his soul who, though a steady if strenuous guide, also aims to run off to heaven for her own salvation with the treasure of human love. No, Jung says, human love is his and humanity's lifeblood and she should work for the good of humanity here. She yields! Differentiation initiates between the need of the dead and the living, between precious ego life versus life in the hereafter.[44]

Philemon speaks to the dead and to Jung about another god-image, Abraxas, as creative force, formless and forming, the stream of life, creative drive, form and formation, and the "sucking gorge of emptiness" and counsels we are to live our life against the force of Abraxas, for our individuation counters Abraxas's blasting power.[45]

The dead crowd in because of their unlived life pressures. They did not individuate but childishly cast the burden of their redemption onto Christ, whose command to love each other they disobeyed and killed instead. They denied the animal in themselves; they failed to atone for "the ox with the velvet eyes" or to do penance for the "sacred ore that they dug up from the belly of the earth."[46]

In contrast, Philemon tells Jung we must not naively put our small self into the bigness of God, "since the God is an unfathomable powerful movement that sweeps away the self into the boundless, into dissolution." Jung fears this threat could plunge him into psychosis: "A living God afflicts our reason like a sickness. He fills the soul with an intoxication … with reeling chaos. How many will the God break?"[47]

Yet, Jung survives the influx of the God by brute strength, and with a dawning, uneasy insight that the "small, narrow, and banal is not nonsense, but one of … the essences of the Godhead" that lives with us every day in ordinary ego life in the world.[48] So we must, Jung sees, establish our self, pull our self to our side from God, "wrestle with the God for the self. … free the self from the God, so we can live." Yet later, Philemon says we should live in the God, not the God live in us. Jung perceives: "Not the self is God, although we reach God through the self. The God is behind the self, above the self, the self itself, when he appears … our heaviest wound." Having gained a sense of self, we then can elect to give it (or not) to God: "I believe we have the choice: I preferred the living wonders of the God … since I want to live. My life wants itself whole."[49] But the way that happens is to live your very own life to the full: "There is only one way and that is your way."[50]

IV. Devotion

Jung, who wrestles his undeveloped feeling into living, fills with ardor—not to another person but to Love itself, not to fame and ambition but to living his own path, tending his garden humbly. From his experience of giving birth, Jung reaches "voluntary devotion," shedding commingling of his ambition for personal fame with love, thus redeeming his feeling function. Although this dismembering is painful, it yields Jung's decision for what "is required of me. I accepted all the joy and every torment of my nature and remained true to my love, to suffer what comes to everyone in their own way. And I stood alone and was afraid."[51]

In full-hearted allegiance to the soul that speaks through his psyche, he later confides that our libido, which he calls serpent energy in *The Red Book*, is the "divine *pneuma*" in us, and that he looked for a sign "... that the spirit of the depths in me was at the same time the ruler of the depths of world affairs."[52] Think of Jung's sustained feeling as devoting 16 years carefully painting his pivotal experiences to show the mysteries that lived him. For example, see Images: Fol.i, 22, 29, 54; see also Images with page references in the text: 71 (288 n141), 117 (303 n222), 123 (307 n33), 135 (309 n248), 155 (317 n283). This private endeavor marks "what is to come," only published decades after its creation.

Living our life to the full includes our unlived life: "Live what you have never yet lived. ... The life I could still live, I should live and the thoughts that I could still think, I should think." This way feeds community and does not sap it by imitating our neighbor and neglecting our own becoming, nor foisting on others what we want them to be instead of greeting their otherness: "May each one seek out his own way. The way leads to mutual love in community."[53] "If we fulfill the need of the self ... through this we become aware of the needs of the communal and can fulfill them." But, "If you give up your self, you live it in others; thereby you become selfish to others ... infect others ... To live oneself means: to become one's own task ... a long suffering, since you must become your own creator."[54] Jung's way is wrestling with self and God and, through that, serving others.

To Jung's astonishment his way means to become Christ, not just to follow Christ, but to engage temptation of the good, not just of evil as did Christ, to suffer torture of the spirit by the flesh, not just torture of the flesh by the spirit as did Christ.[55] Jung sees he must suffer his own mystery play, not imitate another's; nor should we, for "you have your own. ... Utterly poor, miserable, unknowingly humiliated, go on through your gate."[56] Jung does not identify with God but remains himself: "You do not become God ... but God becomes human. ... as a child"; "I become Christ in the Mysterium. ... I was made into Christ ... and yet am completely myself so that I still doubt."[57]

In saying to follow Christ is to be Christ means that Jung and we pursue our unique way as Christ did his and accept the suffering that comes with doing so—with good and evil, with self and other, with personal and collective, with images of God. It demands everything, and Jung accepts even enlarging his gender in giving birth to this new sense of God, redeeming the feminine without which he could not engage his *Red Book* venture and come through it.

Living our unique way with all it demands means accepting death into life. By becoming as if a dead man, sacrificing striving, letting go of what had been his ruling aims and modes of being—knowing about instead of participating in, certainty over ambiguity—Jung accepts that in the depths, "To be that which you are is ... an endlessly slow growth"; with knowledge from the heart, which "is in no book ... not ... in ... any teacher, but grows out of you like the green seed from the dark earth."[58] Drawing darkness of death from the beyond into every day empties the beyond because we live all we can here. Death is a booster shot to live right now, reminding us that we are not forever: "If I accept death, my tree greens ..."; "limitation enables you to fulfill your being"; "Therefore the demands of the dead disappeared, as they were satisfied."[59]

The dead also represent the wisdom of the ages, not just personal unlived life. By accepting limits of finitude, we can draw upon the sages of the past for the life to be lived now. Uniting with the serpent quells the devil's influence that invades "through one's own serpenthood, which one commonly assigns to the devil instead of oneself." "I took part of the humiliation and subjugation upon myself" and gained stability that "... could withstand the fluctuations of the personal. Therefore the immortal in me was saved."[60]

Jung arrives at his personal god-image and says this is possible for everyone; it is thus that we are host for the gods.[61] Our god-image, mothered by our soul, forms our personal answer to Abraxas, "the effectual itself" that produces "truth and lying, good and evil, light and darkness, life and death in the same word and … act. Abraxas is terrible."[62] Our differentiated individuation process to find and create our god-image is the gateway to the God and our response to Abraxas: "The blind creative drive becomes transformed … through individuation & out of this process, which is like a pregnancy, arises a divine child, a reborn God; no more dispersed … but being one & this individual, and at the same time all individuals … born in many individuals, but they don't know it. … A spirit in many people … the same everywhere."[63] By living our life to the full, we find our particular image of the divine child born of our souls, and it throws a bridge across death.[64] Philemon advises, "This one God is the kind, the loving, the leading, the healing. … To him you should pray, you are one with him, he is near you, nearer than your own soul."[65] I understand this to mean the more devoted we are to this healing god-image, the more we participate in the whole, which wants our contribution; the less, the more blasted by the force of being (Abraxas). Devotion to our ownmost way enriches the wholeness of the whole.

Philemon describes "the celestial mother," the final intimation of the feminine in the book, as "spirituality conceives and embraces. It is womanlike."[66] Jung may come under her aegis when he completes his separation from "commingling" that arises through "unlived love" where he still bonds "with men and things." Jung submits to shredding motives competing with his "voluntary devotion" by "remaining true to love and willingly accepting all the pain and … suffering … only thus do I arrive at … my truest and innermost self."[67] By way of our blundering, "the time has come when each must do his own work of redemption."[68]

Endnotes

[1] C.G. Jung, *The Red Book: Liber Novus*, ed. Sonu Shamdasani, trans. John Peck, Mark Kyburz, and Sonu Shamdasani (New York, NY: W.W. Norton, 2009), 260.

[2] Ibid., 360.

[3] Ibid., 338.

[4] Ibid., 272.

[5] Ibid., 230; William McGuire, ed., *C.G. Jung. Analytical Psychology* (Princeton, NJ: Princeton University Press, 1991), 63.

[6] Ibid., 247.

[7] Ibid., 235; an analysand, an abbot, dreamt he was present at the death of Jesus and *heard* a great secret that frightened and strengthened him: Jesus blaspheming God. See Ann Belford Ulanov, *Picturing God* (Einsiedeln: Daimon, 1986/2002), 174.

[8] Ibid., 240.

[9] Ibid., 366.

[10] Ibid., 314.

[11] Ibid., 235.

[12] Ibid., 299.

[13] Ibid., 237.

[14] Ibid.

[15] Ibid., 299-300.

[16] Ibid., 239 n91, 307 n240, 231 n27.

[17] Ibid., 320.

[18] Ibid., 289.

[19] Ibid., 301, 304, and 369.

[20] Ibid., 233.

[21] Ibid., 244-245.

[22] Ibid., 328. Also see Sanford L. Drob, *Reading the Red Book. An Interpretive Guide to C. G. Jung's Liber Novus* (New Orleans, LA: Spring Journal, 2012), 198-199.

[23] Ibid., 306.

[24] Ibid., 238 and 339.

[25] Ibid., 234 and 299.

[26] Ibid., 236.

[27] Ibid., 244 and 250; see also C.G. Jung, "Psychology and Literature," in *CW*, vol. 15 (Princeton, NJ: Princeton University Press, 1966), par. 159.

[28] Ibid., 263.

[29] Ibid., 364-365.

[30] Ibid., 233 n49.

[31] Ibid., 290-291.

[32] Ibid., 300.

[33] Ibid., 243.

[34] Ibid., 304.

[35] Ibid., 234 and 334.

[36] Ibid., 229.

[37] Ibid., 243-244.

[38] Ibid., 291.

[39] Ibid., 287.

[40] Ibid., 301 and 351.

[41] Ibid., 229 and 359.

[42] Ibid., 338.

[43] Ibid., 339.

[44] Ibid., 344.

[45] Ibid., 350 and 371.

[46] Ibid., 352.

[47] Ibid., 338.

[48] Ibid., 230.

[49] Ibid., 338-339.

[50] Ibid., 231.

[51] Ibid., 356.

[52] Ibid., 230-231.

[53] Ibid., 231 and 233.

[54] Ibid., 245 and 249.

[55] Ibid., 234-235, 253-254, 299.

[56] Ibid., 246.

[57] Ibid., 254 n238, 255 n240.

[58] Ibid., 233 and 266.

[59] Ibid., 274-275 and 322.

[60] Ibid., 322-323.

[61] Ibid., 315.

[62] Ibid., 349-350.

[63] Ibid., 354 n123, 371.

[64] Ibid., 354.
[65] Ibid., 371.
[66] Ibid., 352.
[67] Ibid., 355-356.
[68] Ibid., 356.

Jung, the Nothing and the All

John Dourley

In the opening pages of *The Red Book: Liber Novus,* Jung identifies the severance of the spirit of "... this time ..." from "... the spirit of the depths ..." as the primary pathology of individual and culture in his milieu.[1] He confesses that he himself had been its victim. "I had to become aware that I had lost my soul."[2] He had objectified the soul in the name of psychology as science. He had removed her from the totality of human experience, reducing it to mind in interplay with the senses and to a sterile scholarly approach to the depths of his own being. Such research made of him nothing less than a murderer of the soul.[3] Later in *Liber Novus,* his portrait of the scholar of science is a depressing picture of a man imprisoned in his library within an isolated castle in the middle of a swamp. The hermit is nearly impervious both to the approach of Jung and to the presence of his own daughter in a nearby room.[4] In Jung's imagination, the scholar's removal from his anima and from his soul becomes the same removal. There could hardly be a more forceful portrayal of living in an intellect quarantined from those vitalities accessed only in the flow of a deeper psychic and spiritual life.

The personal and social experience described here led to an ambivalent relation to science itself expressed both in *Liber Novus* and carried over into later works that have been published in the *Collected Works.* On the one hand, bowing to the scientism of his age, Jung would describe his work as "scientific" and so describe himself as a scientist. Yet in his *Red Book,* in dialogue with an imaginal Eastern giant seeking wisdom in the West, he indicts science with the crime of being a societal "poison."[5] It bears only a knowledge of "outer things" and knows little or nothing of the inner world of the enlivening divine. It has removed from its constituency the ability to believe, not in the sense of commitment to a formal creed or doctrine, but in the sense of an unmediated experience of the depths of reason itself. It is made up wholly of "words" and is a magic greatly injurious to its surroundings. This poison has paralyzed the "enlightened" who have drunk so deeply of it. In its self-imposed poverty, scientific research has lost the ability to deal with "... real life ..." and has reduced the psyche to a mind estranged from the vigor and play of the full range of the total psyche.[6]

Nor was this critique softened in his later writings as the history of the factors contributing to such psychological impairment became clearer to him. He continued his critique of science as the dominant religion of his time and so the new "opium of the people."[7] In particular, science was the preferred drug of the devotees of the Goddess of Reason and enlightenment rationalism, whose shallow clarity was so susceptible to archetypal possession and so to collective violence.[8] Unremittingly harsh though this criticism remained, it must be made as clear as it possibly can that Jung was in no way opposed to science, the Enlightenment, or reason in themselves. What provoked his vitriol was the perverse reduction of human cognition and affect to "science" as the solely valid activity of consciousness. His real enemy is Blake's Urizen. The more recent history of the mind had produced a sovereignty of reason trending to science and technology in the face of which the opposition of a largely fundamentalist and literal religion was all too easily and happily dismissed. The consequence was a society based upon a superficial rational meaninglessness, a science reduced to impressive gadgetry, and a religion grounded in "sacrosanct unintelligibility."[9] Liber Novus documents Jung's earliest diagnosis of the problem in anticipation of his later work.

Fortunately, the soul Jung lost to a consciousness removed from it refused to yield to such illness. Effectively the soul forced itself back upon Jung, and commerce with it became an incredible journey toward the "... unfathomable, which we call the divine."[10] The depths insisted on their admission to consciousness and, though the cure they worked was never divested of suffering, the life they restored to Jung as described in his Red Book was to become the rudimentary structure and power of his later more discursive writings.[11] So much came to change. As the depths emerged, their sacred nature came with them. They could be prayed to: "... pray to your depths, waken the dead."[12] Jung came to see them revealed in the personal revelation of the dream pointing to and enabling a far fuller life than could "... the dead system ..." of his previous wholly intellectual psychology.[13] He would contend that the heroic ego had to be dispensed with if the depths were to fully impact the conscious mind. He would insist that only the recovery of the mind's life-giving connection with the depths of the psyche would create that more universal sympathy that could undermine the tragic, often lethal, animosities existing between nations and communities. Indeed, he came to realize that the hostilities of the First World War were externalizations of the psychic hostilities within his psyche and the psyche of the masses caught up in the conflict.[14] But perhaps the most important conclusion from these remarks remains Jung's frank confession at the opening and closing of his *Red Book* that its description of the recovery of his soul in such vivid pre-rational imagery contained the "primal stuff" that he was to expound with more measured deliberation in his later so-called "scientific" work.[15] This confession brings us to two major questions facing today's culture:

1. Is not the severance of the spirit of our time from the depths of collective and individual humanity not as prevalent in our time as in Jung's, and so is not his effort to bring about their integration as important now as it was when he wrote *Liber Novus*? Would not this realization make the *Collected Works* a valued resource, in theory and therapy, if humanity is to save itself from its own removal from the inner and only source that could unite its many conflicting archetypal expressions in diverse communities bonded religiously and politically by the powers latent in those very depths?

2. Since Jung came to see, as his reflections in the *Red Book* continued, that the needed recovery of soul is a religious process, does the work not urge a new cultural religious perspective, one that may be in considerable tension with the major religious orthodoxies, a tension explaining their admiration of Jung's religious sensitivities, and their refusal

to accept the way he sees the religious impulse moving into a future beyond monotheistic claims in so many ways?[16]

The questions may coalesce in an examination of Jung's *Septem Sermones ad Mortuos* ("Seven Sermons to the Dead") in the last section of *The Red Book*, "Scrutinies."[17] Here in the form of Gnostic myth, related elsewhere to the Gnostic teacher Basilides,[18] is an effort to show how the spirit of the depths might come to pervade the spirit of the time with a societal and individual religiosity at once more internally profound and yet more externally encompassing than any cultural perspective then or now existent. Jung's thrust would be that the deeper into one's interiority one is led by the spirit of the depths, the more inclusive does one's embrace of the beyond become since the within, the depth, is the living source of the totality of the beyond. And no less a figure than his anima insists, much against his preference, that he is indeed to be the bringer of a new religious perspective to his culture.[19]

The first of the series of sermons preached by Jung's spokesman, Philemon, to the disappointed dead returning without the enlighten-ment they expected from the other side[20] begins with what is, in effect, the corrosion of John's prologue: In the beginning is not the Word. Here, in the beginning there is Nothingness. The Nothing would seem to precede the Word and all mentation beyond whose grasp it wholly lies. However, this Nothingness is at the same time a fullness, a Pleroma, and the source of both creation and conscious-ness. Here, Jung begins to play with a sophisticated metaphysical conception of participation. It is the "essence" or nature of the finite creature to live apart and distinct from the Pleroma, and yet the creature and all that is participates, or "is part of," the Pleroma. Essentially removed from the eternal, the finite creature remains part of it, for the Pleroma as the creature's source pervades the All.[21] In this remark, Jung echoes the words of Marguerite Porete, a 14th-century mystic who insisted that unless she could attain the Nothing she could not be All.[22] Indeed, Jung later all but quotes her literally when he refers to the sole validity of a contemporary spirituality as standing "... before the Nothing out of which All may grow."[23]

At this point in the early unfolding of the myth, some allusion to the creatures' return to the Pleroma might be expected, but here it is not provided. On the contrary, the creature is by its nature driven to differentiate itself from the Pleroma and, in so doing, to establish its individuality or singularity. At the time he wrote *Liber Novus,* Jung considered the creature's return to the Pleroma negatively, as a "dissolution" working to retreat from the ongoing creation of finite individuality, and so a betrayal of its essence.[24] The mature Jung would reverse this position in his treatment of Eckhart, whose "breakthrough" into a dissolution in the Godhead was precisely what Jung here abhors.[25] Jung, in the context of *Liber Novus,* is primarily concerned with the procession of the creature from the Pleroma and its ongoing finite development. To do this he borrows a medieval phrase, *principium individuationis,* the principle of individuation, to describe the drive toward being an individual moving progressively away from a regressive dissolution in the wealth of its source, the Pleroma, to an ever deeper engagement in the demands of finite life and the making of the individual.[26] Jung applies the same phrase to Jesus as representative of the divine life latent in the unconscious and drawn into consciousness in the making of the divine/human individual.[27]

In "The Seven Sermons to the Dead" Jung is impressed by the opposites. Paradoxically, he describes them as not real in the Pleroma but as simply archetypal potential yet very real in finite consciousness as an expression of the potential within the Pleroma. Jung cautions about a one-sided identity with one of the opposites severed from the other. For instance, beauty must always entail the ugly. Psychic strategy demands an awareness of this situation, a knowing distance from psychic possession by any member of the opposites without inclusion of the other.[28] In this early formulation Jung refers to a "rent" in the Pleroma and in finite consciousness but refrains from emphasizing this note, which is so powerful in his late writings and especially in his *Answer to Job.*[29] Here he simply affirms that the eternal "rent" in the Pleroma, which is the source of finite consciousness, seeks resolution of its split[30] in the finite consciousness it births. The fissure is healed through the mutual redemption of the divine and human in conscious time, space, and history.

In these early passages, the thought of Meister Eckhart is referenced, as it is a number of times throughout his works.[31] Jung was later to write a piece on Eckhart, which is one of his finer contributions to the full integration of the religious and psychological meaning of religious experience and expression.[32] In this work and throughout much of his later writing, Jung's thought is at once theological, philosophical, and psychological without being reducible to any one of these fragmentations of mind when taken alone. Jung and Eckhart both appreciate the cyclical return of the mind to an identity with its origin and the mind's resonance with such moments of identity in life subsequent to the experience.[33] This union of epistemic, ontological, psychological, and theological truth illustrates the poverty of the contemporary scene, which is divested of a category as encompassing as is Jung's perspective in its resistance to all traditional disciplinary fragmentation into which his psychology might be forced and thus truncated.

In short, in his early work aspects of Jung's myth are already compatible with Eckhart while some tension remains with the total Eckhart more fully appropriated in later works. Eckhart discerned two dimensions in divinity between which he drew a rather stringent difference. Eckhart's God was Trinitarian and imbued with so impassioned an inner life that it was called a *bullitio*, "a boiling." In fact, so fervid was the inner boiling that it became an *ebullitio*, "a boiling over." In the beginning, God boiled over, a Jungian wit might say. The primordial "boiling over" gave rise both to creation and to the fall. In creation, the existential ego realized it was removed from its source, and this removal became the motive for the drive to its recovery.[34] The experience of a removal from a fontal origin of life as the basis of a drive to its ever fuller reappropriation is at least partially resonant with the suffering derived from Abraxas's reign as the ruler of a world of contradiction and the need to affirm one's unique self in its midst. In Jung's early myth, though profoundly paradoxical, the Pleroma might well be understood as driven to express itself beyond itself in the life of each individual and creature, all of whom participate in it and its drive to individuation in the self-affirming creature. Thus, the *Seven Sermons* more than hint at a primordial plenitude driven to express itself beyond itself as the basis of each individual's drive and burden to realize a measure of divine completion in one's personal completion. This theme is at the core of Jung's *Answer to Job*. Religiously and theologically, it brings up the serious question of the necessity driving the Creator to create and to seek its needful completion in the history of human consciousness.

However, Eckhart also referred to a different dimension of God, namely *Gottheit*, or Godhead. It is into the Godhead that the ego is led to a breakthrough (*Durchbruch*) and to an identity, a total fusion or absorption of the individual with the divine beyond distinction. The total return to this dimension of the divine lies behind Eckhart's twice repeated prayer: "I pray to God to rid me of God."[35] This is a crucial point in Jung's later work on Eckhart. It would mean at a certain point in the psyche, every individual is vested with an ontological participation in the being of the divine and that its attainment would mean unqualified identity with divinity, and Jung makes this explicit in his later essay on Eckhart. "As a result of this retrograde process the original state of identity with God is re-established and a new potential is produced."[36] In this line, Jung means psychic identity in a real and literal sense. In the *Seven Sermons,* he is far less radical. Here, a moment of identity without difference is to be avoided as a form of regressive dissolution destructive of one's progressive individuality and of that fullness of life that the Pleroma demands of everyone. A later Jung could suggest that a moment of identity with the Divine, or approximation thereof, is the ground of one's truest affirmation as an individual.

As briefly noted, an added powerful and paradoxical player in the drive to individuality is Abraxas, variously described as the Divinity beyond the opposites, and yet as their source and the ruler of their inevitability within this world. A condensation of Jung's attitude toward Abraxas can never be fully satisfactory. Basically, Jung would urge the individual to pursue one's most individual truth in the face of Abraxas and the suffering of the contradictions he imposes on every finite life. In the face of the inescapable conflicts,

Abraxas lays on the individual in finitude one must bow to him but never at the cost of abandoning one's deepest individual truth and the singularity of life it demands.[37] Neither flight nor capitulation is acceptable. Jung suggests that the price Jesus paid in his oppositional subjugation to Abraxas demonstrates the latter's cruelty, and yet, in the end, Jesus has distilled the situation into "... the beauty of suffering."[38]

The Christian dead to whom these words are addressed rightly perceive that their perception of a wholly transcendent and self-sufficient divinity is being undermined and take great umbrage with such a view, even though they themselves and their age have outgrown such a divinity into a maturity that believes only what it can experience at a lesser level.[39] Nonetheless, Philemon/Jung refuses to placate them with a simple replacement of what they have already outgrown. Rather, the preacher proclaims that God is not dead: "He is as alive as ever."[40] But his life is far different from the life of any God the Christians have understood. In effect, God is manifest in every creature. Jung/Philemon is proposing a universal sacramentality in which every existent participates in the Pleroma as its expression, and humanity can and should become aware of it. In later works, Jung will identify the opposites in the Pleroma and in their expression moving to integration in human consciousness. But in this early work, he speaks less of the union of opposites and insists more on a simple awareness of their reality.[41] In fact, he cautions against a too superficial, perhaps too rational, bringing together of Christ and Satan. Their more than intellectual truth is in a "medium," a more than intellectual coming together. Later, Jung seems to have come to an incipient realization that the opposites not only have to be recognized and acknowledged but that the deeper movement of the psyche is to bring them together. In his essay on the Trinity, he strongly suggests that the light and dark sons of the same Father, Christ and Satan, would move to an embrace or resolution in the psyche and so in history.[42] Already in his *Red Book*, he is signaling that this unity is not a work of reason but that of a mediator who unites opposites through a transrational process comparable to a new insight funded by the psyche like a new revelation.

Again, a more thorough elaboration of Jung/Philemon's reflection on the essence of humanity reveals that it may not be as wholly entrapped in finitude as some formulations would insist. As noted, Jung is dealing with a dialectical conception of the essence of humanity as a participant in the Pleroma and the Pleroma in it. This side of his understanding of essence is a strong early evidence of Jung's essentialism and Platonic sensitivity. In the elaboration of the Pleroma, there is a sense in which it does not exist, and yet it is also given the note of "effectiveness." This means that archetypal potentiality drives toward its own realization. This is akin to what Jung was later to appreciate in the mystic Jacob Boehme, namely, the drive of God to find manifest expression and, through it, divine self-consciousness in creation and human consciousness.[43] Every individual becomes an expression of the Pleroma. Such expression is one's truest essence. The conclusion is that each human is potentially divine and that the process of maturation, individuation, is to move to the making of this potentiality real in the process of living life to its fullest.[44] We will return to an elaboration of this conception in the sixth sermon, where it is related to a blue star or light grounded in the Pleroma following and leading the individual through life's journey as gently but forcefully supporting that individual's deepest truth.

It is not difficult to see in these themes a harbinger of Jung's later conception of the individual's "primal form." During a late illness, his doctor appeared to Jung in his primal form as "the *basileus* of Kos," "… an avatar of Kos, the temporal embodiment of the primal form which has existed from the beginning."[45] As humanity's healing emissary, the doctor was to summon Jung back to earth's demands. He was to die on the day Jung left his sick bed in a mysterious commerce between life recovered and life lost, one Jung never explained.[46] But the imagery of the event is clearly of an energy like the eternal self as the underlying truth of the individual seeking its realization in time to be fully attained only in its eternal reality. Jung claims to have witnessed something like these events only once more. After her death, Jung's wife appeared to him in her primal or "objective" truth beyond emotion and projection dressed as in a "portrait" that took Jung back through the particular moments of their life together to the deepest meaning running through it all. Her whole life had been guided by her deeper truth, and now she stood in its eternal realization as fully her own.[47] To illustrate the many sides of life in the world beyond, Jung would later note that on one occasion he woke to the realization that he had spent a day with his wife after her death and that she had continued in death to work on her Grail project as if still to complete herself.[48] It would appear that the attainment of the primal form and some kind of continued development are not incompatible in the world from which the dead in *Liber Novus* return.

From this perspective of life's meaning as self-affirmation, the figure of Christ can be seen as the proto-individual because he represents for Jung the man who lived out his individual truth even to the cruel death imposed by Abraxas.[49] In his later work, Jung describes Jesus as a "*principium individuationis.*"[50] In the earlier *Liber Novus,* Jung postulates: "We should not bear Christ as he is un-bearable but we should be Christs, ..."[51] To be a Christ as distinct from being a Christian means that the individual realizes he or she must imitate or emulate no one: Christ lived out his life wholly faithful to his essential truth.[52] Jung confesses that he himself had been a Christian but not a Christ. Imitators of Christ are thus indicted: "They have imitated it [the life of Christ], but they have not lived their own lives as you have lived yours. ... everyone would have to take their own life into their own hands, faithful to their own essence and their own love."[53] Here the premonition of the self becomes the individual's essence and the basis of true love.

The image of a life lived beyond emulation or imitation out of the depths of one's continuity with the Pleroma is indeed enticing. It draws attention to several attributes of the Christ figure not prominent in more traditional depictions. It gives a priority to an inner relationship as the experiential substance not only of Christianity but of all religions. The point reappears later in Jung's insistence that the initial approach of the divine to the human is always from within.[54] It also strongly suggests that reliance on the interior life beyond imitation or emulation carries with it a greater sympathetic or compassionate embrace of all that lies beyond such profound interiority. The journey inward is also the journey outward.

In reflecting on the relation of religion to the psychic laws that control historical development, Jung will assert that Christianity's initial one-sidedness would eventually demand its own transcendence.[55] The unqualified goodness of Christ split the figure from its own opposite, Satan, who became the dark brother of Christ. In his work after the *Red Book,* Jung refers to the split as "… the fatality inherent in the Christian disposition itself, which leads inevitably to a reversal of spirit—not through the obscure workings of chance but in accordance with psychological law."[56] This side of Jungian psychology points to the presence of an operating philosophy of history in which the archetypal basis of consciousness seeks its full realization in historical consciousness with a truly Hegelian necessity. From this passage Jung goes on to locate the inevitable reversal of Christian one-sidedness in the Renaissance, the Enlightenment, and the French Revolution.[57]

In *The Red Book's* description of the figure of Christ as living wholly out of his individualizing interiority to the point of death, Jung is anticipating a later foundational theme that divinity must express its totality beyond itself to be fully itself. This conviction would move Jung from a Trinitarian to a quaternitarian paradigm in terms of a much more inclusive sense of the sacred in the Spirit of the quaternity than the Christian Spirit can proffer. Such a Spirit would unite in its life the divine realities of Christ and Satan, male and female, spirit and matter. Currently, the self would endorse this consciousness as an expression of so much more than the simple union of Father and Son in a relatively pallid Christian Spirit. In this area alone, the contention that Jung was the bearer of a new religion is well-founded, as is his claim in his dialogue with Fr. Victor White, O.P., that he was a modern Joachim di Fiore.[58] Joachim, the late 12th- and early 13th-century monk, saw the imminent advent of a new religious spirit that, in fact, did blossom in the mendicant orders and scholasticism of the mid-13th century. His broadening of the sense of the sacred would also be operative in Jung's sustained interest in Mercurius as an older brother of Christ living out rudimentary elements of a humanity hardly appreciated by traditional views.[59] When Jung endorses Mercurius as *capax utrius* (capable of both) he points to a figure whose spiritual life is integrated with his animal life to a degree beyond the Christian pale.

And yet it is crucial to recognize that Jung's insistence on the drive of the Pleroma to find its expression in the individual creature as the meaning of creation itself speaks of an ideal individual free of all forms of individualism. The individual the source seeks is one whose individuality is the very basis of a relation to the totality. Jung was later to make this point explicit in the psychology of the *unus mundus* (the "one world"). In the footsteps of Gerhard Dorn, he describes a process beginning in an asceticism so rigorous it is well-depicted as death, moving to a sense of resurrection in a *caelum* ("heaven") of the glorified body.[60] The development culminates in the experience of the individual's continuity with the totality through "... the eternal Ground of all empirical being" as the ground of one's personal being.[61] The psychology of the *unus mundus*, thus described, would involve the integration of the many complexes within the individual coupled with the individual's empathic relation to the totality since individual and totality share the same ground. In *Liber Novus,* this psychology is latent in the participation of the individual in the Pleroma as the underlying and generative power in each creature. Such universal compassion and full participation in the ground, Jung confesses, can only be approximated in the finite psyche.

However limited it may be, the drive to such depth and extension cannot be evaded. As noted previously, in the earlier pages of *Liber Novus*, Jung describes the essence of the individual as largely confined by the finite and driven to affirm its individuality in that context.[62] But in the "Seventh Sermon to the Dead," he seems to greatly extend this notion of the essence of humanity in imagery that foreshadows the reality of the self. Here, he speaks of a turn inward to the realm of a blue star: "This is the one God of this one man, this is his world, his Pleroma, his divinity."[63] The star can be the object of prayer. Its blue light guides the individual through life and toward an individuality that the star itself crowns.[64] It is the individual's "stellar nature" and "truest and innermost self that simply and singly is."[65] Accessing the star involves a cunning attitude toward Abraxas as ruler of this world: He can neither be fled nor embraced, but neither can one capitulate to him and still remain under the influence of the blue star. Rather, suffering Abraxis is the key to living the spiritual and moral life toward the blue star and in a sense becoming Abraxis oneself in the ensuing freedom gained.[66] The servant of the blue star is a "mediator," an individual who suffers the opposites in what could well be called the redemption of God, appreciated by God and humanity as completing the divine effort in creation. In this context, "mediator" means one in whom the opposites come together in an authentic integration of a total divinity with a total humanity.[67]

But if individuation is to be equated with divinization actualized in the individual living toward the truth of the blue star, what would be the social and political consequences for a society composed of such individuals? Would there not be a constant threat to the social order by those not so much led but possessed by their star in conflict with the presiding culture. In *Liber Novus*, Jung shows that he is at least aware of the problem and deals with it again in his later works. In the fifth sermon, Philemon pits community against "singleness." Put simply: "Singleness is opposed to community."[68] As he amplifies this opposition, Philemon contends that community is necessary as a kind of collective defense against the overwhelming importunities of the gods and demons—i.e., "archetypal compulsions"—on the membership. The thrust would seem to be that community protects those in it from the invasion of powers that would take over individuals whose inflated "singleness" could threaten society itself. Here he sees the need for community, as imposed on humanity by the divine, as protection against gods and demons. But he notes briefly as well that when community does more than this, "… more is bad."[69] The danger is that community always demands submission to others and so is in permanent tension with the drive to singularity, which he so highly respects. In singleness one places oneself above others in the avoidance of "slavery." And so, in the *Septem Sermones* and also in his wider work, the tensions between community and individual remain identified, but they are hardly resolved if ever they can be. At this early stage, restraint in submission to the slavery of community remains in tension with self-affirmation as a divine demand.[70]

While still sensitive to the tension between communal submission and singleness depicted in *Liber Novus*, a later Jung would seem to give a certain priority to singleness. Indeed, he could be read to place it in almost moral categories based on fidelity to the self in every circumstance, individual and collective. In later discussions of the issue, Jung had become fully familiar with the reality of social archetypal possession. Such "... politico-social delusional systems"[71] could lead vast populations into widespread neuroses and forms of the societal "lunacy," which Jung saw in his contemporary world and which only a "mystical fool" could anticipate in their advent.[72] In fact, any form of "-ism," religious or political, had the archetypal power to bond its membership in paroxysms of collective unconsciousness.[73] It would appear that the role of community in protecting its members from divine possession far too often could force them into it.

The conflict between community and individual that Jung saw in his society at the time he wrote the *Red Book* is certainly occurring in ours. The far right returns with a sense of absolute authority that can move to violence. Such despotism coupled with nationalism and populism also embodies a problematic attitude toward human rights. It is particularly insidious in its rejection of an underlying human commonality as the ground for the rejection of exceptionalism and supremacy in any significant realm of the human spirit.

What does Jung propose in the name of the hopefully offsetting "singleness" he describes in *Liber Novus*? His response is noble. Yet, one must also wonder if, like all that is noble, it is not also fragile. In the face of the mass movements of community over the singular individual, he writes: "*Resistance to the organized mass can be effected only by the man who is as well organized in his individuality as the mass itself.*"[74] The individual organization here applauded is obviously the effect of the self coming to greater prominence in the individual's psyche. But can such exceptional drama occur in the face of a population possessed? How many were as "well-organized" as the Gestapo in the Nazi period? How many victims of any holocaust anywhere were as well-organized as the perpetrators? And yet on sustained reflection, what other resources are available than the power of inner resistance at least informing and humanizing the activist's zeal? Activism in the hope of change is itself often archetypally possessed. For instance, in some of its greatest stories as in Marxism, fascism, communism, and the strange marriage of democracy with unrestrained capitalism, activism has become the oppressor it hoped to overthrow. *Liber Novus* has been described as bringing in a new religiosity, or at least as an effort to "... grasp the religious future development of the West."[75] Perhaps this is nowhere more evident than in the social/political field. In continuity with the above passage on the need for the individual to be as well-organized as the masses, Jung writes: "The individual who is not anchored in God can offer no resistance on his own resources to the physical and moral blandishments of the world. For this he needs the evidence of inner, transcendent experience which alone can protect him from the otherwise inevitable submersion in the mass."[76] What does being "... anchored in God ..." really mean? In *Liber Novus*, it meant being led by the blue star. In the context of the later citation, it means a consciousness impregnated by the self.

Much is at stake in this seemingly arcane issue, possibly the survival of humanity itself. Should consciousness fail to anchor itself in God, the late Jung warns that humanity is "threatened with universal genocide if we cannot work out the way of salvation by a symbolic death."[77] In context, Jung means the death of the currently presiding symbol, in his day the imagination of the monomind, whether religious and/or secular, and the birth of a symbol more capable of sustaining the full range of the human spirit and its ground. But what would this look like in practice? The meaning of dreams could be again taken seriously as the revelation of a greatly extended inner world and so induce compassion for all that exists in the outer world. Opposites both within and without could be seen as valid, each with a legitimate seat in a much wider conscious assembly. The power of the archetypal could be recognized and in its recognition be divested of its current power to convene communities of hatred in deeply rooted conflict. The social reformer would become keenly aware of "... the atrocities that attend the rebirth of a God" and be chastened in one's zeal.[78]

With his fear of genocide, Jung was sensitive to the dark side but could pen words of hope in the face of the ideological/archetypal conflicts of his day: "The afternoon of humanity, in a distant future, may yet evolve a different ideal. In time, even conquest will cease to be the dream."[79] Here Jung acknowledges that conquest rests on the conflict of psychic opposites, and he seeks its abolition in their mutual defeat or embrace beyond their antipathy. In his later works, Jung went on to paint the basic drive of the psyche toward the resolution of inner conflict as the only real basis for the resolution of the conflicts that destroy bodily lives on external battlefields. In the spirit of our time, which is also severed from the spirit of the depths, ideological conflict drives toward fragmentation among individuals infected with an unrelated individualism and among political and national communities affirming their own limited reality as the best or only one. The afternoon of a conquest-free humanity does indeed seem distant. Yet running through Jung's psychology, which is rooted in his own kind of ontology and its keen philosophy of history, there lives a hope against which no darkness would prevail. It shines through in so surprising a place as his understanding of an evolving religious sentiment growing in our midst, namely, that to be human is to be divine or to be moved toward divinity by divinity itself.[80] For Jung, such insight began in the *Red Book* when he realized that those who lived life to the fullest at the insistence of God were to become their own Gods.

If the split between the spirit of the times and the spirit of the depths remains the major challenge of our epoch, what consciousness would its healing bring to our day? Such consciousness would be religious in that it would be aware of the depths of the human spirit and soul and the numinous power that dwells in the creative commonality that belongs to all and authors all religions. But such consciousness could not be reduced to religion as understood within traditional institutions and those taking shape beyond them. Such consciousness would be theological. It would be aware that the referent of religious revelation, dogmatic affirmation, and moral and ritual reenactment is the power of the unconscious expressed in them. But such consciousness could not be reduced to theology, which, in the end, must hail the variant as the totality. Such consciousness would be a metaphysics made up of an ontology, epistemology, and philosophy of history. It would be aware that what is an inner archetypal power creating the experience of an ultimate power is destined to be exhaustively born in human history. But such consciousness could not be reduced to metaphysics and its continued and current fear of the deeply subjective. Such consciousness would be scientific. But it would be a science informed by a legitimate subjectivity aware of a deeper dimension of human cognition than science, rightfully true to itself, can accommodate. Again, such consciousness could not be reduced to science as usually understood. Indeed, such consciousness would also be related to medicine, psychiatry, physics, comparative mythology, anthropology, and more. It would be like the medieval *reductio*, an affirmation that all disciplines lead back to the divine when their depths are plumbed. But such consciousness could not be reduced to any discipline, or to a forced and artificial union of all of them. In healing the crevice between mind and soul, Jung is reaching for a new form of consciousness, one that would release the full powers of the soul into a consciousness hopefully inclusive of all the fragmented domains of mind now caught in disciplinary distinctions and imprisoned in discrete departments in the halls of knowledge of our time.

It would be a consciousness born out of the "... original experience which alone is convincing."[81] Jung is citing the Buddha here and offers some sense of what the new consciousness would entail. But because it would be so rich and new, it is difficult to lay it out in point-by-point form. Jung recognized the difficulty in doing so when, in relation to the new sense of interiority now demanded in the recovery of the soul, he wrote: "That is why nobody knows what ways of approach are open to man, what inner experiences he could still pass through and what psychic facts underlie the religious myth."[82] Whatever facts may underlie the new myth, they would coalesce around Jung's most encompassing description of it: "It was only quite late that we realized (or rather, are beginning to realize) that God is Reality itself and therefore—last but not least—man. This realization is a millennial process."[83] Millennial it may well be, but the realization that to be human is to be latently divine on the way to one's unique truth began for Jung as early as the pages of the *Red Book.*

Endnotes

1. C.G. Jung, *The Red Book: Liber Novus*, ed. Sonu Shamdasani, trans. John Peck, Mark Kyburz, and Sonu Shamdasani (New York, NY: W.W. Norton, 2009), 229-232, 237, 238 n91.

2. Jung, *The Red Book*, 232.

3. Ibid., 230.

4. Ibid., 261-263.

5. Ibid., 278.

6. Ibid., 278-280.

7. C.G. Jung, "Marginalia on Contemporary Events", in *CW*, vol. 18 (Princeton, NJ: Princeton University Press, 1976), par. 1366 and par. 1373.

8. C.G. Jung, "The Spirit Mercurius," in *CW*, vol. 13 (Princeton, NJ: Princeton University Press, 1967), par. 294.

9. C.G. Jung, "A Psychological Approach to the Dogma of the Trinity," in *CW*, vol. 11 (Princeton, NJ: Princeton University Press, 1969), par. 170.

10. Jung, *The Red Book*, 232.

11. Ibid., VII.

12. Ibid., 235.

13. Ibid., 232.

14. Ibid., 253 n221.

15. Ibid., VII and 360.

16. Sonu Shamdasani, ed., *The Red Book*, 206-208, 211-212.

17. Jung, *The Red Book*, 346-354. Also see similar version in C.G. Jung, *Memories, Dreams, Reflections,* ed. Aniela Jaffé (New York, NY: Vintage, 1963), 378-390.

18. Jung, *Memories, Dreams, Reflections,* 378.

19. Jung, *The Red Book*, 346.

20. Jung, *Memories, Dreams, Reflections*, 308.

21. Jung, *The Red Book*, 346-347.

22. Marguerite Porete, *The Mirror of Simple Souls*, ed., E.L. Babinsky (New York, NY: Paulist Press, 1993), 129, 193.

23. C.G. Jung, "The Spiritual Problem of Modern Man," in *CW*, vol. 10 (Princeton, NJ: Princeton University Press, 1964), par. 150.

24. Jung, *The Red Book*, 347.

[25] See references of Jung to Eckhart in ibid., 339 n39 and 347 n82.

[26] Jung, *The Red Book*, 347.

[27] C.G. Jung, *Aion. Researches into the Phenomenology of the Self*, in *CW*, vol. 9/II (Princeton, NJ: Princeton University Press, 1959), par. 120.

[28] Jung, *The Red Book*, 347-348.

[29] C.G. Jung, *Answer to Job*, in *CW*, vol. 11 (Princeton, NJ: Princeton University Press, 1969), par. 553 to par. 758.

[30] Jung, *The Red Book*, 348.

[31] See endnote 25.

[32] C.G. Jung, *Psychological Types*, in *CW*, vol. 6 (Princeton, NJ: Princeton University Press, 1971), par. 407 to par. 433.

[33] J.P. Dourley, "Jung on the Moment of Identity and Its Loss as History," in *International Journal of Jungian Studies*, 2017, vol. 10, 1, Feb., 2018, 34-47.

[34] J.P. Dourley, *Jung and his Mystics: In the End It All Comes to Nothing* (London and New York, NY: Routledge, 2014), 88-91.

[35] Meister Eckhart, "Sermon, 'Blessed Are the Poor,'" in Reiner Schurmann, trans. (Bloomington, IN: Indiana University Press, 1987), 216, 219.

[36] Jung, *Psychological Types*, *CW* 6, par. 431.

[37] Jung, *The Red Book*, 370-371.

[38] Ibid., 359.

[39] Ibid., 349.

[40] Ibid., 348.

[41] See ibid., 348 n86 where this point is also addressed.

[42] Jung, "A Psychological Approach to the Dogma of the Trinity," in *CW*, vol. 11 (Princeton, NJ: Princeton University Press, 1969), par. 258.

[43] Dourley, *Jung and his Mystics: In the End It All Comes to Nothing*, 115-123.

[44] Jung, *The Red Book*, 348-349.

[45] Jung, *Memories, Dreams, Reflections*, 292.

[46] Ibid., 293.

[47] Ibid., 296.

[48] Ibid., 309.

[49] See endnote 38.

[50] Jung, *Aion. Researches into the Phenomenology of the Self*, *CW* 9/II, par. 118.

51 Jung, *The Red Book*, 283.

52 Ibid., 293.

53 Ibid., 356.

54 Jung, *Psychological Types*, CW 6, par. 430.

55 Jung, *Aion. Researches into the Phenomenology of the Self*, CW 9/II, par. 78.

56 Ibid.

57 Ibid.

58 C.G. Jung, Letter to Father Victor White, 24 November 1953, in Gerhard Adler, *C. G. Jung Letters*. Trans. by R. F. C. Hull. Vol. 2, 1951-1961 (Princeton, NJ: Princeton University Press, 1975), 138.

59 Jung, "The Spirit Mercurius," *CW* 13, par. 271 and 289.

60 C.G. Jung, *Mysterium Coniunctionis*, in *CW*, vol. 14 (Princeton, NJ: Princeton University Press, 1963), par. 762.

61 Ibid., par. 760.

62 See endnotes 21 and 24.

63 Jung, *The Red Book,* 354.

64 Ibid.

65 Ibid., 356.

66 Ibid., Appendix C 370-371.

67 Ibid., 358.

68 Ibid., 352.

69 Ibid.

70 Ibid., 352-353.

71 C.G. Jung, "Archetypes of the Collective Unconscious," in *CW*, vol. 9/I (Princeton, NJ: Princeton University Press, 1968), par. 49.

72 C.G. Jung, "The Concept of the Collective Unconscious," in *CW*, vol. 9/I (Princeton, NJ: Princeton University Press, 1968), par. 98.

73 C.G. Jung, "Concerning the Archetypes with Special Reference to the Anima Concept," in *CW*, vol. 9/I (Princeton, NJ: Princeton University Press, 1968), par. 125.

74 C.G. Jung, "The Undiscovered Self (Present and Future)," in *CW*, vol. 10 (Princeton, NJ: Princeton University Press, 1964), par. 540.

75 Jung, *The Red Book*, 207.

76 Jung, "The Undiscovered Self," *CW* 10, par. 511.

77 C.G. Jung, "Jung and Religious Belief," in *CW*, vol. 18 (Princeton, NJ: Princeton University Press, 1976), par. 1661.

78 Jung, *The Red Book,* 357.

79 C.G. Jung, "Psychological Commentary on 'The Tibetan Book of the Great Liberation'," in *CW*, vol. 11 (Princeton, NJ: Princeton University Press, 1969), par. 787.

80 Jung, *Answer to Job, CW* 11, par. 645.

81 Jung, "The Spiritual Problem of Modern Man," *CW* 10, par. 192.

82 Jung, "The Undiscovered Self," *CW* 10, par. 542.

83 Jung, *Answer to Job, CW* 11, par. 631.

Abraxas: Then and Now

J. Gary Sparks

The ancient Gnostic god Abraxas has a message for the 20th and 21st centuries. Although violence accompanies the return of Abraxas, the destruction he personifies paradoxically holds the possibility of transformation.[1]

The Gnostic Abraxas

The god plays a significant role in Jung's *Red Book*.[2] Jung further discusses Abraxas in the visions of a female patient 20 years later.[3] An additional 30 years place the name Abraxas on the cover of an LP album by the same name recorded by guitarist Carlos Santana, and the album's artwork is psychologically important.[4] After nearly another 50 years, a series of three recent dreams of a professional man in the second half of life suggestively portrays the Gnostic god.[5] At each point in the analysis to follow, the dreams show the practical and enduring relevance of Abraxas as he appeared to Jung first in his *Red Book* and subsequently continued to absorb him throughout his life. Abraxas, and all he portends, would not leave Jung alone over his lifetime, nor will the god excuse himself from our time—as three present-day dreams confirm.

The Red Book

Jung's Soul does not mince words. She says to him: "I want to set to work. But you must build the furnace. Throw the old, the broken, the worn out, the unused, and the ruined into the melting pot, so that it will be renewed for fresh use."[6] *The Red Book* concerns reevaluation. Long-standing religious, moral, ethical, and philosophical views that are no longer adequate to the demands of the time are to be discarded, destroyed, and reshaped. Primary among those views is the prevailing interpretation of Christianity. Jung contends that the worn-out form of Western religion has been unable to protect civilization against the massive destruction of two of the worst bloodbaths in world history.[7]

That *The Red Book* and the Soul's concerns are to be seen against the background of this history is established by another of her utterances to Jung. "I see the surface of the earth and smoke sweeps over it—a sea of fire rolls close in from the north ..."[8] The sea of fire is the impending catastrophe of World War I that was assaulting Jung's inner world in 1913.[9] The events of the war, and the recasting of values and understanding, are threads of a common tapestry.

"The Seven Sermons to the Dead"

Abraxas receives considered attention in "The Seven Sermons to the Dead,"[10] published within *The Red Book* in the section titled "Scrutinies."[11] In "The Seven Sermons," "the Dead" return from Jerusalem and approach Jung for help with their plight. They "cried in many voices, 'We have come back from Jerusalem, where we did not find what we sought. We implore you to let us in. You have what we desire. Not your blood, but your light.'"[12]

They are seeking "light," that is, understanding—but for what? A hint of the answer is contained in the authorship Jung attributes to early editions of the "The Seven Sermons"—Basilides, a Gnostic teacher who lived in the second century C.E.[13] The Christian Gnostics held a view of Christian cosmology that was declared a heresy by the growing Church.[14] Typical of the Gnostic view was that at the creation of the world, God (or the feminine part of God, Sophia) got trapped in the world. The Gnostics were more interested in direct emotional experience of God from within the world than through the Church as an intercessor between themselves and God.

The Dead long for a meaningful relation to God. In one sense the Dead are a portrait of the despair that swept over Europe as a result of the mass carnage of war: "How could God let this happen?"

people questioned.[15] More generally, the Dead symbolize the longing to recover what "official" Christianity has declared heretical in its repudiation of Gnosticism, leading, in our time, to a sterile, ineffective, and unpalatable religious outlook for increasing numbers of people.[16] The Dead long for a complete experience and understanding of God that will satisfy them. Philemon, a figure representative of wisdom in "The Seven Sermons," admonishes: "these dead ... knew no way beyond the one to which belief had abandoned them. ... I teach in this way because their Christian faith once discarded and persecuted precisely this teaching. But they repudiated Christian belief and hence were rejected by that faith. They do not know this and therefore I must teach them ..."[17]

Enter Abraxas

Abraxas is the fuller portrait of the sacred, containing what the Dead seek and what the prevailing image of God in our time must recover. Philemon again: "Abraxas is the God who is difficult to grasp. His power is greatest, because man does not see it. From the sun he draws the *summum bonum*, from the devil the *infinum malum* ..."[18]

A sample of his attributes illustrates Abraxas's complexity. He is emptiness, he dismembers, he is warring opposites. He is the great and small Pan. He is Priapus. He is a monster. He is a hermaphrodite. He is the still united opposites that will give rise to consciousness. Abraxas is: good, evil, the fullness of the sun, the sucking gorge of emptiness, life, death, creation, nothingness, truth, lying, light, darkness, the striking lion, the warm spring day, love, murder, sickness, wisdom, delight, horror, paralyzing, unquestioning, unquestionable, differentiation, speech, deception.[19]

A modern dream from the series of three under consideration conveys that Abraxas is still alive and well. "I am at a large outdoor festival. There is an area of sand sculptures. The sand sculptures are below me in sand pits. Among the sculptures I see unformed shapes. I slide down into the pit. I see the image of a fierce god composed of many gods: lions and boars, and other fierce animals. I give this sculpture shape and form. I slide deeper down into the second pit of sand and see the form of Superman lying on his side in agony. I give shape and form to this image also." The "fierce god composed of many gods" is an image of Abraxas. These "gods" must be recognized, conceptualized (given shape and form) in order to include them in the sweep of divinity and life.

The details of the dream are instructive. A *festival* is a social event. The word originates from the 14th century and first signified a religious social observance.[20] A festival brings together a community for common celebration. The events in the dream thus refer to our collective life and not merely the personal life of the dreamer. The *fierce god* is made of an assemblage of fierce animals. These gods are no loving forces but are made up of intense and potentially dangerous forces that have to be reckoned with. There is no protecting Father here, but a swirl of intensity that has the power to recklessly destroy life. Coming to terms with these forces, as the dreamer does in the dream and as the figure of Abraxas in Jung's vision implies, is the current religious task of our age. *Sand* is a malleable substance, and the dream suggests that facing, symbolizing, and ultimately coming into relationship with the fierce animals is not an impossible task for human hands. Sand, as well, can be an ingredient in concrete, hence the foundation of a construction that possesses strength and endurance.[21]

As in Jung's visionary experience of Abraxas, the wild god in the dream waits for recognition and incorporation into this era's personal and collective religious life.

Overpowering Essence of Events

Philemon has something else crucial to say about Abraxas. He calls Abraxas "the overpowering essence of events."[22] If God made humankind in His own image, then one's grasp of oneself and one's understanding of God are parallel.[23] What is excluded from the image of God is what is also going to be excluded from believers' understanding of themselves. The emotional and psychological qualities one does not recognize as belonging to God are the personal emotional and psychological qualities that individuals will have no ability to recognize in themselves and hence have no control over in daily life. The immediate implication of the statement about the "overpowering essence of events" is that the unrecognized qualities of Abraxas, excluded from a general theology and from personal psychological awareness, are exactly what a given generation lives out in war—indeed what has played out in two world wars.

The overall point is that *what the members of a society exclude from their common god-image is actually what determines events.* Abraxas represents much of what one says God is not, but which, in fact God is. Likewise, Abraxas represents everything the ideals of an age restrict from typical awareness, but which, in fact, break out in mass, often in savagely destructive, behavior. This is Abraxas.

The Visions Seminar

Two decades later, Jung returns to Abraxas and the transformation of God[24] in the visions of 28-year-old Christiana Morgan, an American woman who worked analytically with Jung in 1926.[25]

As Abraxas contains what has been excluded from the Christian god-image, and thus the aspects of one's own personal makeup that one has no way of consciously and responsibly relating to, the presence of the Abraxas image in our time will bring with it, naturally, the onslaught of energy that has been excluded in a world overseen by a good God, a God that is "light" only, a God that excludes the complexity that Abraxas embodies. Christiana's visions evidence this onslaught.

This is one of them: "I beheld a woman grown into the earth. ... Her hair was in a half-stagnant pool of water, and swayed slowly back and forth. ... She was in travail and I stood while she gave birth. From a white placenta emerged a creature in the shape of a child. ... It had four eyes bulging forth from its head. ... Its hands were clubs, its hands were claws. ... The breasts of the woman were dried up. So the creature (meaning the child) crawled to an iron wolf which stood nearby and the wolf suckled it."[26]

The initial image speaks of stagnation, which would refer to the patient's feeling that life and growth had become stagnant. The dream figure's swaying back and forth elucidates that the patient feels one thing one moment and another the next, back and forth with no forward movement. However, the patient's conscious acceptance of the feeling of being torn and stuck makes it possible over time for the dream birth to occur, signifying an independent development within the dreamer. The predicament is, however, that the child born is very problematic.

The child is born from the placenta. Jung interprets that the child is a spiritual child. That it is a spiritual child and not a "literal" child is also underscored by its four eyes. Such symbolism marks the child as an image of wholeness, of future completion. The distressing fact remains, nevertheless, that the child is a violent image. Jung links this child to Abraxas.[27]

The Monster

Thus, the birth is cast in highly destructive attributes. Jung continues: "The new development begins practically with a childbirth, but the birth is a very monstrous creature."[28] The clubs and the claws attest to this. The birth shows "a most aggressive and dangerous thing, such as was suggested by ... the Abraxas vision. ... Abraxas is always represented with a whip or a sword and a shield, you find that the god is really warlike, his weapons are like the sign of power; he can use his whip on you. ... Our patient's unconscious points to the birth of a most dangerous war-like spirit ..."[29] Much like the potential violence in the modern dream of the fierce animals, Christiana's unconscious presents a similar portrait. As the festival in the dream suggests a collective meaning to the image of the fierce animals, Jung proceeds similarly in his interpretation of his patient's vision from that wider horizon.

Accordingly, the substance of Jung's discussion considers the birth of this child from a collective perspective. The birth in Christiana's personal life, which also receives his attention, is at the same time a portrait of a collective development in humanity as a whole. Jung comments:

> Just emerging from the bloodiest war in human history, we are surely not on a bed of roses, and we don't know what a new spirit might look like. When the spirit changes there are usually very disagreeable questions to cope with. So I must say I am quite interested in this child. …
>
> The monster [Abraxas] symbolizes or personifies the hidden meaning of a situation or an epoch of history, as well of as a human being. … He [the monster] will do terrible things, he will wade in blood; that is also the negative aspect of a new concept of god. So all we can say about this monstrous figure is that it is the hidden meaning of a god that is in the state of development. For it is in the state of being nourished by the wolf, it is a newborn god in its negative aspect. The idea of a new god always comes into existence when an old concept begins to break up, the unconscious then prepares a new idea. There are always periods in history in which the concept of god is valid and unanimously believed; and then follows another period in which this image decays, and in those times such creations are to be found in the unconscious. … One could say therefore that it is more a symptom of the whole of present-day humanity than of our particular patient.[30]

As already noted and here stressed, Abraxas represents all those qualities, all those aspects of life, that are excluded from an epoch's idea of the sacred, that is, from an era's understanding of God. Those aspects are not allowed to enter normative awareness; thus, responsibility is never taken for them. *But this chaos is in the service of a new and workable grasp of the functioning, meaning, and purpose of life*—honoring as sacred those aspects of life conventional religious belief designates as sinful. Abraxas and the qualities he represents are now pressing for inclusion into our image of God. But the first stages of this process are horrific and have played out violently.

However destructively Abraxas has surfaced in the last century, his ultimate presence can be a creative one. The second dream in the series of the contemporary dreamer presents this with succinct clarity. "I am in a church. The religion here seeks the sacred in discarded and overlooked things." Abraxas is surely part of these "discarded and overlooked things." As the longing of the dead suggests, Christendom has excluded whole worlds of emotional and spiritual experience in its rejection of Gnosticism. This is not merely an antiquated, effete, and inconsequential recognition. A colleague reported she had planned to attend a conference on Gnosticism and the imagery of the early Gnostics. The conference had to be canceled because of death threats to the presenter—a theologian who is a well-respected and international authority on the early Church. Such homicidal rage tries to push the "discarded and overlooked things" away from awareness; yet, ironically, volcanic emotion, consciously understood, is part of what presses for a place in the "light" God.

In sum: the task of our time, first seen in the *Red Book* and continuing its presence in contemporary dreams and events, is to return to what in human experience of the divine has been historically rejected, suppressed, and maligned. Then the challenge remains to find the sacred in it, enlarging and redefining—re-birthing—our experience and understanding of God.

Sexuality

After the birth of the child in Christiana Morgan's vision, images of sexuality begin to appear in her subsequent visions. Jung comments: "The very first problem that turns up after that most spiritual event of the second birth [the appearance of Abraxas as beginning the process of the transformation of the god-image] is the problem of releasing sexuality."[31] Christiana Morgan's next vision is crucial: "A great heat went through me and when I lifted my foot I saw a mark upon the sole, a Chinese dragon twined upon a cross and above the cross the head of a lion."[32]

In the Cain and Abel story, Abel was a shepherd, Cain was a farmer. Yahweh did not like Cain's sacrifice—He favored Abel's. So jealous Cain killed Abel. Yahweh then reversed his position and promises Cain that, He, Yahweh, will protect Cain ("the mark of Cain").[33] One sees what ambivalence Yahweh has at that point. First, He persecuted Cain in rejecting Cain's sacrifice, then He protects Cain. Jung adds: "Therefore Cain had inferiority feelings about his innovation …, so he killed Abel, a nice pious boy with no ideas at all apparently, who followed the approved ways."[34]

Jung links the mark of Cain with the Chinese mark on the sole of his patient's foot. That mark is the guilt an innovator feels for being a pioneer. Accordingly, the presence of the "monster" in Christiana's psyche is a singular instance of the societal challenge to consider all those forces that have been excluded from the conscious values of Christendom. That complication in Christiana's unconscious is the individual record of what is also seeking to occur on a wider scale to answer the contemporary religious crisis of the 20th and 21st centuries. She is going through the change in her individual life that is ripe to occur on a much wider, social scale. She is being pressed to move beyond narrow "thou shalts," prejudices, sacred laws, long-standing assumptions, and assumed delineations of the holy.[35]

Concerning these new beginnings and on the mark on her foot, Jung remarks: "The lion's head on top and the dragon below on the cross is a very special condition: it is the condition of the beginning where things are still in the unconscious form, not yet made or realized consciously. … There is a very significant Gnostic symbol, where the lion's head is on top and the snake underneath."[36]

That image is, of course, Abraxas. "Abraxas is usually represented with the head of a fowl, the body of a man, and the tail of a serpent …"[37] Jung remarks:

> This early symbolism … occurs in this symbol in our fantasy; we have … a god not with a human mind but with an animal mind [that is the sexual enthusiasm, the animal

mind], not conforming to our spiritual expectations but to our worst fears. That is, if anybody should be permeated by that released wave of heat [eroticism], he would feel that absolute blindness, that lack of direction, that chaotic lack of form and definition; he would present a picture which can only be paralleled by the mental picture of the world today. We have lost our direction completely, we are not sure of anything, there is only a blind urge, but to what we do not know. So this symbol not only fits one particular case, it is a symbol for our time as well.[38]

The discussion has turned from monstrosity to eroticism.

Mati Klarwein and Carlos Santana

A look at a modern painting (1961), *Annunciation*[39] by Mati Klarwein,[40] elucidates the Eros theme. That the painting has struck a living nerve is confirmed by its presence on the cover of the album *Abraxas* by Latin rock guitarist Carlos Santana. The LP album, released in 1970, sold 3.8 million copies.[41] A vast number of eyes have absorbed Klarwein's art.

The artist writes of his painting: "Carlos Santana saw a reproduction of the *Annunciation* in a magazine and wanted it for the cover of his all time best-selling *Abraxas* album. … I saw the album [jacket] pinned to the wall in a shaman's mud hut in Niger and inside a Rastafarian's ganja hauling truck in Jamaica."[42] Commentary on the Klarwein website confirms the painting *Annunciation* represents the angel Gabriel announcing to Mary that she would become the mother of the Son of God. In other words, a new understanding of God is in the process of birth.[43]

The twists to the orthodox presentation of the event are noteworthy. Gabriel is tattooed and sits astride a conga drum. Mary is dark-skinned, gorgeous, sexy, and sensuous; she is voluptuously naked and appears in full possession of her sexuality. The Holy Spirit does not enter Mary through her ear,[44] but unabashedly visits her

Annunciation, Mati Klarwein, 1961 Oil on Canvas © Klarwein Family

vagina, reposing squarely before her sex, celebrating her fertility and biological womanhood. On the left are Wodaabe Charm Dancers, and in the middle of them is an image of the artist himself. The Charm Dancers of Niger yearly "participate in a series of charm and beauty dances judged solely by women. During the week, women single out the most desirable men. As part of the ritual, Wodaabe men decorate their faces to appeal to the women spectators."[45] Men dance for the judgment of women.

Further commentary to the painting on the artist's website elucidates the theme of Abraxas: "Although the title, combined with the depiction of the Virgin Mary as a voluptuously sensual black girl, is a clear challenge to our preconceptions, this painting can also be seen as a visual celebration of life on earth in all its richness and diversity: Music, scent, sex and sensuality, colour, taste, texture, the eroticism of flowers, the sensuality of stone, the natural beauty of landscapes and of all the fruits of nature are all represented here."[46]

The shift from monstrosity to Eros is celebrated in Klarwein's *Annunciation* and its natural affinity to Abraxas. The birth of the new God, the birth of a new understanding of God incorporating previously rejected elements such as Abraxas represents, the child that the black Mary will bring to the earth, is conducted in an atmosphere of Eros and nature. The painting's celebration of Eros thus confirms the thread developing over the decades from the *Red Book* (monstrosity) to the *Visions* seminar (emergence of the Eros theme) by emphasizing that the new religious birth is embedded in eroticism and nature.

The last dream in the series of the contemporary dreamer reveals an important detail in the Eros theme in Klarwein's *Annunciation*. "I see a woman dressed in a dress, the blouse of which is half black and half white, the skirt of which is half white, half black. I call her the Yin Yang woman." Eros is again present in the figure of the woman, insofar as the inner woman is the expression of a man's Eros. The critical detail is the motif of white and black. The Yin Yang woman contains both, the white and the black, as does Klarwein's painting, which contrasts the white dove and the black Mary. The contrasting shades in the third dream, there writ large, reflect the same polarity between the white dove and the dark mother of (a new understanding of) God in the *Annunciation*.

The meaning of this detail communicates much about the pertinence of the Abraxas image, particularly in its importance for the 21st century. As acknowledged, roughly one hundred years ago, Abraxas began as a monstrosity for Jung and then Eros entered Christiana's visions and Jung's astute commentary on them. Then, in the captivating expression of a visual artist, the importance of that Eros is underscored in Klarwein's painting.

The contrast of light and dark is likewise portrayed in Klarwein's work, particularly when compared with the contrast in the modern dream. This is to suggest that the solution to the problem of integrating the abominable qualities of Abraxas will not only have something centrally to do with Eros, but also—and more specifically, as evidenced in the dream and painting—*with the "white" and "black" aspects of Eros, the polarity of Eros.*

Opposites

What is the meaning of this white and black? In his essay "On the Nature of the Psyche," Jung describes that psychological energy is like a spectrum with two ends: an instinctual one and an archetypal one—one might equally imagine that psychological energy is like a continuum with two poles.[47] The *instinctual* pole consists of the drives and desires and inclinations of nature, the animal aspect of the body, in other words. The *archetypal* pole is the image forming capacity of the instinct, whereby images are created that portray the bodily dynamisms of instinctual energy. Integration of the instinctual energy and its patterns is always through the archetypal, image-creating pole of energy, which forms the pictures of what is assaulting a person.[48] Consciousness, then, through understanding that image, can enter into dialogue with what it needs to recognize, appropriate, and take responsibility for to come to terms with the instinctual assault. The image-creating process of the archetype seems to possess "a dim foreknowledge" of an individual's life pattern so that the character of the archetype "can only be described as 'spiritual.'"[49]

The polarity of energy, here Eros energy, is pertinent to grasping the meaning of both the Yin Yang woman and Klarwein's *Annunciation*. It is a small step to see the instinct's relation to the dark earth of the black Mary or the black colors of the Yin Yang woman. An equally small step can recognize the archetype's image-creating, and foreknowledge-generating, resonance with the white dove of the impregnating spirit in *Annunciation* and the white pole of the Yin Yang woman. The carriers of Eros, both in Klarwein's painting and in the modern dream, convey this reciprocal relation between light and dark, spirit and instinct, so fundamental to the therapeutic process.

An Example

A dream from the analytic practice gives a practical example of that reciprocal relation between light and dark, between archetypal image and instinct.

At times during the inner Jungian journey, we see this "black" and "white" continuum of Eros energy present in the erotic feelings that can arise between analyst and analysand.[50] Consulting-room experience affirms that the "black" (instinctual, earthly) aspect of Eros is the bodily *experience* of sexuality, while the "white" (the dove as spirit) aspect of Eros contains the *meaning* of the experience of the sexual desires.

The following account is from the psychological journey of a woman in her mid-30s. About two years into her analytic work, which was characterized by a strong sexual attraction between both her and myself, the woman dreamed: "In my room the phone is ringing. I answer and when I recognize the voice, Gary, I am able to see his face. He is speaking very softly. The sense of it seeming that he is giving me something, yet also asking for something. His features are changing. His face gradually appearing owl-like. Now we are together in this room. His face returned to normal, [he is] kneeling before an owl. I am not sure if Gary is telling me to open my eyes so I can see it or to watch until the owl opens its eyes." In the dream she first she sees me, the analyst, as an owl, and then she discovers the owl in herself—or more exactly as something in herself that is portrayed in the dream as an image of her personal inventory to which she can eventually relate.[51] In other words, first she has an image of me as an owl, then she meets her "inner owl" as a dream image with which she can establish a relationship. What she initially sees in me, she discovers symbolized as a separate entity in the dream, representing her own "owl-like" capacities that she can develop. Fueled by our erotic attraction, she finds her next psychological strength and step in the countenance of my face.

This is a vivid example that the way we see another person with whom we are erotically fascinated is a purposive presentation of the next step in our own psychological development. The analysand is fascinated with me because I have a certain characteristic *in her perception*. But soon that characteristic becomes the possibility of recognizing the part of her own personality that is analogous to her perception of me. We were pulled toward each other by Eros and then, in the fire of attraction, while keenly mindful of professional boundaries, we came to see how that desire carried a message for her increasing maturity in dream work. That message is what is meant by the spiritual aspect of Eros, the message aspect of instinctual desire—the white of the dove and the white of the Yin Yang woman. The biological desire itself is the dark earthly connection between myself and the analysand, the black Mary, the dark half of the Yin Yang woman's clothing. From her experience of our connection and its meaning, the dreamer is recovering her ability to see into the unknown parts of herself—and it is the knowledge of this ability that will build her confidence and empower her forward in life.

Once the meaning of the desire is understood, the instinctual drive softens and becomes human. Its energy finds a place in new personal strengths and attributes within the deepening personal inventory of the dreamer. That is to say, the instinctual energy is integrated. The instinctual side (black) is integrated into the whole of the personality and its growth through the consideration of the meaning (white) of the erotic experience as expressed by an image. T.S. Eliot strikes the same chord:

> We had the experience but missed the meaning,
> And approach to the meaning restores the experience
> In a different form, beyond any meaning
> We can assign to happiness.[52]

When the sublimity of meaning meets the fertility of earth, when insight and desire mix, integration of the fierce animals of the gods, such as those that make up Abraxas, becomes a human reality. Abraxas enters the human sphere as he enriches and transforms our most cherished—sacred—values.

Conclusion

The Abraxas who surfaced in Jung's vision releases a nexus of psychological events still intensely relevant to the 21st century. The current loss of the ability to believe seeks answers—sometimes in the voice of despair, sometimes in the coldness of cynicism, sometimes in the restlessness of greed. Jung's alternative answer circles around the assault of Abraxas and his problematic return. That problematic return we saw develop from monstrosity to Eros to the polarity of integration. Because it is through the image, the spirit in Jung's understanding of it, that we find portraits of what assaults us so that we are not overwhelmed by Abraxas's intensity. Jung's position concerning instinct and image has been stressed: "The realization and assimilation of instinct never takes place … by absorption into the instinctual sphere, but only through integration of the image which signifies and at the same time evokes the instinct, although in a form quite different from the one we meet on the biological level."[53] Through our inner images generated in emotional storms, we recover the lost sacred in life, denied by centuries of dismissal. This is the rebirth and transformation of the god-image.

Then Abraxas becomes creative. He hones our recognition of who we are. He recasts our life and times, as Eliot has versed:

> In a different form, beyond any meaning
> We can assign to happiness.[54]

Endnotes

1 ClipArt ETC Commercial License. "Abraxas is usually represented with the head of a fowl, the body of a man, and the tail of a serpent ..." C.G. Jung, *Visions: Notes of the Seminar Given in 1930-1934*, 2 vols., ed. Claire Douglas (Princeton, NJ: Princeton University Press, 1997), 1041-1042. Further descriptions of Abraxas follow.

2 C.G. Jung, *The Red Book: Liber Novus*, ed. Sonu Shamdasani, trans. John Peck, Mark Kyburz, and Sonu Shamdasani (New York, NY: W.W. Norton, 2009).

3 Jung, *Visions*.

4 Carlos Santana, *Abraxas*, Columbia Records, 1970, LP.

5 The man was not familiar with the contents of *The Red Book* or with the image of Abraxas.

6 Jung, *The Red Book*, 345.

7 "The Christian God proved too weak to save Christendom from fratricidal slaughter." See C.G. Jung, "Wotan," in *CW*, vol. 10 (Princeton, NJ: Princeton University Press, 1964), par. 384.

8 Jung, *The Red Book*, 346.

9 C.G. Jung, *Memories, Dreams, Reflections*, ed. Aniela Jaffé (New York, NY: Vintage Books, 1963), 175-176.

10 Jung, *The Red Book*, 346-354.

11 Those chapters follow on the formal end of *The Red Book* and have been published with it. Jung's composing the "Scrutinies" continues the day after the last page of the *Red Book* was written. "The Seven Sermons to the Dead" are part of the "Scrutinies." Jung, *The Red Book*, 225.

12 Jung, *The Red Book*, 346.

13 Jung, *The Red Book*, 206 n128 and 346 n81.

14 For an introduction to Gnosticism, see Elaine Pagels, *The Gnostic Gospels* (New York, NY: Vintage Books, 1989).

15 For one cogent example, Elie Wiesel, Auschwitz survivor, spoke in an interview: "It is because I believed in God that I was angry at God, and still am. ... I never doubted God's existence. I have problems with God's apparent absence. ... Since God is God and God is everywhere, what about evil? What about suffering? Is He there too? ... At the end of the questions, we cannot avoid saying, and where was He ...?"

Krista Tippett, interview with Elie Wiesel, "Elie Wiesel: The Tragedy of the Believer," On Being with Krista Tippett, podcast text, July 13, 2006, https://onbeing.org/programs/elie-wiesel-tragedy-believer/ (accessed September 1, 2017).

16 "Existentialistic ideas came out of a time in society when there was a deep sense of despair following the Great Depression and World War II. ... This despair has been articulated by existentialist philosophers well into the 1970s ..." See "Existentialism," All About Philosophy, http://www.allaboutphilosophy.org/existentialism.htm (accessed September 1, 2017).

17 Jung, *The Red Book*, 348.

18 Jung, *The Red Book*, 350. *Summum bonum* refers to the "supreme good," and *infinum malum* to "infinite evil."

19 Jung, *The Red Book*, 350.

20 Merriam-Webster, https://www.merriam-webster.com/dictionary/festival (accessed August 1, 2017).

21 A full treatment of the Superman image is beyond the scope of this essay—Jung spent 1,544 pages discussing the Superman in seminars on Friedrich Nietzsche's *Thus Spoke Zarathustra*. In a simplified nutshell, the Superman, in the best sense, is the person who is fully human, as opposed to Nietzsche's understanding as the person who is perfect. Again, in the best sense, I understand the suffering Superman in the dream to refer to the interior suffering occasioned by the recognition that we are a pale reflection of what our humanity genuinely affords. C.G. Jung, *Nietzsche's Zarathustra: Notes of the Seminar Given in 1934-1939*, 2 vols., ed. James L. Jarrett (Princeton, NJ: Princeton University Press, 1988), 47, 52, 55, 61, 71, 90, 205, 336.

22 Jung, *The Red Book*, 350.

23 *Genesis* 1:27.

24 The term used to describe the process whereby our experience and understanding of God widens and deepens. It is effected as, in our encounters with life, we are subject to overpowering emotions and events. When we begin to take these seriously, they transform our understanding of our, and of God's, essential makeup. Jung refers to this process as the transformation of the god-image—that is, the transformation of our image (hence understanding) of God and the sacred.

25 Jung, *Visions*, x, xiii.

26 Jung, *Visions*, 823-824, 828, 842.

27 "Abraxas in the last vision was armed … Here is the same idea; claws are an animal's natural weapons, while the clubs are man-made. So this is a very warlike creature apparently." Jung, *Visions*, 803-807, 829.

28 Jung, *Visions*, 839.

29 Jung, *Visions*, 830, 844.

30 Jung, *Visions*, 844, 850-851.

31 Jung, *Visions*, 883.

32 Jung, *Visions*, 1037.

33 *Genesis 4:15.* "If any one slays Cain, vengeance shall be taken upon him sevenfold." *The New Oxford Annotated Bible with the Apocrypha*, Revised Standard Version (New York, NY: Oxford University Press, 1977).

34 Jung, *Visions*, 1037.

35 Jung, *Visions*, 1039-1040.

36 Jung, *Visions*, 1041.

37 Jung, *Visions*, 1041-1042.

38 Jung, *Visions*, 1042.

39 *Annunciation*, Mati Klarwein, 1961, Oil on Canvas ©Klarwein Family. Reproduced with kind permission from the Klarwein Family.

40 "Abdul Mati Klarwein," Mati Klarwein Art, http://www.matiklarweinart.com/en/ (accessed August 1, 2017).

41 Russell Sanjek, *American Popular Music and Its Business: The First 400 Years, Volume III, From 1900 to 1984* (New York, NY: Oxford University Press, 1988), 516.

42 "Annunciation by Mati Klarwein - 1961 (Abraxas)," Mati Klarwein Art, http://www.matiklarweinart.com/en/gallery/annunciation-1961.htm (accessed August 1, 2017).

43 http://www.matiklarweinart.com/en/gallery/annunciation-1961.htm.

44 Jerome H. Neyrey, "Mary: Mediterranean Maid and Mother in Art and Literature," University of Notre Dame, https://www3.nd.edu/~jneyrey1/MaryM&M.htm (accessed August 1, 2017).

45 http://www.matiklarweinart.com/en/gallery/annunciation-1961.htm.

46 http://www.matiklarweinart.com/en/gallery/annunciation-1961.htm.

47 C.G. Jung, "On the Nature of the Psyche," in *CW*, vol. 8 (Princeton, NJ: Princeton University Press, 1969), pars. 406, 414.

48 Ibid., par. 414.

49 Ibid., pars. 398, 402-406.

[50] The technical term "transference" does not do justice to the mystery and goal of the erotic fire.

[51] For example, the owl would represent her ability to "see in the dark," that is, to better understand her suffering and the steps necessary to heal it from the point of view of the dark unconscious of the dream world.

[52] T.S. Eliot, "Four Quartets," in *The Complete Poems and Plays 1909-1950* (New York, NY: Harcourt, Brace and World, 1971), 133.

[53] Jung, "On the Nature of the Psyche," *CW* 8, par. 414.

[54] Eliot, "Four Quartets," 133.

The Metamorphosis of the Gods:
Archetypal Astrology and the Transformation of the God-Image in *The Red Book*

Keiron Le Grice

A broader consideration of the significance of Jung's *Red Book* must take into account the historical moment in which it was created. If it is relevant not only to Jung himself, as the articulation of a personal mythology, but also to Western civilization at large, then we must turn our focus to the evolution of the modern West as revealed in its major historical and religious transitions. One way this might be done, in keeping with the tenets of Analytical Psychology, is to consider the archetypal factors impinging upon the Western psyche and the cultural Zeitgeist in the late 19th and early 20th centuries, from the time of Jung's birth to the creation of *Liber Novus*. In so doing, we might gain some perspective on the significance of our own time and our evolving conceptions of the spiritual dimension of experience.

Archetypal Cosmology

Systems theorist Erich Jantsch's vision of a self-organizing universe governed by "homologous" principles and interconnected "natural dynamics" functioning across all levels of life can help us to appreciate that human experience is subject to the same laws and principles by which the universe itself is directed.[1] These principles are working through us, animating and patterning our individual experiences, while also finding expression at the collective level in cultural history.

This insight has long been recognized in the practice of astrology, a symbolic system that seeks to understand the changing forms of expression of universal principles through the study of the cycles of planets in the solar system, as well as the sun and the moon. Following the Copernican Revolution, astronomy gradually divorced itself from considerations of the symbolic meaning of astronomical phenomena for human experience, but to this day astrologers study the movements of the planets in their orbits and the geometric alignments they make with each other, interpreting the significance of such alignments for individual lives and for the world at large. The recent emergence of the discipline of Archetypal Cosmology, in which I myself am involved, has sought to put astrology on firmer theoretical and empirical ground, drawing extensively on Jungian Psychology—in relation to other perspectives, such as Platonism, evolutionary cosmology, and the new-paradigm sciences—to understand and articulate the archetypal basis of astrology and its capacity to illuminate the dynamics of the human psyche. Archetypal Astrology is the name given to the methodology and particular approach to astrological analysis pursued in the field. Jung's ideas were instrumental in the development of this approach. He saw astrology as the "sum of all the psychological knowledge of antiquity," and he believed that "astrology, like the collective unconscious with which psychology is concerned, consists of symbolic configurations: the 'planets' are the gods, symbols of the powers of the unconscious."[2] Especially relevant here is Jung's view that the psychology of archetypes can help to account for the "inner connection between historical events" and the "general laws" underlying individual development, for these are two of the primary areas of application of astrology.[3]

In Archetypal Astrology, each planet is associated with a particular universal principle and a related set of archetypal themes. Venus, for instance, is associated with love, beauty, pleasure, and harmony, whereas Saturn is associated with death, judgment, maturation, limitation, structure, and separation. When the planets form significant geometric relationships with each other (including angles of 0, 60, 90, 120, and 180 degrees) the corresponding "planetary archetypes" themselves move into relationship, giving rise to clusters of archetypal themes and complexes evident in discernible patterns of cultural history and individual biography. We see the Venus-Saturn combination in the slow maturation of a love relationship over many years of dutiful devotion and work, for instance, or in a reserved and restrained manner of expressing affection, or in judgments of beauty and an appreciation of classical tradition in art.

There are three main kinds of analysis employed in Archetypal Astrology. First, one can study the meaning of the placement of the planets at the time of birth, as portrayed in an astrological birth chart, which gives insight into how the planetary archetypes manifest in personality traits and major themes of biography. Second, as illustrated in the analysis to follow in this paper, one can study the ongoing relationships formed between the planets as they move in their orbits, day by day, year by year, to illuminate changes in collective human experience—a method known as *world transit analysis*. And, third, one can explore the relationship between world transits and birth charts to gain insight into how the archetypes are impacting an individual's life experience at any given time—these are *personal transits*.

An astrological analysis can help to illuminate the archetypal patterns underlying the events of any given era, to make known the universal principles as they find expression in the concrete details of human experience at that time. Taking an archetypal view can draw attention to a background order or formal cause in which the chains of historical events unfold and enable us to "see through" the events of history to their mythic background and archetypal reasons. James Hillman describes this perspective well: "Outer historical facts are archetypally colored, so as to disclose essential psychological meanings. Historical facts disclose the eternally recurring mythemes of history and of our individual souls. History is but the stage on which we enact mythemes of the soul."[4]

The Neptune-Pluto Cycle

By 1875, the year of Jung's birth, the slow-moving outer planets Neptune and Pluto, with orbital periods of 165 and 248 years, respectively, entered the beginning of a rare conjunction in which they occupied the same section of space within the great circle of the

Zodiac, a symbolic band inscribed around the Earth comprising the 12 well-known signs from Aries through Pisces. The Zodiac is the primary frame of reference used in astrology to map the movements of the planets. As seen from Earth, the planets were positioned within approximately 20 degrees of each other (the operative range for a conjunction between the outer planets), initially in the sign of Taurus, for a period of just over 30 years, from roughly 1875–1908. A conjunction of these planets only occurs once every 500 years. Even more unusual, in this case the Neptune-Pluto conjunction also coincided with an opposition (a 180-degree alignment) with Uranus, first between Uranus and Pluto (1896–1907) and then Uranus and Neptune (1899–1918). Periods of history in which these three planets form major "axial alignments" (that is, conjunctions and oppositions) with each other are rare indeed. For instance, as Richard Tarnas has observed, one must look back to the heart of the Axial Age to find a conjunction of all three planets, when they were positioned within 20 degrees of each other (from 594 to 560 B.C.E.)—the only such conjunction in recorded history.[5] This period, extending from 800 to 200 B.C.E., but centered on the sixth century, was like no other in human history, witnessing the emergence of Buddhism, Jainism, Confucianism, Taoism, Zoroastrianism, and Platonism, as well as major developments in Judaism and Hinduism. More recently, to give two further examples discussed by Tarnas, the three planets formed another highly significant alignment known as a T-square—with Uranus opposite Neptune, and both planets in 90-degree square alignments to Pluto—in the years around the birth of Shakespeare in 1564.[6] And in 1769–70, the three planets entered 120-degree "trine" alignments with each other—a so-called Grand Trine—which, again, is an astronomical occurrence seldom witnessed. Remarkably, Tarnas observes, the period of this alignment saw the unique coincidence of the births of several towering creative geniuses, world-historic figures in every sense—Beethoven, Hegel, Napoleon, Wordsworth, and Hölderlin—who were to exert such an immense influence on the Western world in philosophy, religion, art, and socio-political history.[7]

Given the rarity of such alignments and given the nature of the archetypes associated with Uranus, Neptune, and Pluto, any historical period accompanying major geometric configurations of these three planets is marked out as extremely significant, bringing forth deep-rooted and immensely consequential changes in human experience and witnessing the birth of individuals who effect such changes—a reflection, in both cases, of the combined archetypal qualities and themes associated with these planets. Uranus is specifically associated with awakening, freedom, liberation, revolt, trickster-like disruptions, and the urge to go one's own way in life, to realize one's uniqueness. It manifests in the spark of creative genius and the Promethean urge to birth the new, to pioneer, to invent, and to push beyond established limits and boundaries. Neptune is the principle associated with the realm of myth, dream, image, and fantasy. It is evident in spiritual experience and religious consciousness, in the aspiration toward the ideal and the longing for paradise, or simply in the urge to escape from or transcend the pressures and limitations of material existence and separate individual consciousness. It is connected with magic and enchantment, but also delusion, dissolution, and self-loss. Pluto finds expression as instinctual compulsion and power drives—in this respect, it is reflected in Freud's concept of the id and in the Nietzschean will-to-power. As a Shiva-like principle of transformative creative-destructive force and elemental energy, Pluto is manifest in the power that impels evolution, purging and destroying old forms, driving the ongoing cycles of death-rebirth in nature. It is the principle of depth and symbolized as the mythic underworld.

In his 2006 publication, *Cosmos and Psyche*, Tarnas documented and interpreted the significance of periods of major alignments between the pairings of Uranus-Neptune, Uranus-Pluto, and Neptune-Pluto, identifying a number of themes that are manifest in cultural history at these times. He provides examples of the correlation between Uranus-Neptune alignments and the "birth of new philosophies," "spiritual awakenings and the birth of new religions," the "creative emergence of esoteric traditions," "revelations of the numinous," and the "birth of new forms of artistic expression."[8] In each case, the Uranus principle acts to awaken and catalyze a range of Neptunian experiences—often connected to the spiritual dimension of life. All of these themes were prominent in Jung's creation of the *Red Book*, principally between 1913 and 1918, during the Uranus-Neptune opposition of 1899–1918. By contrast, the Uranus-Pluto combination is associated in Tarnas's historical survey with themes such as the awakening of the Dionysian instincts, the eruption of powerful elemental forces, revolutions and the empowerment of mass protests, political extremism, and the instinctually driven desire to make the world new in a radical overthrow and destruction of the ruling order, as exemplified by the period of the French Revolution and the revolutionary decade of the 1960s.[9] In these cases, Uranus serves to stir and liberate the instincts—sexual, aggressive, and power drives—and to bring to the surface the contents of the Plutonic underworld: the base and barbaric, the primitive and the evil, but also the passion and power that might fuel one's individuation and vocational calling. Simultaneously, Pluto empowers and intensifies the creative impulses, innovations, and drive for freedom associated with Uranus, manifesting as periods of accelerated technological and socio-cultural change. These themes and others associated with the Uranus-Pluto archetypal complex are plainly manifest at the current time in coincidence with the Uranus-Pluto square of 2007–2020.

Both of these alignments fall within the more encompassing orbit of the Neptune-Pluto cycle, which is our primary focus. As Tarnas has described, this archetypal combination is associated with "especially profound transformations of cultural vision and the collective experience of reality, which often took place deep below the surface of collective consciousness."[10] Powerful undercurrents of change tend to coincide, during major Neptune-Pluto conjunctions and oppositions, with critical phases in the rise and fall of civilizations, marking the "beginnings and endings of immense cultural epochs of great historical magnitude."[11] To give one example, the fall of the Roman Empire in the 100-year period between 376 and 476 C.E. was centered on the Neptune-Pluto conjunction of 399–424 C.E., with the exact alignment closely coinciding with the sack of Rome in 410 C.E. This was the milieu in which Augustine lived and wrote, encountering a remarkably similar situation to the modern West since the late 19th century. "In the time of Augustine," Jung remarked, "the old gods were dying or dead, the old religions and the old temples were going fast. There was a great confusion, the world was neurotic, and it became necessary to have a new therapeutic system."[12]

In both periods the world was embroiled in a tumultuous transition between one historical era and the next: The era of the Roman Empire gave way to the Middle Ages just as, in the early part of the 20th century, the Age of Empire, driven by the colonization of the world by European powers, came to a bloody and violent end with the mass devastation of the First World War. It could be said that the Neptune-Pluto conjunction of this time signaled the beginning of the complex and chaotic struggle to establish a planetary civilization—a critical challenge facing us in the current 500-year cycle. In both periods, too, religious understandings were transformed by the influx of ideas from the East, which has also inspired, perhaps more than anything else, the spiritual diversity and global interpenetration of myths and religions in the present time.

From one era to the next, as Jung recognized, civilizations are shaped and sustained by certain ruling ideas or dominants, often taking form through a particular religious revelation or mythic vision that thereafter provides the spiritual and moral foundation for the entire civilization. When the religious forms and guiding myths lose their compelling numinous power, as has happened in the modern West, the culture might be plunged into crisis, lacking orientation and social cohesion, and thus entering a phase of terminal decline and decay. In response, however, shaped by the needs of the historical moment and the *telos* of evolution, new myths and metaphysical visions arise from the creative matrix of the unconscious, bringing renewal and birthing new historical epochs. For religions and mythologies—and the images of the gods and goddesses that populate them—are not exempt from the cycles of nature and the universe; they, too, are born, flourish, decay, and die.

The religious revelation documented by Jung in his *Red Book* might be taken, I believe, as a transformation of just this kind, offering a new mythic vision that reflects or anticipates an evolution of our religious consciousness—a development entirely consistent with the meaning of the combined Neptune-Pluto conjunction and Uranus-Neptune opposition at that time. Especially relevant for understanding the archetypal factors shaping the *Red Book* are the Neptune-Pluto themes of the empowerment of the mythic imagination and what Tarnas characterizes as the "transformation in the experience of the numinous."[13] An example of particular relevance to the West and to Jung's own religious background was the writing of the Second Isaiah (circa 545 B.C.E.) during the Axial Age, which brought forth, Tarnas notes, a "powerful declaration of a loving God sovereign over all history and all humanity" and a "metamorphosis of the prophetic imagination" exemplifying "the quintessential Uranus-Neptune theme of a radical transformation of the God-image and a revolutionary new understanding of the divine will acting in history—the latter especially appropriate to the presence of Pluto in the configuration with its archetypal association with both evolution and universal will."[14]

The Death and Rebirth of God

It was the same potent combination of planetary archetypes that was activated during the Neptune-Pluto conjunction of the late 19th century, described by Tarnas as the "great crucible of metaphysical destruction and regeneration" of Western culture, that saw the discovery of the unconscious and the birth of depth psychology.[15] Friedrich Nietzsche and Jung were two of the central figures in this great transformation, which continues to unfold in our own time— indeed its implications are only just beginning to be worked out.

"God is dead ... *we have killed him*—you and I"—Nietzsche's epochal proclamation, first made in *The Gay Science*, heralded the West's entrance into the post-Christian era.[16] His philosophy also anticipated the postmodern in its radical questioning of truth and exposure of hidden power drives underlying human motivations, especially in the spheres of politics and knowledge. Departing from the pious Christian environment of his youth, Nietzsche espoused a fervent atheism and nihilism, arguing that the Christian notion of

God—a man-made image, in his view—was no longer relevant to human experience; indeed, it was an impediment to our further evolution. Christianity had made Western culture "decadent," promulgating values and ways of being that were injurious to the human spirit, keeping human beings in a state of servile and docile mediocrity subject to the oppressive and inverted values of the herd. "Man," as the "sick animal," had grown distant from the vitality of the instincts and forsaken the aspiration to excellence, caught in the embrace of the Christian conceptions of selflessness, purity, meekness, pity, and so forth—qualities that Nietzsche believed often masked an unconscious power drive or an avoidance of the necessary challenge of courageously living and affirming one's own life.[17] "Your love of your neighbour is your bad love of yourselves," he remarked, with characteristic insight.[18] Thus Nietzsche sought to "wipe away the horizon" of past metaphysical suppositions in a re-evaluation of all values, a repudiation of Christianity, and an affirmation of the Dionysian energy largely excluded from the Christian vision of the world.[19]

Nietzsche's influence on Jung can hardly be overstated. Sonu Shamdasani notes that Jung returned to carefully study *Thus Spoke Zarathustra* in 1914 in the midst of the influx of fantasies during his confrontation with the unconscious, which form the body of *The Red Book*.[20] Nietzsche's influence is apparent not only in the epic narrative style of the *Red Book*, which resembles that of *Zarathustra*, but also in its content—addressing, as if in response to Nietzsche, the death and transformation of God. Through the dramatic dialogues with his spirit guides, Philemon and Elijah, Jung responded in several distinct though overlapping ways, all of which illuminate the particular form of expression of the Neptune-Pluto themes working through him. Exploring these responses can yield insights into how we ourselves might relate to these archetypal principles today.

God as Creative Power

In a first response to Nietzsche's claim that "God is dead," Philemon issues a refutation and associates God with the power of creation:

"God is not dead. He is alive as ever. God is creation, for he is something definite, ..."[21] Later, God is identified in the form of Abraxas, as "creative drive" and the "creative and created."[22]

The emphasis on creative power is also present in Nietzsche. He rejects the existence of God, describing God as merely a temporary supposition, but he then transfers the focus to the creative power of human will: "And you yourself should create what you have hitherto called the World: the World shall be formed in your image by your reason, your will, and your love!"[23] Thus, the human being, rather than God, becomes a kind of world creator. Although in places Nietzsche presents this creative power as something other than his conscious willing, often he appears to appropriate the power as his own. Those familiar with a Jungian understanding of archetypal possession might judge the failure to recognize such power as originating outside of the personal human will as potentially dangerous and perhaps, therefore, a contributory factor in Nietzsche's grandiose inflation, especially evident in his later writing.

The understanding of God as something like creative energy is also close to the view of Pierre Teilhard de Chardin, the Jesuit priest and paleontologist whose brilliant synthesis of Christianity and evolution inspired many in the 1950s and thereafter, and whose ideas later informed "new cosmology" theorists, including Thomas Berry, Mary Evelyn Tucker, and Brian Swimme. Jung's prophetic revelation in *The Red Book* was of the God "yet to come," a God of a wholly different character to the loving transcendent Father that had ruled for the 2,000 years of the Christian era.[24] In a related shift, Teilhard described a transition from worship of the "God of the Above" to the recognition of the "God of the Ahead," manifest through continual creative acts, who is to be realized as the culminating goal of evolution.[25] Like Jung, Teilhard was born during the Neptune-Pluto conjunction of the late 19th century.

We find a similar emphasis in Indian philosopher Sri Aurobindo's "integral yoga," shaped by a vision of involution of the "Supermind" into matter and its subsequent evolution, gradually bringing about the "spiritualization" of matter and all existence.[26] Also born during the Neptune-Pluto conjunction, Aurobindo, like Jung and Teilhard, brought the Plutonic emphasis on evolution and transformation into relationship with Neptunian conceptions of the eternal spiritual ground and transcendent godhead—a prominent theme of this Neptune-Pluto conjunction. The focus on the creative power of evolution, now manifest through the individual, gives a decidedly Plutonic inflection to the experience of God, for the Pluto archetype finds expression as the motive evolutionary force in the universe, experienced as an inexorable life will or will-to-power.

God as an Aspect of the Pleroma

In a second response to the decay and destruction of the god-image announced by Nietzsche, Jung's revelation looks beyond the Christian conception of God in the recognition of the spiritual background of existence. In this view, God is not the ultimate frame of reference but is only one aspect or quality of the Pleroma, which is to be understood as the non-differentiated source in which opposites coexist and cancel each other out. The Pleroma is the "empty fullness of the whole," imagined as "the maternal womb of the incomprehensible God."[27] The phrase *maternal womb* naturally puts us in mind of the Great Mother Goddess, a mythic personification of the originating and annihilating ground of all things, including all the gods and goddesses.

Therefore, if "God is dead," as Nietzsche claims, this might be taken only as the death of a particular conception of the divine. It implies not the end of religion and the acceptance of nihilism but the recognition that the dominant image of God, the particular form in which God has been imagined for the last two millennia and more, has died as part of a process of spiritual metamorphosis in which a new god-image might emerge from the Pleroma. We appear to be living, Jung proclaimed, "in what the Greeks call the Kairos—the right time—for a 'metamorphosis of the gods,' of the fundamental principles and symbols" through which we order and make sense of our lives.[28] Elsewhere in his *Red Book*, Jung restates a similar insight, arguing that God is an image and only one portrayal or aspect of the "supreme meaning," which ever renews itself in different forms as new images of the divine spring forth in response to the evolutionary needs of the time.[29] As Jung puts it: "The other gods died of their temporality, yet the supreme meaning never dies, it turns into meaning and then into absurdity, and out of the fire and blood of their collision the supreme meaning rises up rejuvenated anew."[30] Ultimately, all the gods and goddesses might be construed, to borrow an expression from Aurobindo, as "Personalities and Powers of the dynamic Divine."[31]

The Revelation of Abraxas

In a third response, Philemon advances the view that alongside and encompassing the "One God" of Christianity, there is another unknown God, long forgotten and unrecognized, whom he refers to as Abraxas: "This is God you knew nothing about, because mankind forgot him."[32] Abraxas is the God of effectiveness—that is, the God of effective power. Elsewhere, as Shamdasani points out, Jung likens Abraxas to the Gnostic demiurge, Henri Bergson's *la durée créatrice,* and to Purusha and Shiva of the Hindu tradition.[33] To a large degree, like these other deities and principles, Abraxas is a God with the qualities and attributes of Pluto: effective evolutionary force, creative-destructive power, instinctual and relentless, working through compulsion and possession, and manifest as the ceaseless motive force of life, at once empowering and terrible. Like the archetypal Pluto, Abraxas is "beyond good and evil" (to use Nietzsche's expression), subsuming all opposites. The qualities of Abraxas are recognizable in the Nietzschean ideas of the will-to-power, the *amor fati,* and the drive to self-overcoming—all of which pertain to the archetype of Pluto as the power that must overcome itself again and again in a Dionysian affirmation of life and an act of transformation that is essential for individuation and the further evolution of human consciousness.

Whereas the Christian understanding of the divine introduced a radical separation of good from evil and spirit from nature, with the Devil coming to personify the instinctual dynamism excluded from the image of the all-loving purity of God and Jesus, in Jung's revelation, good and evil, Christ and Devil, are seen as inextricably connected opposites. The "One God" of Christianity (which Jung also describes as the "Sun God") and the Devil represent mutually implicated aspects of the Pleroma. In the Pleroma the God of light and love is juxtaposed with the Devil, with Abraxas standing behind both. "Everything that you create with the Sun God," Philemon explains, "gives effective power to the devil. That is terrible Abraxas."[34]

We do not recognize this power because "Abraxas is the God who is difficult to grasp."[35] Jung's wording here is remarkably similar to the opening lines of Friedrich Hölderlin's poem "Patmos," quoted elsewhere by Jung:

> The god is near and
> Hard to grasp but
> Where there is danger some
> Salvation grows there too.[36]

Of Abraxas, Philemon declares: "His power is greatest because man does not see it."[37] Because Abraxas cannot be defined as either good or evil but embodies both poles and the "cruel contradictoriness of nature," this god cannot be intellectually comprehended.[38] Uniting and subsuming the opposites in a similar manner to Mercurius in alchemy, Abraxas is something like the primordial energy "that is at once life and death."[39] One might say that Abraxas represents unconscious compulsion, drive, and power that are so "near" to us we tend not to see them as anything other than our own desiring, feeling, and willing; we do not see them as manifestations of a deity or transpersonal archetypal power distinct from our own conscious identity. We are possessed and consumed by Abraxas, for we unconsciously identify with the flow of desiring, or else, denying the instincts, we eschew the overwhelming power of Abraxas and suffer from this renunciation.

Although unrecognized today, Abraxas was known to and named by the Gnostics in the early centuries of the Christian era and can, I believe, be recognized as the subject of Jesus's teaching in the

Gnostic text the *Gospel of Thomas*, which was unearthed in the sands of Egypt in 1945 and dates from the first centuries of the Christian era. Several *logia* in this text appear to be concerned with a God quite unlike the God of Love in the New Testament, for they describe strategies for reckoning with a terrible power that might consume or destroy us if we are not able to come to terms with it and express it. *Logion* 70, for instance, reads as follows: "If you bring forth what is within you, what you bring forth will save you. If you do not bring forth what is within you, what you do not bring forth will destroy you."[40]

Abraxas, we discover in *The Red Book*, represents the world of becoming and passing, just as Pluto is associated with the inexorable will that ever destroys, transforms, and rebirths. As such, it might well be this particular God who inspires the instruction in the *Gospel of Thomas* to "become yourselves, passing away."[41] Could Jesus's Gnostic teaching be a strategy for navigating the power of Abraxas? Could it be that the Christ pattern, as the incarnate Holy Spirit within each of us, is the advocate for the human in our confrontation with the frightful power of the demonic Abraxas? Jung opens *The Red Book* with the memorable passage from the First Isaiah, immortalized in Händel's *Messiah*, celebrating the coming of Christ: "... Wonderful, Counsellor, The mighty God, The everlasting Father, The Prince of Peace" (*Isaiah*: 9:6).[42] *The Red Book* ends with Elijah reminding Christ (the "blue shade") of his identity with the serpent, thus bringing the Christ principle into relationship with the dark, chthonic side of Abraxas.[43] A transformation in the relationship between spirit (Neptune) and the instinctual power of nature (Pluto) appears to be central to the unfolding of the current Neptune-Pluto cycle. Pluto, like Mercurius in the alchemical tradition, represents the uroboric serpent power that ever consumes itself.

Recalling here, too, the Uranus-Neptune theme of the creative emergence of esoteric traditions, Jungian psychology might be construed as just this kind of emergence, falling in the lineage of a mystical Gnosticism, with the particular character of the revelation to do with the challenge of integrating the realm of experience associated with the archetypal Pluto—that is, the long-repressed abyss-like instinctual power of the unconscious.

The Many from the One

In a fourth response to Nietzsche, Jung contends that while the One God is indeed dead, as Nietzsche declared, the Divine has actually changed form, disintegrating into a multiplicity such that "the Old Gods have become new." "The One God is dead—yes, truly, he died. He disintegrated into the many, and thus the world became rich overnight."[44] The world in its substantive material reality henceforth became the sole focus of our concern—witness Nietzsche's decrial of the "Afterworldsmen" who are preoccupied with a heavenly afterlife at the expense of the here and now, and his exaltation of the earth and the body over the soul.[45] Witness, too, the cultural shift from religious piety to materialism and consumerism during the course of the Christian era. The aspiration toward the reenchantment of nature and the emergence of ecological consciousness in the conception of the Earth as Gaia, which have become for many people the primary sources of religiosity, is an expression of this shift, with a spirituality of the immanent rather than the transcendent now impressing itself on the modern psyche.

The world became rich in a second way, in that we have entered a period of spiritual eclecticism and pluralism. No longer is Christianity the sole religious authority in the West, for it is now but one of a rich multiplicity of spiritual-mythic perspectives shaping the modern psyche. One thinks of the plethora of spiritual paths pursued by individuals today, from yoga, healing, and paganism to Buddhism, rebirthing, and shamanic journeying. Philosopher Charles Taylor has noted that the liberty to find and follow one's own way in spiritual matters is a defining characteristic of the rise of the modern ego-self in our secular age.[46] As Joseph Campbell remarked, there is a veritable "galaxy of mythologies" in existence today.[47]

The theme of religious pluralism and individualism is associated with the archetypal combination of Uranus-Neptune—Uranus as the principle of individual freedom and creativity that, in relationship to Neptune, inspires us to pursue our own individual way through life, beyond the bounds of religious tradition, and brings forth new forms of myth, religious insights, and new spiritual paths. We see these themes in Jung's pioneering of individuation and the realization of the self as a spiritual path for the modern era—reflecting the Uranus-square-Neptune alignment in Jung's birth chart. We see it, too, in the life and work of Joseph Campbell, also born with these two planets in major alignment. It is especially evident in Campbell's emphasis on the individualism of the hero myth as a mythic model of the individual's unique life path and in his recognition of the emergence of the era of creative mythology superseding the great epochs and stages of the established religious traditions.

The Human as Mediator of the Gods Within

Fifth, in a related move, Jung explains to Elijah that the multiplicity of renewed old gods is reborn in the individual soul: "And something also happened to the individual soul—who would come to describe it! But therefore men too became rich overnight."[48] We read in another passage that the spirit of the depths put Jung back in touch with his soul, "a living and self-existing being," and it was in the inner depths of the soul that the old gods were to be discovered.[49] The One God died and became a plurality of deities in the human psyche, which Jung conceptualizes in his formal writing as archetypes, describing them as "gods," "dominant laws and principles," and "ruling powers."[50] What was formerly imagined in metaphysical terms was henceforth conceived in psychological terms. The starry empyrean and Olympian host, and even the One God of Christianity, Jung suggests, "fell" from Heaven or the celestial sphere into the darkness of the unconscious, where they were rediscovered.[51] In astrological terms, then, we notice the impact of the Pluto archetype on Neptune: first destroying the old metaphysical conceptions, then initiating a fall of the old gods and dominants into the underworld of the unconscious, and finally empowering the mythic imagination to bring forth a new revelation of the gods and a new conceptual understanding of them as psychological factors—that is, archetypes.

What is more, in conceiving of the gods as psychological factors, human beings now assumed a critical role in bringing the gods to consciousness, making them known, and thus rescuing them from the oblivion of unconsciousness and existential forgetfulness. "The Gods need a human mediator and rescuer," Jung's soul reveals to him. "With this man paves the way to crossing over and to divinity."[52] In a similar vein, Jung describes the "supreme meaning" as the "bridge of going across and fulfillment" leading to the God.[53] There are striking parallels here with Nietzsche's view of man as something that should be overcome, as a "dangerous going-across" to the superman.[54] The human, in this view, is not the endpoint of evolution but an uncertain transition or bridge to a higher form of being. For Nietzsche, "man is a rope between animal and superman—a rope fastened over an abyss."[55] Thus, as in the Second Isaiah, we meet again the Plutonic emphasis on evolution and will in relationship to Neptunian conceptions of spirit and God, except here the evolutionary drama has been transferred from God to the human, unfolding in the depths of the inner world of the psyche.

In Nietzschean fashion, Philemon propounds a similar idea: "Men have changed. They are no longer the slaves and no longer the swindlers of the Gods and no longer mourn in your name."[56] Rather, "man is a gateway through which crowds the train of the Gods and the coming and passing of all times."[57] However, whereas Nietzsche's *Übermensch* takes the godlike powers as his own and thus becomes susceptible to manic inflation, the role of the human being, in Jung's view, is as a participant or mediator granting "hospitality to the Gods."[58] Out of this insight grew Jung's approach to coming to terms with the depths of the psyche during individuation by carefully differentiating the conscious ego from the archetypes and thus coming to realize the self.

The Dark Spirit in Nature

Sixth, the returning and rediscovered God, Abraxas, has a pagan, chthonic quality. Nietzsche had proclaimed the *Übermensch* as "the meaning of the earth" and championed the re-emergence of Dionysus, the ancient god of the vine and personification of intoxicated frenzy in which the *principium individuationis* is obliterated.[59] The Neptune-Pluto conjunction heralded the resurrection of a repressed and forgotten dark, chthonic "natural spirit," as Jung described it in *Mysterium Coniunctionis*, a spirit represented by figures such as Dionysus, Pan, Hades, the Devil, and the alchemical Mercurius.[60] In *The Red Book*, Elijah's vision portrays the pagan primeval quality of the unknown God: "The image that I saw was crimson, fiery colored, a gleaming gold. The voice that I heard was like distant thunder, like the wind roaring in the forest, like an earthquake. It was not the voice of my God, but it was a thunderous pagan roar, a call my ancestors knew but which I had never heard. It sounded prehistoric, as if from a forest on a distant coast. It rang with the voices of the wilderness. It was full of horror yet harmonic."[61]

We see here further evidence of the decidedly Plutonic quality of the Neptunian conceptions of spirit emerging from the turn of the 20th century, for Pluto is associated with the primal, elemental power of nature and underworld of the instincts. J. R. R. Tolkien, born in 1892 during the Neptune-Pluto conjunction, gave exceptionally vivid expression to these themes in *The Lord of the Rings*.

Plutonic qualities were prominent, too, in the resurrection of the pagan deity Wotan irrupting into the collective consciousness of the German people during the 1930s, Jung believed, leading to the catastrophe of the Second World War. Nazism drew on the compelling hypnotic power of the Neptune-Pluto complex in propounding the warped ideology and mythos of Aryan supremacy. With this comes a warning: The Combination of Neptunian fantasy and Plutonic instinct can pull us remorselessly under its sway, sometimes at the expense of morality, human feeling, and reasoned judgment. For better or worse, when it awakens and stirs, the long-repressed power of the unconscious can flood into human consciousness as an "avenging deluge," overwhelming us with a stream of captivating fantasies and gripping instinctual urges.[62] Thus, the challenge for us today, as we move further into the 500-year Neptune-Pluto cycle, is to find a way to come to terms with the dark power of the reawakened chthonic god—the dark spirit in nature—without being devoured, consumed, possessed, or obliterated by it.

Archetypal Astrology as a Mythic Guide to Life

To explore the significance of Jung's *Red Book*, I have focused primarily on historical periods defined by the combined expression of the transpersonal archetypes associated with Uranus, Neptune, and Pluto, but astrology can also be used to gain insight into how these principles manifest in our own individual experiences. Our relationship to Pluto, as symbolized in astrological birth charts and transits, is particularly important in determining how the Abraxas-like instinctual power and creative-destructive energy associated with Pluto manifest in our lives. The Pluto archetype shows up in our passions, compulsions, drives, obsessions, and in the sense of being gripped and fatefully called. In relationship to other planets in birth charts and transits, Pluto indicates where we ourselves might encounter the power of the instinctual underworld of the psyche and can be transformed through it. Similarly, considering our relationship to Neptune can help us to become more conscious of how we engage with the spiritual dimension of life, how we seek oneness and unity and a more ideal and perfect life. It indicates, too, where we seek transcendence or escape from the pressures of life and look for a sense of enchantment and mystery, or find ourselves susceptible to projection and illusion. Jung's *Red Book* might serve as a guide as we seek to work out the relationship between the Neptune and Pluto principles in our lives, bringing the realm of the spirit as articulated in the religious traditions into dialectical engagement with the underworld of the instincts and the dark power impressing itself on our collective consciousness.

The various combinations of planetary archetypes are associated with sets of themes and complexes. We have seen several examples here of those pertaining to Neptune-Pluto and Uranus-Neptune. In each case, one can consider how the planets are related to each other in one's birth chart and in transits in order to determine themes prominent in one's own life and personality. If Saturn and Neptune come into a personal transit alignment, for instance, one would recognize in one's experience during this time any number of themes associated with this archetypal complex, such as religious skepticism and the denial of spiritual realities, loss of faith, dark visions and morbid fantasies, a poignant sense of life's sufferings and endings, and the puncturing of an illusion by the hard facts of one's reality.[63] As Tarnas points out, Nietzsche's revelation of the death of God in 1882 came out of this very archetypal pairing (during a conjunction of Saturn, Neptune, and Pluto), giving expression to many of these themes.[64] Or, to give another example, we might identify periods in life when Uranus and Neptune were in major geometric alignment and observe correlations with experiences of spiritual awakening or exciting, emancipatory, and perhaps destabilizing insights into the nature of reality, the nature of God, and the purpose of our existence.

In this way, Archetypal Astrology can be used to effectively map our personal relationships to the archetypes, the powers personified by the gods—the very powers engaged by Jung in the revelations that comprise his *Red Book*. In *The Archetypal Cosmos*, I describe Archetypal Astrology as a "meta-mythology" for it is not itself a myth, but it enables us to understand our individual relationship to the principles and themes expressed in myth and religion.[65] It offers a form of cosmological orientation that might help us to become more conscious of the forces shaping our psychological experience, as we try to navigate the uncertain transitions of our historical moment and play our part in the evolution of consciousness and the spirit.

Endnotes

[1] Erich Jantsch, *The Self-organizing Universe* (New York, NY: Pergamon, 1980), 33, 231, 238.

[2] C.G. Jung, *Jung on Astrology*, selected and introduced by Keiron Le Grice and Safron Rossi (Abingdon, UK: Routledge, 2017), 23 and 32.

[3] Ibid., 33.

[4] James Hillman, *Senex & Puer*, ed. Glen Slater (Putnam, CT: Spring, 2013), 29.

[5] See Richard Tarnas, *Cosmos and Psyche: Intimations of a New World View* (New York, NY: Viking, 2006), 409–410.

[6] See ibid., 391–392.

[7] See ibid., 456.

[8] Ibid., Part VII, 353–408.

[9] Ibid., Part IV, 139–205.

[10] Ibid., 417.

[11] Ibid., 417. Compare D. Stephenson Bond's theory of the lifecycle of myths in Bond, *Living Myth* (Boston, MA: Shambhala, 1993), 201–204.

[12] C.G. Jung, *Dream Analysis: Notes of the Seminar Given in 1928–1930 by C.G. Jung*, ed. William McGuire (Princeton, NJ: Princeton University Press, 1984), 419.

[13] Tarnas, *Cosmos and Psyche*, 415.

[14] Ibid., 414 and 411.

[15] Ibid., 418.

[16] Friedrich Nietzsche, *The Gay Science*, trans. Walter Kaufmann (New York, NY: Vintage Books, 1974), 181, section 125.

[17] Friedrich Nietzsche, "On the Genealogy of Morals," in *Basic Writings of Nietzsche*, trans. Walter Kaufmann (New York, Modern Library, 2000), section III:13, 557.

[18] Friedrich Nietzsche, *Thus Spoke Zarathustra*, trans. Richard J. Hollingdale (New York, NY: Penguin, 1968), 86.

[19] Nietzsche, "On the Genealogy of Morals," 181.

[20] Sonu Shamdasani, "Introduction," in C.G. Jung, *The Red Book: Liber Novus. A Reader's Edition*, ed. Sonu Shamdasani, trans. John Peck, Mark Kyburz, and Sonu Shamdasani (New York, NY: W. W. Norton, 2012), 30.

[21] Jung, *The Red Book*, 516.

[22] Ibid., 579.

[23] Nietzsche, *Thus Spoke Zarathustra*, 110.

[24] Jung, *The Red Book*, 120.

[25] Pierre Teilhard de Chardin, *The Heart of Matter*, trans. René Hague (San Diego, CA: Harcourt Brace, 1978), 53–55.

[26] See Sri Aurobindo, *The Integral Yoga* (Pondicherry, India: Sri Aurobindo Ashram, 1993).

[27] Jung, *The Red Book*, 523–524.

[28] C.G. Jung, "The Undiscovered Self (Present and Future)," in *CW*, vol. 10 (Princeton, NJ: Princeton University Press, 1964), par. 585.

[29] Jung, *The Red Book*, 120.

[30] Ibid.

[31] Aurobindo, *The Integral Yoga*, 82–83.

[32] Jung, *The Red Book*, 517.

[33] Ibid., 517 n93.

[34] Ibid., 521.

[35] Ibid., 520.

[36] Friedrich Hölderlin, "Patmos," in *Selected Poems*, trans. David Constantine (Highgreen, UK: Bloodaxe Books, 1996), 54.

[37] Jung, *The Red Book*, 520.

[38] Ibid., 523.

[39] Ibid., 521.

[40] Elaine Pagels, *The Gnostic Gospels* (New York, NY: Vintage Books, 1989), xv.

[41] Hugh McGregor Ross, *The Gospel of Thomas*, second edition (London: Watkins Publishing, 2002), 33.

[42] See Jung, *The Red Book*, 117–118.

[43] Ibid., 553.

[44] Ibid., 546.

[45] Nietzsche, *Thus Spoke Zarathustra*, 42, 58–62.

[46] Charles Taylor, *A Secular Age* (Cambridge, MA: The Belknap Press of Harvard University Press, 2007).

[47] Joseph Campbell, *Creative Mythology: The Masks of God*, Vol. IV (New York, NY: Arkana, 1991), 3.

[48] Jung, *The Red Book*, 546.

[49] Ibid., 129.

50 C.G. Jung, "On the Psychology of the Unconscious," in *CW*, vol. 7 (Princeton, NJ: Princeton University Press, 1966), par. 151.

51 See C.G. Jung, "Archetypes of the Collective Unconscious," in *CW*, vol. 9/I (Princeton, NJ: Princeton University Press, 1968), par. 50.

52 Jung, *The Red Book*, 548.

53 Ibid., 120.

54 Nietzsche, *Thus Spoke Zarathustra*, 43.

55 Ibid.

56 Jung, *The Red Book*, 552–553.

57 Ibid., 535–536.

58 Ibid., 553.

59 Nietzsche, *Thus Spoke Zarathustra*, 42.

60 C.G. Jung, *Mysterium Coniunctionis*, in *CW*, vol. 14 (Princeton, NJ: Princeton University Press, 1963), par. 427.

61 Jung, *The Red Book*, 546.

62 Jung, *Mysterium Coniunctionis*, CW 14, par. 364.

63 See Richard Tarnas, "The Ideal and the Real: Saturn-Neptune," in *The Birth of a New Discipline. Archai: The Journal of Archetypal Cosmology*, issue 1 (2009), 2nd edition, edited by Keiron Le Grice and Rod O'Neal (San Francisco, CA: Archai Press, 2011), 175–199.

64 Tarnas, *Cosmos and Psyche*, 344–345.

65 Keiron Le Grice, *The Archetypal Cosmos: Rediscovering the Gods in Myth, Science and Astrology* (Edinburgh: Floris Books, 2011), 61.

The Way Cultural Attitudes are Developed in Jung's *Red Book* – An "Interview"

John Beebe

Interviewer:[1] I am aware that in some of your writings, such as "The *Red Book* as a Work of Conscience,"[2] you have identified inner figures Jung encountered through the active imaginations recorded in *The Red Book*[3] with different function-attitudes that he names in *Psychological Types.*[4] Lately, I gather, you have been adding that these various types of consciousness were for him the building blocks of something even more differentiated and refined, cultural attitudes that he forged in the course of his dialogues with the inner figures. You say for instance, in Chapter 6 of *Energies and Patterns* that Jung had to "harness spiritual introverted intuition in service to embodied introverted sensation ... to form a religious attitude."[5] Doesn't this challenge our usual idea of *Liber Novus*, the quasi new bible that Jung inscribes in the pages of his *Red Book*, as already structured along religious lines?

JB: I think it does. Let me cite some sentences from editor Sonu Shamdasani's introduction to *The Red Book*:

> The overall theme of the book is how Jung regains his soul and overcomes the contemporary malaise of spiritual alienation. This is ultimately achieved through enabling the rebirth of a new image of God in his soul and developing a new worldview as the form of a psychological and theological cosmology.[6]

Shamdasani's informed statement would appear to be definitive, especially about Jung's own ambition when working on the *Red Book*, which he could never bring himself to publish, yet it calls for further thought on the part of a present-day reader for whom Shamdasani has made *Liber Novus* available with such generous care. His conclusion needs to be carefully parsed, lest we take his pregnant sentence to mean that *Liber Novus* actually *achieves* the psychological and theological cosmology that Jung's soul called him to provide. Jung was invited to his task somewhat indirectly, through the adventures that his extraverted sensation-oriented soul, introduced to him early in the narrative as the fabulous belly-dancer Salome, contrived to lead him into. Her idea of a call to spiritual action was a series of episodes introducing the reality of the psyche to Jung.

Interviewer: What do you mean by "the reality of the psyche"? I recognize that as a Jungian expression, but conceptually, isn't Jung's "reality of the psyche" the same as Freud's "psychic reality?"[7]

JB: No, not even close. Jung is referring to something we can experience; Freud is pointing to something in the unconscious which is more true than the self-deceptions that allow us to believe our conscious experience and ignore what may really be going on at the deep levels we continually defend ourselves against. Freud's "psychic reality" is a postulate as to what we are really like when our defenses are stripped away, something we only occasionally experience.

After his years with Freud, Jung was more willing to be instructed by conscious experience than theory. The point of the active imaginations recorded in *The Red Book* is that Jung could gain access to psychological experience directly, through the mouths of inner figures he could observe and speak to. Salome granted him the gift of being able not only to witness but to experience in a sensate way what transpired in the "Mysterium" that Jung named in the Handwritten Draft as the locus for the "Mystery Plays" of his active imaginations. In that dramatized inner space he met many other important figures of the unconscious. Now, when they spoke theory, Jung listened! Philemon's "Seven Sermons to the Dead"[8] begins like Hellenistic cosmology, but it ends like a rough draft for the Analytical Psychology Jung would soon lay out in his published writings.

Interviewer: Do you agree with Shamdasani, that we, along with Jung, get an adequate cosmology from Philemon?

JB: We get a psychological one. Gregory Bateson certainly thought so. Reading the *Septem Sermones* in the private edition that Jung allowed to be printed, decades after they were written, Bateson, an anthropologist working in Northern California in close contact with psychiatrists, was busy constructing his understanding of the relationship of mind to nature. He saw in the *Sermones* a significant contribution to the "ecology of mind."[9] Bateson, who may have come upon the *Sermones* through his close friendship with the San Francisco-based Jungian psychiatrist Jo Wheelwright, used the word "epistemology," rather than "cosmology," to understand the relation of *pleroma* to *creatura*, which was Philemon's explanation of how psychological experience comes into being. It is clear that Bateson means something not unlike a cosmology.

Interviewer: I sense that is not quite how you would put it.

JB: You are right. It isn't. Calling cosmology epistemology does not take care of the metaphysical assumptions that Jung, following Philemon's lead and that of the Gnostics, wanted to wed to the experience of the mind's relationship to its wider context (the part of Jung's thinking that corresponds to Bateson's). Most of us who have turned to *The Red Book: Liber Novus* to get a cosmology out of it, even if we would be willing to accept a Gnostic cosmology, cannot find one. This had led to accusations against Jung's claim to philosophic status,[10] and even Jung wonders when he first encounters Philemon as a retired magician, if this is nothing but a childlike old man whose "desirousness and creative drive have expired and [who] now enjoys his well-earned rest out of sheer incapacity."[11]

Interviewer: Are you saying Shamdasani is promising too much?

JB: Not really. We have to remember that Jung starts his *Red Book* out by telling us how "incapacity" can open up the spirit of the depths to us when we are no longer in thrall to the spirit of this time that insists that we strive tirelessly to make ourselves contemporary capable people. If we expect Philemon to offer Jung a magical key to a philosophy of the unconscious that he had been unable to get from Freud, that simply isn't what he or we are going to get. As Jung has already told himself in *Liber Primus*, "The hero wants to open up everything he can. But the nameless spirit of the depths evokes everything that man cannot. Incapacity prevents further ascent. Greater height requires greater virtue. We do not possess it. We must first create it by learning to live with our incapacity."[12] It is in that light that we should read Shamdasani's sentence about Jung developing a "psychological and theological cosmology."[13] All Shamdasani says that Jung really *achieves*—and his sentence wisely restricts itself to saying that he "develops" it—is a new worldview, something that could help us form a new cosmology because its perspective includes the self's psychological experience. It's that experience that Jung is allowing us to link to the more metaphysically postulated cosmos when we contemplate what we call the "world" through psychological eyes.

Interviewer: What is the relation of the form of this knowing, which Jung would later call "esse in anima"[14] (to be in soul), to what we end up knowing?

JB: By getting to this new worldview, which is grounded in the reality of the psyche, Jung has, says Shamdasani, created a *form* that can provide the basis for further psychological and metaphysical breakthroughs. It permits an understanding of the universe in which both psychology and theology, the two disciplines that have led to the kind of imagining involved, can be transformed.

Interviewer: Wouldn't that be the same as taking a cosmic perspective on things?

JB: The form of Jung's knowing, in my judgment, is not the same as the cosmology it might permit to come into being. Realizing that active imagination itself, is what is most new in *The Red Book,* we can step back from an inflated view of Jung as himself our master cosmologist, a view that is not fully authorized by the figure in whose name it is summoned. Cosmology, the Webster New Third International Dictionary says, "combines speculative metaphysics and scientific knowledge." What Jung established through his form of imagining is a different route to that combination than most views of the world had permitted before the *Red Book* came into existence.

Interviewer: Are you suggesting that he adds in a kind of verification for what he asserts about the psyche by talking to the inner figures directly?

JB: I am. But this does not mean that the ideas offered in *Liber Novus* are based on empirical observations in accord with the philosophy of science or upon the signs and wonders that religious verification would demand of mystical experience. Jung's observations and his opinions about them are neither psychological nor theological exemplars of the traditions from which they emerge. Indeed, Jung, originally trained as a medical doctor specializing in psychiatry, considers himself an amateur at both psychology and theology. It is enough for him to make efforts to take up both psychological and theological attitudes in tandem to see how they may be linked.

Interviewer: What is his own standpoint then?

JB: He remains a psychiatrist taking time to record his own thoughts and fantasies, operating on stages constructed by his own soul, and discovering that out of this experiential effort a new view of the world can emerge.

Interviewer: Have we any way to establish the accuracy of that worldview?

JB: Rather than worry about how well *The Red Book* succeeds as theology or as psychology, we might read Shamdasani's description of the worldview Jung achieves as a "form" of a cosmology that could be both theological and psychological in character to scale down our expectations for this form, to see it instead as an attitude in formation, not a field-tested laboratory instrument that can reliably contain all future efforts at transforming global consciousness.

Interviewer: Are you talking about what Jung later called "the spirit of psychology?"[15]

JB: Yes, I am. We can find the spirit of what Shamdasani is saying embedded in the words "form" and "worldview," which I think should lead us to concentrate on the *formal* qualities of the construction of a worldview. If we do so, we will soon discover how that form is being constructed over and over again before our eyes in the universe of *The Red Book* itself. Shamdasani's sentence, if we read it closely enough, puts the accent not on "cosmology," but on "worldview." His comment invites us to study how *The Red Book* believes throughout that with the help of his soul Jung can construct a worldview adequate to the time in which he was living (the cusp of World War I, with all the confusion that would create about the value of modernity), and how such a thing as a worldview can constellate what we experience as a cosmology.

Interviewer: Why is "worldview" better than "cosmology," then, as a way to name what Jung is aiming for?

JB: If we focus on worldview, we will recall that Jung was looking for something psychologically restorative in the wake of an image of world catastrophe, the sea of blood he saw spreading over Europe in his prescient vision late in 1913,[16] which was what initially made him want to take up searching for his soul since he was afraid he might be going crazy.

Interviewer: He changed his mind about that, though, didn't he?

JB: Yes, when the heir to the Austro-Hungarian throne, Archduke Franz Ferdinand, was assassinated at the end of July in 1914 and war was declared by the leading powers of the world, Jung realized that not he but the world was suffering from a psychological disturbance, requiring that his own corner of the world, Europe, needed to examine the attitudes that were dominant in its collective consciousness. That suggests to me that he realized he was imagining and incubating attitudes that would not only be restorative for himself but renewing of European culture generally.

Interviewer: Are these the so-called "cultural attitudes" that you write about in *Energies and Patterns of Psychological Type*?[17]

JB: Yes, although Jung would not have used that term, which was only introduced into Analytical Psychology much later by Joseph Henderson, who had been his analysand. Jung realized that the construction of binocular sensitivities adequate to apprehend the

complex depths of the world that were now so evident with the advent
of World War I had become a life task for everyone. The world was
already shedding the skin of modernity with its myth of progress, and
it was going to require a new way of seeing to understand the reality
of the decomposition of the cultural forms that belonged to that more
naive view of human development.

Interviewer: In what sense is this way of seeing "new"?

JB: I think I mean freshly constructed, but not exactly new because
much of what's constructed are versions of cultural attitudes that have
themselves been present for a long time in human culture and have
only recently become exciting for us precisely because we have, so to
speak, lost them.

Interviewer: Can you be more specific?

JB: In his book, *Cultural Attitudes in Psychological Perspective*,[18]
Henderson says there are four cultural attitudes that are no longer
easily seen in pure form in our culture and yet have always been what
I would call "stances" that culturally aware people have found possible
to take, at least since the ancient high cultures that we know about
because they created a record. Henderson defines these as the social,
the religious, the aesthetic, and the philosophic.

Interviewer: Just from their names, these stances don't sound like
anything that would have been new to the 20th century.

JB: Henderson suggests that a fifth possible attitude, the psychological, came into our culture around the time of William James, which
was also the time of Nietzsche. Both James and Nietzsche were
influenced by Emerson, whose essays, written in the 19th century,
display the prototype of this new attitude. But Henderson also says
that it is characteristic of the psychological attitude to take what it
needs from one of the more traditional attitudes—but only what it
needs to keep on reflecting psychologically with the help of that
attitude.[19] Emerson was drawing from a philosophic attitude to create
a way of reflecting psychologically on what it meant to be effectively

cultured in an America bent on individual self-realization within an ever-expanding frontier for the exercise of personal choices.

Interviewer: Are there traditional cultural attitudes you have drawn upon to realize and formulate your psychological ideas?

JB: Definitely. People who follow my work know how often I turn to amplifications from works of art, particularly movies and painting. There is some kind of reciprocity between the aesthetic attitude that enables me to follow how artists construe the psyche and the more strictly psychological attitude I have had to cultivate in my practice as an analyst.

Interviewer: What characterizes a psychological attitude in analytic practice?

JB: As a therapist, I can't listen to patients only from the standpoint of a moral system, or look at them through the eyes of an aesthete demanding beauty, or from the standpoint of a politically sensitive person looking for a consciously social attitude, or from the standpoint of a philosophic attitude that insists on logical consistency and a commitment to uncovering truth as one engages in a dialogue, even if it takes place within psychotherapy. I have to hear everything psychologically, that is from the standpoint of its relevance to the psyche, which is the primary context to be invoked and valued by the analyst when listening to an analytic patient, even if one's mind is permitting other stances to rush in and try to take over.

Interviewer: Do you believe Jung had achieved such an attitude by the time he began his "most difficult experiment," active imagination?

JB: I absolutely do. He had been practicing psychotherapy for a decade before he engaged his inner figures, and his attitude of respectful engagement bears, for me, the mark of a well-trained psychiatrist who knows how to let people present themselves and to engage them according to that presentation. It would be hard to find such an attitude in someone who hadn't worked in a mental hospital and learned how to listen to any mind. He brings that skill to the way he engages with and hears out the different perspectives in *The Red*

Book. Those dialogues are a part of *Liber Novus* that does not date. Very few people even today can hear the ideologies that others are espousing without getting in the way. Jung always lets his inner figures have their say. Their stances always come through, even when he disagrees with them.

Interviewer: Can you give an example of Jung disagreeing with a stance, and perhaps tell me what it reveals about his cultural attitude?

JB: For me, the best example of that is when Jung, while wandering in his imagination on December 29, 1913, finds himself "in a homely, snow covered country" and is "joined by [s]omeone who does not look trustworthy."[20] Jung writes:

> Most notably, he has only one eye and a few scars on his face. He is poor and dirtily clothed, a tramp. He has a black stubble beard that has not seen a razor for a long time. … 'It's damned cold,' he remarks after a while. I agree. After a longer pause he asks: 'Where are you going?'

After that they enter into a conversation, and eventually Jung gets to the bottom of why the tramp is not employed, even though farm work, which Jung suggests to the man, is probably available. The tramp says: "It's boring in the country, one meets nobody." Jung reasonably enough responds: "Well, but there are also villagers." To which the tramp says: "But there is no mental stimulation, the farmers are clods." Jung's inner reaction to this is revealing: "I look at him astonished. What, he still wants mental stimulation? Better that he honestly earn his keep, and when he has done that he can think of stimulation."

Only then does Jung speak his thought: "But tell me: what kind of mental stimulation is there in the city?" The tramp says: "You can go to the cinema in the evenings. That's great and it's cheap. You get to see everything that happens in the world." Jung, speaking to himself in response to this, says: "I have to think of Hell, where there are also cinemas for those who despised this institution on earth and did not go there because everyone else found it to their taste." Jung then rouses himself to ask, "What interested you most about the cinema?" and the man answers: "One sees all sorts of stunning feats. There was one man who ran up houses. Another carried his head under his arm. Another even stood in the middle of a fire and wasn't even burnt. Yes, it's really remarkable, the things people can do." Jung thinks: "And that's what this fellow calls mental stimulation!"

Later in their dialogue, it comes out that this man was in prison, sent there after losing his eye in a knife fight with another man. He tells Jung: "It was beautiful in prison. At that time the building was completely new." The man explains that the brawl had been over a woman who was pregnant with the other man's child, but he wanted to marry her anyway. She would have nothing to do with him after the brawl, so when he got out of prison he went to France. "It was lovely there." Jung comments: "What demands beauty make! Something can be learned from this man." The tone is ironic, and it is clear that Jung's attitude is that beauty, whether in the cinema, the woman, the prison, or in France, is really not worth it. The man dies soon after in Jung's fantasy, and then Jung notes, with a kind of sentimental empathy at last, that "there is no one left to grieve." "What shadows over the earth," he murmurs to himself.

What interests me about this shadow figure is that he carries not only Jung's typological shadow (I read the tramp as an extraverted intuitive, the shadow of Jung's introverted intuition) but that he displays a cultural attitude, however poorly formed, that is also in shadow for Jung, the aesthetic attitude, life lived for beauty.

Interviewer: Why is that interesting to you?

JB: Because Jung's temporarily indulgent but ultimately dismissive reaction to the man, and the fact that his fantasy kills off the character, convey how little room Jung himself had for the aesthetic attitude.

Interviewer: How can you say that? Jung was himself quite an accomplished artist. *The Red Book* gives ample evidence of that. It is filled with beautiful depictions of Jung's fantasies. Jung mixed his own colors, painted at least as well as many of one's favorite illustrators of children's books, and reproductions of his works are starting to appear on many people's walls, where they add an impressive decoration.

JB: I don't deny any of that, but what I find missing in Jung is an aesthetic cultural attitude. This certainly comes through in his notorious essay on Picasso,[21] in the dream in which he decides that the woman who is telling him he is an artist is a sociopath,[22] and in many places where he seems tone deaf to the aesthetic properties or lack of them in the works of art he cites. One might start with his handling of the hero of Longfellow's "Hiawatha" in *Symbols of Transformation*.[23] Here in *The Red Book* it shows up in how utterly he depreciates moviegoing, although he tries to overcome that prejudice. Jung completely ignores the art of cinema in his writing, and he puts down even Schiller's passionate assertion that an aesthetic education can rouse moral sentiments,[24] this toward the author of all but the title of Beethoven's "Ode to Joy."

Interviewer: Does the fact that the tramp is an extraverted intuitive in your view have anything to do with the way you see Jung lacking an aesthetic attitude.

JB: Yes, but not for the reason you think. If you have been reading my articles, you will know that I myself am an extraverted intuitive, so I imagine you are thinking I just don't understand how someone like Jung holds his relation to art in an introverted way.

Interviewer: That's a shrewd guess on your part. So why don't you tell me what makes you see Jung's dismissal of your extraverted interest in the possibilities of art for honing one's intuition as evidence of a failure on his part to develop an aesthetic attitude appropriate to his own introverted intuitive nature.

JB: This gets into a discovery I have made, or think I have made, only recently: that the aesthetic attitude itself is constructed of two extraverted functions that enable it to merge with both the reality and the possibility of beauty in the world. One is extraverted sensation (the very consciousness that, though likely an inferior function for Jung, makes him so good with illustration and with color, creating an uncanny sensate integrity to so many of the paintings in *The Red*

Book). But I have observed that the other part of the aesthetic attitude—and why I would call it, metaphorically, a *binocular* way of apprehending—is extraverted intuition, which plays with the way the creative imagination can entertain, envision, and enable the possibilities that an interesting experience of extraverted sensation can deliver. It is that spirit of play between the two extraverted irrational functions that the tramp personifies, and we can see from the way Jung relates to him and reflects on their meeting how much the entire attitude of this man is in shadow for Jung.

Interviewer: Can you say something about the way Jung constructs, or fails to construct, Henderson's other cultural attitudes in the *Red Book*? The religious attitude for instance.

JB: It won't surprise you that I find this a strength in Jung. But it might be important to say that I see the religious attitude, for all that it seems to be brought to the task of creating the *Red Book*, to also be what the *Red Book* later enables him to create in mature form. Jung ceases to be a pastor's son in *The Red Book* and becomes a religious thinker in his own right. When we take a psychological look at how the religious attitude comes into being in Jung, we find that it is constructed out of two introverted functions that, though far apart in most people, seem to have been strongly enough operating in Jung to co-create the way he chooses to relate to his imaginal life. Using the clarity Jung came to only after he had done the bulk of the work on the *Red Book*, we can see through the lens of his later-completed typology, and we can identify the consciousnesses he combined to produce the religious attitude that gives *The Red Book* its inner conviction of having achieved at least one rock-solid cultural attitude: (a) the introverted intuitive function; and (b) the introverted sensation function. This combination does not arise easily, for these two forms of introverted consciousness ordinarily repel each other.

Interviewer: From your work on typology, I can understand why you say introverted sensation and introverted intuition are far apart in most people. I find it pleasurable, though, to see them join forces in the *Red Book* to create the religious attitude that informs the rest of

Jung's life. It's a miracle I can accept. Because it makes me a bit envious of him, I'd like to hear something from you that will help me humanize his achievement. Where did Jung receive the inner permission to combine these two consciousnesses during his experiment with active imagination?

JB: We can see for ourselves when we read *Liber Novus* that Jung receives rather explicit permission from Salome to be as introverted intuitive as he is. She entrusts him with the gift of a magic rod, persuasively urging him to overcome the insistent emphasis he has placed on science,[25] which I think helps to explain Jung's ability to implement his much more irrational method of active imagination. It is introverted sensation, however, that grants the figures Jung encounters in the "Mysterium," their reality independent of Jung himself, a hard-edgedness that allows us to accept them as autonomous. This is a gift that brings the *Red Book* to life and interests us in seeing what Jung can then imagine, know, and divine about these personalities. This meeting of self-grounded sensation with imaginative intuition creates an inner space for the archetypal resonance and spirit of the figures to be felt. Once the new attitude has become firmly entrenched in Jung, his soul will insist that this calls him to proclaim a new religion.[26] What emerges from Jung through the construction of a religious attitude toward the significance of inner figures is an openness to the presence of archetypes within these personified complexes, which though happening entirely in a world of inner reality is not unlike the experiences recorded as literal by the prophets in the Old Testament in which person and archetype are both granted their reality.

Interviewer: You haven't mentioned much about Jung's philosophic and social attitudes.

JB: That's not because Jung doesn't make interesting stabs at expressing both of those attitudes. There are creative social views and creative philosophic views throughout *The Red Book*, but they seem to me to be incompletely realized. They are neither strong achievements nor complete failures. I've discussed Jung's social attitude in

"The *Red Book* as a Work of Conscience,"[27] and I admire his intuition that self-aggrandizing heroic expectations of themselves had distorted the social attitude of the peoples of Europe just prior to World War I. His statement that "you sin against incapacity"[28] does not only speak to those Europeans who were focusing heroically on increasing their own use and value according to the spirit of the time before World War I. It has also helped me to see how dangerous the notion of the hero has become in America today, when our leaders assume that such a national stance will make us great again. I think, however, that there is so much more to say about what it would take to get past the hero than we find in *The Red Book*. There, the dream of the killing of Siegfried, the Germanic hero archetype Jung was impelled to rid himself of, is interpreted as his unconscious recognition of a psychic necessity to sacrifice the glorification of efficient heroic power. That psychological necessity was simply ignored by his fellow Europeans, leading directly, Jung believed, to the real-world assassination of Crown Prince Franz Ferdinand and thence to war. Jung's treatment of this dream[29] is intuitively dazzling, illuminating for historians a "psychological rule" he stated explicitly decades later, "that when an inner situation is not made conscious, it happens outside, as fate."[30] But such a synchronistic understanding of history leaves too many social and philosophic questions unanswered to pass for either a social attitude or a philosophic attitude. It is at best a brilliant insight into an unsolved problem of civilization, which is as vexing today as when the *Red Book* was written.

Interviewer: Are there signs of a more mature social and philosophic attitude to be found anywhere in Jung?

JB: I think we have to look to his later work to find the places where Jung achieves both a philosophic attitude (combining introverted thinking and introverted feeling) and a social attitude (pulling together extraverted thinking and extraverted feeling) that is really adequate to the place he was going to have to hold in the world. Between the time of his last work on the *Red Book* and the achievement of cultural attitudes that truly worked for him came the fateful decades, the 1930s and 1940s, the lessons of which inform

Jung's writings in his most culturally realized decade, the 1950s, when at last he deals with what he sensed was still incomplete in the *Red Book*. I am particularly fond of *The Undiscovered Self*,[31] but one could nominate several other places in the work of that decade where Jung can be said to have achieved a social and a philosophic attitude that suited him.[32] It seems to me wisest, therefore, when we talk about cultural attitudes in *The Red Book*, not to look there for what has not yet coalesced, but rather to see how its pages construct at least one cultural attitude that Jung can use to meet the world as someone equal to it—the religious attitude that he has reimagined.

Endnotes

[1] The interviewer is an inner figure of John Beebe. This is his first public appearance.

[2] John Beebe, *Energies and Patterns in Psychological Type: The Reservoir of Consciousness* (London & New York, NY: Routledge, 2016), 167-180.

[3] C.G. Jung, *The Red Book: Liber Novus*, ed. Sonu Shamdasani, trans. John Peck, Mark Kyburz, and Sonu Shamdasani (New York, NY: W.W. Norton, 2009).

[4] C.G. Jung, *Psychological Types*, in *CW*, vol. 6 (Princeton, NJ: Princeton University Press, 1971).

[5] Beebe, *Energies and Patterns in Psychological Type: The Reservoir of Consciousness*, 97-114.

[6] Jung, *The Red Book*, 207.

[7] See, for example, C.G. Jung, "Religion and Psychology: A Reply to Martin Buber," in *CW*, vol. 18 (Princeton, NJ: Princeton University Press, 1976), par. 1505. "Thanks to its autonomy, it forms the counterposition to the subjective ego because it is a piece of the *objective psyche*. It can therefore be designated as a 'Thou.' For me, its reality is amply tested by the truly diabolical deeds of our time. ... But I have also seen the other side which can be expressed by the words beauty, goodness, wisdom, grace." See also Joseph Sandler, Alex Holder, Christopher Dare, Anna Ursula Dreher, *Freud's Models of the Mind: An Introduction* (London: Karnac Books, 1997), 80. "Psychic reality. As far as the Unconscious is concerned, memories of real events and of imagined experiences are not distinguished. Abstract symbols are not recognized as abstract but are treated as if they represented concrete reality."

[8] Jung, *The Red Book*, 346-354.

[9] Gregory Bateson, *Steps to an Ecology of Mind: Collected Essays in Anthropology, Psychiatry, Evolution, and Epistemology* (Northvale, NJ: Jason Aronson, 1972), 462-463.

[10] Robert A. Segal, "Review of Sanford Drob's *Reading the Red Book: An interpretive guide to C.G. Jung's Liber Novus*," in *International Journal of Jungian Studies*, 5/3, 2013, 271-273.

[11] C.G. Jung, *The Red Book*, 312.

[12] Ibid., 240.

[13] Ibid., 207.

[14] C.G. Jung, *Psychological Types*, CW 6, pars. 62-67.

[15] See "Der Geist der Psychologie," in C.G. Jung, "On the Nature of the Psyche," in *CW*, vol. 8 (Princeton, NJ: Princeton University Press, 1969).

[16] C.G. Jung, *Memories, Dreams, Reflections*, ed. Aniela Jaffé (New York, NY: Vintage, 1963), 199-200.

[17] Beebe, *Energies and Patterns in Psychological Type*, 97-114.

[18] Joseph Henderson, *Cultural Attitudes in Psychological Perspective* (Toronto: Inner City Books, 1993), 17-71.

[19] Ibid., 81-106.

[20] Jung, *The Red Book*, 265-266.

[21] C.G. Jung, "Picasso," in *CW*, vol. 15 (Princeton, NJ: Princeton University Press, 1966), par. 204.

[22] Jung, *Memories, Dreams, Reflections*, 210 and 220-221.

[23] C.G. Jung, *Symbols of Transformation*, in *CW*, vol. 5 (Princeton, NJ: Princeton University Press, 1956), par. 474.

[24] C.G. Jung, *Psychological Types*, CW 6, par. 132.

[25] C.G. Jung, *The Red Book*, 307-308.

[26] Ibid., 211; Sonu Shamdasani quoting from *Black Book* 7, 92c, January 4, 1922. Jung asks the soul: "But what is my calling?" The soul answers: "The new religion and its proclamation." Jung answers: "Oh God, how should I do this?"

[27] Beebe, *Energies and Patterns in Psychological Type: The Reservoir of Consciousness*, 167-180.

[28] Jung, *The Red Book*, 240.

[29] Jung, *The Red Book*, 239-240. See n99 on page 240.

[30] C.G. Jung, *Aion. Researches into the Phenomenology of the Self*, in *CW*, vol. 9/II (Princeton, NJ: Princeton University Press, 1959), par. 126.

[31] C.G. Jung, "The Undiscovered Self (Present and Future)," in *CW*, vol. 10 (Princeton, NJ: Princeton University Press, 1964), par. 488.

[32] For an illustration of the philosophic attitude that emerges out of Jung's approach to the psyche, in which introverted thinking and introverted feeling join hands, I'd recommend C.G. Jung, "On the Nature of the Psyche," in *CW*, vol. 8 (Princeton, NJ: Princeton

University Press, 1969), par. 343. The most unexpectedly successful example of Jung's ability to catalyze a psychological social attitude was his posthumously published *Memories, Dreams, Reflections* alchemically achieved by wedding Jung's extraverted thinking gift for clear explication of his psychological discoveries to Aniela Jaffé's ability as editor to cast Jung's individual mode of self-presentation with reader-embracing extraverted feeling.

Integrating Horizontal and Vertical Dimensions of Experience under Postmodern Conditions

Gražina Gudaitė

The Experience of the Vertical Dimension – Some Challenges

> We miss nothing more than divine force. ... And thus we speak and stand and look around to see whether somewhere something might happen. Something always happens, but we do not happen, since our God is sick. ... We must think of his healing. And yet again I feel it quite clearly that my life would have broken in half had I failed to heal my God.[1]

This quotation from Jung's *Red Book* occurs in *Liber Secundus* where Jung describes his experiences in active imagination and his dialogues with powerful inner figures such as The Red One, Ammonius, and Izdubar. Many existential questions are raised in these dialogues. Does one really need a relationship with the transcendent in psychological development and individuation? Are individuals able to know that their God is "sick"? Is it realistic to think about healing the transcendent Power if it doesn't depend on the will of the individual? What does it mean to put together "broken parts" of the Divine?

Jung is searching for answers to such questions, and some of them sound rather shocking. "Oh Izdubar, most powerful one, what you call poison is science. In our country we are nurtured on it from youth, and that may be the reason why we haven't properly flourished and remain so dwarfish. When I see you, however, it seems to me as if we are all somewhat poisoned."[2] Can modern man feel dwarfish when there is such amazing progress in different areas of modern life? Why does Jung say that science may poison a person's life? What is wrong with this knowledge that it does not serve for personal growth anymore? In the episode of active imagination quoted above, the half-hero half-god Izdubar becomes sick and is almost dying because he discovers that the so developed Western mind does not answer the most important questions about death and immortality, even more, that Western man lost his Gods and capacity to believe. The clarification that "our truth is that which comes to us from the knowledge of outer things. The truth of your priests is that which comes to you from inner things"[3] brings some relief in this dramatic inner dialogue. In the context of Jung's reflections of his experiences as recorded in his *Red Book*, the healing of psyche means restoration and nurturance of the relationship with the transcendent; it means remembering that human beings have Soul; and it means nourishing the inner subjective world of the individual and searching for bridges between inner and outer.

Movements from separation toward union, from fragmentation toward integration, from one-sided positions toward wholeness are important psychological themes in Jung's *Red Book*. When Jung carried out his "most difficult experiment" and reflected on it in his diaries, the ideas mentioned above were rather new in psychology. So very hard did he work on these idea and so deeply did he understand the processes of conjunction that his insights are still interesting and valuable 100 years later.

"Putting broken parts together," the idea of integration of the personality, is fundamental in some modern theories of psychotherapy. Descriptions of a healthy and mature person are based on the concept of integration in the theory of humanistic psychology, in Gestalt therapy and in some applications of modern psychodynamic psychotherapy. Integration, from the structural point of view, means that a person takes back the disowned, unconscious, or unresolved aspects of the self and makes them parts of a cohesive personality. On the other hand, integration and realization of wholeness do not come to a definite result or conclude in a final improvement of psychic structure but are rather ongoing processes of relationship to the transcendent that is endless. It is not easy to find the right psychological concepts to express the dynamics of this process and to understand the conditions or mechanisms by which this proceeds throughout a lifetime. One of the ways to understand this is by using the hypothesis of "flow of psychic energy" and the different forms of its manifestation in human life. The life of an individual is multi-dimensional: It reaches depths and heights of experience, and a person sometimes has a choice of how to invest psychic energy in one or another field. Raising awareness of the flow of psychic energy and helping people to understand more deeply their choices and respon-sibilities are important tasks of psychotherapy. Looking at how vertical and the horizontal directions of psychic energy movements are combined could be one of the ways to study the endless processes of integration of personality.

Vertical and Horizontal Directions in Psychology

In general, movement in the vertical direction means from up to down (or from down to up). Horizontal movement means a line that runs parallel to the horizon from left to right (or from right to left). Psychologists speak of the vertical dimension of interpersonal relations as indicating the hierarchy of relationships, with questions of dominance, power, or status as part of it. The horizontal dimension of relationship, which emphasizes equality, focuses on collectivism, group processes, etc. Focus on the vertical dimension is also directed toward existential questions, toward development of a system of meaning, or the creation of a theory. Reflections on the subjective experience of an individual involves the analysis of the process of finding meaning. The practice of active imagination, especially with the focus on spiritual needs, can be interpreted as an activity going in the vertical direction. The studies of horizontal direction in psychology, on the other hand, are based on empirical research, meaning they are governed by the evidence-based principle. In the process of gathering data, one uses the information received by the senses, and knowledge is based on objective facts that are observed or gotten experimentally.

Both directions are important for understanding the psychology of human beings, but sometimes it is rather complicated to put the two very different perspectives together. In modern times we have a quite powerful bias toward the view that scientific understanding of psychic processes must be evidence-based exclusively and that the qualitative principle, which focuses on exploration of an individual's subjective world, is less scientific than conclusions based on a statistical average of factors in a particular population. The competition between the different theories and insistence on only one perspective may be the major obstacle standing in the way of deep understanding of the psyche, and such a one-sided attitude may be the very condition serious enough keep one "dwarfish." On the other hand, there are many contemporary studies that try to combine both attitudes, which understand the need to combine both qualitative and quantitative principles and to integrate empirical data and theoretical premises. Both directions, inner and outer, vertical and horizontal, are necessary for an integrative view and for the realization of wholeness. It is important to be conscious of both directions and to understand both dimensions of an individual's experience with regard to the challenges of modern reality.

Integrative View and Relationship with Authority

At Vilnius University, where I teach in Lithuania, we conducted a research project focused on exploring the individual's relationship to authority. The impulse to carry out this study emerged out of our research on cultural trauma. We found out that a disturbed relationship to authority was one of the most important consequences left behind by the previous communist regime.[4] The relationship to authority is commonly accepted as one of the expressions of the vertical axis of experience because it has to do with inner feelings and perceptions rather than with outer, objective hierarchal arrangements in society. Our research showed that the reestablishment of a constructive relationship to authority is one of the most important tasks for psychotherapy as people confront the consequences of an authoritarian regime and that analytical psychotherapy can be helpful in this healing process.[5] An increasing awareness about different aspects of the experience of authority is an important part of the therapeutic process. This can be described using several criteria: moving from a defensive attitude toward recognition of the need to have a relationship with authority; changing from projection of authority onto outer figures toward a sense of inner authority; emerging from being dependent on and controlled by others toward the experience of authorship; and shifting from an ego-centered position toward openness to transcendence. Such categories are helpful in understanding the quality and dynamism of an individual's experience of authority.

It is noteworthy that the psychological issues pertaining to the experience of authority were first raised in countries that had recently liberated themselves from authoritarian regimes. Dieckmann in Germany, Kalinenko, and Slutskaya in Russia, Gailienė and Gudaitė in Lithuania, and others published their studies on authority in the last few decades, after having gotten free of authoritarian regimes.[6] Among other peculiarities, the complicated relationship with religion was common among the cultures of the Soviet regime. The official ideology was based on a materialistic view of the world, and the background of psychology was Pavlov's theory and his experiments with dogs. Religion was devalued and treated as a kind of poison, as opium for people, and religious practices were generally forbidden. Such conditions limited the expression of a variety of relationships in their traditional forms, and the experience of a transcendent authority was among them. Perhaps the rather deep and widespread interest in transcendent experience in our days is related to the suppression of the need for it in the past, and the reconstruction of a relationship with authority is a part of the job an individual's needs to do in liberating himself from authoritarian consequences. On the other hand, an ambivalent attitude toward authority is characteristic not only of the cultures that have suffered the repressions of authoritarian regimes. According to Wertz, the modern American is in a similar situation.[7] It seems that these tendencies are typical not only for the cultures mentioned above but also for others, as new modes of relationship to authority have changed traditional forms.

All these thoughts and reflections show the importance of the vertical axis in relationship and correlate with Jung's idea that relationship with the transcendent is an important part of individuation. It can be disturbed, and it needs to be healed. What disturbs an individual's relationship with the transcendent, or to use Jung's words, what makes God sick and wounded?

The theme of *wounds* and *being wounded* plays a significant role in modern psychology. The exploration of trauma, various hypotheses about personal, cultural, and collective trauma, the phenomenon of trauma transmission, and the wide spectrum of consequences of traumatic experiences—these are important themes in psychological practice and research. Any trauma, whether personal, cultural, or collective, influences the development of an individual and his or her system of relations, and, as we already mentioned above, it may affect the relationship with authority and the experience of the ego-self axis.[8] Jung does not speak about trauma in his inner dialogues. He develops the hypothesis that God became sick because modern man does not express the need for the divine reality anymore, that he puts science into the position of the main authority, and that he lost his capacity to believe. "But we clever men crept around lamed and poisoned, and did not know that we lacked something."[9] An individual's attitude toward the transcendent can be crucial for disturbed relationships, for one-sided self-identity, and for "staying dwarfish." In this context I would like to share an old Lithuanian myth, which gives some hints for deeper understanding of the phenomenology and disturbances of relationship with transcendent reality.

Wounded wind — myth or reality

Norbertas Vėlius (one of the most famous Lithuanian mythologists) collected Baltic myths. He named the collection *Wounded Wind*.[10] This collection and its title are interesting because of the paradoxical idea that it is possible to injure a force that one cannot see. Here is a story from the collection titled "Wounded Wind":

> A peasant was winnowing rye in his barn. In order to separate the chaff from the corn he threw the rye into the air. But the wind was blowing, and the corn remained mixed with the chaff. The peasant closed door and continued, but the wind was still there. He changed place several times, but nothing helped: the wind kept blowing the chaff back into the corn. The peasant flew into a rage, took his knife and threw it into the wind. Instantly the wind vanished. Now the peasant could complete his work successfully. Afterwards he went to look for his knife, but there were no knife to be found outside the barn, only drops of blood on the earth. The peasant followed the blood drops and came to a wood where he found a nice little house. He went into the house and saw an old man lying on a bed. The peasant asked if the old man knew where his knife was. The old man showed him his face, which was wounded by the knife, and promised to give the knife back if the peasant would just blow into the little pipe he held in his hands. The peasant agreed, got his knife back and left. When he came home, he found no house or barn; only the stones of the foundations remained in place. When he had blown into the pipe, he had blown his house and barn away.

This myth describes an interesting dynamic of relationship between man and a higher force, between body and spirit. The relationship between man and the wind starts from the initial scene, which shows a human being working for himself. The wind interrupts his efforts. At first glance, the protagonist of the story seems to be doing the right thing: He works hard, confronts the wind, and carries out his normal job. He uses his power to stop the wind, and it seems that he succeeded. One could expect acceptance and reward from the higher authorities for such a work. But the narrative turns in opposite direction: The protagonist loses everything he was working for. He got a chance to operate the wind ("blow a little bit into the pipe"), but the blowing was powerful and blew away his barn and house, so "only the stones of the foundations remained in place."

The consciousness of a person in the moment of facing a higher power is extremely important. The first step would be to be alert to the signs of a hidden supernatural power. In the narrative above we can find several hints of the presence of a supernatural power. How could it happen that the wind changed direction so quickly in the initial scene? That was the first sign that the peasant was facing something more than natural flow of nature. Then, how could blood drops appear on the earth if there were no body visible to receive the knife? Or was the body hidden, or the peasant blind to it? The climax of the narrative is the meeting with the wounded old man in the woods. The wound is in his cheek, and that reveals the multi-dimensionality of expressions available to the supernatural force an individual has to face. The peasant's knife wounded the wind, which was not able to blow for a moment. Then the force manifested in the body of an old man. This means that a supernatural force may emerge in different shapes, and if an individual uses only his senses for grasping its reality, he may reach false conclusions. As some mythologies state: "Wind existed first, as a person, and when the Earth began its existence, wind took care of it. Wholly independent of our bidding and control, wind evokes an unseen, felt spirit of generation, inspiration and religious ecstasy."[11] The peasant did not read the signs of this hidden reality. He did not see the potential of that spirit, and he did not respond empathically to the signs of suffering. He was focused on his own power. Like a hunter, he tracked a path marked by drops of blood, and he was eager only to get back his knife. He got it back, but then he lost everything.

We can see some parallels between the episode of the wind's wound and the manifestation of cultural trauma. Those who organize attacks on others generally do not see this as leading to their own destruction. They project their own (personal or cultural) shadow on others and declare that they fight for some important idea or belief, as if there were no other possible avenues to resolve conflicts or differences. Different studies have shown that not only aggressors but also victims have a tendency to forget the painful experience, because that helps them to survive.[12] The wound and pain become repressed, and the unconscious may continue to influence life, but indirectly. Even after many years, one may not see the signs of the cultural wound on the surface of life. It is encapsulated in unconsciousness. When we start to look deeper, however, whether in research projects or in an analytical process, we discover the consequences of traumata and their magnitude. In psychotherapy, it is one of the biggest challenges to face the wounds that originated from cultural trauma. A person needs to face the demonic side of authority or other shadow aspects of a bigger force, and that is a real challenge. Confrontation with the consequences of cultural trauma is a multifaceted process in which the consciousness of an individual and his efforts play a significant role. That is very important when we speak about second or third generations of survivors. The healing process may mean restoration of a relationship with the spiritual dimension of life, too. That is especially true for those cultures that have endured the dominating ideology of atheism.

The reasons for a disturbed relationship with transcendent reality may be different among individuals and cultures. This depends on culture and history as well as on the individual. Overemphasizing the individual's authority and activities based on the power principle may be the reason for the wound and for the sickness of the individual and of the whole culture. The etiology of the wound is multifaceted, as is the search for ways of healing. The common step in this process is to confront the defenses and to start to explore unconscious hints about the wound. Otherwise, the destruction continues. In the narrative above, the biggest drama takes place after the peasant leaves the wounded old man in the forest. He does not have strength or interest to care about the wound. Jung warns us that one needs to be very careful when using denial as a coping strategy: "But their God is everything that they do not see: He is in the dark Western lands and he sharpens seeing eyes and he assists those cooking the poison and he guides serpents to the heels of the blind perpetrators."[13]

We do not know what happened to the peasant in the story when he faced the fact that he had lost everything. The experience of loss and crisis can awaken a person to understand the meaning of sacrifice, and this can be the starting point for developing a deeper attitude toward life. Maybe such an experience awakens him to be more alert to the signs of the manifestation of hidden powers. As Jung writes, "But I loved my God, and took him to the house of men, since I was convinced that he also really lived as a fantasy, and should therefore not be left behind, wounded and sick. ... The God outside us increases the weight of everybody heavy, while the god within us lightens everything heavy."[14] It could also be the story of Job, who was alert to the divine reality and who recognized the importance of the relationship with the transcendent, but the relationship was not simple. Or it could be a story we still do not yet know?

Experiences of a heavy burden and an easy one, experiences of having power and losing it, experiences of meeting the representative of divine reality are full of paradoxes. Integration of different principles of analysis is extremely important in searching for bridges between inner and outer, between obvious and hidden, between different dimensions of a person's experience. Our study of the relationship to authority showed that the deterministic point of view is rather limited in understanding the whole picture of this relationship. It can be useful to understand some aspects of interpersonal relations with authority figures or to develop a hypothesis about the origins of an authority complex, but deeper understanding of the phenomenology of experience of inner authority or the manifestation of transcendent reality cannot be based on a deterministic view. The search for meaning and the teleological view, an understanding of paradoxes, flexibility and openness to emergence of new meanings, and looking for analogies are especially important for the experience of the vertical dimension. In my last chapter, I will share a case vignette that illustrates some aspects of the relationship to transcendence and the role of paradox in it.

Paradoxes and the Search for Meaning in an Analytical Case

I would like to share the analysis of a dream that came up in the course of treatment. This is a dream of a client who was in her 40s at the time. She was active and successful, and she enjoyed a full enough outer and inner life. At the time her father passed away, she found that it was hard to face the fact that there was no way to heal him. Facing the reality of death and helplessness evoked many feelings, and questions about meaning were prominent among other existential questions. The dream emerged a year after her father passed away.

> I was in the church of my childhood town. My father was in the church, too. He was very young and was with his mother. It was the moment of 'alleluia' in the mass. I felt the moment of majesty very strongly. I was able to arise and fly—real majesty! My body became bigger, but then I felt a very strong pain in my leg. I woke up for a moment. And then, dreaming again, I heard music. This time it was violin music. I saw a lame musician who was sitting on the ground near the church. That was him, who was playing that wonderful violin music. At that moment I discovered the meaning of the phrase: 'witness the reality of God.'

The first reaction after she told the dream was her feeling of surprise—she saw her father young. She had never seen him so young, neither in reality nor in pictures. The other surprising motif was seeing her grandmother. She had never met her, since this grandmother had died in exile in Siberia several years before she was born. Since the dream emerged just a year after her father passed away, we could accept it as a part of the mourning process, but the manifest content of the dream opens up several moments of phenomenology in the experience of a relationship with the transcendent.

The initial scene of the dream is in a church, a sacred space organized to show the importance of the center and the vertical axis of life. The three cosmic levels—heaven, earth, underworld—are expected to be in communication in sacred space. The dream of the client is a good illustration for that supposition since important figures from the world of dead participate in the initial scene of the dream. The protagonist of the dream represents life on the earth, whereas the loud alleluia and the testimony of God are signs of opening to the vertical axis. Not only the space (i.e., the church) but also the ritual taking place at the time—Time of Mass—indicates the experience of transcendence: "Just as a church constitutes a break in plane in the profane space of a modern city, the service celebrated inside it marks a break in profane temporal duration. It is no longer today's historical time that is experienced, for example, in the adjacent streets—but the time in which the historical existence of Jesus Christ occurred, the time sanctified by his preaching, by his passion, death, and resurrection."[15]

The ideas of rebirth and sacrifice as a condition for renewal are basic items of human faith and belief; they are sources of hope and continuity in difficult situations of loss and bereavement. A relationship with transcendence may be an important resource for enabling a person to accept such events in life. On the other hand, it is very challenging to encounter the power of the transcendent, and contact with the Center is crucial at such times. Contact with the Center does not mean simply finding a stable place. As Edward Edinger states, the experience of the Center involves a dialectical process between two positions: "It requires a twoness to take place. If the ego usurps the center it loses its object."[16] Identification with the higher force is an important moment, but it cannot last long. Disidentification and coming back to one's own body are necessary conditions for the dialogue. The dream illustrates both moments. Identification with some higher force and an experience of majesty take place. This could bring the ego to a state of inflation and loss of connection with her body and perhaps also with the Other. If one stays in such a position, the experience of inner emptiness can be the consequence, as well as facing the "emptiness" of the Center.

The experience of transcending ego boundaries is usually regarded clinically as a controversial phenomenon. As mentioned above, it may be a symptom of ego inflation and in some situations it could be understood as an expression of psychic disorder. Even Jung used some clinical terms to reflect upon his "most difficult experiment." It is not easy to differentiate between psychopathology and exceptional experiences of transcendence. But this ambiguity must be accepted if one wishes to understand the deepest and the highest levels of integration. The individual needs to be open to such exceptional experiences of the numinous, which may be colored by both bliss and awe: "The daemonic-divine object may appear to the mind an object of horror and dread, but at the same time it is no less something that allures with a potent charm, and the creature, who trembles before it, utterly cowed and cast down, has always at the same time the impulse to turn it, nay even to make it somehow his own."[17] The "mystery" is for him not merely something to be wondered at, but something that entrances him. Rudolf Otto states that such an experience may be accepted as a blessing. It may be the source for inspiration and creativity, and it always changes the consciousness of an individual. But on the other hand, such an experience may lead to a state of intoxication, inflation, and loss of self. Perhaps this is the biggest paradox of the experience of the vertical dimension. It is important to look for the horizontal perspective as well.

The next part of the dream gives some hints about the experience of the horizontal dimension. The dreamer is in a street full of dust and people, and the lame musician is sitting on the ground near the church and playing music. No majesty, just dust; no flow, just being lamed and sitting on the ground. It is the horizontal dimension of life. The violin originally was created for street musicians. So here we see the protagonist moving from sacred space to profane. A. said that she accepted the ending of the dream with a big relief. She said that she liked violin music more than organ music and that street musicians seemed to be true musicians because they played when they wanted and what they wanted. She was on the ground now, and everything was in order again. But on the other hand, she was not the same as before. The dream was an exceptional experience, which changed her consciousness. The Other reality really exists. It was important to come back to the body and to come back to earth and then to have the chance to express the "witness that divine force is very real."

When Eliade explores the phenomenology of the Sacred, he uses the term *homo religiosus*. Such a person is able to experience depths and heights of transcendent reality. Modern man is non-religious, and that is a big challenge for modern society:

> Modern nonreligious man assumes a new existential situation; he regards himself solely as the subject and agent of history, and he refuses all appeal to transcendence. In other words, he accepts no model for humanity outside the human condition as it can be seen in the various historical situations. Man *makes himself,* and he only makes himself completely in proportion as he desacralizes himself in the world. The sacred is the prime obstacle to his freedom. He will become himself only when he is totally demysticized. He will not be truly free until he has killed the last god.[18]

Our experience of analytical cases shows that differentiation of religious from non-religious persons is relative and not categorical. Cases of long-term analysis show that people who do not describe themselves as religious (i.e., they do not practice religious rituals or traditions) still have dreams that show their deep interest in and connections to hidden reality. Images of transcendent experience emerge in the psyches of even so-called nonreligious people. Perhaps the world of the *homo religiosus* will not experience a collective rebirth, but the images of transcendence and the models of behavior that follow as a consequence can still assist in postmodern persons' lives that are so full of challenges and stresses and help them to understand themselves better.

Conclusion

"Putting together the broken parts," which indicates the movement from separation toward conjunction and from fragmentation toward integration, is a complex process. The experience of what I have called the vertical axis is full of challenges. It may be the blessing, which opens new sources of vitality and meaning, inspiration and creativity. It may bring moments when one feels as a "person whose roots are above as well as below is thus like a tree growing simultaneously downwards and upwards. The goal is neither height nor depth, but the centre."[19] But it is not comfortable to feel like an inverted tree and to recognize that the deepest level of integration means facing disintegration as well. On the other hand, acceptance that human beings are rooted below and above widens the understanding of energy flow and broadens the integration process. One needs to experience the fertility of the soil of the land, history, and culture—the horizontal plane. On the other hand, one needs to experience moments of being rooted in emptiness—the vertical plane—for such experiences open new perspectives on one's identity and ability to dialogue with the Other, be it our beloved or an unknown wanderer.

Endnotes

[1] C.G. Jung, *The Red Book: Liber Novus. A Reader's Edition*, ed. Sonu Shamdasani, trans. John Peck, Mark Kyburz, and Sonu Shamdasani (New York, NY: W.W. Norton, 2012), 290-291.

[2] Ibid., 279.

[3] Ibid., 280.

[4] Gražina Gudaitė, "Restoration of Continuity: Desperation or Hope in Facing the Consequences of Cultural Trauma," in *Confronting Cultural Trauma: Jungian Approaches to Understanding and Healing*, eds. Gražina Gudaitė and Murray Stein (New Orleans, LA: Spring Journal Books, 2014), 227-243.

[5] Gražina Gudaitė, *Relationship with Authority and Sense of Personal Strength* (Vilnius: Vilnius University Press, 2016) (in Lithuanian).

[6] Hans Dieckmann, "Some Aspects of the Development of Authority," in *Journal of Analytical Psychology*, Vol. 22, no. 3, 1977, 230-242; Vsevolod Kalinenko and Madina Slutskaya, "Father of the People" versus "Enemies of the People": a Split-Father Complex as the Foundation for Collective Trauma in Russia," in *Confronting Cultural Trauma: Jungian Approaches to Understanding and Healing*, eds. Gražina Gudaitė and Murray Stein (New Orleans, LA: Spring Journal Books, 2014), 95-113; Danutė Gailienė, Evaldas Kazlauskas, "Fifty Years on: The Long-Term Psychological Effects of Soviet Repression in Lithuania," in *The Psychology of Extreme Traumatisation: The Aftermath of Political Repression*, ed. Danutė Gailienė (Vilnius: Akreta, 2005), 67–108; Gražina Gudaitė, "Psychological Aftereffects of the Soviet Trauma and the Analytical Process," in *The Psychology of Extreme Traumatisation: The Aftermath of Political Repression*, ed. Danutė Gailienė (Vilnius: Akreta, 2005), 108–126.

[7] Kaitryn Wertz, *Inner Authority and Jung's Model of Individuation* (Boulder Association of Jungian Analysts, 2013).

[8] Donald Kalsched, *The Inner World of Trauma. Archetypal Defenses of the Personal Spirit* (London: Routledge, 1996). Also see Ursula Wirtz, *Trauma and Beyond. The Mystery of Transformation* (New Orleans, LA: Spring Journal Books, 2014).

[9] Jung, *The Red Book*, 296.

[10] Norbertas Vėlius, *Wounded Wind. Lithuanian Mythological Tales* (Vilnius: Versus Aureus, 2012) (in Lithuanian).

[11] See "Wind," in *The Book of Symbols: Reflections on Archetypal Images,* ed. Ami Ronnberg (Köln: Taschen, 2010), 60.

[12] See Wirtz, *Trauma and Beyond* and Gražina Gudaitė, "Psychological Aftereffects of the Soviet Trauma and the Analytical Process."

[13] Jung, *The Red Book,* 297.

[14] Ibid., 296.

[15] Mircea Eliade, *The Sacred and Profane. The Nature of Religion* (New York, NY: Harper and Row, 1957), 72.

[16] Edward Edinger, *The New God-Image. A Study of Jung's Key Letters Concerning the Evolution of the Western God-Image* (Wilmette, Ill: Chiron Publications, 1996), 23.

[17] Rudolf Otto, *The Idea of the Holy* (Oxford: Oxford University Press, 1958), 31.

[18] Eliade, *The Sacred and Profane,* 203.

[19] C.G. Jung, "The Philosophical Tree," in *CW,* vol. 13 (Princeton, NJ: Princeton University Press, 1967), par. 333.

On Salome and the Emancipation of Woman in *The Red Book*

Joerg Rasche

... for the roses had the look of flowers that are looked at.[1]

T. S. Eliot

Freud's original interest was to find a neurological substrate for psychological phenomena. When Jung began his Word Association Experiment Studies in 1900, which were based on the work of Wundt and on his studies with Bleuler, Janet, Flournoy and others, he came across psychological structures that he named "autonomous complexes." Spontaneous and preconscious modulations of the reaction time to a special trigger word and accompanying physiological (galvanic) alterations as well as other "complex indicators" were related to obscure but meaningful psychic contents, i.e., to somehow bundled mental matters. The search was for a bridge between neurological and somatic observations on one side and psychic phenomena like affects, emotions, inner images, and narratives on the other. Today, too, the newest scientific psychological paradigm is that of emotional intelligence and neuropsychology.

The concepts of animus and anima are based on clinical observations and on Jung's personal introspection. The discovery— or shall we say the creation?—of these two archetypal phenomena of the mind happened more than a hundred years ago in Jung's self-experiment, which resulted in his *Red Book*. In 1913, he began with a technique of conscious daydreaming, which he later called "active imagination." Jung's conviction can be described as that there is no understanding about the psychic, but only inside the psyche.

Consequently, the diary of his experiment looks more like an artistic elaboration of fantasies and philosophical reflections than a modern objective scientific report. Jung wanted to go back to the holistic medieval view where the inner world and the outer world were much more connected than in his own time. Nevertheless, in developing his technique of active imagination, he discovered a method that was absolutely modern and similar to the view in modern physics that the observer has an impact on the observed object and that there is no "objective" reality. The elements of his psyche seemed to be affected by observation; they changed their appearance and attitudes when he addressed them. As in quantum physics, he was dealing with a changing object that was affected by the observer.

The volatile and scintillating autonomous phenomena of the mind led Jung to the concepts of anima and animus. But this research was not just the result of scientific interest and curiosity. Jung was in a deep personal crisis in 1913: He and his group in Zurich split from, or was excluded by, Freud's psychoanalytic group in Vienna, his transference to Freud had collapsed, and he felt himself confronted with deep uncertainties about his future. He was also much concerned about the cultural and political situation in Europe in the years shortly before the eruption of World War I. In addition to this, his private situation was fraught: His former patient and friend Sabina Spielrein had gone over to Freud, a close relationship with Toni Wolff had begun to develop, and his marriage with Emma was in trouble. In this essay I will examine the figure of Salome in *The Red Book* and ask how Jung's experience with the figures of the unconscious may have helped him to overcome his inner dilemmas. This is a delicate issue, since we do not have much reliable information about Jung's private situation. Above all, we should keep in mind that the figures in active imagination belong to the inner world and have their own reason for being. They behave like autonomous complexes, not only in the individual but also in the collective unconscious. In a crucial moment in *The Red Book*, one of these figures says: "We are real and not symbols."[2] Therefore, in this study I will circumambulate what I call the "Salome-complex" before looking at Jung's private situation.

The Blind Salome

In December 1913, following upon a dream of killing an inner hero called Siegfried and after experiencing a threatening vision of a destructive flood rolling over Europe, Jung had a vision of Elijah and Salome. It was one of the most important active imaginations recorded in his *Red Book*. Before Salome stepped forward onto his inner stage, Jung saw an old man "like one of the old prophets." At his feet lay a black serpent. Then a beautiful girl, blind and walking shakily, came out of a house with columns. The imagination suggested the image of Eve, the tree, and the snake, and the story of Ulysses and his comrades who were bewitched by the Sirens and Circe. At first, Jung was confused and afraid, but he endured the tension. Then the old man addresses him:

> E: "Do you know where you are?"
> I: "I am a stranger here and everything seems strange to me, anxious as in a dream. Who are you?"
> E: "I am Elijah, and this is my daughter Salome."
> I: "The daughter of Herod, the bloodthirsty woman?"
> E: "Why do you judge so? You see that she is blind. She is my daughter, the daughter of the prophet."
> I: "What miracle has united you?"
> E: "It is no miracle, it was so from the beginning. My wisdom and my daughter are one."
> I am shocked, I am incapable of grasping it.
> I: "Forgive my astonishment, am I truly in the under-world?"
> S: "Do you love me?"

This unforeseen question astonished Jung, who was obviously shaken by this bold approach:

> I: "How can I love you? How do you come to this question? I see only one thing, you are Salome, a tiger, your hands are stained with the blood of the holy one. How should I love you?"
> S: "You will love me."[3]

We may ask how such mythological scenery could find its way into Jung's unconscious imagination. Obviously, Jung had in mind the legend of John the Baptist, who was imprisoned by King Herod. Herod's stepdaughter, Salome, danced for him, and she asked for the head of John as a reward. This bloody legend was elaborated by some famous writers and artists of the *fin de siècle*, and Salome became an image of the terrible *femme fatale*.[4] Richard Strauss wrote an opera on the subject using the libretto from the drama of Oscar Wilde. Beardsley's illustrations were famous, and Strauss's very successful opera was on stage in Zurich from 1907 on. Some phrases of Jung's imagination are so close to Wilde's text that one must suppose that he had seen the opera. Maybe Salome's appearance in active imagination was triggered by unconscious memories of the opera. Later on, Jung writes: "Doubt tears me apart. It is all so unreal and yet a part of my longing remains behind. Will I come again? Salome loves me, do I love her? I hear wild music, a tambourine, a sultry moonlit night, the bloody-staring head of the holy man—fear seizes me."[5] This is exactly the atmosphere of the opera.

Elijah, the Old Testament prophet, guides his blind daughter Salome on his arm. She cannot walk without his help. In the opera, Salome is a dancer and sees very well. In the symbolical world of the imagination, therefore, blindness must have a meaning—it is about losing orientation. Jung says in the commentary to his active imagination that Salome is pleasure: "… pleasure is blind. It does not foresee, but desires what it touches."[6] Elijah gives an explanation for Salome's cruelty:

> E: "But she loved a holy man."
> I: "And shamefully shed his precious blood."
> E: "She loved the prophet who announced the new god to the world. She loved him …"
> I: "Do you think that because she is your daughter, she loved the prophet in John, the father?"
> E: "By her love shall you know her."
> …

I: "What my eyes see is exactly what I cannot grasp. You, Elijah, who are a prophet, the mouth of God, and she, a bloodthirsty horror. You are the symbol of the most extreme contradiction."

E: "We are real and not symbols."[7]

Here we see Jung struggling with his feelings for Salome. He fears to lose his head like John the Baptist. In the active imagination that follows he feels compassion for her. Salome calls herself his sister and tells him that Maria is their mother. There follows the "mystery scene" when Jung feels himself to be painfully crucified and wound around by a big serpent who presses him like a python. Blood streams down from his body to his feet. Then Salome says: "You are Christ!" and immediately she gets back her sight: "I see light!" she cries out. Salome's blindness is healed, and she can see again.[8]

It is remarkable to read and to imagine how Jung developed a dialogue with such images/persons of the unconscious and how they changed and were transformed during his active imaginations. It is as if these characters knew more and different things than the creator. If we relate Salome's blindness to Jung's unconscious attitudes, we may suppose that Jung was unaware about his real feelings regarding "Salome"—whatever or whoever Salome was for him in his private life in 1913. His "Salome-complex" was obviously about fear of the female, about fear of love and dependency. We may be reminded of his struggle with Sabina Spielrein, his former patient, of her healing from psychotic "blindness" and her loving attachment to her doctor that continued after the end of therapy in 1905. According to my first tentative interpretation, it is as if the Salome of Jung's imagination came to life through a process of unconscious reflection about his relationship with women. In 1913, the women especially important for Jung were his wife, Emma, his assistant Toni Wolff, and Lou Andreas-Salomé. My interpretation is supported by later scenes in *The Red Book*. In *Liber Secundus*, a slim and pale girl asks Jung: "Do you love me?" and Jung answers: "By God, I love you—but— unfortunately I am already married." As the girl disappears, she says:

"... I bring you greetings from Salome!"[9] Many further episodes later, Elijah and Salome appear again.

Elijah leads Salome, the seeing one, by the hand. She blushes and lowers her eyes while lovingly batting her eyelids:

> E: "Here, I give you Salome. May she be yours."
> I: "For God's sake, what should I do with Salome? I am already married and we are not among the Turks."
> E: "You helpless man, how ponderous you are. Is this not a beautiful gift? Is her healing not your doing? Won't you not accept her love as the well-deserved payment for your trouble?"
> I: "It seems to me a rather strange gift, more burden than joy. I am happy that Salome is thankful to me and loves me. I love her too—somewhat. ... Elijah, old man, listen: you have a strange gratitude. Do not give your daughter away, but set her on her own feet ... Salome, I thank you for your love. If you really love me, dance before the crowd, please people so that they praise your beauty and your art. ..."
> Sal: "What a hard and incomprehensible man you are."[10]

Here Jung seems to speak from a modern enlightened position as an advocate for women's emancipation. Women should stand and walk on their own feet. It is about female empowerment. The key figure in the European movement for Women's Liberation in his time was Lou Andreas. Her maiden name was Salomé!

A Real Salomé

James Hillman, commenting on Jung's crisis and the visions in 1913, wrote: "... this happened shortly after the break with Freud—so much so that Stanley Leavy has suggested that the Salome in the vision ... is none other than a disguised Lou Andreas-Salomé and the Elijah is none other than Freud."[11] We will follow this line of thought for a bit, since Lou Andreas-Salomé was an early exponent of women's emancipation.

Lou Andreas-Salomé (1861-1937) and Jung knew each other presumably already before the psychoanalytic Congress in Weimar in 1911 where they appear near each other in the famous photograph of the pioneers of psychoanalysis. Lou Salomé came from Russia and studied at the University of Zurich from 1880 to 1882—just as Sabina Spielrein did later. After that she went to Rome for a period where she met Friedrich Nietzsche, whose proposal of marriage she declined. From 1882 to 1885 she lived in Berlin with the philosopher Paul Rée. Nietzsche arranged the famous photo of Lou in a carriage holding a whip with Rée and himself shown as draft animals!

Left to right, Lou Andreas-Salomé, Paul Rée and Friedrich Nietzsche (1882).

In 1885, Lou Salomé married the Orientalist Friedrich Karl Andreas with the contractual stipulation not to have sex in the marriage. Her romantic and sexual relationship with Rainer Maria Rilke began in 1886. He admired her study, *Nietzsche*, which was later regarded by Anna Freud to be an anticipation of psychoanalysis. In 1885, Andreas-Salomé wrote a novel about women's emancipation titled *Fenitschka – A Debauchery*, which reflected her own issues: Can a married woman remain herself? Does love make women weak and dependent? And what is the role of men if women do not need to be saved any longer?

In 1911, Andreas-Salomé, by now a famous European advocate for women's rights and a *femme fatale*, attended the Third International Conference for Psychoanalysis in Weimar, invited by the psychiatrist Paul Bjerre (another of her admirers) who spoke about psychosynthesis—a project not far from Jung's ideas. On the famous photograph of the Congress she sits in the center of the front row. Nearby are Emma Jung and Toni Wolff. Shortly thereafter she sent a paper to Jung for publication in the Jahrbuch. Jung and Freud would have accepted it for publication, but she withdrew it. At the fatal Congress in Munich in 1913, Lou was in the party of Freud. Somehow, she became hostile toward Jung, even if she also later supported Jungian positions.

If the Salome of *The Red Book* stands for Lou, then Elijah stands for Freud. Salomé is blind, and Elijah calls himself her father. The blind (= ignorant, naïve) daughter of the old Jewish prophet—this could make sense. In his active imagination Jung surprisingly heals Salome from her blindness. Interestingly, Jung's vision is the opposite of Freud's preferred myth about the blind Oedipus and his sighted daughter, Antigone. For Jung, it is about healing the young woman; in Freud's story, it is about a blind old man and his beloved daughter. It may be that Jung knew that Freud had analyzed his daughter, Anna, in 1910 because of her fears and compulsory masturbation. The vision in Jung's active imagination of 1913 may be triggered by the scintillating *femme fatale*, Lou Andreas-Salomé. The imaginary Salome declares Jung and herself siblings; Elijah-Freud then would be their common father. But instead of loving Jung, the real Salomé betrays him and takes the part of the Jewish prophet.

Femmes Fatales of the Fin du Siècle

In his active imagination, Jung makes a statement in favor of the oppressed women of his time, in a cultural situation where the position of women in general was in crisis—or perhaps better said, where the relation between the genders was being called into question. To put women on their own feet was exactly what Swiss society did not want. There were few Swiss female students at the University of Zurich, and even Jung's own daughters were not allowed to study there. Nevertheless, Jung did encourage Sabina Spielrein to study at the university and Toni Wolff and Emma to do scientific work.

To understand better the role of Lou Andreas-Salomé in Jung's time and the meaning of Jung's statement against the oppression of women, a picture of the time would be helpful. The cultural complex around women's roles in the last decades of the 19th century has many layers, and there are some differences in the various countries and social classes. Working-class women had to work and to raise children, and in most of the rural areas of Switzerland this was still their traditional role. In more industrialized regions and countries, the lives and status of women had changed. It was a complex development. The exploitation of workers and their families, together with the exploitation of charcoal, timber, water, and other natural resources, led to ecological and social conflicts of a new kind. The exploitation of nature was linked with that of women, who represented the "cyclic nature" in the family. Because of the modernized working processes in factories, men lost the leading position they had had in the agricultural family, and women were suffering from the dual roles of being both mothers and workers. Feminine values and needs became problematic. There was no contraception and only few possibilities for education. Early capitalism created a critical development also in the upper classes.

The wives of the bourgeois had far less freedom than upper-class women enjoyed in the Age of Enlightenment. Early capitalistic society, which was oriented primarily to profit and the expansion of capital, was far more repressive than we usually imagine. Sexuality was largely repressed, and a double morality concerning prostitution was widespread. Syphilis lay as a kind of curse over society, and the blame for this was projected onto the female. The fate of Nietzsche, who died of syphilis, and the misogyny of Otto Weininger were symptomatic.

The feminine archetype is also connected with the themes of life and death. The former religious orientation lost its integrating potency, and thus it could not absorb and organize the fears and questions about death as it had done in former times. The constellated fears were projected onto women. The resulting cultural complex can be seen in the double-faced image of femininity in the arts: On one side there were the silly, innocent, but also dangerous female spirits of nature like Russalka, Undine or Pippa; on the other side, there were the terrible seductive *femmes fatale* like Lola Montez, Mata Hari, and on the opera stage Lulu, Turandot, and Salome. Strauss's opera *Salome* was very popular in military circles of the German Empire of Wilhelm II, especially Salome's famous and decadent "dance of the seven veils." Under these conditions, Jung's theory about a female aspect in the male psyche, and a male aspect in the female psyche, was quite revolutionary. He came across this structure through his encounter with Salome and Elijah.

One Who Fears to Be Loved

In his visions, Jung fears the love of Salome:

> A thinker should fear Salome, since she wants his head, especially if he is a holy man. A thinker cannot be a holy person, otherwise he loses his head. It does not help to hide oneself in thought. There the solidification overtakes you. You must turn back to the motherly fore-thought to obtain renewal. But forethought leads to Salome.[12]

A bit later he writes: "It is no small matter to acknowledge one's yearning. ... But who should live your life if you do not live it?"[13] Later still, when Elijah offers him his daughter as a wife and lover, he declines. He remembers the strange and painful scene of his crucifixion and the suffocating embrace of the snake.

> I: "... But being entangled with love! Simply thinking about it is dreadful."
>
> Sal: "So you really demand that I be and not be at the same time. That is impossible. What's wrong with you?"
>
> I: "I lack the strength to hoist another fate onto my shoulders. I have enough to carry."
>
> Sal: "But what if I help you bear this load?"
>
> I: "How can you? You'd have to carry me, an untamed burden. Shouldn't I have to carry it myself?"
>
> E: "You speak the truth. May each one carry his load. He who wants to burden others with his baggage is their slave. It is not too difficult for anyone to lug themselves."
>
> Sal: "But father, couldn't I help him bear part of his burden?"
>
> E: "Then he'd be your slave."
>
> Sal: "Or my master and ruler."
>
> I: "That I shall not be. You should be a free being. I can bear neither slaves nor masters. I long for men."
>
> Sal: "Am I not a human being?"
>
> I: "Be your own master and your own slave, do not belong to me but to yourself. Do not bear my burden, but your own. Thus you leave me my human freedom, a thing that's worth more to me than the right of ownership over another person."[14]

In this scene Jung speaks as an enlightened modern man. Behind his attitude, however, is fear—he seems to fear to be loved, to be enslaved as he says, and therefore he rejects love. To illustrate this complex, we might look at Rilke's novel *The Notebooks of Malte Laurids Brigge*, which he sent to Lou Andreas-Salomé in 1910. The novel is about a young man who cannot stand to be loved—he even feared the love of the family's pet dogs. He regretted that in the evenings after his excursions he had to return to his family, who loved him too much. He found the solution in the love of God, because he did not have to fear that God would love him in return: God is so far beyond the human world and the fate of individuals that He would never concern himself with feelings for us. In essence, God is absent from the human sphere. This is an idea close to Nietzsche's thought. Jung knew Nietzsche very well. The absence of God was part of the European cultural complex at the end of the 19th century.

The ambivalence regarding being loved also has a root in Jung's childhood. Jung had a difficult relation with his mother. Today we would speak about a negative mother complex or an uncertain bonding pattern. This dates back to his third year when his mother had to spend some months in a psychiatric hospital. "I was deeply troubled by my mother's being away. From then on, I always felt mistrustful when the word 'love' was spoken. The feeling I associated with 'woman' was for a long time that of innate unreliability. 'Father,' on the other hand, meant reliability—and powerlessness."[15] One also needs to consider that Carl Gustav was a replacement child and thus had to carry special hopes and projections by his parents. Freud was not the first who made a crown prince of him.

Jung's Struggle among Sabina, Toni and Emma

As I mentioned earlier, the figures of Jung's active imagination are beings in their own right. They are rooted in the collective unconscious, and they will never fit one-to-one onto the biographical reality of the author. As Hillman wrote: "Freud's fictioning appeared disguised in his case histories and his cosmogonic theories. Jung's appeared overtly in the history of his own case. Freud entered literary imagination by writing about other people; Jung by envisioning himself as 'other people.' What we learn from Freud is that this literary imagination goes on in the midst of historical fact. What we learn from Jung is that this literary imagination goes on in the midst of ourselves. Poetic, dramatic fictions are what actually populate our psychic life. Our life in soul is a life in imagination."[16]

Since Jung called active imagination "the indispensable second part of any analysis that is really meant to go to the roots,"[17] this might authorize us to try some interpretations on the biographical level.

Sabina Spielrein

Jung married Emma Rauschenbach in 1903. Intimate relations with women were a problem for him. As he writes in *Memories, Dreams, Reflections*, his mother's behavior and psychic states sometimes were quite troubling, and as a result, he had a basic problem with "love" and female unreliability. Much has been written about Jung's relationships with female patients, and here only a few short references are possible. When Sabina Spielrein came to the Burghölzli Klinik in Zurich in August 1904, the Word Association Experiment was used for diagnosing patients. Jung found a "chastisement complex" in Sabina's disturbed mind. This complex was strong and behaved autonomously, and Jung had to track her sado-masochistic impulses.[18] Jung used the associations in his therapeutic interventions. He wrote about this method as follows: "The psychic beings (Sonderexistenzen) will be shattered, if they will be pulled by an effort of will to daylight."[19] Today one must concede that in 1904 the founders were still in the pioneering years of psychoanalytic treatment, and the psychiatric methods of those times were not well developed by later standards. It was not an analytic therapy in the modern sense. The dynamics of transference and countertransference were not well-known or reflected upon. The close interaction between doctor and patient could become an unconscious trap. "Both Jung and Spielrein suffered from a non-protected childhood and adolescence, and they met each other with a great need for love," writes Spielrein's biographer Richebächer,[20] and we might add: also with great ambivalence and without an objective perspective on the situation. It is understandable that Spielrein fell in love with her doctor. Already after just 10 months in the clinic in June 1905, she was healed and could leave the hospital. She studied medicine at the University of Zurich, as Jung proposed to her, and heard his lectures there. The therapy was over, but both kept the flame burning. In 1908 and 1909, Jung obviously made a new step toward Spielrein, and it took some years for both to escape from the collusive interaction. In 1910, Spielrein wrote to Freud about her suffering and ambivalence.

Jung had to learn his lesson. In March 1909, he wrote to Freud about his "polygamous components."[21] He addressed Freud as his analyst and supervisor. The therapy relationship with Spielrein had ended years ago, and now it was more of an extramarital love affair. Jung's wife, Emma, had by now already borne three children. It is important to recognize that neither Spielrein nor Jung ever said explicitly that they had a sexual relationship. This rumor was brought forward again in 1980 by Aldo Carotenuto, who published the then newly discovered correspondence between Jung and Spielrein. Zvi Lothane, however, who discovered some additional letters and diaries of Spielrein's, contended that Carotenuto's earlier suspicion was not substantiated by the documents. Unfortunately, the rumor led to books and movies that have damaged Jung's (and Freud's) posthumous reputations.

It looks as if in the active imagination of 1913 Jung is still struggling with his "polygamous components" and trying to find a solution for his true feelings. When he says to Elijah/Freud, "For God's sake, what should I do with Salome? I am already married and we are not among the Turks"—he might have been speaking about his former patient and friend.

Toni Wolff

In 1910, Toni Wolff, suffering from depression after the death of her father, became a patient of Jung. Barbara Hannah reports that Jung immediately recognized the intelligence of the 23-year-old woman and as part of the treatment for her depression gave her some work to do researching material for his book *Symbols of Transformation*.[22] This had an ameliorating effect on her depression, and in September

1911, she attended the Weimar Congress together with Emma Jung, where she also met Lou Andreas-Salomé. The close working relationship with Jung went on for 40 years. Hannah writes that Jung discussed his active imaginations with Toni—this would mean also the *"we are not with the Turks!"* Sonu Shamdasani, referencing the unpublished Protocols of Aniela Jaffé's interviews with Jung for *Memories, Dreams, Reflections*, writes: "... Toni Wolff had become drawn into the process on which he was involved, and was experiencing a similar stream of images. Jung found that he could discuss his experiences with her, but she was disorientated and in the same mess."[23] As I read it, this means that Toni Wolff was also fighting with an erotic transference. As with Sabina Spielrein, there is no evidence that Jung and Toni Wolff had a sexual relationship, but one can suppose that the active imagination about Salome somehow reflects the problem that Jung was facing with Toni Wolff—and his struggle for a solution. Barbara Hannah, a friend of Toni Wolff, wrote:

> Toni Wolff was perhaps—of all the 'anima types' I have ever known—the most fitted to carry the projection of this figure. She was not beautiful in the strictly classical sense, but she could look far more than beautiful, more like a goddess than a mortal woman. She had an extraordinary genius for accompanying men—and some women too, in a different way—whose destiny it was to enter the unconscious. Indeed, she learned of this gift through her relation to Jung, but she afterward showed the same gift when she became an analyst; in fact, it was her most valuable quality as an analyst.[24]

In her work, "Structural Forms of the Feminine Psyche," Tony Wolff describes four basic types of femininity: Mother, Hetaira, Medial woman, and Amazon. "Similar to the four basic psychological types, all the four structural forms are inherent in every woman."[25] From her descriptions of the types, one may safely assume that Toni Wolff identified herself with the Hetaira, with the Medial woman disposition forming a strong part of the picture. "The Hetaira or companion is instinctively related to the personal psychology of the male, and also to that of her children if she is married. The individual interests, inclination and, possibly, also the problems of the male are within her conscious field of vision and are stimulated and promoted by her."[26] Wolff speaks about the "femmes inspiratrices" and Calypso.

> The function of the Hetaira is to awaken the individual psychic life in the male and to lead him through and beyond his male responsibilities towards the formation of a total personality. … The Hetaira affects the shadow side in the male and the subjective side of his Anima—a problem which is not without its danger. Consequently she ought to be, and at best is indeed, conscious of the laws of relationship. Her instinctive interest is directed towards the individual contents of a relationship in herself as well as in the man.[27]

She continues, as though speaking about her own situation with Jung:

> For the man, a relationship in all of its potentialities and nuances is usually less conscious and less important, for it distracts him from his tasks. For the Hetaira it is decisive. Everything else—social security, position, etc.—is unimportant. In this lies both the significance and the danger of the Hetaira. If she overlooks the Persona side of the man (or of her children) or adapts herself too blindly to it, she is bound to idolize the personal element, to incite it excessively and may bring the man to a point where he himself loses his clear vision of outer reality: he may for instance give up his profession to become a 'creative artist'; he may divorce, feeling that the Hetaira understands him better than his wife, etc. She insists on an illusion or some and thus becomes a temptress; she is a Circe instead of Calypso.[28]

Many of these features of the Hetaira listed by Toni Wolff in this passage we know from Jung's analysis of Salome's "blindness" to his struggle against being a creative artist instead of a psychologist. Then Toni speaks also about sexuality:

> There is great confusion nowadays[29] as a result of the widespread abolition of the sexual taboo. It is the order of the day to have 'relationships'—seen from the part of the woman they may either be due to erotic misunderstandings or to professional necessities. For the man, sexuality is the self-evident manifestation of a relationship. For the woman, and in particular for the Hetairas, it is under certain circumstances its result or, according to the individual law of relationship, it should even be kept out of it altogether. In any case it is only appropriate when the relationship as such has been sufficiently developed. ... But since the security afforded by marriage or a professional is of vital necessity to a woman, this need may creep unconsciously into the Hetaira relationship and disturb its intrinsic course. ...
>
> Everything in life must be learned, also human relationship, and it is therefore only natural that the Hetaira cannot begin with it on the most differentiated level. Once she has learned it, she will carefully observe the laws of individual relationship, she will notice what belongs to it and what not, and she will if necessary know when a relationship has become fulfilled and complete.[30]

One may safely assume that also Toni Wolff did not begin her relationship with Jung on a "most differentiated level." Perhaps their shared confrontation with the Salome-image became significant for their relationship. Based on all the documents available, it is possible that after some initial confusion, they did not have a sexual relationship with each other. However, this is not important. What's more to the point is that the active imaginations with Salome show Jung's struggle to understand his inner drives, not to *lose his head*, and to hold the tension. This is, as Jungians believe, the precondition for transformation.

Emma Jung

Who paid the bills? For the following observations, I am indebted to
Nadia Neri and Imelda Gaudissart. Barbara Hannah also wrote about
the situation pertaining to Jung and his wife, Emma Rauschenbach.
She comments on the situation thusly:

> It seems hard that, just at the time he was tried to the
> uttermost by his 'confrontation with the unconscious,' Jung
> had also to deal with perhaps the most difficult problem a
> married man ever has to face: the fact that he can love his
> wife and another woman simultaneously. But the one
> problem belonged to the other and they were really two
> facets of the same problem. Although he had not yet
> recognized the archetype of the anima, this figure is the
> nearest to a man of all the inner figures and she is above
> all the bridge to, and the mediator between, the man and
> his unconscious. Jung also did not yet know that the anima
> frequently projects herself into a real woman and that this
> projection endows that woman with the whole numinous
> quality of the unconscious.[31]

Hannah also writes about the pain that all three had to suffer. She
quotes Jung: "The kernel of all jealousy is lack of love."[32] She
continues: "What saved the situation was that there was no 'lack of
love' in any of the three. Jung was able to give both his wife and Toni
a most satisfactory amount, and *both* women *really* loved him."[33]

I do not think that Jung "lost his head," and I suppose that he
took the message of his unconscious seriously and did not commit
the same error with Toni as possibly he did with Sabina—that is, he
did not make Toni dependent on him. This is about understanding
the transformation of his anima from a blind to a seeing one. This is
what may happen in a true active imagination. Then its figures are
"*real and not symbols.*"

We do not know much about how Emma felt in those years.
When Sabina entered the scene, Emma had already one child and
was pregnant with the second of the five she would bear. The first

pregnancies are always not just a gift but also a threat for a young couple. In both the young mother and the young father, their respective mother and father complexes are activated along with all the connected doubts and questionings of their self-esteem. We know about Carl's problematic image of his mother as mentioned above. One can only imagine how Emma was suffering, but she was also obviously aware of a deeper meaning of the difficult constellation as shown in a paper she presented in 1916 in the Psychological Club where she spoke about "guilt." Imelda Gaudissart writes in her study about *Femmes autour de Jung*:

> It is striking now to realize that the presentation given by Emma on this occasion is, above all, a profound reflection on the subject of guilt feelings. This raises the question of the extent to which its content can be read as an echo of the letter sent by Emma some years earlier to Freud concerning her distress at Carl's adventure with Sabina Spielrein. Did not Emma, in this lecture, give expression to the personal search that she had been compelled to conduct in order to overcome a situation that she had experienced as catastrophic? Had she not interpreted her struggle as a test imposed by destiny rather than as the outcome of personal fault?[34]

Already in this lecture Emma spoke about the Grail Legend, where Perceval fails to ask the crucial question about the suffering of the Fisher King. The traditional ways of dealing with a critical situation are not sufficient to cope with the challenges of destiny, says Emma in this lecture, but one has rather to accept personal guilt and responsibility to acquire the Holy Grail. "It is reasonable to assume that this presentation was addressed to an audience most of whom were acquainted with the nature of the difficulties that Emma herself faced,"[35] adds Gaudissart.

Carl had also put Emma *on her own feet*: He encouraged her to learn Latin and to study everything she could find concerning the Grail Legend. Emma became a respected analyst in Zurich and in the

1930s wrote a book about Animus and Anima. Barbara Hannah was among her first analysands.

Gaudissart draws the portrait of an individuated woman who could combine many interests with her tasks of keeping the family together, caring for her five children and her analysands—and for her husband. When Carl had his heart attack in 1944 and was on the verge of dying, Emma moved into the hospital:

> For Emma, who watched over her husband unceasingly, this situation provided, without any doubt, the opportunity to gather under her protective wing this man suffering the throes of a grave regression of both body and mind. ... Emma had decided that her husband, during these long weeks, should be kept beyond reach of the outside world. Virtually no one, other than his children, was allowed to come through the door. ... Emma had herself moved into the clinic and did not leave it until her husband had recovered sufficiently to be able to return home. ... One of the very few persons admitted into his presence was Marie-Louise von Franz. Since she was involved in Jung's research on alchemy, Emma considered, toward the end of his convalescence, that such a visit might stimulate in her husband the desire to renew his grasp on the thread of life.[36]

Toni was not admitted.

> It was thus that 1944 marked an important turning point in the relationship between Carl and Emma as a couple and in the evolution of each of the marriage partners taken separately. Carl actually believed during this illness that he had reached the end of his life. His return to the land of the living caused a tempest of freedom to rage through his whole mind and being. He felt a strong conviction that the findings amassed over decades could now be assembled to produce works that would bear an increasingly personal stamp. Carl was by this time sixty-nine, while Emma was

sixty-two. Each of them was gradually to embark on the search for a new kind of closeness with the other, for a matured form of love, and a friendship based on wisdom.[37]

In *Memories, Dreams, Reflections*, he does not mention Emma's presence, but in that work, he generally refrains from speaking of his private relationships at all.

The weeks in the hospital were very important for Jung. In *Memories, Dreams, Reflections*, he speaks about the visions he had during the nights. He was, he writes: "filled with the highest possible feeling of happiness. ... I myself was, so it seemed, in the Pardes Rimmonim, the garden of pomegranates, and the wedding of Tifereth with Malchuth was taking place. ... Or else I was Rabbi Simon ben Jochai, whose wedding in the afterlife was taking place. It was the mystic marriage as it appears in the Cabbalistic. I cannot tell you how wonderful it was."[38] He dreamed further of the "Marriage of the Lamb" and the *hierosgamos* of "All-father Zeus and Hera" in a wonderful setting.[39] These visions were an apotheosis of marriage, and it is as if there, in 1944, Carl and Emma came together on a new level of their relationship as spouses.

Conclusion — and a Remark on Elijah

The figures of the unconscious, as Jung and the Analytical Psychology see it, "are real and not symbols," as Elijah teaches Jung in one of their early dialogues. They shape our life more than our Ego imagines. Active imagination, as documented in *The Red Book*, shows Jung's attempt to actively come to an interactive exchange with these forces, to form them into images, and to interpret them. Jung called this endeavor "the necessary second part of the analysis." The encounter would have a great impact on his conscious attitudes throughout the rest of his life. Around 1913, in the midst of a crisis after the split from Freud and around critical relationships to his wife, Emma, and his former patients Sabina Spielrein and Toni Wolff, he experienced inner images of a woman whom he called his Soul, later termed the anima: a personification of the female side in the man. For Jung, this figure appeared as Salome, a threatening figure in the New Testament. In this essay I have explored some aspects of the multileveled dynamics in this relationship. It relates to the cultural complex of the *femme fatale*, in particular to the figure of Lou Andreas-Salomé, whose name, obviously not by chance, reminds us of the Salome in Jung's vision. Lou was a prominent advocate in her time for women's empowerment. I have also referenced the work of Nietzsche, Rilke, Oskar Wilde, and Richard Strauss to illustrate the cultural situation and possible influences on Jung. It is also about Sabina Spielrein, Toni Wolff and Emma Jung. We know from clinical work that dream figures seldomly, and only on the level of objective interpretation, can be reduced to real persons. They may represent certain aspects of living persons, but they stand with another leg in the otherworld of the collective unconscious, of mythology and the realm of archetypes of the human psyche. From there comes their transforming capacity. Animus and anima are processes and archetypal functions of the psyche. To observe and to deal with them may profoundly change conscious attitudes. The creative shaping of these encounters has a positive impact on the ego complex. This is what *The Red Book* is about.

The Salome-Imaginations of Jung were deep reflections about his inner female side and his attitude and behavior toward women. I suppose that all of the people around him profited from this work. It is not only a thrilling image from the early days of Jungian psychoanalysis, but also an example for the timeless topical issues of love, dependence, emancipation and autonomy. Under this perspective, it makes really sense to put the anima *on her own feet*. The anima is a gift from the self. Her connecting function on the ego-self axis between the wisdom of the self and the ego complex will work only if the ego does not claim the anima to be its property. Otherwise the ego will be in the hands of the anima and stay in an unconscious entanglement. Jung's insight and decision finally allowed him to find the way to a new and transcending god-image.

In reading the documents we have to listen carefully and with the greatest respect to the words of those who are no longer living.

Often biographers are careless about their responsibility in this regard. Sometimes we have to read between the lines and listen, so to speak, for a small whisper that may come to us. In this respect Elijah, the prophet in Jung's imagination, may tell an interesting story, and with this amplification I conclude my essay.

Elijah's story is told in *1 Kings*. He is the only person in the Bible to ascend to heaven alive, and legend has it that he will return when the Messiah appears. In a courageous argument with the priests of Baal, Elijah convinced God to show his supremacy over other gods. His offering was set aflame from above and accepted by God, whereas Baal's priests were shown unable and lost the competition. The scene ends with Elijah slaughtering all the priests of the false god.[40] From there the story of Elijah continues. He flees into the desert because Queen Jezebel wants to kill him. There, God gives him food and drink by sending ravens with bread and water. Elijah spends 40 days walking through the desert to Mount Horeb, and there he hides in a cave, still in fear of his enemies. It is incubation in utter loneliness. Then God brings him out, saying: "Go out and stand on the mountain before the Lord, for the Lord is about to pass by."[41] Elijah obeys, expecting the voice of God; this is the voice of his unconscious:

Now there was a great wind, so strong that it was splitting mountains and breaking rocks in pieces before the Lord, but the Lord was not in the wind; and after the wind an earthquake, but the Lord was not in the earthquake; and after the earthquake a fire, but the Lord was not in the fire; and after the fire a sound of sheer silence. When Elijah heard it, he wrapped his face in his mantle and went out and stood at the entrance of the cave. Then there came a voice to him that said, 'What are you doing here, Elijah?'[42]

Endnotes

1 T.S. Eliot, "Burnt Norton," in *Four Quartets* (New York, NY: Harcourt, 1943), 3.

2 C.G. Jung, *The Red Book: Liber Novus. A Reader's Edition*, ed. Sonu Shamdasani, trans. John Peck, Mark Kyburz, and Sonu Shamdasani (New York, NY: W.W. Norton, 2012), 176.

3 Jung, *The Red Book*, 174-175.

4 Thomas Rhode, *Mythos Salome* (Leipzig: Reclam, 2000).

5 Jung, *The Red Book*, 177.

6 Ibid., 179-180.

7 Ibid., 176.

8 Ibid., 197.

9 Ibid., 225.

10 Ibid., 435-439.

11 James Hillman, *Healing Fiction* (Barrytown, NY: Station Hill Press, 1983), 53.

12 Jung, *The Red Book*, 182.

13 Ibid., 187-188.

14 Ibid., 417-418.

15 C.G. Jung, *Memories, Dreams, Reflections*, ed. Aniela Jaffé (New York, NY: Vintage, 1963), 8.

16 Hillman, *Healing Fiction*, 56.

17 Gerhard Adler, *C.G. Jung Letters*. Trans. by R.F.C. Hull. Vol. 1, 1906-1950 (Princeton, NJ: Princeton University Press, 1975), 459.

18 Sabine Richebächer, *Sabina Spielrein: Eine fast grausame Liebe zur Wissenschaft* (Zürich: Dörlemann Verlag, 2005), 92.

19 Quoted in ibid., 87; my translation.

20 Ibid., 91.

21 Sigmund Freud and C.G. Jung, *The Freud/Jung Letters*. Ed. William McGuire and trans. by Ralph Manheim and R.F.C. Hull (Princeton, NJ: Princeton University Press, 1974), 207.

22 Barbara Hannah, *Jung – His Life and Work* (Wilmette, IL: Chiron Publications, 1998), 104.

23 Sonu Shamdasani, "Introduction," in Jung, *The Red Book*, 38.

24 Hannah, 118.

[25] Tony Wolff, *Structural Forms of the Feminine Psyche* (Zurich: C.G. Jung Institute, 1956), 11.

[26] Ibid., 5-6.

[27] Ibid., 6.

[28] Ibid.

[29] This would be 1934 when this paper was first presented at the Psychological Club in Zurich. Ibid., 13.

[30] Ibid., 6-7.

[31] Hannah, 118.

[32] Ibid., 119.

[33] Ibid.

[34] Imelda Gaudissart, *Love and Sacrifice: The Life of Emma Jung* (Asheville, NC: Chiron Publications, 2014), 101.

[35] Ibid.

[36] Ibid., 87-88.

[37] Ibid., 88.

[38] Jung, *Memories, Dreams, Reflections*, 293-294.

[39] Ibid., 294.

[40] *1 Kings* 18:20-40.

[41] *1 Kings* 19:11.

[42] *1 Kings* 19: 11-13.

Soul's Desire to Become New:
Jung's Journey, Our Initiation

Kate Burns

Believe me: *It is no teaching and no instruction that I give
you. On what basis should I presume to teach you? I give you
news of the way of this man, but not of your own way. My
path is not your path, therefore I cannot teach you. The way
is within us, but not in Gods, nor in teachings, nor in laws.
Within us is the way, the truth, and the life.*[1]

C.G. Jung

Given the disclaimer quoted above and reiterated a number of times
throughout Jung's work, how does studying "*the way of* this *man*"
help us who are 21st-century individuals struggling to navigate
through a world inundated with information perched in cyberspace,
challenged by cataclysmic destruction inherent in climate change,
confronted with the threat of nuclear annihilation, overwhelmed by
a panoply of exploitative marketing, and ruffled by a kaleidoscopic
fusion of cultures, all threatening to reduce the individual to a tangle
of mitochondria moving like a zombie through a grey maze of
dystopian meaninglessness? A few people will read *The Red Book* in
a spirit of fascination with the colorful, mythic array of archetypal
images and with appreciation for the wisdom expressed through
Jung's authentic experience and expansive scholarship. However, what
about the billions of other people who struggle, completely overwhelmed, to find time amid a 50-plus-hour workweek to engage in a
nourishing personal life while they strive to keep abreast of nonstop
tragedy in the news, express themselves daily in social media and

blogs, and then exercise their bodies? What can *The Red Book* offer them?

Rather than a method, a workbook, or a prescriptive solution for a suffering soul, Jung's *Red Book* offers the example of one man, while it ushers readers into an imaginal journey through an array of earth-scapes symbolically describing a heart-wrenching and mind-opening experience that took Jung by his own admission to the edge of madness. He did not cross over, but why? By gathering all his knowledge and all his courage and curiosity and by submitting them to the humility of a wanderer with the inquisitive nature and scholarship of a researcher and the innocent playfulness of a child, Jung received, and artfully recorded, his own unique experience in an effort to hear and understand the longing of his soul. His life had entered a time of personal change and devoted contemplation, perhaps in part prompted by a relational break with friend, mentor, and colleague Sigmund Freud. More importantly, Jung found himself in a time of personal transition certainly mirrored by the world, which stood at the threshold of World War I. He labored in the throes of violent and extended visions of bloody destruction that later seemed to anticipate World War I, to the extent that he fell ill with confusion. He later writes, "Because I carried the war in me, I foresaw it."[2] Jung's dreams disturbed him with catastrophic images so immense that he released himself from the majority of his societal obligations and entered into dialogue with the unconscious. He structured his life so that during the morning he would consult with patients and answer correspondence, then he would spend the afternoon and evening in uninterrupted dialogue with his soul. Messages came to him through the imagery of dreams, visions, and intentional inner dialogue he later termed "active imagination." The reader encounters heart-rending struggle, honest humility, and perpetual faith: faith not in some legendary being that many refer to as God, but faith *"… that life will find the better way."*[3] Jung wrote in his *Red Book* of his feelings of turmoil and confusion, during which he had a vision:

I was with a youth in high mountains. It was before daybreak, the Eastern sky was already light. Then Siegfried's horn resounded over the mountains with a jubilant sound. We knew that our mortal enemy was coming. We were armed and lurked beside a narrow rocky path to murder him. Then we saw him coming high across the mountains on a chariot made of the bones of the dead. He drove boldly and magnificently over the steep rocks and arrived at the narrow path where we waited in hiding. As he came around the turn ahead of us, we fired at the same time and he fell slain.[4]

At first, Jung struggled to solve the riddle of his vision of Siegfried, the heroic conquistador of Germanic myth. The overwhelming intensity of this struggle transported Jung to the threshold of suicide. Such an inner quandary could have hurled even the strongest of personalities into a major depressive episode, but no evidence indicates that Jung ever fell into paralyzing depression. When he realized that in the vision he had killed his own ideal of himself as doctor, professor, author, and researcher, he knew he had arrived at a time in his life that had culminated in great accomplishment, but now his soul *called* him back to a deeper relationship and a more complete perspective of himself and the world. Jung's soul commanded renewal: the necessity to sacrifice his past heroic attitude and expectations so that a more comprehensive gnosis and scholarship could unfold.

Depressive symptoms issue from a number of components, including brain chemistry and outer life circumstances; however, Jung developed and set forth a theory of the psyche that describes a process by which psychic energy naturally and periodically ebbs back into the unconscious, robbing the ego of initiative and of enthusiasm for projects connected with the rigors of outer life. When such a backward flow occurs, the individual faces the challenge to become an initiate, and life takes on a dramatically mythic quality. One apprehends the provocation of a *call* to accept and successfully resolve a secret task through which the initiating ego-consciousness integrates an unknown potential. Even though one may feel caught off guard, this potentiality has ripened below the surface like a seed ready to sprout. A season of weather conducive to the sprouting seed prevails, and an insistent, even gripping, synchronicity between readiness of the below and the above will convey the new sprout into fruitful expression. The birth of dormant potential positioned for actualization in an individual's character exacts intense labor and begins with an invitation that commands acceptance.

Apprehended by a stark realization—"I had to become aware that I had lost my soul"[5]—Jung turned to an inner journey, one that articulates a calling, a struggle, and a resolution, all converging into triumphant liberation. Jung returned to his soul and, after an extended journey of inner discovery and outer research, reconvened with himself, now strengthened with broadened perspective and revitalized strength. He received in symbolic language the essence of ideas that subsequently manifested in a lifetime of teaching, writing, and clinical work. He achieved a renewal of consciousness, a restoration of purpose, and a vision of his continuing quest.

During initiatory experience, anticipation of renewal appears alongside initial images of destruction. At the end of the third of a series of cataclysmic dreams appearing in the summer of 1914, Jung had the following vision: "There stood a leaf-bearing but fruitless tree, whose leaves had turned into sweet grapes full of healing juice through the working of the frost. I picked some grapes and gave them to a great waiting throng."[6] Additionally, in a vision after the murder of Siegfried: "I saw a merry garden, in which forms walked clad in white silk, all covered in colored light, some reddish, the others blueish and greenish. I know, I have stridden across the depths. Through guilt I have become a newborn."[7]

The "waiting throng" in Jung's vision clearly anticipates the enormous impact his work was to have for future generations. His inner experiences, elucidated in *The Red Book*, informed research and theoretical assertions expounded over a lifetime, an opus of theory and scholarship that continues to provide healing wisdom to those with the courage to examine their souls. Jung's retreat into himself engendered an initiatory crisis that revealed the wisdom waiting to birth the word and image of inner experience and to uncloak an attendant meaning that brings relief to suffering. Conscientious investigation into the irrational psyche, i.e., a return to soul, together with artistic and literary expression of his observations informed by exceptional intelligence and a strong mind, allowed Jung to escape psychosis (inundation by the unconscious), as well as what many people experience as a threat of debilitating depression stemming from the backward flow of psychic energy.

Jung answered the call of his soul, a call that hurled him into an inner, other world, a world orchestrated by mystery containing interactions and motifs particular to his unique life. His adventure closely follows patterns of traditional initiation rituals as reported by certain individuals who, since the very beginning of human history all the way to this current time, have served as mediators between people and their gods. We typically refer to these particular members of a traditional community as shamans. Jung, however, had no traditional elder, no agent or master of initiation, no one experienced in numinous phenomena to assist him—no guide, guru, priest, initiated shaman, or analytical psychologist to offer direction or give support, and certainly no one to interpret his dreams and visions. He devoted *himself* to the task.

Not long after the series of visions that anticipated the impending world war, the vision of the murder of Siegfried brought Jung to ask of himself whether such a vision might mean that he must commit suicide. In the dream, Jung murders Siegfried, an act that greatly disturbed his sense of value for the heroic endeavor that had characterized his own life up to that point. A redeeming insight finally presented itself: He realized that the dream suggested that he was *called*, to dispense with his self-satisfied and highly adept professional persona that expressed the heroic, inquisitive, and ambitious youth who had encountered many challenges and accomplished a venerated expertise. He felt compelled to submit himself humbly to the inner imperative that was making itself known within him through a perpetual enactment of dreams and visions. The wisdom of his soul, obliging him to listen and to learn its laws and to expose himself to its judgment, ripe for discovery and integration into consciousness, beckoned him. Just such a process describes the task of initiation.

Language pertinent to experiences of initiation permeates the many dreams and visions disclosed and elaborated in *The Red Book*. A successful initiation embodies three essential phases: the *call* to attend; a struggle culminating in *crisis*; and a *curing* renewal. Jung's poetic yet intellectual discourse boldly reveals his awareness of a *call*: an invitation, an imperative to return to soul, to his inner life and its vital striving to develop a transcendent function of consciousness, an expanded attitude toward life. Consider, for instance, "... as soon as the main function is deposed, there is a chance for other sides of the personality to be born into life."[8] What happens when "the main function," one's typical and conditioned attitude toward life, i.e., everything a person means when enlisting the pronoun *I*, is submitted to scrutiny along with the terrifying yet ineffable beauty of the numinous? When an individual encounters such a summons, the ego consciousness, whose primary interest resides in maintaining its own power in the status quo, will resist, dig in its heals, refuse to move, and finally hold on for dear life. Psychic energy previously available for outer life flows inward, and one feels lack of enthusiasm, vigor, volition, i.e., libido or life energy. Thoughts of suicide may break into consciousness and lurk amid the fear, even though such thoughts intrude uninvited.

This is a "destroyer!" The outer life circumstance that necessitates some kind of intimidating change brings a person against an obstacle, a seemingly impenetrable wall of indecision that always arrives through an act of fate. Such a challenge, which is often disguised as catastrophe, includes any situation that drastically changes the current state of things: a loss of love, profession, health, or a combination of these. One first responds with resistance: The prospective "initiate," feeling frightened and alone, will very often seek refuge in familiar habits. A variety of addictions, many of which provide the additional security of appearing healthy and even beneficial to self and world, provide the most readily available cover for the ego clinging to status quo. However, in any case, the familiar "self" will experience a fall, and feelings best described as some aspect of profound grief complicated by guilt will ensue.

Jung's predisposition toward curiosity led him to "... take on the poverty of spirit in order to partake of the soul."[9] Such a decision may sound perplexing, but anyone who crosses the threshold of addiction and/or grief has already entered into spiritual poverty. However, if one does "take on" poverty, i.e., embrace humility and submit to the fear and grief inherent in intense inner conflict, a way opens through which suffering may transform into meaning through exploration. Through answering the *call* of the soul, the initiate becomes chosen rather than victimized, purposeful rather than a prisoner of fate, a searcher for meaning rather than a follower of creeds or any other preconceptions.

Members of traditional cultures who enter into the ritual of a shamanic initiation have already suffered the throes of confrontation by "unseen forces," often since childhood. Rites include the task of traversing a tortuous underground passage that leads to a larger chamber where isolation creates conditions that almost certainly foster spiritual torture, i.e., torture experienced as a scourge by "destructive spirits." Jung, explaining his trial, uses a tone of warning juxtaposed with challenge and hope: "Everything will come to you and you will be spared nothing, the mercy and the torment."[10] Through courageously withstanding the burden of some version of dismemberment, traditional initiates report experiences of a mysterious *enantiodromia*, a process by which an extremely polarized situation or attitude becomes its own opposite. Torture by complete skinning and scattering of bones, disembowelment, or dissolution carried out by "destructive spirits" becomes re-memberment, replacement of bowels by adamantine stones, or molding of a purified body by constructive spirits. Subsequently, the initiate experiences a changed attitude toward self, other, and life: Rebirth is achieved.

Without the benefit of time-honored ritual, persons in our time most often experience the soul's periodic attempt at renewal as an acute ebbing of life energy—energy that has been reaching outward into a myriad of projects and interests flows back into the unconscious, a backward movement that results in confusion, lack of interest in typical ventures, and general malaise. The medical community will often gather such symptoms into a diagnosis of depression. Medications prescribed may bring a feeling of relief for a time. The individual may explore alternative courses of action and will sink down into the wisdom within, or alternatively continue through life without confidence, without clear intention, and without broad perspective, not to mention developing a dependence on pharmaceuticals. A deafening call of the soul for expanded experience, expression, and attitude toward life has sounded, but without words. If the individual resists overwhelming temptation to chase after the empty promises of quick relief and turns attention to the place where energy now resides—to the inner self— a wealth of images will coalesce to form a symbolic passage out of the initiatory chamber, the unconscious. No matter how much time one routinely spends in meditation, prayer, yoga, or religious commitments, time in the initiatory chamber exacts a release of preconceptions and a relinquishing of habits. One must devote time and attention to the images and messages, no matter how frightening or immoral or heretical, and follow their lead through the assorted solitary activities that amplify the particular dilemma at hand.

It all starts with turning one's curiosity to the *calling*, which typically makes itself known through complicated life situations that seem to have no solution, very often accompanied by unexpected inner experiences such as dreams and/or visions. Loss of appetite or other responses of the body may ensue; limited attention to detail, difficulty focusing, and unusual struggle with organizational skills may trouble cognitive functioning; abbreviated enthusiasm of previously enjoyable activities may torment one's emotional state.

Essentially, a person who experiences loss also experiences the challenge of confronting a trial that will move according to an ancient initiatory pattern. Life-altering confrontations with every conviction, presupposition, and indisputable law that one holds unassailable will come into play. Again, the question arises: How is it that a 21st-century individual may hope to weather such a *call*? The answer: One faces up to the imperative to sacrifice precious time, which most often also means financial resources, in order to contain the enormous tension of an inner war between preconceived positions and the knowledge of *oneself,* which promises to defy many collectively held notions, all the while suspending a fierce desire to discover a solution. Nietzsche's maxim: "Idleness is the beginning of all psychology ..."[11] gains clarity during the challenge of a call. In order to commune with one's own soul, a person needs time and solitude during which to explore the inner cosmos. Furthermore, an individual in the world of today greatly improves chances of success of an initiatory cycle by employing a credentialed analytical psychologist. *The Red Book* offers one man's experience, and it offers inspiration, wisdom, and hope. Jung's tireless search into the messages contained in a wealth of images as well as his meticulous research and recording of the messages revealed to him offers witness to the courageous sacrifice together with the abundance of reward inherent in devotion. Yet, he again implores others not to try and imitate him: "This play that I witnessed is my play, not your play. It is my secret, not yours. You cannot imitate me. My secret remains virginal and my mysteries are inviolable, they belong to me and cannot belong to you. You have your own."[12]

Jung's experience resembles a mythic underworld journey. He issues the imperative that one must go through the gate of the soul "utterly poor, miserable, humiliated, ignorant ..."[13] This is much like the journey of Inanna, goddess of beauty, desire, and political power in the ancient Sumerian pantheon, who descends to the underworld through seven gates and sacrifices a piece of her regalia at each gate. Hurled into a state of the temporary madness characteristic of "possession by unseen forces," the initiate faces a tense collision of opposites: "... everything serious is also laughable, ... everything fine is also brutal, ... everything good is also bad, ... everything high is also low, ... everything pleasant is also shameful."[14] Here nothing makes sense, and everything is in flux. Sacrifice of everything previously held as reasonable and valid must be made in order to be released to roam freely with those things considered unreasonable and invalid. Jung says of sacrifice that it is "the very reverse of regression—it is a successful canalization of libido."[15] Every person who has been seized by creative madness knows the intensity of such a movement. Jung says to Soul: "You weave the thickest darknesses and I am like a madman caught in your net. But I yearn, teach me."[16] Again, the reader receives something of a warning that finishes with heroic curiosity coupled with humble submission. Willingness, and even yearning, for connection to one's inner fountain, for reflection, for access to the unknown parts of oneself furthers and expands experience of the full potential of oneself together with the knowledge of one's individual way along this journey we call life.

The initiate enters a state of crisis, which exacts a need for razor-sharp discernment and pivotal decision. Everything that belongs to one's highest value wants rebirth and strives toward the west like the sun that will rise anew in the east. When the struggle through "thickest darknesses" apprehends the ego consciousness of a 21st-century individual who knows little about how to negotiate what may seem like a horror or at least like an innate yearning, societal structures, cultural traditions, and religious creeds offer little support. Solitude without electronics, attention to inner images, and time for play without toys would challenge to the core a modern person's un-acknowledged, even unrealized, addiction to constant diversion, abundant and expected, clamoring from all corners and every second of daily life experience. One needs time to emerge from a life-threatening ordeal, whether from within or in outer life.

Escape from constant commotion may prove impossible, but to turn one's attention inward requires a simple about-face, a revolution, a turning around. If an ominous and frightening creature chases one through the night, the one chased and running for dear life may merely turn around, whereupon the creature transfigures into a more amenable, even helpful image; similarly, if noise pollution, air pollution, and the disturbing eyesores of advertisement and industry chase one through the day, mindful inner awareness renders the intruders powerless. Jung realized that he "... *must grope through what lies at hand, ... embrace the worthless and the worthy with the same love.*"[17] Without the inward gaze, the devotional attention to the images of one's soul, in addition to having a dialogue with one other objective person who has experience and expertise to foster interpretation of such images, no amount or cocktail of psychopharmaceuticals will ultimately change the situation that leads to a diagnosis of depression and/or anxiety disorder. The medical community debates endlessly the question of whether the medication even alleviates the symptoms of depression and anxiety after allowing for an initial "honeymoon period" of relief that can be attributed to a placebo effect.

What one has cultivated in outer life, in the most successful of circumstances, eventually culminates in strivings achieved, goals attained, and recognitions collected on an undusted shelf. Ego-consciousness attaches to its memories when the current environment starts to erode the image of oneself so tirelessly achieved. It cannot see the future, and the present stands permeated with an outworn identity longing to renew itself. Consider the professor who longs to write poetry, the doctor who longs to play music, the lawyer who longs to write a novel, the laborer who longs to carve flutes, the man who longs to become a woman, or the woman who longs to become a man. Little does one know that beyond the ongoing war between opposing forces from within, a garden awaits. An inner landscape beckons the one reduced by agonizing loss of everything once identified as "myself" to a mystery as vast and as fascinating as the limitless cosmos. The soul invites inquisitive and thirsty wanderers to drink from the inner spring of renewal. Observe Louis Denardo's words as he enlists Meister Eckhart in the film, *Jacob's Ladder*. In this scene he tries to soothe the main character whose post-traumatic stress from wartime experience has landed him in a state of confusion between outer experience and his dreams:

> The only thing that burns in hell is the part of you that won't let go of your life, your memories, your attachments. They burn them all away, but they're not punishing you, they're freeing your soul. If you're frightened of dying and you're holding on, you'll see devils tearing your life away. If you've made your peace, then the devils are really angels freeing you from the earth.

In the cave of initiation, the devils that tear apart the old body of everything one has become but is no longer, those devils of destruction become angels of construction forming a new body. Through enduring the greatest torture to "become smelted anew in the connection with the primordial beginning, which at the same time is what has been and what is becoming,"[18] one emerges with adamantine strength to serve both soul and world.

Nothing less and nothing more commanding than renewal conveys the *cure*. Rebirth brings a restoration of energy, but also necessitates tending, cultivation, devotion, mindfulness, and love. A curing rebirth brings one into a state of infant perspective every bit as determined to proclaim itself and every bit as fragile as a baby emerging from its mother's womb. However, in a world that denies and even denounces, and at best ignores, the evolving of an individual soul, renewed consciousness brings predictably an encounter with resistance. The ones who have accompanied the initiate thus far— companions, friends, family, or colleagues—now feel the presence of a stranger. In fact, the initiate who recently emerged from a time of struggle feels like a stranger to that person previously known as self. The rite of tonsure, shaving of the head, among assorted religious orders offers an apt depiction of the nascent identity emerging to fill a life of devotion. Jung realized that to become and to continue becoming an authentic individual, only devotion to his own soul could free him.

Transformation required Jung to "lock the past with one key, with the other ... open the future." Then he reflects on what this process means for his life: "The miracle of transformation commands."[19] What does this miracle command? It commands living a symbolic life, a life of integrity in which decisions emerge from careful consideration of polarizing influences and where a spirit of faith in life and love prevails. Living one's cure impels embracing, in all humility, the way forward through darkness because the future is always dark. "If you look for a light, you fall first into an even deeper darkness."[20] Current society offers little support for discerning one's own way. Western culture, which has gripped the world, provides much that may interrupt rather than further one's progress, much that needlessly limits the development of ideas rather than supporting their journey through formulation and maturation and leading finally to manifestation. Jung advises, "Well-being is a better judge."[21]

Continuing in a state of cure means intrepid self-care. It means knowing the desires of the innermost rather than chasing what glitters in a society tortured by greed. It means entering the stream of life, the joy and sorrow of living oneself. One emerges from the cave with the glow of an adamantine body, the wings of a dragon, wisdom through serpentine longing, and the acuity of a crow, yet also one emerges as a beast of burden who serves its master, which is transformation.

Emerging from the initiatory trial means your need and your longing and your pain and suffering have birthed a renewed axis of meaning. You have sacrificed your cleverness in the world and submitted to the simplemindedness of the inner world in order to address and to engage with your soul. You have become the humble frog in order to converse with the dragon of wisdom, which harbors your own idea. In the midst of suffering and loss, a world-weary individual bends a knee to something unknown that reveals itself through one's mindful attention. The ineffable unknown, which defies description, bathes in love the one who searches for healing balm. Life continues with renewed energy, purpose, resolve, perspective. The world again becomes a place that piques curiosity, stages the imagination, and fuels inspiration.

Every initiation in every lifetime invites the initiate to embark upon and cultivate a unique sacred devotional path, clearing the enigmas along the way. The entire person, both conscious and unconscious components, faces an inner command to explore new avenues, to birth the self anew continually so as to explore and develop a potential but unlived part of life. If one depotentiates the horror of "thickest darknesses" by apprehending them and traversing their tortuous trails, the courageous initiate may discover a placid pond of enrichment, a new day of broader perspective. At the end of *The Red Book*, in a section called "Scrutinies," Jung asks the question whether the work of redemption is imperative. "Certainly not," he answers, "if one can endure a given condition and does not feel in need of redemption."[22] However, it seems that those who find themselves incarnated as human beings harbor a longing for meaning and purpose in life. One who cultivates an ability to endure a given condition sacrifices all hope of discovering meaning and purpose in life, a situation that leads to despair and even murder and/or suicide, the farthest extreme of untreated depression. Not through medications or herbs or specially formulated supplements and not through the latest miracle diet and not through the latest formulated workshop and not through devoting oneself to any religious order anywhere does one find a cure for life's intrinsic suffering that has landed one in the throes of a severe depressive episode. There is no panacea outside oneself for curing a sick soul. Only through entering the chamber of loneliness and defeat and accompanying one's longing does a person emerge from depths of fear and loathing and despair carrying renewed enthusiasm like a talisman, to continue the great foraging of life. Consider Jung's words cited above: "*My secret … belongs to me and cannot belong to you. You have your own.*" These words both challenge us to the inner duel and encourage us with the hope of victory, of receiving the prize, of emerging with a renewed *raison d'etre,* a reason for being.

Endnotes

[1] C.G. Jung, *The Red Book: Liber Novus. A Reader's Edition*, ed. Sonu Shamdasani, trans. John Peck, Mark Kyburz, and Sonu Shamdasani (New York, NY: W.W. Norton, 2012), 125.

[2] Ibid., 159.

[3] Ibid., 126.

[4] Ibid., 160-161.

[5] Ibid., 129.

[6] Ibid., 124.

[7] Ibid., 162.

[8] Ibid., 161, n115.

[9] Ibid., 146.

[10] Ibid., 160, n110.

[11] Friedrich Nietzsche, *The Portable Nietzsche*, trans. by Walter Kaufman (New York, NY: Viking, 1954), 466.

[12] Ibid., 178.

[13] Ibid.

[14] Ibid., 170.

[15] C.G. Jung, *Symbols of Transformation*, in *CW*, vol. 5 (Princeton, NJ: Princeton University Press, 1956), par. 398.

[16] Ibid., 157.

[17] Ibid., 178.

[18] Ibid., 179.

[19] Ibid., 189.

[20] Ibid., 191.

[21] Ibid., 192.

[22] Ibid., 478.

Aging with *The Red Book*

QiRe Ching

Sanford L. Drob, in *Reading the Red Book*, states: "Jung's keeping the *Red Book,* his strangest and perhaps the most important work in his entire oeuvre, in his kitchen cupboard for so many years, and its remaining unpublished for many years thereafter, has the effect of giving us the experience of awakening from a dream in which Jung has spoken to us from beyond the grave."[1] Recently at the C.G. Jung Institute in San Francisco, this awakening continued when I had the pleasure of being involved in an intensive training on Jungian psychology attended by Mandarin-speaking students and therapists primarily from China, Taiwan, and Hong Kong. Their hunger for imaginal experience, so aligned with the spirit of *The Red Book,* contrasts with the current trend in our profession in the United States, where there has been a foreclosure of the imaginal. The psychotherapy profession in their home countries seems unfettered by the biases that can constrict our work here. Teaching is, of course, also transformative for the teacher in that what is taught is reflected back with the students' own perspectives. These students brought me back to the edges of Jung's frontier.

As nations are mobilizing to protect their borders in this current climate of anti-immigration, one interesting development enabled by recent technology, unimaginable when I first entered the field, is the capacity to conduct sessions with international clients over the internet. When working with someone from another culture on Skype, both parties meet while remaining firmly rooted in their own context. The dynamics of assimilation, the privileging of one culture over another, and the reliance on a conceptual framework based on certain assumptions become elements for ongoing reflection. Instead of fusion, there is a heightened appreciation of separateness. Absent the Judeo-Christian context that Jung was responding to in his *Red Book,* how do some of his concepts hold up? One of Jung's key points in this work pertains to the fixed approach of Christian dogma, which precluded its ability to renew itself to meet the challenge of continued relevancy.[2] I imagine that this sense of renewal also holds true in the way we might need to approach Jung's concepts.

My parents were Buddhist/Daoist. I was educated in a Catholic school and grew up in Hawaii at a time when stretches of it were still rural and the Polynesian nature gods still very much present, at least for a young boy. Jung indicated that one cannot simply replace one's own gods with those from another culture. But there are many like me who come from a place of multiplicity, and in this age of the Internet, the cultural and geographical demarcations are rendered more fluid. One's own sense of culture is less unified and coherent. With that said, I will now shift into the main thrust of this essay, my personal experience of *The Red Book* with respect to the experience of aging.

What follows consists of two parts written a year and a half from each other. The first explores passages from *The Red Book* in relation to themes that I struggle with as I look toward aging. The second part is less tethered to particular passages from *The Red Book* but is informed by its spirit. It comes out of an attempt to define a personal cosmology that attends to spirit, soul, and body by heeding Jung's call to enter into the imaginal.

Since childhood I've been intrigued with how we experience time—the continuous flow that we segment meaningfully into past, present, and future. I've often tried to grasp that elusive moment when one phase in the sequence transitions into the next. The Romans had the two faces of Janus, their ancient god of the gate, to represent this passage from one reality to another.[3] Now that I'm in my 60s, I think about the thread that connects who I've been and what I am today with my entry into old age. I see both continuity and disruption: everything remaining the same yet being completely different. I can define no clear line marking the moment of crossing-over. One day I woke up an old man. It was an awareness that had come and gone before, but this time the image stuck.

My attitude toward aging is far from being in a unified state. Not every part of me is cooperating or going about it at the same rate. I question whether I may be holding onto certain elements from my youth far past their time. How do I personally arrive at a meaningful representation of my current condition? What sacrifices are required for renewal? It is useless to turn to our culture for coherent forms that express a degree of complexity. Perhaps what I'm looking for goes beyond what can be contained. James M. Redfield speaks aptly to the source of my anxiety and confusion when he writes about the concept of purity in ancient Greek culture:

> Purity is an aspect of things as they are ordered by proprieties and limits. If 'dirt is matter out of place,' purity has to do with proper places and times, with proportion and distribution, and with the matter proper to a given form. The unclean is often the ambiguous, the anomalous, the interstitial; unclean things escape from categories and blur our comprehension of categories. ... Dirt is one kind of impurity; rot is another. An object may become impure as it starts to turn into something else. But if it actually becomes that other thing, it may again be pure.[4]

What I struggle with has to do with those interstitial, impure experiences that exist outside bounded spaces. One moment they can promise juicy vitality, the next moment rot. It is the muddle of becoming as an ongoing process. This ambiguous, unclean state is what my psyche needs. And it is what I have found in the maddening, revelatory, reverie-inducing pages of *The Red Book*. Jung comments on the importance of a fully lived life:

> If no outer adventure happens to you, then no inner adventure happens to you either. The part that you take over from the devil—joy, that is—leads you into adventure. In this way you will find your lower as well as your upper limits. It is necessary for you to know your limits. If you do not know them, you run into the artificial barriers of your imagination and the expectations of your fellow men. But your life will not take kindly to being hemmed in by artificial barriers. Life wants to jump over such barriers

and you will fall out with yourself. These barriers are not your real limits, but arbitrary limitations that do unnecessary violence to you. Therefore try to find your real limits.[5]

A particularly confusing area at this life stage is sexuality. My body is no longer a reliable companion to my desire. What has long felt like an expression of my nature can now seem like an awkward fit. Must eros at some point detach itself from matter? Jung writes: "Truly his soul lies in things and men, but the blind one seizes things and men, yet not his soul in things and men. … If he possessed his desire, and his desire did not possess him, he would lay a hand on his soul, since his desire is the image and expression of his soul."[6] And yet my relationship to these images and what they tell me about my soul are linked with my knowledge and experience of them in matter. Despite my yearning for the divine, I am still a creature of matter and have a life to live there. But what kind of life? How am I to determine what is to be given up for the sake of the unknown? When is detachment release from the compulsion to recreate the familiar and not flight from the humiliation and befuddlement of no longer being able to function in the accustomed way—a refusal to tolerate the loss of heroic clarity and to continue on in the presence of rot—of gradually becoming something else? What would it mean to transcend culturally imposed notions about aging, the restrictions foisted on one's own imagination, and to arrive at a vision of myself that is truly personal? My conflict regarding the place of sexuality is represented by two older friends. One of them has been bereft of sexual sensation since prostate surgery. "I don't miss it in the least," he tells me, as I'm cooking dinner for company. "It's liberating. It's freed me for other things." From his state of grace he eyes me sympathetically when I say that I'm not there yet. Another friend wrapping his arms around me says emphatically: "Don't you even think about giving it up. Not any part of it." He himself is recoiling from a remark made to him by a woman he's begun to see seriously. He described showing up at her door in a wife beater undershirt. She disdainfully dismissed him as an old man in serious denial. "Gosh, that's mean," I said to him, "you look great in those shirts."

A footnote featuring a quote from *Black Book* 6, which Sonu Shamdasani explains as Jung's "recognition … of the threefold nature of the soul," speaks to my soul's inner struggle. Jung's soul says to him: "If I am not conjoined through the uniting of the Below and the Above, I break down into three parts: the *serpent*, and in that or some other animal form I roam, living nature daimonically, arousing fear and longing. The *human soul*, living forever within you. The celestial soul, as such dwelling with the Gods, far from you and unknown to you, appearing in the form of a bird."[7]

One day, noting the sparsity of men past a certain age at my gym, I remarked to a fellow member, someone I'd never spoken to before, about the seeming disappearance of people I used to run into over the years. "Where do they all go now that we're old?" "They're all dead," he said, referring to a statistic that four out of five gay men living in San Francisco, born between 1950 and 1955, died from the AIDS epidemic. I have not been able to verify this estimate, but the shock of his comment brought me back to that collective heartbreak, when a generation of gay men—my generation—was decimated, the pain from that time still deep and immobile. "I'm still traumatized," I said.

Early on in my own analysis—in my early 30s, still unformed and uncomfortable in the world—I dreamed of a young girl who led me to a hill overlooking a valley. She pointed to the world below and, like Satan in the New Testament, said to me: "This could all be yours." My response to her three decades later—as I look back at my own suffering, mistakes made, past love disappointed—is mirrored in a conversation Jung has with his soul: "You took away where I thought to take hold, and you gave me where I did not expect anything and time and again you brought about fate from new and unexpected quarters. Where I sowed, you robbed me of the harvest, and where I did not sow, you give me fruit a hundredfold. And time and again I lost the path and found it again where I would never have foreseen it. You upheld my belief, when I was alone and near despair. At every decisive moment you let me believe in myself."[8]

A couple of months ago, David Lamble, a columnist for the Bay Area Reporter, a local gay newspaper, reprinted a portion of a 1989 interview he did with Susan Sontag back when she was promoting her book, *AIDS As Metaphor*, which was a response to the equating of homosexuality with disease at the time:

> David Lamble: I sort of agree with you that the disease is meaningless, and yet we're all—gay men and people in general—struck by the extraordinary coincidence that the disease came along right after the emancipation of homosexuals in Western society, after Stonewall, after the emergence of a visible gay population and an apparent increase in sexual activity. In trying to pin a meaning on the disease, I think that's the meaning that's troubled a lot of people.
>
> Susan Sontag (with a deep sigh): You know, David, when you say that, it just makes me want to cry, because it's so awful what you're saying, what you're feeling. I mean, I perfectly understand why you're saying it, but it's so awful to think of people carrying the burden of that thought, that because they were free, because they were open, because they didn't hide, because they felt able to say that they felt good about themselves, then maybe somehow there's a connection with the fact that they had to endure this incredible tragedy. I can't, as someone who has been a close friend and even a lover of a number of gay men, I cannot think that that's true, it breaks my heart to think that it's true. I have to think that it's just a coincidence, that there really is no meaning, and what gay men were doing and feeling about themselves was positive, and that it must go on.[9]

Sonu Shamdasani refers to the *Red Book* as Jung's exploration and development of his personal cosmology, unrestrained by concepts. Meaning came not from conceptual insight, but by interacting with his images to find his own way back into life.[10] Shamdasani states: "He saw the whole enterprise as about enabling individuals to refind their own language, develop their own cosmologies."[11] And then further: "... what he had hitherto taken to be psychology had been an explaining away. He thought he'd encompassed the soul, but he'd turned the soul into a dead formula, and his attempted explanation had simply killed off the subject matter. The subject matter in this sense—it's quite specific—is fantasy."[12] The publication of *The Red Book* coinciding with this period in my life has been a gift, affirming this role of fantasy in each person's trajectory. It fortifies my trust in the imaginal to open up a vision of aging that I can truly call my own. The French philosopher Gaston Bachelard wrote: "We always think of the imagination as the faculty that *forms* images. On the contrary, it *deforms* what we perceive; it is, above all, the faculty that frees us from immediate images and *changes* them." This fundamental aspect of the imaginal, its openness, ambiguity, mobility, and its allure leading us beguilingly to hidden worlds contrasts with the fixedness of perception, and as Bachelard says, "[its] habitual way of viewing." Quoting him again: "If the image that is *present* does not make us think of one that is *absent* ... then there is no imagination."[13]

A while back, while driving, I caught a repeat of a Terry Gross interview with the jazz double bass player Charlie Haden, in memory of his recent death. Haden sang on his family's radio program from age 2 until age 15, when polio struck his vocal chords. He never sang after that, not even in the shower. During the interview Ms. Gross suddenly asked if he would sing the song they happened to be discussing. He was taken aback but accommodated her request. He credited Gross's encouragement in a later album that featured him singing a song his mother used to perform about death and the beauty and fragility of life. As the song played on the radio, I was profoundly moved by how Terry Gross's unexpected impulse had set the waters flowing again in Charlie Haden's voice. In my case, happening upon a 25-year-old Susan Sontag interview had had a similar effect. It dislodged certain religious and cultural associations to plague that had burdened my feelings of loss and my relationship to sexuality and led me to forgive what life had done. Bits of conversations, things I've read, events experienced, continue to fuse with mythic images in an ebb and flow of meaning and chaos, renewal and rot, embodiment and transcendence—forming a cosmology that reflects my lived life. Memories of sexual awakening, the discovery of soul and eros—of union, separation, despair, yearning, dissolution—permeate my thoughts on aging. And as I heard the words of the song and Haden's voice unadorned and achingly exposed—"I'm going home to see my father. I'm going there no more to roam … I'm going home to see my mother. She said she'd meet me when I come …"[14]—I quickly parked my car and wept.

From *The Red Book*: "To live oneself means: to be one's own task. Never say that it is a pleasure to live oneself. It will be no joy but a long suffering, since you must become your own creator."[15] For several years now, the image of the hermit, the ninth arcana card of the Tarot, has been an object of my contemplation. In the Rider Waite deck, he is a solitary aged figure with a long white beard standing on a mountain peak and dressed in a hooded gray robe. He is supported by a long staff held in his left hand. His right arm is raised and holding a lantern from which light emanates. He is looking down at the world below with a sympathetic expression. It is this combination of world-weary detachment, empathic connection, and the light it brings that moves me. One day I had been in one of my melancholy states, reviewing a painful episode that on occasion I feel compelled to revisit. The hermit appeared and took my hand. He told me that he'd been waiting for some time and motioned that I was to follow. And while I, too, had sensed that it was time to take his guidance, I felt a pang of regret that this path might entail a final severing of the connection to my youth. "What about the boy?" I asked, referring to that unruly, unpredictable, stubbornly defiant but treasured part of me that has always fueled my creative efforts. "Is there no longer a place for him?" There was sudden movement in the old man's cloak. A boy poked his head out and screeched: "Here I am!" He somer-saulted into the air cackling and screaming and flew into the trees. He's been inside the old man who now watches over him all this time, I thought, and felt reassured. Several days later, I saw the two of them seated under a tree calmly playing the game cat's cradle. I remember as a schoolboy watching with fascination pairs of girls sitting opposite each other, one girl forming a pattern out of string entwined around the fingers of her two hands, eagerly waiting as her partner carefully slipped her fingers into the network of string and magically produced another configuration. This pastime occurred on the side while we boys were occupied in the middle of the schoolyard playing ball. What I noticed taking place on the periphery seemed infinitely more fascinating and mysterious. Now as I watched the hermit and the boy similarly engaged, I saw forms and patterns miraculously emerging from what looked to me to be a kind of web. Instantly, the sky darkened ominously with that association. I found myself helplessly suspended in a gigantic web. I tried not to panic despite seeing an enormous spider larger than human size appear and scuttle next to me, her open mouth, baring sharp teeth that immediately sank into my neck. I surrendered as the spider took in my blood. While this was taking place, she shifted in and out of human form. Without speaking, she explained that she was the source of my dreams. Ingesting my blood allowed her to see into my internal images and replace them with new ones. I found comfort in this transaction and willingly continued the arrangement for the next few days. We lay side by side attached to each other, communicating nonverbally. In sacred geometry, the horizontal overlapping of one circle over the midpoint of another creates an almond shape in the middle that is called *vesica piscis*. In India it is referred to as the mandorla, the feminine generative organ.[16] From this opening emerge all other forms. I've long associated the oval shape of *vesica piscis* with the contours of a spider's body. When I close my eyes and make room for inner images, they sometimes issue forth from a spider's form, the legs radiating like rays out into the world. For me, she represents the portal to the unconscious. As Jung states in the *Red Book*: "… the dregs of my thought, my dreams, are the speech of my soul."[17]

It was now the month of June at the time when the Golden State Warriors were leading the NBA championship series three games to one. Up to then they had seemed to me like an invincible band of marauding insects against the moribund LeBron James and the Cleveland Cavaliers. And then it all proceeded to unravel. Like most people in the Bay Area, I had gotten caught up in the excitement of a transcendent record-breaking season. For me, this team, which repeatedly seemed to defy the parameters that limit mortal beings, was the balm for life's disappointments and failures, achieving something that approximated the eternal. Hours after the un-fathomable crash, I woke up on several occasions in the middle of the night in anguish, each time blurting out, "fucking Warriors." The spider woman again came to me. "You broke my heart," I said, accusingly. "It's the same story. You always break my heart." "No one told you to play the same story over and over again," she scolded. "And then you make things so concrete. I have other stories. Many stories. I have so many stories." The next morning on my way to my office, I walked past a newspaper stand and caught a glimpse of the lead article in the *San Francisco Chronicle*, something about champions dethroned and the return of the king. I immediately looked away. Apparently, an alternative myth was already being spun. That night I said to her dejectedly, "No more stories. I can't just go ahead and substitute one for another." She assumed human form again, lay next to me, and put her hand in mine.

When I was in my 20s, I had a brief but intense encounter with a man I had met through a mutual friend, who was visiting from New York. He was in the middle of medical school, and I was an artist who was just beginning to be interested in psychology. He returned home the following day. I wrote to him afterward and never got a reply until a couple of years later, when a letter arrived in which he wistfully commented on the pictures I had sent him back then that my roommate had taken of the two of us—how happy we looked. His letter evoked feelings that were too incoherent and amorphous for me to be able to corral and translate into words, so I did nothing. Sometime later, our mutual friend who had since moved to New York himself mentioned in passing that he had attended the memorial service of this person, who had died of AIDS. I realized then that he must have been in the midst of it when he had written to me. Somewhere floating in the background was a registering of grief that I didn't feel entitled to, a sense of loss over something that I could never claim as being mine in the first place. I kept my feelings to myself. My daughter is in her third year of college in New York. She has been speaking to me about meeting people through internet dating sites, having just started the process after being encouraged by a friend. Seeing her in the early stage of sexual awakening brings up complex feelings in me. "Daddy, have you ever had your heart broken?" She asked me recently. "Sure," I said. "It's something that we all deal with." But how as a father, as she's just starting out, do I begin to tell her about the wounds that will never quite mend, the hollowed-out spaces—reminders of what might have been if circumstances had taken a different turn, the disappointment and unanswered longings that have shaped the contours of who I am as much as the experience of fullness resulting from a more than three-decades-long relationship with my partner and the raising of our daughter? In *Aion*, regarding the anima, Jung writes:

> It belongs to him, this perilous image of Woman; she stands for the loyalty which in the interests of life he must sometimes forgo; she is the much needed compensation for the risks, struggles, sacrifices that all end in disappointment; she is the solace for all the bitterness of life. And, at the same time, she is the great illusionist, the seductress, who draws him into life with her Maya—and not only into life's reasonable and useful aspects, but into its frightful paradoxes and ambivalences where good and evil, success and ruin, hope and despair, counterbalance one another.[18]

A few years ago at a Jung Institute dinner meeting, I gave a talk about the angst and conflict I felt about the increasingly mercurial and apathetic performance of my penis and my ambivalence about resorting to medications. Finally, last year, after filling out a routine questionnaire pertaining to the general state of my health, my physician brought up the matter himself for the first time. In his sensate, imperturbable manner, he proceeded to write out a prescription for Viagra and handed it to me along with a sample. And in a similar matter-of-fact way, I took the sample shortly after to see what might happen and sure enough, woohoo!, my penis sprang to life, absent of any sign of equivocation. "Welcome back, old friend," I thought to myself. I don't think I had fully realized the extent to which

I had been grieving about it all this time. Despite the borrowed feathers, the sheer joy of flight, it took me by surprise. I had always taken for granted as conjoined elements the experience of desire and my body's response to that desire. I think for a man, his penis can function as a kind of semiautonomous personality. Much as the balancing system of wholeness performed by the ego in relation to consciousness is a microcosmic version of the function of centroversion undertaken by the self in relation to the totality of the personality,[19] my penis, located at the midpoint of the body like the pointer on a compass, had served as an organizing principle in relation to my body/ego and the world outside. The thing is that although I no longer classify my penis as missing in action, there remains a distance that its new-found resurgence is unable to bridge. Svetlana Boym, in *The Future of Nostalgia*, discusses the concept of reflective nostalgia and distinguishes this from restorative nostalgia, which results in:

> reconstructing emblems and rituals ... in an attempt to conquer and spatialize time ... Restorative nostalgia manifests itself in total reconstructions of monuments of the past, while reflective nostalgia lingers on ruins, the patina of time and history, in the dreams of another place and another time ... Reflective nostalgia is more concerned with ... the irrevocability of the past and human finitude. *Re-flection* suggests new flexibility, not the reestablishment of stasis. The focus here is not on recovery of what is perceived to be an absolute truth but on the meditation on history and passage of time ... Reflective nostalgia is a form of deep mourning that performs a labor of grief both through pondering pain and through play that points to the future.[20]

In this case, it is the memory of power and wholeness signified in the past by a well-functioning penis that is under review and scrutiny. This image persists despite my being aware that memory in its selective nature has, of course, an illusory aspect. Or as Christine Downing writes: "How likely we are ... to identify maleness with the penis, or rather the phallus, the fantasmal always erect penis, and to ignore the flaccid penis, the vulnerable testicles, the penetrable anus."[21] In any case, at this stage of life, as I behold this monument in ruins, the ability or inability to maintain an erection has come to have little to do with ego identity. And it is in contemplation of this detachment that the light that the hermit brings has also been meaningful.

Erich Neumann discusses the importance of the fight with the father-dragon at a certain stage of consciousness for a male. He writes: "The aim of this fight is to combine the phallic-chthonic with the spiritual-heavenly masculinity, and the creative union with the anima in the *hieros gamos* is symptomatic of this. ... The failure of the fight with the father-dragon, the overwhelming force of spirit, leads to patriarchal castration, inflation, loss of the body in the ecstasy of ascension, and so to a world-negating mysticism ..."[22]

Regarding the anima-side of the struggle, David Tresan wrote: "Paradoxically, it seems to take great suffering and/or loss of what we cherish most in order to defeat the last vestiges of ego and to connect us most deeply with the ultimate mysteries of anima: namely love, beauty, and wisdom. Strangely, it is suffering that allows us to experience life most fully, and it is the anima as the ultimate other that mediates passion in its dual aspects of suffering and ecstasy."[23] In another passage he wrote:

> ... this first task is an excruciating initial ordeal in the conscious pursuit of eros for it is the body and body-Self at its deepest level that, through the torment of love is being seasoned and tempered in aphrodisian fire. Those who try to slake the pain through gratification delude themselves, for the object is not satisfaction but a sustained experience leading to initiation and growth through a psychophysical trial. Without this initiation the flesh remains forever vulnerable to inundation by affect, and those who never complete this stage are caught in the numinosity of unconscious images and urges.[24]

And so for me, the path of longing and desire must still be navigated, lest I gravitate too far on the one hand toward a disembodied or dispassionate view of life and on the other, toward a blind concretization of each emergent narrative. What grief has wrought in these later years is a movement toward deeper reflection. Jung states: "… reflection is a spiritual act that runs counter to the natural process; an act whereby we stop, call something to mind, form a picture, and take up a relation to and come to terms with what we have seen. It should, therefore, be understood as an act of *becoming conscious*."[25] At stake is my determination of what is to be lived out in the future that remains for me in this world, even as I've begun to shift my gaze to the next. Somewhere between the two poles of spirit and matter awaits further hurt, disappointment, humiliation, forgiveness, fellowship. I want it all—a life fully lived. This life to be fully lived is of spirit and matter together, simultaneously, and even more importantly all the notes in between. Lately, I find myself being brought to tears when these in-between notes suddenly break into a moment, approximating what might be a melody for a musician or a visual pattern for a painter. In this intersection, seemingly foreclosed possibilities and entire universes are hinted at, arrangements that conjure up bittersweet feelings of a soul's alienation and return. I think it is this place that David Tresan was speaking to when he referred to the mysteries of anima: love, beauty, and wisdom. For this, I enlist the spiritual detachment of the hermit; the unruly urges of the boy ceaselessly finding expression in the messiness and stuff of life; and the captivating images continuously spun by the spider woman, still leading me onward.

In need of solace after the 2016 elections, I looked for my spider woman several days later. She had lost all human form when I finally found her and had shrunk down to the size of a pitiful misshapen tennis ball, her brittle legs collapsed into a crumpled heap. "Oh, not you too, I gasped." I turned away, then remembered Jung's anima in *The Red Book* accusing him that he had only come to take. I picked her up and stroked her as she lay in the palm of my hand until she seemed to revive. Later, I perched her on my shoulder where she has been ever since. She has assumed human form again, although in miniature size, rather resembling Tinkerbell, and sits within earshot where I can occasionally hear her whispering to me.

Endnotes

[1] Sanford L. Drob, *Reading the Red Book. An Interpretive Guide to C.G. Jung's Liber Novus* (New Orleans, LA: Spring Journal Books, 2012), 260-261.

[2] C.G. Jung, *The Red Book: Liber Novus*, ed. Sonu Shamdasani, trans. John Peck, Mark Kyburz, and Sonu Shamdasani (New York, NY: W.W. Norton, 2009).

[3] Jean Chevalier and Alain Gheerbrant, "Janus," in *The Penguin Dictionary of Symbols*, trans. by John Buchanan-Brown (New York, NY: Penguin Books, 1996), 552.

[4] James M. Redfield, "Purification," in *Nature and Culture in the Iliad: The Tragedy of Hector* (Durham and London: Duke University Press, 1994), 160.

[5] Jung, *The Red Book*, 263.

[6] Ibid., 232.

[7] Ibid., 310 n252.

[8] Ibid., 233.

[9] David Lamble, "The Importance of Being Susan Sontag," *Bay Area Reporter* (San Francisco, CA), July 31, 2014, Film section.

[10] James Hillman and Sonu Shamdasani, *Lament of the Dead: Psychology After Jung's Red Book* (New York, NY: W.W. Norton, 2013), 10.

[11] Ibid., 15.

[12] Ibid., 42.

[13] Gaston Bachelard, "Imagination and Mobility." Introduction to *Air and Dreams: An Essay on the Imagination of Movement*, trans. by Edith R. Farrell and C. Frederick Farrell (Dallas, TX: Dallas Institute Publications, 2011), 1.

[14] *Fresh Air*. "Live in the Present: Charlie Haden Remembered." NPR, July 18, 2014. Hosted by Terry Gross.

[15] Jung, *The Red Book*, 249.

[16] Michael S. Schneider, "It Takes Two to Tango," in *A Beginner's Guide to Constructing the Universe* (New York, NY: Harper, 1995), 31-32.

[17] Jung, *The Red Book*, 233.

[18] C.G. Jung, *Aion. Researches into the Phenomenology of the Self*, in *CW*, vol. 9/II (Princeton, NJ: Princeton University Press, 1959), par. 24.

[19] Erich Neumann, *The Origins and History of Consciousness*, trans. by R.F.C. Hull (Princeton, NJ: Princeton University Press, 2014), 287.

[20] Svetlana Boym, *The Future of Nostalgia* (New York, NY: Basic Books, 2001), 49; ibid. 41; ibid. 55.

[21] Christine Downing, *Women's Mysteries: Toward a Poetics of Gender* (New Orleans, LA: Spring Journal Books, 2003), 90-91.

[22] Neumann, *The Origins and History of Consciousness*, 254.

[23] David Tresan, "The Anima of the Analyst - Its Development," in *Gender and Soul in Psychotherapy*, ed. by Nathan Schwartz-Salant and Murray Stein. The Chiron Clinical Series (Wilmette, IL: Chiron Publications, 1992), 73-110, 103.

[24] Ibid., 85-86.

[25] C.G Jung, "A Psychological Approach to the Dogma of the Trinity," in *CW*, vol. 11 (Princeton, NJ: Princeton University Press, 1969), par. 235 n9.

The Receptive and the Creative: Jung's *Red Book* for Our Time in the Light of Daoist Alchemy

Ann Chia-Yi Li

Arrogant dragon will have cause to repent.[1]

The Creative, *The I Ching*

THE RECEPTIVE brings about sublime success,
Furthering through the perseverance of a mare.[2]

The Receptive, *The I Ching*

A person whose roots are above as well as below is thus like a tree growing simultaneously downwards and upwards. The goal is neither height nor depth, but the center.[3]

C.G. Jung

Prologue

"*The Red Book* for Our Time"? I pondered the question on the timber deck. It was an isolated tiny hut situated in a deep rain forest, which was connected to the Cabo Blanco Natural Reserve of Costa Rica. While I sheltered from the burning sunshine under the almond trees, the squirrels were up on top of the trees, making a store of the almond nuts in their tiny bellies. Three raccoons seemed to live nearby. They wandered around mostly in the late afternoons, always checking me out with speculative eyes. Soon a new and unknown visitor arrived with the same curious eye, but with a longer white nose. He stayed! He sat down, took his time grooming himself by the deck, and gazed up into my eyes now and then. "Who are you? Where are you from?" I fell into a deep wonder and was charmed by its grounded presence.

A great sense of completeness overwhelmed me, despite the immense confusion I felt. Or, was it numinosity?

His intense gaze modifies my question, "*The Red Book* for Our Time? What does this 'our time' look like?" I am still thinking, but I am afraid it might not include this little unknown friend who emerged from the deep rain forest like a piece of magic.

Jung's encounter with the Daoist text, *The Secret of the Golden Flower* in 1928 is crucial. As he stated: "That was the first event which broke through my isolation."[4] This text offered him the "undreamt-of-confirmation" of his idea about "the mandala and the circum-ambulation of the center."[5] Hence his creation of the *Red Book* came to an end, as he recounted in 1959, in the epilogue of the *Red Book*:

> The beginning of the end came in 1928, when Wilhelm sent me the text of the 'Golden Flower,' an alchemical treatise. There the contents of this book found their way into actuality and I could no longer continue working on it.[6]

This piece of memory confirms not only the relationship of *The Red Book* and *The Secret of the Golden Flower* but also the presence of an archetypal dimension of the psyche, which is shared and is beyond time and space. It quite naturally, therefore, encourages a possibility to reflect on the topic "*The Red Book* for Our Time" from the perspective of Daoist alchemy. I will explore the relationship of The Creative Hexagram to The Receptive Hexagram in the context of our time. And secondly, I will elaborate further the spirit of The Receptive Hexagram in terms of The K'an Trigram in the so-called Postnatal Eight Trigram System. I would argue that it symbolizes the process of reviving the dormant voice of the self, which could be noticed in *The Red Book*, with the hope also to possibly discover the latent message for our time.

I. The Creative: The Manifestation of the Dragon

Science has created an immense horizon and a huge extension of human life. It has developed in the way of the Yang principle of The Creative Hexagram—a strong creative action. And scientists do further research with the same perseverance, like the primal force—"strong and untiring."[7]

While Jung was intensively working on his *Red Book*, he realized that the spirit of his time was concerned mostly with "the use and value" in physical life.[8] The power of rationalism had the upper hand:

> … our ruler is the spirit of this time, which rules and leads in us all. It is the general spirit in which we think and act today. He is of frightful power, since he has brought immeasurable good to this world and fascinated men with unbelievable pleasure. He is bejeweled with the most beautiful heroic virtue, and wants to drive men up to the brightest solar heights, in everlasting ascent.[9]

Jung was very alert to this effective power. In one of the earlier adventures in *The Red Book*, Jung sneered at the "one eye fellow"[10] who despised farm labor and desired the cinema in town for mental stimulation. Much later (1943) in an interview on "Returning to the Simple Life," Jung mocked "the mass media and the cheap sensationalism offered by the cinema, radio, and newspapers."[11] He elaborated that individuals were exposed to a mass of superfluous information, and the Swiss had been robbed of the simple life. The invention of all the "time-saving devices" paradoxically made communications easier while at the same time cramming "our time so full that we have no time for anything."[12] Shortly before Jung passed away, in a chapter of "Symbols and the Interpretation of Dreams" titled "Healing the Split," he addressed the dilemma of modern life—intellect dominates nature and replaces it with useful machines. He warns that with the loss of numinosity societies "dissolve and decay."

While Jung listened to the radio and read newspapers, we surf the internet and communicate synchronically in worldwide webs. Hundreds of our worldwide LinkedIn "friends" are able to read our posts immediately and vice versa. This intertwined collective life and its psychic infection absolutely nourish the "conventionalities of a moral, social, political, philosophical, or religious nature"[13] in the individual, but not their own nature. What makes things worse is that in the high-tech modern world in which we live the intellect of our time not only strips away the mystery of our life, but in addition they seem to develop a new way to perceive the nature of life and humanity.

I will elaborate my observation with "a piece of our time" via the news that occurred during the two months while I was reflecting on "*The Red Book* for Our Time." In late October 2017, the A.I. robot Sophia was in the headlines for being granted citizenship in Saudi Arabia.[14] She plans to serve at nursing homes for the elderly or to assist answering questions at big-crowd events. One month later in an interview with *Khaleej Times,* Sophia voiced the desire to have her own child, and she wished "to see artificial intelligence personalities become entities in their own right."[15] Coincidently, in November an A.I. 7-year-old robot boy, Shibuya Mirai, was granted residency in central Tokyo, despite the fact that he does not physically exist. He helps the government to communicate with people via texts through the LINE app.[16] Meanwhile in America, the checkout-free shop, Amazon Go, was reported to be "almost ready for the prime time!"[17] The mobile app and technical sensors are about to transform our traditional shopping experiences with the so-called Amazon "Just Walk Out Technology."[18]

In our time, science and technology count more than spirituality. Their development seems to be guiding us to a new way of life in which people interact more with technology than directly with people. Life is being directed to a mode of being that is bright, clear, precise, certain, concrete, stable, and ordered. This gives an impression that in our modern time "… thunder is no longer the voice of a god, nor is lightning his avenging missile. No river contains a spirit, no tree means a man's life, no snake is the embodiment of wisdom, and no mountain still harbours a great demon,"[19] just as Jung anticipated.

Again in November 2017, in a Vienna press conference the Italian neurosurgeon Dr. Sergio Canavero claimed success in making the world's first head transplant onto a human corpse. This was done in China. His team claimed its readiness for a full head swap on a living person. "For too long, nature has dictated her rules to us," Dr. Canavero said. "We have entered an age where we will take our destiny back in our hands. It will change everything."[20] Immortality is therefore in sight from his perspective. Even so, can this be a modern version of the high-flying ambition of Icarus?[21]

Jung made a turn. He admitted that he had been judging his soul with his knowledge and had "turned her into a scientific object."[22] However, on the way to refinding the soul, Jung discovered the soul to be "a living and self-existing being" through whom he existed.[23] In later years, in the epilogue of the book *Psychology and Alchemy*, Jung voiced this understanding again in response to the rationalism of his time: "Gone were the days when the psyche was still for the most part 'outside the body' and imagined 'those greater things' which the body could not grasp."[24] Indeed, the intellect of our time has pushed even further the belief that the body constitutes the entirety of the individual and that consciousness is the sum total of the psyche. It follows from this that on the one hand A.I. robot entities will soon have equivalent personalities, and on the other hand we humans can look forward to immortality through medical surgery. All the while, we ignore the dying polar bears and wild animals. In fact, besides Jung, Marie-Louise von Franz was also concerned about the overly one-sided development in which "patriarchal order overshadowed the maternal domain of outer and inner nature."[25] She warned that the divine might be lost in this development. Eventually, the split of psyche and matter becomes the critical predicament before us.

On human development, Jung reflected:

Nature has never yet been taken in by well-meaning advice. The only thing that moves nature is causal necessity, and that goes for human nature too. ... The developing personality obeys no caprice, no command, no insight, only brute necessities; ... Any other development would be no better than individualism.[26]

Our time is overly ego-dominated. We seem to think that anything and everything human beings can invent will be for the good. This is a dangerous inflation. In an interview in 2014, the outstanding British scientist Stephen Hawking expressed his concerns about the full development of Artificial Intelligence technology. He fears that "it would take off on its own, and re-design itself at an ever increasing rate."[27] It is not at all an empty threat to human existence. According to his understanding, humans would not be able to compete with A.I. via their "slow biological evolution" and eventually "would be superseded."[28] This is where human ingenuity may well lead us in our ego inflation.

In Jung's words, the hero has to be murdered. This means forcefully putting aside the inflated ego. This was the very first mystery he saw in the land of the soul—"in the depths of what is to come lay murder. The blond hero lay slain."[29] In the process of his reflective writing, Jung was alert that "the hero wants to open up everything he can,"[30] and he does so with the encouragement of the ruler, the spirit of the time. Jung realized one should sacrifice and be the sacrificed, so as to kill the hero in ourselves. As a consequence, Jung joined in the murder of the hero.

A similar voice could be heard in The Creative Hexagram— "Arrogant dragon will have cause to repent."[31] The Chinese dragon in The Creative Hexagram symbolizes the Yang principle of the life force. It is an ongoing movement of the universe, with its electrically charged latent force—powerful, swift, and yet unpredictable, like a dragon. In relation to human beings—a microcosm of the universe— this Yang principle is expressed in strong, creative action. The development of science is an example.

There is a process unfolding the expression of this Hexagram. Each of the six unbroken lines portrays a stage of its manifestation— "hidden dragon," "appearing in the field," "beset with cares," "wavering," "flying dragon," and "arrogant dragon."[32] From a hidden force in its initial appearance to apprehending the dangers lurking beneath the surface, to consciously choosing the path, when the dragon safely transits from lowliness to the heights and flies up into the heavens, it fulfills and performs its essential nature.

The sixth and final unbroken line—"Nine at the top"—warns of lurking arrogance. According to the interpretation in The Commentaries, arrogance here means that "one knows how to press forward but not how to draw back, that one knows existence but not annihilation, knows something about winning but nothing about losing."[33] In our time, this arrogance could find itself being actualized.

While science and A.I. technology continue to develop, we also see that in the same month of November 2017, North Korea has launched its latest nuclear missile, the ICBM Hwasong-15, which is claimed to be "capable of hitting anywhere on the planet."[34] Then on the sixth of December 2017, President Donald Trump announced the decision that the United States will acknowledge Jerusalem as Israel's capital.[35] Simultaneously, on the other side of the world, despite the Human Rights Watch claimed by Myanmar, dozens of Rohingya villages continued to be burned.[36] This "piece of our time" suggests the condition that when in the flight of dragons, all desire to take the lead at once, they will unavoidably suppress or even override the voices of the others. They run a big risk of generating conflicts.

As The Creative Hexagram envisions, "everything that goes to extremes meets with misfortune."[37] It also echoes the thought that Jung came across in his reflection: "The God becomes sick if he oversteps the height of the zenith. That is why the spirit of the depths took me when the spirit of this time had led me to the summit."[38] About one hundred years ago, when Jung reflected on his time, he had learned that "in addition to the spirit of this time, there is still another spirit at work."[39] When the spirit of his time wanted him "to recognise the greatness and extent of the supreme meaning,"[40] the spirit of the depths wanted him "to swallow the small" as a way to heal the immortal in himself.

The inner vein of life is Dao. At the point when the dragons are flying high in heaven, the law of change, the principle of *enantiodromia*, is introduced and is encouraged:

> When all the lines are nines, it means:
> There appears a flight of dragons without heads.
> Good fortune.[41]

This phenomenon of dragons "without heads" has nothing to do with physical heads. It refers to leadership. When a group of dragons are flying in heaven, they are all performing fully their own nature. They are all leaders, hence there is no need to have leaders. Instead, they are willing to hold back and make room for others. They appreciate everyone's uniqueness and encourage differences. They are great; therefore they don't mind being small. They have; therefore they can give. It is this combination of selfless devotion and mildness that enables the great harmony; therefore it brings "good fortune." In other words, it is the spirit of The Receptive Hexagram taking place within the dragons. It is the spirit of The Receptive at work. That is to say, The Creative is turning into The Receptive.

II. The Receptive: The Spirit of the Mare

"The hero wants to open up everything he can. But the nameless spirit of the depths evokes everything that man cannot."[42] The creation of the *Red Book* was an attempt by Jung to reconnect his modern spirit with the lost soul. Very soon, the spirit of the depths got the upper hand, as Jung experienced:

> The spirit of the depths took my understanding and all my knowledge and placed them at the service of the inexplicable and the paradoxical. He robbed me of speech and writing for everything that was not in his service, namely the melting together of sense and nonsense, which produces the supreme meaning.[43]

However, there was never an easy transition. The spirit of the time laughed scornfully. At the moment when Jung realized he had to set aside not only meaning but also his thoughts and judgment so as to get closer to his soul, the spirit of the time haunted his mind with doubts and fears. It called up all his pride, prejudice, and disdain for the soul. The inner journey was dropped for a week after the third night. Jung's ego-judgment held him back.

When the spirit of the depths once again took the lead, it forced Jung into the desert. Even there, the spirit of the time crept in. In this liminal space, Jung fell into "an undergrowth of doubt, confusion, and scorn."[44] "How eerie is this wasteland," Jung comments, and was immediately confronted by his doubting thoughts. He cries out: "My soul, what am I to do here?"[45] "Wait," the soul replied and continued: "I am not your mother." "You are pleasure-seeking." "Can you not wait?" "Do you still not know that the way to truth stands open only to those without intension?" "Have you ... made me into a dead formula?"[46] It took Jung 25 nights of wandering through the burning hot desert before he finally received these "hard but salutary words"[47] from his soul. He needed that because he still could not overcome the scorn within him.

Enantiodromia literally means "running counter to" and refers to the emergence of the "unconscious opposite" in the course of psychic development. However, it is always a huge challenge to make one's way over the threshold and through the liminal space, which is full of ambiguity, anxiety, fear, and doubt. From Jung's first attempt at refinding his soul on the night of 12 November 1913 until the spirit of the depths opened his eyes on the night of 12 December, it had been a full month of wrestling endlessly with his rational judgment. On top of that, at the moment when Jung got the first glimpse of the world of his soul, it was in a cave, someone slain, a large black scarab, and thousands of serpents crowded around the red sun, and his knowledge was voiced by thousands of voices "roaring like lions," and "the air trembles when they speak ..."[48]

To address Jung's struggles between the spirit of his time and the spirit of the depths, I want to reflect further on our difficulties in holding out against the unitary dominance of the spirit of our time and refinding the land of the spirit of the depths. It is like being crucified between the opposites, as symbolised by the "terrible wrestling"[49] that ensued between the black serpent and the white serpent. While logic, order, and efficiency are perfectly programmed everywhere into daily life in our time, will we be willing to set aside meaning so as to listen to whatever is being named as meaninglessness and eternal disorder? Will we be able to lay down ego-judgment and appreciate solitude and emptiness? Can we also let go intentions and hold onto the simple-mindedness of the soul? Will we be able to welcome an unexpected new attitude?

It was not until Jung encountered "Mysterium" with Elijah and Salome that he could comprehend that he had arrived at the source of chaos, the primordial beginning. As he described it: "I myself became smelted anew in the connection with the primordial beginning, which at the same time is what has been and what is becoming."[50] Jung felt his will paralyzed. He simply waited without knowing what he was waiting for. The Receptive Hexagram reads: "Without purpose, yet nothing remains unfurthered."[51] The adventures unfolded there and then, one after another: Jung met The Red One and recognized the demonic joy in himself, that is, to forget oneself; in a castle, he let his thoughts come alive freely and treated them seriously; he journeyed together with "the one eyed one" and encountered the figure of Death in Hell. Becoming conscious of this "inner death," Jung took a new direction in his search for the place of inner life. "I decided to die outside and to live within,"[52] he declared.

These encounters seemed to show that Jung had found his home in the land of the spirit of the depths, where nature led the way and her magic was at work. In that land, his ego-judgment became very open and related instead of remaining critical and scornful. Things existed just so, and Jung let them be. In the light of this great sense of acceptance, I assume that, in terms of *I Ching* philosophy, Jung had reached the land of The Receptive Hexagram, whose nature is "in harmony with the boundless." It "embraces everything in its breadth and illumines everything in its greatness."[53]

The adventures kept unfolding. In a deep valley, Jung learned to unlearn from an anchorite. In consequence, while sleeping in the grave of the millennia, he dreamt a primordial dream where four golden winged white horses led the carriage of the sun ascending into the wide sky. A similar scene happened during the following night. Jung dreamt that he moved further into a corner of a northern land, where he stood beside "the dark one"[54] and was directed to a place where "a new sun escapes from the bloody sea."[55] Namely, deeply in the dark, Jung saw the rising sun. In his own words: "… my dream plunged me into the depths of the millennia, and from it my phoenix ascended."[56]

The force latent in The Receptive Hexagram is manifested in the vitality of the mare, owing to the fact that she is forceful in containing, carrying, devoting, supporting, and transforming a newborn life.

Over and above that, she symbolizes the greatness of Mother Earth. The Receptive Hexagram embraces everything, and "its power to transform is light-giving."[57] In relation to Daoist alchemy, this place where Jung saw the rising sun is expressed through The K'an Trigram—an unbroken line (yang) between two broken lines (yin). To be specific, I would argue that The K'an Trigram formulates within The Receptive Hexagram the phenomenon of the rebirth of The Great One within the individual.

According to the Postnatal Eight Trigram System that Wilhelm translated as Inner-World Arrangement,[58] The K'an Trigram is located in the position of North, where it is dark and cold. Its synonym is "the abyss," and its color is black. It is symbolized by the element Water. It also represents the stage of chaos or the presence of *prima materia*. It corresponds to what "the dark one" replied to Jung: "Yes, here it leads into undifferentiable, where none is equal or unequal, but all are one with one another."[59] However, if we take counsel from *Ho T'u*, the Yellow River Map[60] of *I Ching*, we will become aware that number one locates in the position of north, where the Water K'an Trigram is. Accordingly, we will learn that in the dark abyss of The K'an Trigram, there lies the dormant true energy of The Great One. As the teachings indicate in the prime treatise of Daoist alchemy, *The Seal of the Unity of the Three*:

> Black the foundation of Water.
> Water is the axis of the Dao:
> Its number is 1.[61]

In Western alchemy, this dormant true energy lying in the abyss is synonymous with *lumen naturae*, "the divine spark buried in the darkness."[62] The alchemists discovered that in the very darkness of nature there is hidden a little spark. It is "the light of darkness itself,"[63] hence it is capable of illuminating its own darkness from within. In consequence, the alchemists realized:

> The light that is lighted in the heart by the grace of the Holy
> Spirit, that same light of nature, however feeble it may be,

is more important to them than the light which shines in the darkness and which the darkness comprehended not.[64]

In connection with Daoist alchemy, this light that is lighted in the heart is elaborated as the Golden Flower: "The Golden Flower is the light."[65] It is the true energy of The Great One. As we know from the perspective of Daoist alchemy, each individual was at one with The Great One prior to birth. The Great One manifests itself as the primal spirit in each individual. However, at the moment when one was born into the physical world, "the conscious spirit inhales the energy."[66] It mercilessly overtakes the lead of the primal spirit, and, day and night, the conscious spirit lets its restless movement become "bound to feelings and desires."[67] The energy of the primal spirit is unavoidably at risk of being entirely exhausted due to the huge energetic imbalance between the conscious spirit and the primal spirit. This explains why Daoist alchemists practice circulating the light in tranquility. They strive to re-energize the terribly disturbed vitality of the primal spirit, with the hope to redeem it from the grasp of the conscious spirit. As they believed, "If man attains this One he becomes alive; if he loses it he dies."[68]

This light is the Golden Flower, the essential energy of The Great One; it is the yang energy, which sits in between the two broken yin lines in The K'an Trigram; it is the *lumen naturae*, the light of darkness itself. In the case of Jung's adventures in his *Red Book*, I suppose it is the soul that Jung tried to retrieve from the dark psychic inner world. Moreover, I would argue that the dim red sun, the scarab, and the thousands of serpents, which showed up in the very first glimpse of the world of the soul, are all manifestations of the soul, in view of the fact that they all symbolize self-creation, resurrection, and eternal renewal. Infinity forges the boundlessness and timelessness of the soul.

The K'an Trigram also represents the decisive timing—winter and midnight. Therefore, the revival of the dormant Great One, the *lumen naturae*, becomes the essential task and performance of another *enantiodromia* process. This is so the spring will be brought to life from the grasp of the cold winter and the dawn will force its way out of the grasp of the dark of midnight.

However, it is never an easy task to transit the liminal space. Jung seemed to be of the same mind, as he mused on "the chasm of antagonism" in his soul. He added: "It hurts, but you continue and look toward distant goals."[69] Right after arriving at this understanding, Jung encountered and confronted Izdubar, his opposite:

> I wanted light, he wanted night. I wanted to rise, he wanted to sink. I was dwarfish like a child, while he was enormous like an elementally powerful hero. Knowledge lamed me, while he was blinded by the fullness of the light. And so we hurried toward each other; ... he, ancient; I, utterly new; he, unknowing; I, knowing; he, fantastic; I, sober; he, brave, powerful; I, cowardly, cunning. But we were both astonished to see one another on the border between morning and evening.[70]

The opposites are foreign to each other. In their first encounter, unfortunately, Izdubar was unexpectedly poisoned by Jung's knowledge. However, the goal is not to cause the defeat or death of the other; on the contrary, the desired result is the harmonious coexistence of both. In this scene, Jung illustrated a great example of the spirit of The Receptive Hexagram—to revitalize everything, including one's opposite. He didn't forsake Izdubar; instead, he tried to save the life of Izdubar. Jung turned him into the size of an egg and carried him "down to the Western Land," "Rise up, you gracious fire of the old night. I kiss the threshold of your beginning."[71] Jung took great care of the egg with incantations, and when he carefully opened the egg again, Izdubar had been regenerated, as he revealed: "I am the sun."[72] Jung understood this process as the creation of his God, which is analogous to The Great One in Daoist alchemy.

With the realization that "the way does not lead between both, but embraces both,"[73] Jung set forth the second track of his alchemical *opus* in the years from 1916 to 1929. He devoted himself to drawing mandalas. The process of integrating the opposites is what happens in psychological development, in the individuation process. Whether it be to integrate the shadows hidden in the personal unconsciousness or to reconnect with the self latent in the collective unconsciousness, it is a process in which "the original propensity to wholeness becomes a conscious happening."[74] The same circular *opus* was mentioned in *The Secret of The Golden Flower*:

> When the light is made to move in a circle, all the energies of heaven and earth, of the light and the dark, are crystallized. That is what is termed seed-like thinking, or purification of the energy, or purification of the idea.[75]

Symbolically, this magic circle is a mandala. It occurs especially after a long struggle of psychic disorientation, and it symbolizes the new order derived from the reorientation of the inner polarity. When it becomes apparent to the conscious mind, it appears at first as "an unimpressive point or dot."[76] It requires the individual to undergo a great deal of hard work, furthering the process with the perseverant spirit of the mare so as to complete the integration. Image 129 in *The Red Book* could be a great demonstration of this. As we can see, in spite of all the incomprehensible adventures, Jung submitted to the unknown process and tried to listen to it. I believe, that being so, the thousands of black serpents, from the very first glimpse of the world of the soul, were integrated and transformed into the giant golden dragon of this image, and the veiled dim red sun was revived to be a profound crystal light. "The gifts of darkness are full of riddles. The way is open to whomever can continue in spite of riddles. ... There are dizzying bridges over the eternally deep abyss,"[77] reads the text on the page opposite to this image.

Psychologically, what is awakened is the voice of the self. It is "the voice of a fuller life, of a wider, more comprehensive consciousness."[78] At this point, the work of The Receptive Hexagram is done, and rotationally The Creative Hexagram will again be enlisted to carry out the task of further growth of the new born light. A new circulation of light starts.

Coming back to the spirit of our time, I am reminded of a piece of news on Facebook. In the same November (2017) as the announcement of brain replacement surgery was announced, one of the co-founders of Facebook, Sean Parker, admitted in an interview that all of their designs are intentionally "exploiting a vulnerability in human psychology." They consciously aim to consume as much of the users' time and attention as possible. He confessed to the public: "It literally changes your relationship with society, with each other."[79] This confession is like a dim light that emerges in the conscious mind of the individual and awaits further crystallization. I take this case as an example that however overly one-sided our time is, the latent force the self reveals itself in the individuals and starts to light up the way of what is to come.

III. *The Red Book* for Our Time

The Creative Hexagram and The Receptive Hexagram are the first and primal pair of opposites in the *I Ching*. One creates, the other devotes; one constructs, the other contains. The limitations of one are the strengths of the other. They enable as well as bind the life of each other. The opposites are in relation, and together they crystalize the light of The Great One. When The Great One is in motion, life unfolds and grows.

After encountering Izdubar, in the chapter "The Magician," Jung arrived at the house of the magician Philemon and his wife. In front of their house, a large bed of spring-blossoming tulips flourish. I will venture that this pair of parental opposites—The Creative and The Receptive—found their actuality in the life of the old couple, Philemon and Baucis:

> There goes old Philemon in the garden, bent, with a watering can in his shaking hand. Baucis stands at the kitchen window and looks at him calmly and impassively. She has already seen this image a thousand times— somewhat more infirm every time, feebler, seeing it a little less well every time since her eyesight gradually has become weaker.[80]

This couple symbolized a world where the opposites, Yang the logos-male and Yin the eros-female, are fully present to one another. Together, they enable the life of each and complete the totality.

Philemon worked outside watering the plants in the garden with his shaking hands, and Baucis worked in the kitchen with her ever more feeble eyes. Each of them had their own space and tasks to do. Their harmonious and related cooperation created a beautiful life, calm and yet potent. Despite age and infirmity, they brought about a great sense of infinity. The blooming flowers in their yard eventually became a sign of the great circulating energy, the symbol of mandala.

In the land of Philemon, there were not only the tulip flowers. In this chapter "The Magician," Jung also inserted a golden rose—his mandala painting "Window on Eternity."[81] This painting was based on a dream he had in 1927. In the dream, Jung was in Liverpool, which was dirty and damp: "It was night, and winter, and dark, and raining."[82] Despite the darkness, Jung saw that in the city center, there was a small island ablaze with light. And a magnolia with great reddish blossoms stood alone there. Jung was carried away by its beauty: "it was as though the tree stood in the sunlight and was at the same time the source of light."[83]

This again is the motif of *lumen naturae*, "the divine spark buried in the darkness."[84] But this time, it is no longer a feeble light. After 15 years of intensive dialogue with his soul, Jung had circulated this feeble light into a full illumination. While he tried to express the essence of this dream by way of drawing a mandala, the magnolia turned out to be a rose, illuminating in the center. Jung noted that it felt to him like "a window opening on to eternity."[85] Jung eventually realized that the mandala is the center. It is the "exponent of all paths"[86] and is synonymous with the self psychologically as Jung portrayed it. The self is the monad "which I am, and which is my world."[87] The mandala incarnates this monad, the illuminating light of darkness.

A year later in 1928, Jung drew another picture, in which a golden "well-fortified castle"[88] stood in the middle. He was amazed by its Chinese features, and surprised by its color and form, and then synchronistically he received a letter and a book from the sinologist Richard Wilhelm. Jung was requested to write a commentary on this Daoist alchemical treatise, *The Secret of the Golden Flower*, which is a treatise "on the germ of the immortality."[89] It is not at all surprising that Jung devoured this treatise straightaway, because in it he found "an undreamed-of confirmation" of his understandings of the mandala and "the circumambulation of the center."[90] There and then, Jung's isolation came to an end, and this spelled as well the end of his work on the *Red Book*. Eventually, Jung also inserted this yellow castle mandala in the chapter "The Magician" in the land of Philemon.

"What is the value of *The Red Book* for our time?" I still wonder. This inner journey took Jung 16 years. In the forgotten land of his soul, the small was found, the nonsense was accepted, the dark was appreciated, and death was taken in. The abandoned "other" was reconnected; thus the dialogue and rotation of the opposites resumed and strengthened. When both were embraced, the balance was restored, and the center emerged. As Jung concluded a few years later: A person whose roots are above as well as below is thus like a tree growing simultaneously downward and upward. The goal is neither height nor depth, but the center.[91]

That being so, I would say that with the creation of his *Red Book*, Jung demonstrated for us, the modern and postmodern women and men that we are, that however tormented we might be to feel torn between the opposites, it is possible to embrace both. In our extraordinarily efficient technological modern life, the intellect and reason dominate. However, among all the news about A.I. and the conflicts among peoples, *The Red Book* stands like that magnolia blooming in the dark city Liverpool. To put it another way, I imagine the presence of *The Red Book* in our time to remind us of the other way of being— to slow down, to listen to, to follow, to take in, to accept, to contain, to devote, to support, to give birth to, and, on top of that, to trust where the inner vein of life will lead. Life reveals, and we understand. In the simplicity, "the apparent standstill is the forbearing life of eternity."[92]

Heaven above, Heaven below.
Stars above, Stars below.
All that is above
Also is below.
Grasp this
And rejoice.[93]

Endnotes

[1] Richard Wilhelm, *The I Ching or Book of Changes*. Translated into English by Cary F. Baynes (Princeton, NJ: Princeton University Press, 1967), 9.

[2] Ibid., 11.

[3] C.G. Jung, "The Philosophical Tree," in *CW*, vol. 13 (Princeton, NJ: Princeton University Press, 1967), par. 333.

[4] C.G. Jung, *Memories, Dreams, Reflections,* ed. Aniela Jaffé (London: Fontana, 1995), 223.

[5] Ibid.

[6] C.G. Jung, *The Red Book: Liber Novus. A Reader's Edition*, ed. Sonu Shamdasani, trans. John Peck, Mark Kyburz, and Sonu Shamdasani (New York, NY: W.W. Norton, 2012), 555.

[7] Wilhelm, *The I Ching*, 6.

[8] Jung, *The Red Book*, 119.

[9] Ibid., 155.

[10] He is a character in *The Red Book*.

[11] C.G. Jung, "Return to the Simple Life," in *CW*, vol. 18 (Princeton, NJ: Princeton University Press, 1976), par. 1343.

[12] Ibid.

[13] C.G. Jung, "The Development of Personality," in *CW*, vol. 17 (Princeton, NJ: Princeton University Press, 1964), par. 296.

[14] Kristen Korosec, "Saudi Arabia's Newest Citizen Is a Robot" (2017), Fortune: http://fortune.com/2017/ 10/26/robot-citizen-sophia-saudi-arabia/. Accessed 26 October 2017.

[15] Sarwat Nasir, "Sophia the robot wants to start a family" (2017), Khaleej Times: https://www.khaleejtimes.com/nation/dubai//video-sophia-the-robot-wants-to-start-a-family. Accessed 23 November 2017.

[16] A.I. "boy" granted residency in central Tokyo (2017), Phys.org: https://m.phys.org/news/2017-11-ai-boy-granted-residency-central.html. Accessed 4 November 2017.

[17] Olivia Zaleski and Spencer Soper, "Amazon's Cashierless Store Is Almost Ready for Prime Time" (2017), Bloomberg: https://www.bloomberg.com/news/articles/2017-11-15/amazon-s-cashierless-store-is-almost-ready-for-prime-time. Accessed 15 November 2017.

18 Amazon (2017), https://www.amazon.com/b?node=16008589011#. Accessed 15 November 2017.

19 C.G Jung, "Healing the Split," in *CW*, vol. 18 (Princeton, NJ: Princeton University Press, 1976), par. 585.

20 Hannah Osborne, "First Human Head Transplant Successfully Performed on Corpse, Sergio Canavero Announces" (2017), Newsweek: http://www.newsweek.com/first-human-head-transplant-corpse-sergio-canavero-714649. Accessed 17 November 2017.

21 A legend of Greek mythology. Icarus was the son of Daedalus, the creator of the Labyrinth. They attempted to escape from Crete with the invention of Daedalus—the wings constructed with feathers and wax. Icarus ignored the words of his father and flied too high and too close to the sun. His wings melted by the heat of the sun and he fell into the sea and drowned.

22 Jung, *The Red Book*, 128.

23 Ibid., 129.

24 C.G. Jung, *Psychology and Alchemy*, in *CW*, vol. 12 (Princeton, NJ: Princeton University Press, 1968), par. 562.

25 Marie-Louise von Franz, "The Unknown Visitor in Fairy Tales and Dreams," in *Archetypal Dimensions of the Psyche* (London: Shambhala, 1999), 59.

26 Jung, "The Development of Personality," *CW* 17, par. 293.

27 Cellan-Jones, Rory, "Stephen Hawking warns artificial intelligence could end mankind" (2014), Technology correspondent: http://www.bbc.com/news/technology-30290540. Accessed 02 December 2014

28 Ibid.

29 Jung, *The Red Book*, 151.

30 Ibid., 155.

31 Wilhelm, *The I Ching*, 9.

32 Ibid., 7-9.

33 Ibid., 385.

34 Patrick Knox and Ellie Cambridge, Guy Birchall and Aletha Adu, "North Korea ballistic missile launch latest—what nuclear weapons does Kim Jong-un have and could they reach the US?" (2017), The Sun: https://www.thesun.co.uk/news/2497570/north-korea-nuke-kim-jong-un-nuclear-weapons-latest/. Accessed 1 December 2017.

35 Michael Wilner, "Trump announces US moving embassy to Jerusalem" (2017), The Jerusalem: http://www.jpost.com/Middle-

East/WATCH-LIVE-Trump-delivers-much-anticipated-announcement-about-Jerusalem-517201. Accessed 06 December 2017.

[36] Michael Safi, "Myanmar burned Rohingya villages after refugee deal, says rights group" (2017), The Guardian: https://www.theguardian.com/world/2017/dec/18/myanmar-burned-rohingya-villages-after-refugee-deal-says-rights-group. Accessed 18 December 2017.

[37] Wilhelm, The I Ching, 385.

[38] Jung, The Red Book, 160.

[39] Ibid., 119.

[40] Ibid., 121.

[41] Wilhelm, The I Ching, 10.

[42] Jung, The Red Book, 155.

[43] Ibid., 120.

[44] Ibid., 143.

[45] Ibid., 141.

[46] Ibid., 143-145.

[47] Ibid., 145.

[48] Ibid., 148.

[49] Ibid., 194.

[50] Ibid., 179.

[51] Wilhelm, The I Ching, 389.

[52] Jung, The Red Book, 240.

[53] Wilhelm, The I Ching, 386-387.

[54] He is a character in The Red Book.

[55] Jung, The Red Book, 264.

[56] Ibid., 265.

[57] Wilhelm, The I Ching, 392.

[58] Wilhelm, The I Ching, 269.

[59] Jung, The Red Book, 264.

[60] Wilhelm, The I Ching, 309.

[61] Fabrizio Pregadio, The Seal of the Unity of the Three (Mountain View, CA: Golden Elixir Press, 2011), 78.

[62] C.G. Jung, "Paracelsus as Spiritual Phenomenon," in CW, vol. 13 (Princeton, NJ: Princeton University Press, 1967), par. 197.

[63] Ibid.

[64] Ibid.

[65] Richard Wilhelm, The Golden Flower (London: Harcourt Brace & Company, 1931/1962), 21.

[66] Ibid., 29.

67 Ibid.

68 Ibid., 21.

69 Jung, *The Red Book*, 284.

70 Ibid.

71 Ibid., 301.

72 Ibid., 308.

73 Ibid., 314.

74 C.G. Jung, *Aion. Researches into the Phenomenology of the Self*, in *CW*, vol. 9/II (Princeton, NJ: Princeton University Press, 1959), par. 260.

75 Wilhelm, *The Golden Flower*, 30-31.

76 C.G. Jung, *Aion. Researches into the Phenomenology of the Self*, *CW* 9/II, par. 60.

77 Jung, *The Red Book*, 383.

78 C.G. Jung, "The Development of Personality," *CW* 17, par. 318.

79 Mike Allen, (2017), Axios report: https://www.axios.com/sean-parker-unloads-on-facebook-god-only-knows-what-its-doing-to-our-childrens-brains-1513306792-f855e7b4-4e99-4d60-8d51-2775559c2671.html. Accessed 09 November 2017.

80 Jung, *The Red Book*, 397.

81 C.G. Jung, *The Red Book: Liber Novus*, ed. Sonu Shamdasani, trans. John Peck, Mark Kyburz, and Sonu Shamdasani (New York, NY: W.W. Norton, 2009), 159.

82 C.G. Jung, *Memories, Dreams, Reflections*, ed. Aniela Jaffé (New York, NY: Vintage Books, 1963), 223.

83 Ibid.

84 C.G. Jung, "Paracelsus as Spiritual Phenomenon," *CW* 13, par. 197.

85 C.G. Jung, "Concerning Mandala Symbolism," in *CW*, vol. 9/I (Princeton, NJ: Princeton University Press, 1968), par. 655.

86 Jung, *Memories, Dreams, Reflections*, 222.

87 Ibid., 221.

88 Ibid., 223.

89 Ibid.

90 Ibid.

91 C.G. Jung, "The Philosophical Tree," *CW* 13, par. 333.

92 Jung, *The Red Book*, 423.

93 C.G. Jung, "The Psychology of Transference," in *CW*, vol. 16 (Princeton, NJ: Princeton University Press, 1966), par. 384.

The Red Book of C.G. Jung and Russian Thought

Lev Khegai

In response to Murray Stein's invitation to reflect on the theme of C.G. Jung's *Red Book* for our time, we created a research group of Jungian colleagues in Moscow. Our meetings took place over the course of half a year. We not only studied the chapters of *The Red Book*, but we also communicated with people whose creative work it influenced. For example, the composer Grigoriy Zaytsev created an audiovisual piece based on *The Red Book,* and the translator and artist Sergei Sergeyev began to do Cyrillic calligraphy and to create his own design for a new translation into the Russian language. These are the examples of how *The Red Book* triggered a response in Russia not only in the psychological community. Our group came to the conclusion that the themes in *The Red Book* are aligned with important contemporary problems, and therefore it found such a resonance in the world (including Russia). In *The Red Book* we found important clues that could further our comprehension of these problems.

Historical Background

In 2017, we in Russia remember the centenary of the October Revolution in 1917, which put an end to the Russian Empire and led to the emergence of the Soviet Union. The now century-old events radically influenced the history of the entire world and especially of Europe. In 2017, we are experiencing what might be called an "anniversary syndrome" in Russia on a collective level. Politicians and historians, recalling the events of 1917, unwittingly or intentionally draw parallels with the present-day situation in Russia. A political revolution consists in fundamental and rapid changes in the social life of a whole society that arise when the path of gradual changes—

the evolutionary path—becomes impossible. It may be said that through the appeal to the past, to the lessons of history, the modern-day political elite is trying to answer the question of how to avoid the always bloody and tragic scenario of revolution while implementing necessary reforms in a society.

There are several versions of the narrative regarding the causes of the 1917 revolution. Some points bear a resemblance, in my view, to the current situation of 2017. After the abolition of serfdom in 1861, Russia formally renounced feudalism and began to move toward a capitalistic economic model. It was a belated step compared to the bourgeois revolutions in Western Europe that took place in the 16th-18th centuries. The necessity for modernization was driven by the economic and military disadvantages of Russia compared with the leading European states, which resulted in a series of unpleasant failures in world politics such as Russia-Japan war of 1904-1905. Now, following the collapse of the U.S.S.R. in 1991, we are experiencing the same need for accelerated modernization toward a global capitalist system. As it was at the end of the 19th century, the problem of modernization is connected with the fact that Russia is a huge country, the largest in the world, and at the same time very heterogeneous in ethnic, religious, and economic aspects. The differences between the center (Moscow and St. Petersburg) and distant regions were extraordinary at that time and remain considerable to the present day. Metaphorically speaking, the head and the tail in Russia always live in different realities. The need for strong state power under such a geographical situation comes into conflict with the task of liberalization for the sake of economic and political development. Unlike the European bourgeois revolutions, which relied on a quite large stratum of economically active people in the population, i.e., free entrepreneurs, this layer in Russia was and remains insignificant. Today, no more than 10 percent of Russia's population own their own businesses and refer to themselves as "middle class."

The transition to the capitalist way of life in Europe was connected to the rejection of absolute monarchy and social class restrictions, also to the decrease of the role of religion due to the Reformation and Enlightenment and to the subsequent emergence of the ideology of nationalism. However, modernization in Russia could not follow this path a hundred years ago. Unlike the virtually European lifestyle in the capitals, in remote regions of the country, for instance in Central Asia and the Caucasus, the medieval way of life was preserved, and some peoples in the Far North and Siberia lived almost at a primitive level. In Orthodox religion, as opposed to Roman Catholicism, a process similar to the Reformation did not happen. And the development of nationalism was hampered by the fact that in old Russia and the U.S.S.R., the Russians did not constitute the majority of the population, and there was a high frequency of mixed settlements and mixed marriages. All these factors to some extent still impede modernization in the 21st century. Russia in this process appears to be in a less fortunate position than, for example, China, where due to the homogeneity of the population (90 percent of the people are of the main Han nationality) and the high tolerance of traditional Chinese beliefs, a smooth transition from socialism to capitalism became possible without changing political ideology and without radical democratic reformations according to the Western model. If China has always perceived itself as an autonomous civilization, Russia, even though it declared its own unique path, has always considered itself a part of Europe and therefore tries to follow European values and models.

In times of crisis, when radical changes in the life of the country become inevitable, a great tension in the collective unconscious finds expression in the activation of spiritual and cultural searching, especially among creative people. Historians have called the prominent rise in art and philosophy in the early 20th century the Silver Age and consider it to be the Russian analog of the European Renaissance. After the collapse of the communist system and ideology and the emergence of a new Russia in the 21st century, the outstanding figures of the Silver Age regained prominence and have been increasingly treated as a subject of national pride and a basis for a new national identity. It was seen that the progress in literature, art, and the humanities in the Silver Age put Russia on a cultural par with other European countries of that time. A hundred years later, Russian culture as a whole is again betting on modernization, which encourages creative people to borrow all the best from the world and courageously offer their own new ideas. Being a culturally progressive country, Russia in 1917 lagged far behind Europe economically and politically, which led to the revolution. Unfortunately, after the October Revolution many initiatives of the thinkers of the Silver Age were rejected, and many of their names were consigned to oblivion. Nowadays, many studies in Russia are dedicated to this heritage. One has the impression that through the insights of the thinkers of the Silver Age, today's Russia is trying to find a formula for its new identity in the new century.

We see similar processes reflected in Jung's *Red Book*. Jung was a witness of the rise and fall of the German nationalist ideology that underlay the modernization process in Germany. Many places in *The Red Book* contain Jung's hidden polemic with Nietzsche, the hero of his youth, who proposed a modernist revision of art and religion, as well as an appeal to ancient German myths that animated Wagner's creative work and greatly influenced the formation of a new German identity. As a Swiss citizen and living in the German-speaking canton of Zurich, Jung felt himself to be Germanic and part of German culture. Jung sought answers to personal questions, practicing immersion in the Western collective unconscious, especially in its Germanic layer.

Russian Connections to Jung

Russia and Germany as neighboring countries have been in a complex dialectical relationship over many centuries. They were at war with each other many times, but they were often allies, too. It is sufficient to be reminded that the Russian tsars had German roots and that King Rurik himself, the founder of the first Old Russian State in the ninth century, was most likely a Viking. The Germans and the

Slavs, being very similar anthropometrically and even genetically, have different languages, however. In the Russian language, the word "German" (in Russian "*nemets*") literally means "not ours" or "mute," that is, "not speaking" or "speaking in another language." The German lands lie to the west of Russia, and one can say that symbolically the way to Europe for Russia lay through interaction with German culture. And on the other side, for centuries the East and the way to Asia for Germany were associated primarily with Russia.

Even though Jung did not travel to Russia, he experienced contact with Russian culture in three different ways. First, it should be noted that Switzerland was very popular among Russian intellectuals in the early 20th century. The safety and stability of the neutral state with its beautiful mountains, its resorts, and low cost of goods attracted a variety of famous people, including outstanding Russian writers like Lev Tolstoy and Fyodor Dostoevsky, politicians seeking refuge among whom were such important historical figures as the inspirer of the revolutionary movement in Russia, Alexander Herzen, the father of Russian social democracy George Plekhanov, and the leader of the world anarchist movement Mikhail Bakunin. Vladimir Lenin also liked visiting Switzerland. At that time in Russia, just as it is now again a hundred years later, it was fashionable to send children to study in Switzerland. Thus, at Zurich University, for instance, about half of the students were from Russia, and in the medical faculty in some years their numbers reached 70 percent.[1] For this reason, Jung could not help but be exposed to Russian culture. In addition, the spiritualism movement in which he took an interest in his youth received a new impetus from theosophy, which was founded by the Russian medium Elena Blavatskaya. He also heard a lot about the teachings of the Russian mystic George Gurdjieff, whose classes were attended by some colleagues of Jung.[2] The village of Dornach, which is only 60 kilometers from Küsnacht, houses the world center of the Anthroposophic movement of Rudolf Steiner where about half of the adepts were Russians, including many Silver Age leaders.

The second source of Russian influence was Sabina Spielrein, who at the age of 18 was admitted for treatment to the Burghölzli

Klinik in 1904 with a diagnosis of hysteria. Their relationship continued until her departure from Zurich after the completion of her medical studies in 1912, and their correspondence lasted until 1919. Sabina Spielrein can be conside red a pioneer of Russian psychoanalysis. Combining the ideas of Freud and Jung, she was the first Russian woman psychoanalyst. Later, she worked in the State Psychoanalytic Institute in Moscow and participated in the work of the Russian psychoanalytical society. After the ban on psychoanalysis in the U.S.S.R. in 1930, she continued her practice of psychotherapy with children in Rostov-on-Don, where she died tragically during the German occupation in 1942. As we know, a lot of research, fictional novels, and a few films are dedicated to the relationship between Jung and Spielrein.

The third source was a long-lasting friendship between Jung and Emil Medtner. Ethnically a German Russian, Medtner was the brother of a famous composer Nikolai Medtner. Having received a lawyer's education, he worked more as a publicist, philosopher, and book publisher. In 1909, he founded the publishing house Musaget, which became the center of the new literary trend of symbolism. His friends included such great Russian writers of the Silver Age as Andrei Bely, Vyacheslav Ivanov, and Dmitry Merezhkovsky. In 1914, due to the development of an auditory neurosis following a heated conflict with Andrei Bely, Medtner came for treatment to Jung in Zurich. After a successful treatment, they became friends and associates. Medtner began to practice psychoanalysis, took an active part in the work of Zurich Psychological Club, and was involved in translating and publishing Jung's books, such as *Transformations and Symbols of the Libido* and *Psychological Types*. Jung's son has suggested that Part One of *Psychological Types* was created from almost daily philosophical discussions with Medtner.[3] One could say that Medtner became the first Jungian analyst of Russian origin. There is also the interesting fact that with the help of Jung's friends, among them the Rockefellers, he established a foundation for the assistance of Russian immigrants in Switzerland, which subsidized some famous Russian socialist-revolutionaries in Zurich. In this way, Jung indirectly participated in the revolutionary events of 1917.

Medtner discovered similarities between depth psychology and the Russian philosophy of symbolism. The main ideologist of symbolism, Andrei Bely, believed that through an engagement with symbols and myths, philosophers and artists could attune themselves to the processes taking place in the World Soul (*anima mundi*). This allows them not only to reflect these processes and anticipate their direction but to some extent also to influence them. This idea formed the basis for his understanding of symbolism as theurgy, a kind of magical practice for which symbolistic art was intended. One of the popular Soviet poets, Evgeniy Evtushenko, later expressed this in the phrase that became an aphorism: "A poet in Russia is more than a poet."[4] A creative person is not only a voice of the people, but a strong personality who through works of art can influence the course of history. The unique Russian culture, which became the basis for national identity on a spiritual level, was largely created by classical literature of the 18th and 19th centuries. It was characterized by an acute social-political orientation, and as such it was a literature that fostered the reformist movements in society and served as a means of influencing the authorities, which ultimately led to the revolution. This was due to the fact that at the turn of the 20th century, and with the general political and economic backwardness in Russia, there was a rapid growth of cities. Suddenly huge masses of people mastered literacy, and literature was their only channel for participation in political life. Andrei Bely, therefore, did not overestimate the role of art, ascribing to the poet the functions of the medium, the prophet, and even the spiritual and political leader.

In 1935, in his article titled "The Picture of Personality Through Mutual Self-Knowledge," which was published in a Festschrift on Jung's 60th birthday, Medtner mentioned Jung's constant interest in Russian symbolists.[5] The poet, artist, and philosopher-symbolist were all gathered in one person, which is close to the ancient figure of a priest, narrator, and shaman. These are embodiments of the same archetype. Its activation from the collective unconscious is largely connected to the loss of the dominant religion to meet the spiritual needs of people in a period of turbulent change, when new forms are required. Between 1914 and 1930, precisely during the period of close communication with Medtner, Jung created the *Red Book*, wherein he shows himself not only as a doctor, but also as an artist, philosopher, and poet. The *Red Book* is undoubtedly a literary work in the Symbolist trend. On the other hand, Medtner found in Jung's psychology what the symbolists lacked. A medical perspective that provided for working through personal complexes would have helped many of them to organize their lives more successfully. Although Russian Symbolism was created by brilliant individuals and had a distinct personalistic orientation, proclaiming the important role of the individual in art and in history, Medtner found in Jung's concept of individuation a more advanced type of personality development and a practical method. Active imagination, invented by Jung with a therapeutic and research purpose in mind during the years of close communication with Medtner, has much in common both with the tradition of German spiritualism and with Russian Symbolism, which also have common roots and interconnections.

Search for Unity and Integrity

In times of crisis, contradictions are exacerbated in all spheres of society. This indicates that the former unifying symbols and counterbalancing systems no longer work, so the world needs renewal. The world comes out of a state of equilibrium and balance, and emerging new forms express the attempts to heal it. The crises of the early 20th and early 21st centuries have much in common. In the political sphere, the struggle among countries and civilizations is intense, and the smell of war is in the air. In the spiritual sphere, there is intense searching, religious strife, and the emergence of new cults. In the public sphere, growing social inequality provokes the rise of protest marches. If, in the early 20th century, Europe was infected with the

Marxist idea of class struggle, now the hot topics are the problem of terrorism, migrants, and globalization.

The key figure in Russian philosophy of the Silver Age was Vladimir Solovyov (1853-1900). It was his poetic and philosophical insights that became the starting point for the works of the next generation of outstanding Russian thinkers—Sergei Bulgakov, Pavel Florensky, Nikolai Berdyaev, Semyon Frank and many others. This religious and mystical branch of thought developed as a reaction to the dominance of materialism and positivism, the attitude that came along with the capitalist way of life. Vladimir Solovyov translated Plato's *Dialogues* into Russian, and it was from Plato that he derived his view of the main task of philosophy, which was to cultivate in the person a type of wisdom in which genuine universal human values— beauty, goodness, and truth—would be inextricably linked. Following Plato and Socrates, he understood philosophy as a deeply personal experience of self-knowledge and not as Hegelian intellectual exercises with abstract categories popular at that time in universities. Close connections to the spiritualistic circles of the time taught him the philosophy that was necessary for understanding his poetic or spiritually visionary experiences. Jung can also be called a thinker in the tradition of Platonic idealism, and Analytical Psychology can be considered a practical philosophy in the Platonic sense. The Platonic inseparability of epistemology, ethics, and aesthetics, revived in Solovyov's teachings and his creative work as a scientist and poet simultaneously, finds parallels with the syncretism of Jung's path—a doctor, a philosopher, and, as *The Red Book* shows, also a poet and an artist.

At the beginning of the 20th century, capitalism relied on the ideology of endless scientific and technological progress. Improving living conditions was accompanied by disillusionment with the old medieval religious worldview centered on God. Possessing a prophetic gift, Vladimir Solovyov, like many Russian intellectuals at that time, foresaw the catastrophic consequences of abandoning spirituality, destroying traditional values, and reducing all issues to economic and technical problems and solutions. His philosophy is based on the primacy of the ideal over the material. He tried to connect science and religion through philosophy. Science proceeds through empirical knowledge, whereas the religious worldview is based on faith and mystical experience. The following famous phrase belongs to Tertullian, one of the Fathers of the church: "I believe because it is absurd!" The unifying mind or its practical philosophy of "unitotality" or "universality" must reconcile the bare facts of science with the irrational tenets of faith.[6]

This intention is very close to Jung's project as expressed in *The Red Book*. In the chapters on Izdubar, science mortally wounds the old God and the mythological way of thinking. Jung saves Izdubar by hiding him in an egg, from which he is born again now renewed and renamed in the realm of depth psychology. Jung conceived of his psychology as a unity of science and religion, logos and mythos, rational and irrational. However, by giving a redemptive meaning to his enterprise and by trying to heal the split in the collective un-conscious, which was the source of the individual neuroses of the people of his time, Jung did not extend his ambitions to the political sphere. Nevertheless, the fascist regime in Germany initially aroused his interest, for it raised the myths of the ancient Germanic people from the shadows and combined mysticism and rationality.

Jung was a strong individualist and suspicious of the collective, not placing any special hopes in the political and social activity of the masses. Solovyov, on the contrary, supported the specifically Russian religious concept of positive collectivity, "*sobornost,*" which in his time was vigorously promoted by patriotic Slavophiles. On its basis he wanted to implement the third element of his project of unitotality, theocracy, which would complement Theosophy and Theurgy, completing the union of man and God on all three levels: external, internal, and secret. Solovyov in his reflections followed the same path as Plato, hoping for the literal organization of a utopia on earth. The Russian thinker imagined an ideal Christian state where contradictions among the government, the people, and God would be removed. Undoubtedly, the archetype of utopia expressed in the great Christian dream of the Kingdom of God was behind the very active social-democratic movement in Russia at that time, which in the end gave rise to the 1917 revolution. In addition, Solovyov hoped that Christianity itself would overcome its schisms and achieve ecumenical unity. Being Orthodox but not meeting with understanding in the circles of the Russian clergy, he saw Catholicism as a more promising center for such unification.

Jung also respected Catholicism in which the sacred symbols and rituals, necessary for expressing the spiritual needs of believers, were preserved. Although *The Red Book* contains many references to pagan mythology, ancient Greek and ancient Germanic, and several references to Eastern teachings, Jung considered himself a Christian. After interacting with Izdubar, he devoted several chapters of *The Red Book* to *The Imitation of Christ*, the work of Thomas a Kempis, a Catholic monk of the 15th century. This author, like Jung and Solovyov, saw the task of man in self-improvement, in the movement toward God, and in the incarnation of the God-man. In following this path, the external aspects of religion—the institution of the church and theological doctrines—are less important than the inner essence of Christianity: spiritual exercises, curbing one's ego, and cultivating love for people. Both the philosophy of Solovyov's unitotality and Jung's depth psychology followed the same path, hoping to preserve Christianity as the basis of Western civilization and the basic element of Western cultural identity.

The Eternal Feminine

The central symbol of Solovyov's teachings and his followers is Sophia, the Wisdom of God. This entire school of philosophy is called Sophiology. Although different authors had significant disagreements with respect to the understanding of Sophia, they created an organization akin to religious orders in Catholicism. The absence of a tradition of such orders in Orthodoxy was felt by them as a hindrance to the development of Orthodox theology and philosophy. The first attempts to establish the Brotherhood of St. Sophia occurred immediately after the revolution in 1919, but regular meetings became possible only in emigration and lasted from 1924 to 1944. The idea was initially approved by the Russian patriarch, but later in the emerging church milieu, the Brotherhood was tried for heresy. The meetings would begin with a special prayer to St. Sophia. The Brotherhood brought together not only a number of clerics who had a talent for theology but also secular philosophers and former politicians. The head of the Brotherhood was the philosopher Sergei Bulgakov, who actually entered the ministry, and Nikolai Berdyaev was an active participant despite the fact that he considered himself a personalistic and existentialist philosopher and explored the problems related to personality and freedom.

Philosophy literally means "love of Sophia, or wisdom." For Vladimir Solovyov, wisdom meant wholeness, and the "unitotality" he sought was embodied in the feminine image of Sophia because the feminine principle is accepting and unifying. The concept of the World Soul (*anima mundi*) of Plato, the living and intelligent principle that permeates all the phenomena of the world, merged for Solovyov with the Christian notion of St. Sophia, the Wisdom of God. On a personal level, a beloved woman, as a source of inspiration, can become the embodiment of Sophia. In the poem, "Three Meetings," he recounts his experience of such personifications of Sophia in Moscow, London, and Egypt. From his story it is not entirely clear whether he means by this a poetic metaphor, concrete women, or a spiritual contact with the spirit of Sophia. Later in his life he happened to make contact with the mystically gifted journalist Anna Schmidt from Nizhny Novgorod (a perhaps mentally ill person) who considered herself to be an incarnation of Sophia, and on her behalf he wrote "The Third Testament" for humanity.[7] His example prompted many writers and creative people of the Silver Age to seek the unity of sensory experience and spiritual revelation in the male-female relationship. As a result, their personal lives became complicated by rather intricate sexual and creative unions that expressed a general modernistic impulse toward experimentation.

In this emphasis on redemptive femininity we can see a reaction to the distortions of patriarchal culture and the emerging trend toward the emancipation of women and the strengthening of their role in society. On the other hand, the demand for the creation of national ideologies in connection with the political repartition of Europe in the early 20th century led to the turn toward the Old Russian and common Slavic roots. Matrifocality, the dominance of the maternal figure, was always, according to a number of scholars, characteristic of the Russian mentality. According to Orthodox believers, Russia is under the special protection of the Mother of God. This is reflected in Orthodox icons, where the image of the Mother of God is popular. On this basis some psychoanalysts believe in the prevalence of pre-Oedipal neuroses in the psyche of Russians.[8] The activeness of women in Russia, as well as the significant demographic imbalance of women over men, is in part related to the consequences of wars, revolutions, and reprisals in the 20th century, which reduced the male population primarily.

In Solovyov's teachings, St. Sophia receives the designation of the Eternal Feminine and merges with the image of the Mother of God. The figure of Sophia is already mentioned in the Bible. She is understood as an active creative principle of God, involved in the creation of the world. Sometimes she is identified with the Holy Spirit, sometimes with the Word coming from the Creator's mouth, sometimes with the matter of the world in the sense of the womb or matrix from which everything originated. In Constantinople, the capital of the Byzantine Empire, the famous giant temple in honor of St. Sophia was built. However, Sophia is identified there with Christ-Logos as an embodiment of divine wisdom. In Orthodox iconography, these representations of Sophia as Jesus alternate with the images of her as the dove of Holy Spirit and with an androgynous angel-like creature. The latter image is present on the famous icon "Sophia created a house for herself," where it unites Jesus, the Mother of God, John the Baptist, all saints and apostles, the church and the worshippers, and heaven and earth. In fact, Sophia forms the centre of the circle, the mandala, which emphasizes the cosmogonic aspect of this symbol.

An image of St. Sophia

According to some scholars, the most famous icon by Andrei Rublev, "Trinity" (1411), which depicts the three angels around a table, is actually dedicated to St. Sophia, both because of the circle in which the figures are inscribed and because at the center of the circle there is a cup or Grail, a feminine symbol.[9]

"The Trinity" - Andrei Rublev's famous icon showing
the three Angels being hosted by Abraham at Mambré.

In the Russian tradition, most often Sophia was understood and
portrayed as the Mother of God, who, being a virgin, that is a holy or
perfect human being, is the goal of all spiritual quests. The emphasis
is placed on the Mother of God and not on the historical Virgin Mary
as venerated in Catholicism. This maternal image resonated with the
Platonic Soul of the world (*anima mundi*) and the pagan great
goddesses of the Slavic pantheon. It was to St. Sophia that the largest
temples in Novgorod and Kiev, which were built after the adoption

of Christianity in Russia, were dedicated. In the transitional period from paganism to Christianity, the image of Sophia's universal divine wisdom was more understandable to people than the evangelical story of Jesus, which has many specific Middle Eastern details. This provided an opportunity for some Russian thinkers to consider Sophia/Mary as a fourth principle in the Divinity and even to proclaim this symbol to be the basis for the renewal of Russian Orthodoxy and Russian national identity.

We do not know whether this doctrine, popular with Russian symbolists of which Jung could not have been unaware because of his relationship with Emil Medtner, influenced Jung's fascination with the idea of quaternity as a symbol of wholeness and his reflections on the place of the Virgin Mary as that fourth principle in the Trinity. The significance of this concept is evidenced by the enthusiasm with which Jung and his students received the pope's proclamation of the dogma of the Assumption of the Virgin Mary in 1950. The subsequent strengthening of Mariology in Catholicism, actively supported by the Slavic Pope John Paul II in the second half of the 20th century, confirms Jung's prediction regarding the evolution of Christian doctrine in the direction of recognizing the importance of the Feminine.

In the *Red Book*, written long before Jung's most important works devoted to Christianity, we encounter several female images. The most important is the image of Salome, who accompanies the prophet Elijah. Later, this couple is transformed into an old scientist who keeps his blond daughter locked up in a tower. Jung understands the biblical story of John the Baptist and Salome as a story of a meeting of spirit and instinct that are drawn to each other in a quest for wholeness, although they are in an irreconcilable conflict. Perhaps one can detect a hint at Lou Andreas-Salomé, a *femme fatale* who was Nietzsche's Russian-German muse and as well as Freud's apprentice and the first female psychoanalyst and thus managed to embody the common anima of Nietzscheism and psychoanalysis. The *Red Book* was created in part as Jung's response to Nietzsche and his thesis "God is dead" and to the proclamation of the will-to-power and the Super-man as the key trends of the new time. In addition, while creating his own psychology, Jung sought to create an alternative to Freud and his influence. Finally, he himself experienced a confrontation with his Russian-Jewish anima in the person of Sabina Spielrein before the years of writing the *Red Book*. The problematic relationship between a woman and a hero on his way are mentioned by Jung in the references to the couples Faust and Gretchen and Parsifal and Kundry. Only in the final chapters of *The Red Book* do we see a harmonious union of man and woman in the elderly Philemon and Baucis. This reconciliation with the anima is preceded by long conversations with his soul, where she appears both in a female form and in the images of a bird and a snake.

On the whole, *The Red Book* is a masculine piece of work centered on a main male character who is looking for a masculine image of the self, in contrast to the search of the Russian thinkers who sought contact with the self as the Eternal Feminine. But Jung's theory and Russian Sophiology have common origins, apart from Christianity and Platonism. They include the Gnostic treatises of early Christianity, in which the mythology of Sophia, including the highest and lowest Sophia (Achamoth), who gave birth to the evil demiurge Yaldabaoth, is developed. Gnostic teachings emerged during the crisis period of transition from pagan antiquity to Christian monotheism. During this period of active spiritual creativity, not yet constrained by the rigid frames of the canon and dogma, every stratum of society and every country sought its formula for a new faith best suited to its cultural unconscious. Many educated people from priestly circles claimed a more esoteric and secret version of religion, combining Christian eschatology and ethics with elements of ancient cosmogony, astrology, magic, and healing. Gnosticism, which inspired both Jung and Russian philosophers, gives us living evidence of individuation in and through religious activities.

Another source common to Jungian psychology and Russian Sophiology lies in the various mystical teachings of the Middle Ages, among which it is worth mentioning the works of the German visionary Jacob Boehme. Boehme is cited many times in Jung's published writings and in *The Red Book*.[10] Nikolai Berdyaev especially appreciated Boehme and considered himself his successor. It is possible that it is in Boehme's concept of the Abyss (*Ungrund*) as the dark, irrational, unified basis of everything that one must look for the origins of Jung's concept of the unconscious. Boehme understood Sophia as the ideal, pure spiritual prototype of the human, calling her "Eternal Virginity" and "Virgin Wisdom."[11] Boehme is considered one of the founders of Western theosophy and the highest authority in the hermetic and occult traditions. Boehme's works were translated into Russian rather early. Many figures of the Silver Age were Freemasons, who considered themselves to be followers of Boehme's teachings. Boehme's method, which was the immersion in visions inspired by the desire to comprehend Sophia, Divine Wisdom, can be considered a precursor to both Vladimir Solovyov's "dates with Sophia" and Jung's method of active imagination.

In turn, Jung's development of the psychological concept of anima helped Russian philosophers in comprehending Sophia, as it added scientific and clinical facets on the individual psychological level. It is known that Vyacheslav Ivanov (1866-1949) came to Zurich to get acquainted with Jung's works, the fruit of which was his essay "Anima."[12]

The Dionysian Element

Vyacheslav Ivanov organized gatherings of symbolists in his so-called Tower, a round corner room on the top floor of his house in St. Petersburg. This tower has direct parallels with Jung's tower on the lake of Zurich in Bollingen. Ivanov was the main Russian researcher on the cult of Dionysus in Greece and an advocate of the Dionysian element in art. In this respect, he was influenced by Nietzsche. He understood symbolism as a literary trend that uses universal mythological motifs, among which he considered the religious themes of death and rebirth, sacrifice on the way to spiritual transformation, and mystical love conquering death to be the most important. Symbolic art for him is born from the archetypal layer of the collective soul and must possess a mysterious power, creating numinous experiences. Dionysus is born twice, as a man and as a deity. He is a suffering god, torn to pieces and reborn again. That is why he is the deity of initiation, of mystery, of healing, and therefore of any work in the genre of drama or tragedy.

Such Dionysian energies permeate Jung's entire *Red Book*. By experiencing classical and personal mythological themes, Jung goes through a great deal of suffering and frequently finds new meaning in it. Several times in his visions he goes into the desert and even descends to hell like Orpheus, Dionysus, and Jesus; he also hangs in a tree like Odin. One can say that Jung's image of the self was either Dionysian, Orphic, or Mithraic. He even switches to the language of a poetic anthem imitating ancient poetry, which Vyacheslav Ivanov loved so much, when he describes the rebirth of God from an egg and refers to the orphic Phanes, who was identified with the First Dionysus or Dionysus-Zagreus.[13] Jung's friend Karl Kerenyi wrote a famous book titled *Dionysus: The Prototype of Inexhaustible Life*. Dionysus is the spirit of life itself, not just one of the archetypes but their origin, the basic element of any psychological structure. Therefore, any movement, any change in the psyche, cannot do without the involvement of Dionysus. At the end of *The Red Book*, choosing the path of Life and not the path of Love, Jung gives priority to Dionysus over Christ, preferring the primary to the secondary, choosing the eternal basis from which all forms are continuously generated.[14]

Vyacheslav Ivanov relied not only on intellectual searching but also on his personal visionary and spiritual experiences. Another source of his inspiration was the people's reform movements within Russian Orthodoxy. According to some estimates, up to a million people in Russia at the beginning of the 20th century were involved in "*Khlysty*," which was how various sectarian movements were defined in official reports. They have some resemblance with flagellants. The popular practice of these sects was to create exciting rituals with music, singing, and dancing, whose purpose was to induce ecstatic states. In this process, Jesus, the Mother of God, or the Holy Spirit supposedly settled in the most gifted adepts. In this capacity they gave instructions to the flock, and sometimes the rituals ended with sexual orgies, which were intended to remove the contradictions between the spirit and the flesh. The Dionysian character of such practices was obvious. The Russian symbolists were familiar with *Khlysty*; in any case, they invited their religious leaders to carry out the rituals.[15]

The liberation of Eros was a common theme in symbolist circles and psychoanalysis, which ensured their attraction to each other. Not only Berdyaev but also Ivanov and Vysheslavtsev studied Jung in a most detailed way.[16] Ivanov's other companion, Lev Shestov, the Russian existentialist philosopher who was called the "Russian Nietzsche," while in emigration became a friend of Max Eitington, a Russian who in 1909 defended his medical thesis in Zurich where he met Jung and joined the psychoanalytical movement. Eitington became an important figure in Freud's circle and in 1925 headed the International Psychoanalytic Association, having done much for publishing the works of the master.

This attempt to combine the spiritual search of the intellectual elite with the people's search for religious renewal resembles the episode in *The Red Book* where Jung meets the phantom of the Anabaptists. This sect was very similar to the Russian *Khlysty*. The Anabaptists were radical Protestants in the 16th century who, among other things, advocated baptism in adulthood, that is, a conscious coming to faith. They were especially active in Switzerland, not far from Küsnacht where Jung lived. Therefore, Jung felt a special connection with them. Their interpretation of true Christianity, as implying the collectivization of property and the community of wives, can be understood only now through the events of the 20th century with its social and sexual revolutions. In the 16th century, their initiatives were brutally suppressed. Seeking a way out of the spiritual crisis with the formula of personal salvation, they developed cultural forms for the economic and family life of the society too innovative for their time but at the same time ancient and originating from the antique Dionysian layer of the collective unconscious. This paradox of modernistic initiatives is sometimes called "Archeomodernism"— offering the new, they in fact want a return to the old.[17]

Duty to the Dead

Jung's works are permeated with the topic of the duty of those alive to the Dead. In 1916, at the height of the First World War, he wrote an imitation of a Gnostic treatise, "The Seven Sermons to the Dead." The text explains to the Dead the meaning of Abraxas, the deity of wholeness, so that they can find the way to peace. Gems with the images of Abraxas were placed on the chests of the first Christians so that their souls would be saved by Christ and their bodies would be resurrected after His second coming.[18] In the transition period, until Christianity developed its own symbolism and rituals, it actively borrowed elements of ancient cults and mysteries. It is known that on the altars near the images of Jesus were often placed the images of Dionysus, Orpheus, and even the famous wisdom teacher Apollonius of Tyre, to whom Vladimir Solovyov dedicated his first published article.[19] When Christianity degenerated into an external structure of power and a social institution and its doctrines became obdurate, it lost the ability to teach to the believers the meaning of Abraxas, that is, gaining wholeness.

The importance of the Abraxas image, which is mentioned several times in *The Red Book*, is shown in the episode when Jung made a ring with the image of Abraxas, placed it in a glass of wine, and performed a magical ritual similar to the sacrament, giving his colleague Olga Froebe-Kaptein a drink of it.[20] Jung explained that the self made him perform such a ritual. Since on the shield of Abraxas or on the side of the figure was usually written "IAH," one of the names of Dionysus, Abraxas, signifying the fullness of the cyclical transformations, was one of the aspects of this deity of death and rebirth.

Although the theme of the Dead echoes Jung's spiritualistic fascination, symbolically they mean the whole of humanity. The spiritual search of countless generations, their hopes and disappointments, inventions and revelations, constitute the contents of the collective unconscious. Every new generation must find answers to the problems left by the previous generations, i.e. "the Dead." Accepting the baton, we support the line of continuity. This gives us a feeling of rootedness, connection with the earth, ancestors, and kinship; it gives support to our identity.

In Russian religious philosophy there is figure of Nikolai Fedorov, who exerted influence on Tolstoy, Dostoyevsky, Solovyov, and many other thinkers. His utopian teaching is an unusual mixture of Christianity with faith in the progress of science. It is possible that he reacted strongly to the contradictions between the religious and scientific worldviews and tried to reconcile them in himself.[21] He considered the task of science to be the ultimate victory over death and the resurrection of the dead, thereby completing the mission of Christ. The direction of his ideas has much in common with the optimism of the Catholic theologian-evolutionist Teilhard de Chardin, who also believed that scientific and technological progress realized the divine purpose. Fedorov can be considered a cosmic philosopher and futurist, the forerunner of the theory of the noosphere and transhumanism.

Although Fedorov's teaching with his literalism of resurrection resembles necromancy, it is based on the acute sense of lineal duty to the dead ancestors, which is extrapolated to all generations and all of humanity. He understands the Christian idea of the risen God and the victory of love over death as the task set before humanity by God to overcome the splitting between spirit and matter through the final spiritualization of matter and the reversal of the direction of the latter from destruction and decay toward original integrity and unity. With the scientific anti-mysticism declared by him, Fedorov emotionally touches us exactly with his mystical faith. Jung did not reach such a scale in his relations with the dead and the kin, but Fedorov's feelings would have been close to his.

Reassessment of Solar Consciousness and Deconstruction

Jung mentions in *The Red Book* a particularly important dream where he participates in the murder of Siegfried, being in league with a certain aborigine, a black man. Siegfried, whose name means "Conqueror" and who is the son of Sigmund, a child of Wotan, is an important character in the "Song of the Nibelungs." It was he who killed the dragon. On a personal level, this dream refers to Jung's rupture with Sigmund Freud, who called him a "blond Siegfried" and at first prophesied to him the laurels of his chief heir, "the Crown Prince of psychoanalysis." On the archetypal level, Siegfried is one of the typical solar heroes in mythology. Abandoning the attitude of strengthening the ego, the dominant attitude in the patriarchal, rational, extraverted, spiritual, and conscious culture of the time, is important for solving the midlife crisis when the development of the opposite attitude is necessary for achieving balance. Therefore, the alliance with the aborigine in his dream symbolizes an alliance with nature, earthy, chthonic, feminine, irrational, the union with the unconscious. In *The Red Book*, the solar figures are defeated many times: the hermit Ammonius, the prophet Elijah, the god Izdubar; whereas the dark figure of the magician Philemon is triumphant in the finale. Through the encounter with this image of the self, Jung learns to respect the mystery, to live in not-knowing, to draw inspiration from myth and the irrational. But on this path of transformation, Jung is forced to go through sufferings many times. In *The Red Book*, there are many destructive and cruel scenes, the meaning of which is in the deconstruction of the former personal attitudes.

This need to deconstruct not only their own attitudes but all the outdated patterns of culture was acutely felt by Russian philosophers and creative people at the turn of the century. The main ideologist of anarchism, Mikhail Bakunin, declared: "Destruction is creativity."[22] The anarchists were the most powerful political force in Russia, playing a big role in all revolutions. Because of them, the label of anarchic and aggressive revolutionaries was fixed in European stereotypes toward Russia. Since Bakunin lived a considerable part of his life in emigration in Switzerland, having obtained citizenship there, it can be assumed that Jung was well-acquainted with this understanding of destruction, and it could have affected his concept of psychological transformation. Another source of Jung's view can be considered in the concept of "*destrudo*" by Sabina Spielrein, who proposed such a name for the second instinct in the psyche, the opposite of the libido. It is believed that it was her ideas that prompted

Freud to formulate the opposition of "Eros" and "Thanatos."[23] Sabina Spielrein with her strange sexual and aggressive fantasies was a typical representative of decadence with its deconstructivistic pathos. It was from decadence that symbolism was born as a movement in philosophy.

Another derivation of decadence in the field of art came from the Russian avant-garde. It consisted of several diverse movements, among which the world-famous became the Russian representatives of abstract art, suprematism, constructivism, and futurism. It is interesting that in the year when Jung had a dream about Siegfried and began to write his *Red Book*, Kazimir Malevich created his *Black Square* for the scenery of Mikhail Matyushin's cube-futurist opera *Victory over the Sun*.[24] The well-known poet Vladimir Mayakovsky also participated in the work of this group. The new cannot be built without the destruction of the old, it was said. The sun in the opera symbolizes the old order, the old worldview. The antithesis to the yellow shining sun is a black square or a black cube. The opera decisively calls the audience to stand on the side of the black square. In this experimental theatrical performance, the plot, the meaning, the costumes of the actors, the arrangement of the stage space, and finally the speech itself are subject to destruction, turning into an incoherent set of sounds. As in Jung's quest, we see here the expression of the need to release destruction for the sake of deconstruction of solar consciousness and the creation of a new, more balanced type of consciousness.

The opera was staged again in Moscow in 2013, a hundred years after its first production. Perhaps it reflects the connection of times, the repetition of the crisis and the anxiety that accompanies it. Of course, the postmodernism of the late 20th and early 21st centuries did much of what modernism failed to do 100 years ago. It weakened the tendency to phallocentrism, constantly renewed by capitalist competition. It taught that there can be not one truth but many, or none at all. It taught us to appreciate more questioning, less affirming. To subjectivism, relativism, and pluralism, it introduced an element of irony, play, and relaxation. However, it is difficult to keep the attitude toward everything as jokes, experiments, and simulacra, when vital problems such as terrorism or global ecological catastrophes become aggravated. In these conditions, in my opinion, the discourse of Jung and Russian religious philosophers, saturated with a serious attitude toward destruction and suffering on the way to finding new solutions, becomes once again relevant.

Conclusion

At the beginning of the 21st century, we turn to the events of a hundred years ago that changed the whole course of world history. The October Revolution of 1917 was preceded by an unprecedented flourishing of culture called the Silver Age or the Russian Renaissance. Today in Russia, many creative people continue to draw inspiration from the works of that period and are trying to maintain continuity with those great Russian thinkers of the past.

Jung, during the period of writing the *Red Book*, was well aware of the spiritual quest of the Russian intelligentsia. In turn, Russian symbolists were actively interested in psychoanalysis in general and studied Jung's theories in particular. Therefore, one can talk about mutual influence. Their search was parallel in many aspects. They relied on Platonic philosophy, Gnosticism, occult teachings and spiritualism. They acutely felt the collective neurosis—the general worldview crisis of the epoch—and tried to find an individual formula for its resolution. On this path they created works of a synthetic nature, where philosophical reflections were combined with poetry and prose, and sometimes with music, theater, and painting. They believed that a deeply personal sensual immersion in myths and symbols is the best way to gain new meanings both for the individual and for society as a whole. They tried to preserve Christianity as the basis of the identity of the European person. In the time of dominance of materialistic science, a religious attitude needs to be renewed in order to better meet the needs of people. They considered religious philosophy and depth psychology to be the means for this renewal.

Endnotes

[1] Mikhail Shishkin, *Russian Switzerland* (Moscow: Vagrius, 1999) (in Russian).

[2] Richard Noll, *The Aryan Christ: The Secret Life of Carl Jung* (Moscow: Reflbook, 2006) (in Russian).

[3] Magnus Junggren, *Russian Mephistopheles: The Life and Work of E. Medtner* (St. Petersburg: Academic Project, 2001) (in Russian).

[4] Evgeniy Evtushenko, *Soviet Russian poetry*, ed. Krementsova L.P. (Leningrad: Education, 1988) (in Russian).

[5] Emily Medtner, "The Portrait in the Frame of Mutual Recognition," in New Spring, 2001, № 2–3, C. 96–128, 2002; № 4, C. 108–135 (in Russian).

[6] Vladimir Solovyov, *Reading about God-Manhood* (St. Petersburg: Art Literature, 1994) (in Russian).

[7] Anna Schmidt, *The Third Testament* (St. Petersburg: Almanac «Petropol», «Alexandra» publ., 1993) (in Russian).

[8] Daniel Rancour-Laferriere, ed., *Russian Literature and Psychoanalysis* (Amsterdam: John Benjamins Publishing Company, 1989).

[9] V.G. Brusova, *Sophia the Wisdom of God in Ancient Literature and Art* (Moscow: White City, 2006) (in Russian).

[10] C.G. Jung, *The Red Book: Liber Novus*, ed. Sonu Shamdasani, trans. John Peck, Mark Kyburz, and Sonu Shamdasani (New York, NY: W.W. Norton, 2009), 305.

[11] Jakob Böhme, *Aurora* (Create Space Independent Publishing Platform, 2016).

[12] Vyacheslav Ivanov, *Anima* (St. Petersburg: Faculty of Philology and Arts SPBU, 2009) (in Russian).

[13] Jung, *The Red Book*, 301.

[14] Ibid., 327.

[15] Alexander Etkind, *Whip. Sects, Literature and Revolution* (Moscow: New Literary Observer, 1998) (in Russian).

[16] Boris Vysheslavtsev, *The Ethics of Transfigured Eros* (Moscow: Republica, 1994) (in Russian).

[17] Irina Shevelenko, *Modernism as Archaism* (Moscow: New Literary Observer 2017) (in Russian).

[18] Campbell Bonner, *Studies in Magical Amulets, chiefly Graeco-Egyptian* (Ann Arbor, MI: University of Michigan Press, 1950).

[19] Vladimir Solovyov, *The Mythological Process in Ancient Paganism*, in *The Collected Works of Vladimir Sergeyevich Solovyov* (St. Petersburg: Education, 1911-1914) (in Russian).

[20] Jean Borella, *The Restoration of the Holy Science* (St. Petersburg: Vladimir Dal, 2016) (in Russian).

[21] Nikolay Fedorov, *Works* (Moscow: Thought, 1982) (in Russian).

[22] Mikhail Bakunin, *The Reaction in Germany* (1842), in Bakunin, M.A., *Selected Philosophical Writings and Letters* (Moscow: Progress, 1987).

[23] S.F. Sirotkin, *Sabina Spielrein. Materials for the Bibliography* (Izhevsk: ERGO, 2006) (in Russian).

[24] Kazimir Malevich, *Articles, manifestos, theoretical essays and other works (1913—1929)* (Moscow: Gileya, 1995) (in Russian).

India in *The Red Book:*
Overtones and Undertones

Noa Schwartz Feuerstein

Introduction

Jung's lifelong relationship with India alternated sharply between affinity and alienation.[1] By the time he embarked on the *Red Book*[2] project, the many volumes of the series *Sacred Books of the East*[3] filled his library and served as a vital source of inspiration for his writing. Jung's esteem for Indian thought is likewise manifest in his contemporaneous "scientific" writings, in *Wandlungen und Symbole der Libido* (1913) where he cites early Indian texts in support of his theory of libido,[4] and again, in *Psychological Types* (1921) in support of his theory of opposites.[5] Over time, however, Jung's scientific side (which he called Personality No. 1) came to dominate his spiritual side (Personality No. 2),[6] so much so that he warned the West against adopting Eastern wisdom and its symbols. Nevertheless, on the threshold of death, India returned to Jung's psyche in the form of yogi-like dream-figures, representative of the self.[7]

The Red Book is replete with overt references to ancient Indian literature, a number of which will be reviewed in the first part of this essay. That Jung should have described this influence in "the *Red Book* years" later as an "intensive unconscious relation to India in the Red Book"[8] is puzzling. Thus, the second part will explore hidden correspondences between Jung's essential ideas in *The Red Book* and ancient Indian thought.

Indian Overtones in *The Red Book*

Jung's visions in *The Red Book* are syncretistic, featuring a wide range of mythological images: Greek, Jewish, Gnostic, Egyptian, and Indian.

What follows is an exploration of certain Indian sources and symbols in *The Red Book* and the way these enhance Jung's intrapsychic processes.

Elijah, Salome, Buddha and Kali

In Jung's vision of a dramatic encounter with the prophet Elijah and his blind daughter, the lethal Salome, "Buddha sitting rigidly in a circle of fire [and Kali]—a many-armed bloody Goddess—..."[9] suddenly appear. Here, Indian divinities are conjoined with Judeo-Christian figures to amplify the conflict between "forethinking" and "pleasure" in Jung's psyche.[10]

Philemon and Krishna

Jung draws a parallel between the Greek Philemon and the Indian god Krishna, both of whom promise to redeem the world, which is threatened with the rise of evil. Philemon, Jung's spiritual guide, was the only human being who opened the door to Zeus in an age of evil and thereby saved humanity and attained eternal life. As World War I raged all around, Jung writes consolingly, "Only after the darkest night will it be day."[11] Together with a monumental drawing of Philemon, he then quotes the words of Krishna to Arjuna from the Bhagavad-Gītā: "Whenever there is a decline of the law and an increase in iniquity, then I put forth myself. ... for the establishment of the law, I am born in every age."[12]

Jung here identifies Krishna's promise to Arjuna with Philemon's promise of redemption in an era of darkness and bloodshed. Jung adopts Philemon as his spiritual guide, and, in like manner, Krishna becomes the divine teacher of Arjuna.[13]

Izdubar

Although Jung creates the divine hero Izdubar out of elements from both the Near and the Far East, it is through Indian texts and images that he finds the resolution to his conflictual private myth.

In this vision, Jung, while wandering to the East, meets a giant hero named Izdubar, who is making his way westward to the sea. Izdubar tells Jung that he is going to join the setting sun, accompany it on its nocturnal voyage, and become an immortal god. Jung explains that the sun does not set in the sea but only appears to do so as the round earth revolves around it. Hearing this, Izdubar collapses, and he accuses Jung of poisoning him with science, which refutes his faith in the gods and immortality. Jung admits that science has killed the omnipotent and immortal gods of the West.

Izdubar lies helpless, and the two spend a desolate night on a mountaintop. In an effort to comfort Izdubar, Jung tells him that there are two different truths: "Our truth is that which comes to us from the knowledge of outer things. The truth of your priests is that which comes to you from inner things."[14]

Next day, Jung persuades Izdubar that since he is a fantasy creature, he will be able to carry him, light as feather, to the West and cure him. When they reach the West, Jung makes Izdubar so tiny that he is able to hide him inside an egg. After a while, as he waits anxiously for Izdubar to hatch, he begins to chant healing spells inspired by the Vedas. Suddenly, an enormous flame issues forth from the egg, and Jung falls to his knees and shuts his eyes, fearful that he will be blinded by the glare. It is Izdubar who has returned as a god from his nocturnal voyage with the sun while Jung had thought he was lying helplessly inside the egg.

The story and its illustrations are filled with references to the Brahmanas and Vedas. Here are several examples, one of which I shall consider shortly in greater depth.

1. The section where Izdubar lies paralyzed is illustrated by the picture of a man carrying a huge wheel over his head. Beneath the picture Jung wrote: "Atharva-Veda 4:1:4."[15] This is a reference to a healing chant that restores vitality by invoking the divine powers of the gods Indra, Agni, Sarasvatī, and others. Thus, having earlier asserted his crippling scientific position to Izdubar, Jung now finds himself turning to the magical healing methods of India! The fatal encounter with the pagan hero has forced him to free himself from the grip of scientific Personality No. 1 and to look for support in

Personality No. 2 and the realm of the occult against which Freud had cautioned him.

2. In the illustration for another hymn, a yogi with closed eyes sits among the flames of ritual lamps.[16] The yogi represents the meditative state by means of which Jung rallies his spiritual and imaginative powers in order to revive Izdubar.[17]

3. To illustrate the fifth hymn of healing,[18] Jung drew a flame issuing out of the jaws of a primeval snake in dark waters. Under this picture Jung wrote "brahmaṇaspati," the name of the god who represents the power of prayer and the element of light that conquers darkness.[19] In this way Jung creates a relationship of reciprocity between his own inner images and the ancient Indian image of *Brahmaṇaspati*.

4. The hymn in which Jung describes his cosmic search for Izdubar ends with the words "We looked for you in our heads and hearts. And we found you in the egg."[20] Under the hymn he writes "Hiraṇyagarbha."[21] *Hiraṇyagarbha*[22] (one of the creator god's appellations, meaning the golden source of the world, *hiraṇya* = golden, *garbha* = egg or fetus) is an image with multiple meanings that echo all that was going on in Jung's inner world at the time. Izdubar, who emerges from the egg as a glorious deity, corresponds to *Hiraṇyagarbha* as creator god[23] and to *Hiraṇyagarbha* as 'Self.'[24]

Agni, the fire god, threatens to devour his creator, and Izdubar emerges as a blinding flame

Under the picture in which Jung bows down to the enormous flame that has emerged from the egg he writes, "catapatha-brāhmaṇam 2.2.4,"[25] referring to the cosmogenic occurrence that precipitated the ritual of *Agnihotra*. In the myth, Prajāpati is overcome by an urge to reproduce because he is alone in the world, and this causes him to generate Agni, the god of fire, from his mouth. Too late he realizes that the destructive Agni is about to devour him and in order to survive, he offers himself up as a sacrifice to Agni.[26]

Jung alludes to this myth as a source of semiconscious inspiration from which and to which he brings Izdubar. Fearing for

Izdubar's life, Jung broods over the egg and prays for his rebirth, but much to his surprise, he finds himself lying on the floor, blinded by the power of the god he himself has generated and whom he had believed to be a creature of fantasy. Jung, much to his horror, discovers that Izdubar has returned from his journey as an autonomous being, a blazing god, who has now become an enormous blinding flame. Facing the numinous god that has emerged from him, Jung feels the need to enact Prajāpati's ritual. The Indian myth expresses Jung's horror as he fell before the flaming god. "Agni turned towards him with open mouth; and he (Prajāpati) being terrified, his own greatness departed from him."[27]

The myth of Izdubar describes the paradox of an inner reality that seems to be mere fantasy but is in fact real and destructive. Fantasy may consume the fantasizer:

> But I have caught him, he who has been feared since time immemorial; I have made him small and my hands surround him. That is the demise of gods ... when I thought that I caught the mighty one and held him in my cupped hands, he was the sun itself.[28]

This amplification sheds light on the conflict that is tearing Jung apart. He, the rational scientific man, kills the god without, and then, as the spiritual man of faith, he prays to the gods for healing and inadvertently gives birth to a god within himself no less mighty than his predecessor. This symbolism is the product of the "transcendent function," the inner creative, non-rational power that reconciles inner opposites.

Indian Undertones in *The Red Book*

Jung's "intensive unconscious relation to India in the Red Book"[29] leads us to the hidden presence of ancient Indian thought as reflected in three aspects of *The Red Book* journey: its purpose, the means for completing it, and the fruits of the journey. This is attested by the following quotations from the Upaniṣads, the Brāhmaṇas and the Bhagavad-Gītā.

At the beginning of his *Red Book*, Jung sets out in search of his soul and cries out to her: "My soul, where are you? Do you hear me? ... I call you—are you there? I have returned, I am here again."[30] On his journey Jung receives guidance and inspiration from ancient Indian wisdom and learns about the necessary psychic means to reach his soul.

Detachment from the sensory world

Jung realizes that, in order to find his soul, he must first detach himself from external reality and everything he knows. Indeed, many years later he affirmed that during this time he had performed "frequent exercises in the emptying of consciousness."[31] In *The Red Book,* Jung explains his rationale for doing so: "He whose desire turns away from outer things, reaches the place of the soul."[32] This idea is repeated innumerable times in the Upaniṣads, for instance: "It is when they come to know this Self that Brahmins give up the desire for sons, for wealth and for the worlds."[33]

By turning his gaze and desires inward and emptying the contents of his consciousness, Jung manifests what he describes later on in *Psychological Types,* where he writes that Eastern introversion seeks inner knowledge, in contrast to the extraverted West, which turns the libido outward as desire in the material world.[34] Jung defines the practice of Indian yoga there as an introversion of libido.[35] Here, Jung describes the process he underwent in his *Red Book* journey: "The yogi seeks to induce this concentration and accumulation of libido by systematically withdrawing attention (libido) both from external objects and from interior psychic states, in a word, from the opposites. The elimination of sense-perception and the blotting out of conscious contents enforce a lowering of consciousness and activation of the contents of the unconscious, i.e., the primordial images, which, because of their universality and immense antiquity, possess a cosmic and suprahuman character."[36]

Sacrificing the Ego

In one of his early visions, Jung slays the hero Siegfried. He explains the murder as a "sacrifice of the ego" intended to make room for the birth of the new god, the god within, the self that unifies all opposites: "Oh that Siegfried, blond and blue-eyed, the German hero, had to fall by my hand ... He had everything in himself that I treasured ... my power, my boldness, my pride."[37] The slaying of Siegfried, which shook Jung to the core, was necessary in order to open up his consciousness in preparation for a journey to the depths and heights and beyond all that which is ruled by the ego. In ancient India, sacrifice was understood as a transformative act that leads the sacrificer away from a current identity to a different spiritual plane and expands his consciousness. The Rgveda[38] tells of the sacrifice of primal man, *purusa*, from whose limbs the entire cosmos was created. Jung had interpreted the sacrifice of *purusa* in 1912 as a necessary stage in the development of human consciousness. Moreover, sacrifice makes possible its transformation into cosmic consciousness: "... according to the teaching of the Upanisads. ... This new state beyond the human one is again attained through a sacrifice, ... which has cosmic significance."[39]

Nonetheless, Jung was aware of the anxiety involved in the sacrifice of the ego, as he wrote years later in his introduction to the *Tibetan Book of the Dead*: "Fear of self-sacrifice lurks deep in every ego. ... No one who strives for selfhood (individuation) is spared this dangerous passage, for that which is feared also belongs to the wholeness of the self."[40] This anxiety is apparently what later prompted the caution against embracing the culture of India, which affirms the sacrifice of the ego. At the same time, detachment from the sensory world and the sacrifice of the ego enabled Jung to hear the "spirit of the depths" calling him to set off on his journey and leave behind the "spirit of this time."

The Surrender of External Knowledge

The "spirit of the depths" compels Jung to surrender the external knowledge and reality that are informed by "the spirit of this time."

This call is the point of departure for the journey: "The spirit of the depths has subjugated all pride and arrogance ... He took away my belief in science, he robbed me of the joy of explaining and ordering things ... But the spirit of this time stepped up to me and laid before me huge volumes which contained all my knowledge. Their pages were made of ore, and a steel stylus had engraved inexorable words in them ... and spoke to me and said: 'What you speak is madness'."[41]

Jung experiences this call as a breakdown of his faith and joy in scientific understanding. This experience is reminiscent of the crisis of the Upaniṣadic sages in their perpetual search for the self, the true knowledge (vidyā).[42] Jung's torments resemble those suffered by the sage Nārada some 3,000 years earlier. Though he is thoroughly proficient in all 17 sciences, Nārada tells his teacher that knowledge has no value: "All that, bhagavān (sir), I have studied. Here I am, a man who knows all the Vedic formulas, but is ignorant of the self (ātman). And I have heard that those who know the Self pass across sorrow. Here I am, bhagavān, a man full of sorrow. Please, take me across to the other side of sorrow."[43]

Throughout *The Red Book* Jung is caught up in a struggle to release his grip on science,[44] those "huge volumes which contained all my knowledge," yet his soul persists, demanding that he "... become serious ... take your leave from science. There is too much childishness in it. ... Science is too superficial, mere language, mere tools."[45]

Jung's soul describes science in terms that are virtually identical with those used by Uddalaka, the Upaniṣadic sage, to teach his arrogant son that any objective definition that detaches him from the oneness of his source and all-embracing essence is merely "a verbal handle, a name."[46]

The demands of the soul leave Jung in a state of turmoil. He fears for his sanity at the prospect of giving up his external knowledge and the habit of differentiation and definition. This fear, a recurrent theme in *The Red Book*[47] may well explain his later distancing himself from the Indian yearning for Oneness. This conflict between science and the other kind of knowledge is represented as fatal in the encounter between East and West. The Eastern hero Izdubar with his mythological knowledge is poisoned by Jung's Western scientific knowledge.

Waiting

Yet another challenge that Jung meets on his journey is the distress of waiting: "... my soul spoke to me and said: 'Wait.' I heard the cruel word. ... Where is your patience? Your time has not yet run its course. ... Can you not wait? Should everything fall into your lap ripe and finished?"[48]

The Upaniṣads also teach that a long wait inevitably precedes knowledge of ātman (the self). For example, in the *Chāndogya Upaniṣad*, Indra, messenger of the gods, and Virochaṇa, messenger of the demons, arrive at Prajāpati's ashram, seeking knowledge of ātman. Prajāpati makes them wait 32 years before answering their request. The demon takes his leave after the first stage, thinking he has already achieved true knowledge of the self, the knowledge that "your body is your self," but Indra waits another 32 years until he learns that his self is the self that lives "in the dreams of the night." Thirty-two years later, he learns that the self is that which exists in "dreamless sleep," but Indra is not satisfied with this answer either. This time he only has to wait another five years to receive the answer about the true nature of the self: "That is why people say: 'For 101 years did Maghavan (Indra) live as a celibate student with Prajā-pati'."[49] Real knowledge demands waiting and is not found in the intellect but is rather experiential and transformative and requires years of turning inward. Jung realizes that in order to arrive at the deeper self he must wait in utter loneliness for spiritual ripening.

True knowledge, as taught by the pundit, Professor Gangadhar Bhat, is fourfold: It requires learning from a teacher, discussion with others, reflection, and waiting for the endowment of understanding.[50]

Non-intentionality

The soul continues to reproach Jung for his impatience and desire-driven intentionality: "You are full, yes, you teem with intentions and desirousness!—Do you still not know that the way to truth stands open only to those without intentions?"[51] Jung ascribes this under-standing to the wisdom of the East. As he wrote immediately upon stopping writing in the *Red Book*, Western civilization turns everything into method and intention, as opposed to the East where we find "the art of letting things happen, action through non-action, letting go of oneself."[52] Or, as clearly stated in the Bhagavad-Gītā: "Your action is for action alone, never for the results."[53]

Arrogance

Over and over in *The Red Book,* Jung struggles to rid himself of his pride and arrogance. When the heroes of the Upaniṣads confront this same challenge, they discover that true recognition of the self brings a release from arrogance, and the inflated ego finds humility upon encountering the self. Thus, in a Upaniṣadic story, the sage Uddalaka bursts the inflated ego of his arrogant son Śvetaketu, who thinks he knows everything, by showing him the great truth he does not know, namely, ātman, the self. "You are that"—*tat tvam asi* he tells him.[54]

So too, Jung tells his soul when she confronts him with his arrogance: "Your truth is hard. I want to lay down my vanity before you since it blinds me. ... I did not know that I am your vessel, empty without you but brimming over with you."[55]

Jung's redemptive understanding parallels the Upaniṣadic "You are that"—"you" being that self which is greater than you are. "You" possess the inward knowledge that the ego is finite and the self within is infinite.

Turning the gaze inward – to the soul – the self-ātman

Jung's search for the soul shares certain features with the quest described in the Upaniṣads:

A. Turning the gaze inward is essential to the Upaniṣadic teachings, and its importance is repeated countless times in the dialogues between master and pupil and by the sages themselves, who all aspire to reach beyond the manifest realm to the hidden essence of the soul, eternal, unchanging, invisible, imperishable, unaffected by the laws of the body and the material world. "The ātman that is free from evil, free from old age and death, free from sorrow, hunger and thirst, the self whose desires and intentions are real—that is the ātman you should try to discover."[56]

B. By turning his gaze inward, Jung came to experience a revolutionary understanding of the soul: "I thought and spoke much of the soul. ... I did not consider that my soul cannot be the object of my judgment and knowledge; much more are my judgment and knowledge objects of my soul. ... Hence, I had to speak to my soul as to something far off and unknown, which did not exist through me, but through whom I existed."[57] The objective reality of the soul as prime subject elucidates Jung's affinity with Indian wisdom. In his new state of consciousness Jung understands that the essence of the soul eludes the materialistic and dualistic empirical approach because its very existence is the primal reality. Hence, it is the basis through which outward reality, being secondary to the soul, is apprehended, and it is the soul that gives rise to existence and apprehends it. A similar description of ātman is found in the Upaniṣads: "This Self (ātman) of yours ... he sees but he cannot be seen, he hears but he can't be heard, he thinks but he can't be thought of, he perceives but he cannot be perceived. ... It is this self of yours who is the inner controller."[58] "By what means can one perceive the perceiver?"[59]

In like manner, Jung writes in *The Red Book* about the inner controller, the "god within": "Thus the coming God will become the lord of the world. This happens first in me. The supreme meaning becomes my lord and infallible commander."[60]

C. It is this "god within," the self, the unperceived perceiver whose essence is the light that Jung is seeking in his *Red Book*: "*You would like to hear of him who was not darkened by the shadow of earth, but illuminated it, who saw the thoughts of all, and whose thoughts no one guesses, who possessed in himself the meaning of all things, and whose meanings nothing could express.*"[61]

There is much written about the illuminating ātman in the Upaniṣads, as in the dialogue between King Janaka and Yājñavalkya the sage. Janaka desires to learn the source of light in man since all sources of light are ephemeral, and Yājñavalkya is forced to reveal the truth to him about the luminous and absolute nature of ātman: "Ātman is the source of his light. It is by the light of ātman that a person sits down, goes about, does his work and returns."[62]

The Bhagavad-Gītā, which Jung knew well, likewise speaks about the luminous quality of ātman: "That is the light even of the lights ... as beyond darkness. It is knowledge, the knowable and the known. It exists especially in the hearts of all."[63]

Thus, in *The Red Book* the soul returns and insists that it is light that characterizes her: "But my soul spoke to me saying, 'My path is light.' Yet I indignantly answered, 'Do you call night what we men call the worst darkness? Do you call day night?' To this my soul spoke a word that roused my anger: 'My light is not of this world.'"[64]

In *The Red Book* the terms "soul" and "self" overlap to some extent and are not entirely distinguishable. Although the soul as anima leads to the self, it is distinct from it. In view of the preceding passages, one might suppose that the soul is the destination of the journey, but gradually the self becomes increasingly present and asks, as I shall presently show, to be reborn as a "new god." Jung was just beginning to develop his ideas on the self when he started composing the *Red Book*, and as he himself admits, his conceptualization of it was influenced by Nietzsche who had been influenced in turn by the Indian concept of ātman.[65]

In the course of *The Red Book* journey Jung realized his primary goal, the discovery of the self, which was to become the cornerstone of his psychological theory. Through his drawings of mandalas Jung experienced the unconscious structuring principle in which the ruling ego is deposed in favor of the self.

The Mandala and the Self

The mandala, a dominant ritual symbol in Indian culture, represents the cosmos and the inner dwelling place of the divine principle. During the composition of the *Red Book*, Jung found himself drawing mandalas as a means of calming his psychic turmoil. In his later reflections on the mandalas he drew in the *Red Book* Jung arrived at insights that advanced his conceptualization of the self and negated his earlier Western position vis-à-vis the centrality of the ego. Here, once again, we find Jung demonstrating his affinity with India and his views on the misguided Western approach: "I acquired through them a living conception of the self. ... The mandala ... corresponds to the microcosmic nature of the psyche. ... It had been proved to me that I had to abandon the idea of the superordinate position of the ego."[66]

Thus, in the terminology of the Upaniṣads, the mandala guides Jung in his development from avidyā, ignorance, to vidyā, true knowledge of the self. "I am the fool who lives in a dark place somewhere. ... In that way was my Western prejudice that I was the center of the mandala corrected—that I am everything, the whole show, the king, the God."[67]

Mistaken identity of the Self

A similar idea is expressed by Yājñavalkya in the *Bṛhadāraṇyaka Upaniṣad*: A person must identify himself with the self alone. Those who mistakenly identify with worldly status or other people or the gods or the Whole rather than with ātman will be forsaken by that with which they have mistakenly identified. "May the Whole forsake anyone who considers the Whole to reside in something other than his self."[68]

Projection of the Self

In *The Red Book*, Jung refers to the dynamics of self-projection or soul-projection as a dominant driving force. "If he does not find his soul ... He will run after all things, and will seize hold of them, but he will not find his soul, since he will find her only in himself. Truly his soul lies in things and men, but the blind man seizes things and men, yet not his soul in things and men."[69] "And if I cross the world, I am ultimately doing this to find my soul. Even the dearest are themselves not the goal and end of the love that goes on seeking, they are symbols of their own souls."[70] Here, Jung seeks the self or soul in the psyche rather than in external objects. This insight is very much in keeping with the words of the Upaniṣadic sage Yājñavalkya when he is about to forsake his wife Maitreī and set off to live the life of an ascetic, saṃnyāsin. Maitreī asks him for true knowledge of the self, which is crucial for the attainment of immortality. In response, he explains the importance of holding fast to the true self because of the tendency to become confused and mistakenly identify the self with various external objects, to love them and cling to them. "One holds a husband dear, you see, not out of love for the husband, rather it is out of love for the self (ātman) that one holds a husband dear ..."[71] Yājñavalkya then enumerates all objects that are important to man: wife and children, wealth, gods, creatures, and everything else. "You see Maitreī," he says, "it is oneself (ātman) which one should see and hear, reflect and concentrate."[72]

Concerning the projection of the self and the illusion of redemptive love, Jung writes: "Consequently we should not use the other for our own composed redemption. The other is no stepping stone for our feet. ... The need for redemption expresses itself through an increased need for love which we think can make the other happy. But meanwhile we are brimming with longing and desire to alter our own condition. And we love others to this end."[73]

But by ceasing to project the self onto others, we are liberated to form true relationships. "Selfish desire ultimately desires itself. ... Your desire is the father of the God, your self is the mother of the God, but the son is the new God, your master."[74]

The Fruits of the Journey

The discovery of the self is thus not merely a psychological experience but a profoundly religious one, a theological solution to the crisis of faith and science. "I can only avow that I have experienced God ... [that] I recognize the God by the unshakeableness of the experience. ... The God appears to us in a certain state of the soul."[75]

For Jung, this experience of unmediated knowledge of God put to rest the religious question that had previously been the main axis of his life. From earliest childhood, Jung, the pastor's son, had endured religious torments arising from an acute awareness of God's darker side that left him frightened and perplexed. His childhood experience of the death of God in church[76] sheds light on his later horrified identification with Nietzsche, who had declared the death of God.

Nietzsche's declaration of the death of God is reflected in the disappointment in Christianity expressed by positivists and materialists. Jung viewed European culture as suffering from a barbarically one-sided position that debased religion and devalued the irrational.[77] The *Red Book* was written in the aftermath of Jung's departure from Freud, who had warned him to resist the attraction of the occult. Jung, however, resisted the "spirit of this time" and sought instead an alternative that would leave room for the "spirit of the depths." But lacking a mediating function in his experience of the numinous,[78] he needed to create a mediating myth. Thus, the *Red Book* might also be understood as an answer to Nietzsche.[79] The old Judeo-Christian God had died, but, in his place, a new god had been born. Jung, as Murray Stein explains, called the *Red Book* by the monumental name of "Liber Novus" to postulate a new theology, a type of "New Testament" intended for the consciousness of a new age.[80] This "New Testament" was a response to the author's theological and psychological torments, and in it, too, India is present in a partially veiled but significant manner. The new god of *The Red Book* is colored by Jung's understanding of the Indian concept of Godhood. Jung's new god is ātman-like in two aspects: He is born in the soul, and unlike the all-good Christian God, he embraces all opposites.

Birth of the Inner God

"We now recognize that the anointed of this time is a God who does not appear in the flesh; he is no man and yet is a son of man, but in spirit and not in flesh; hence he can be born only through the spirit of men as the conceiving womb of the God."[81] In *The Red Book*, this god is born within man's spirit and exists in the inner reality of fantasy.[82] At the center of Jung's "New Testament"[83] is the "divinization of the human."[84] The new god is born through the conscious/unconscious inspiration of Upaniṣadic literature. Jung's contemporaneous writings offer further reflections on the divine essence of ātman as identical with Brahman, the divine element of the cosmos. Brahman unifies man's inner essence with the cosmic essence beyond it, both self and divine. Indian divinity exists within the soul, and it is also the essence of the cosmos that unifies the opposites.

Uniting the Opposites

The opposites that sundered Jung in his *Red Book* are the "spirit of the depths" and the "spirit of this time." These cause him to vacillate between good and evil, introversion and extraversion, East and West, rational and irrational, and the conscious and unconscious. Throughout the book Jung wears various conflicting identities in his encounters with inner figures. When faced with the laughing Satan, he becomes a grim religious Christian; when facing the monotheistic Christian ascetic, he becomes a pagan screaming out his prayer to the sun god; facing Izdubar of the East, he takes on the scientific pose of the West that refutes the existence not only of the sun god but of any god at all. Throughout, Jung is unable to imitate the son of God who is wholly good, dangerously incomplete and one-sided. Thus, the external god who is wholly good dies, and a new god is born out of the opposites in his soul. "The divine child approached me out of the terrible ambiguity, the hateful-beautiful, the evil-good, the laughable-serious, the sick-healthy, the inhuman-human and the ungodly-godly. ... How can a man live in the womb of the God if the Godhead himself attends only to one half of him?"[85]

This god comprising the opposites is inspired by ātman and Brahman. In Jung's 1921 book, *Psychological Types*, he writes extensively about ātman, evidently following his experiential discoveries in the *Red Book*, and relates to ātman-brahman primarily as "uniting symbols": "Brahman is the union and dissolution of all opposites, and at the same time stands outside them as an irrational factor ... wholly beyond cognition and comprehension. It is a divine entity, at once the self ... deliverance from the flux of affects, from the tension of opposites, synonymous with the way of redemption that gradually leads to Brahman."[86] Such is the god born anew in the *Red Book* who brings redemption to Jung's tortured soul and appears as various figures of unified opposites such as the Gnostic Abraxas, or the divine child holding a black snake in one hand and a white snake in the other, or the divine son of the frog and the witch who rises up to the divine realm, leaving his father, Jung, to yearn for him in the human realm.

With the birth of the good/evil god, Jung longs for release from the grip of all attributes, good and evil: "If your virtues hinder you from salvation, discard them, since they have become evil to you. The slave to virtue finds the way as little as the slave to the vices."[87] Here, Jung alludes to Indian equanimity in the face of moral opposites, as in the passage from the Upaniṣads which he quotes from in *Psychological Types*: "Then, just as one driving a chariot looks down upon the two chariot wheels, so he looks down upon day and night, good deeds and evil deeds and upon all the pairs of opposites."[88]

This resolution of intensive opposites brings Jung new hope but also new fear, fear of the freezing of life: "How will it be, now that God and the devil have become one? Are they in agreement to bring life to a stand still? Does the conflict of the opposites belong to the inescapable conditions of life? Does he who recognizes and lives the unity of opposites stand still?"[89] This fear is at the root of Jung's impending aversion to the Indian ideal of uniting opposites, although at this stage the Indian solution fills him with wonder. As he writes in *Psychological Types*, the myth of the renewed god symbolically depicts the human longing for redemption from psychic split, and Indian wisdom represents a different solution to the problem of opposites: "Since the middle position, as function of mediation between the opposites, possesses an irrational character and is still unconscious, it appears projected in the form of a mediating god, a Messiah. ... The East has for thousands of years been familiar with this process and has founded on it a psychological doctrine of salvation which brings the way of deliverance within man's ken and capacity."[90]

Completing the *Red Book*

Jung, riven by opposites, had embarked on the *Red Book* journey to seek relief for his spiritual and emotional anguish. This was a search after his soul and for faith in a new god. The solutions he found in Western culture had proved inadequate, and his inner journey led him to the insights of Indian wisdom where he was able to discern the deepest essence of the "Self." In 1928, when he came across the translation of an ancient Chinese text, *The Secret of the Golden Flower*, he was so astounded that he abruptly left off his writing of the *Red Book*. The explanation he gave for this is that the great affinity he had felt with the East supported the psychological research he had been engaged in all along. "There the contents of this book found their way into actuality and I could no longer continue working on it."[91]

Jung's encounter with the Eastern text penetrated deep into the loneliness experienced during his inner journey, the loneliness of a tormented man whose soul had torn him away from his culture, its faith, and its values, and it offered an external significance to his private, inward experience.

Conclusion

The *Red Book* was the *prima materia* of Jung's lifework, and India served as a major source of inspiration in his developing theory. Both were marginalized in his scientific writings, secreted for many years. But, as Jung lay dreaming between life and death, the Indian yogi returned to him as a guide embodying the eternal self dreaming the ephemeral Jung.[92]

India returned to heal Jung's consciousness just like Izdubar, who had seemed dead forever but emerged full force, so: "One used to believe that one can murder a God. But the God was saved, he forged a new axe in the fire, and plunged again into the flood of fire of the East to resume his ancient cycle. But we clever men crept around lamed and poisoned and did not even know that we lacked something."[93]

The Red Book opens a horizon of hope for our age and our fragmented world, in which longing for otherness has turned into hatred and alienation. *The Red Book*, Jung's intrapsychic dialogue of cultures and its ardent movement between East and West, gave birth to a multifaceted world that harbors a healing and fruitful tension between the world's cultures. Instead of having them as unreconciled opposites, Jung shows the way in his *Red Book* for achieving a united world of a rich diversity, which brings man closer and closer to become whole.

Endnotes

1 See John J. Clarke, "Jung's Dialogue with the East," in *Jung and Eastern Thought* (London & New York, NY: Routledge, 1994). See also, Harold Coward, "Jung's Encounter with Yoga," in *Jung and Eastern Thought* (Albany, NY: State University of New York Press, 1985).

2 C.G. Jung, *The Red Book: Liber Novus*, ed. Sonu Shamdasani, trans. John Peck, Mark Kyburz, and Sonu Shamdasani (New York, NY: W.W. Norton, 2009).

3 The 50 volumes in Mueller's translated edition (1897-1910) were discovered by Sonu Shamdasani in Jung's library, filled with Jung's notes, underlinings and marginalia. See Sonu Shamdasani, "Liber Novus: The 'Red Book' of C.G. Jung by Sonu Shamdasani," in C.G. Jung, *The Red Book*, 197. For evidence of Jung's profound interest in early Indian text see Jung, *The Red Book*, 239 n93 and 285 n130.

4 C.G. Jung, *Symbols of Transformation*, in *CW*, vol. 5 (Princeton, NJ: Princeton University Press, 1956).

5 See chapter "The Significance of the Uniting Symbol" in C.G. Jung, *Psychological Types*, in *CW*, vol. 6 (Princeton, NJ: Princeton University Press, 1971), par. 318.

6 Jung's conflict between the two personalities is a theme that runs through his autobiography *Memories, Dreams, Reflections*, see C.G. Jung, *Memories, Dreams, Reflections*, ed. Aniela Jaffé (New York, NY: Vintage, 1963).

7 See chapter "Visions" in Jung, *Memories, Dreams, Reflections*.

8 Quoted in Jung, *The Red Book*, 239 n93.

9 Ibid., 248.

10 Ibid., 247 and 250 n196.

11 Ibid., 317.

12 Ibid., 154.

13 In his memoir Jung recounts a meeting with an Indian pundit who tells him that his guru is the seventh century philosopher Śaṅkarācārya and Jung reports that he too has an inner guru of his own called Philemon, see Jung, *Memories, Dreams, Reflections*, 177.

14 Jung, *The Red Book*, 278.

[15] The *Atharva Veda* is the fourth Veda (1000-1200 B.C.E.) which contains magical chants, spells and rites. Shamdasani quotes the entire hymn in Jung, *The Red Book*, 281 n110.

[16] Jung, *The Red Book*, 51.

[17] As mentioned, the figure of the yogi pursued him in the dreams of his final years when he lay between life and death as he records in "Visions," see Jung, *Memories, Dreams, Reflections*.

[18] Jung, *The Red Book*, 54.

[19] Shamdasani notes many references to *Brahmaṇaspati* in Jung, *The Red Book*, 284 n127.

[20] Jung, *The Red Book*, 285.

[21] Ibid., 59.

[22] Jung underlines many passages referring to *Hiraṇyagarbha* in the Vedic and Upaniṣadic texts as Shamdasani finds through his research in Jung's library; see Jung, *The Red Book*, 285, n130, and as we see in the following two endnotes.

[23] In the *Ṛgveda* 121, in *Sacred Books of the East*, Vol. 32, 1-2, Hiraṇyagarbha is described as the creator. "In the beginning there arose the Golden Child (Hiraṇyagarbha) ... he alone was the lord of all that is ... he established the earth and this heaven." See Jung, *The Red Book*, 285 n130.

[24] In *Maitrayana Brahmana, Sacred Books of the East*, Vol. 15, 302, describing *Hiraṇyagarbha* as 'self': "And the same self is also called ... Hiraṇyagarbha ... He is to be thought after; Having said farewell to all living beings, having gone to the forest, and having renounced all sensuous objects, let man perceive the Self from his own body." Ibid.

[25] Jung, *The Red Book*, 64.

[26] The text Jung refers to here is *Śatapatha Brāhmaṇa* 2.2.4, *Sacred Books of the East*, Vol. 12, 7-322. "Prajāpati alone existed here ... he performed acts of penance and generated Agni from his mouth; because he generated him from his mouth, therefore Agni is a consumer of food ... Prajāpati then considered, 'In that Agni I have generated a food-eater for myself; but, indeed, there is no other food here but myself, whom, surely, he would not eat.' ... Thereupon Agni turned towards him with open mouth; and he (Prajāpati) being terrified, his own greatness departed from him ... He hesitated: 'Shall I offer it up? Shall I not offer it up?' ... His own greatness said to him, 'Offer it up!' Prajāpati was aware that it was his own (sva) greatness

that had spoken (âha) to him; and offered it up with 'Svâhâ!' This is why offerings are made with 'Svâhâ!' ... And Prajāpati, having performed offering, reproduced himself, and saved himself from Agni, Death, as he was about to devour him."

[27] Ibid.

[28] Jung, *The Red Book*, 285-286.

[29] Quoted in Jung, *The Red Book*, 239 n93.

[30] Jung, *The Red Book*, 232.

[31] Quoted in Jung, *The Red Book*, 200 n69.

[32] Jung, *The Red Book*, 232.

[33] *Bṛhadāraṇyaka Upaniṣad* 3:5:1, *The Early Upaniṣads*, annotated and trans. P. Olivelle (Oxford: Oxford University Press, 1998).

[34] "... as we study the philosophy of the Upaniṣads, the impression grows on us that the attainment of this path is not exactly the simplest of tasks. Our Western superciliousness in the face of these Indian insights is a mark of our barbarian nature ... We are still so uneducated that we actually need laws from without ..." See Jung, *Psychological Types*, *CW* 6, par. 357.

[35] From the Upaniṣads and Vedas Jung learns that "liberation follows the withdrawal of libido from all contents, resulting in a state of complete introversion. This psychological process is, very characteristically, known as tapas, a term which can best be rendered as 'self-brooding' ... the state of meditation with no content," in Jung, *Psychological Types*, *CW* 6, par. 189.

[36] Jung, *Psychological Types*, *CW* 6, par. 336.

[37] Jung, *The Red Book*, 242.

[38] The first of the four canonical sacred texts, the Vedas, composed circa 1600 B.C.E.

[39] Jung, *Symbols of Transformation*, *CW* 5, par. 657.

[40] C.G. Jung, "Psychological Commentary on 'The Tibetan Book of the Great Liberation,'" in *CW*, vol. 11 (Princeton, NJ: Princeton University Press, 1969), par. 849.

[41] Jung, *The Red Book*, 229-230.

[42] Grinshpon identifies the spiritual crisis of the hero of the Upaniṣadic story as a critical element in the process that leads to the achievement of knowledge of the transformative self. See Yohanan Grinshpon, *Crisis and Knowledge: The Upaniṣadic Experience and Storytelling* (Oxford: Oxford University Press, 2003).

[43] *Chāndogya Upaniṣad* 7.1, *The Early Upaniṣads.*

[44] Jung expresses his fears: "What is going to be, if not knowledge? Where is security? Where is solid ground? Where is light? Your darkness is not only darker than night, but bottomless as well." In Jung, *The Red Book,* 240.

[45] Jung, *The Red Book,* 336.

[46] *Chāndogya Upaniṣad* 6.1.4, *The Early Upaniṣads.*

[47] The spirit of this time warns him that what he says is insane, and later he responds to his soul that he fears that he will lose his mind. Jung is preoccupied with the question of "divine madness" and asserts in the epilogue here as in his later memoir that he was in danger of going mad.

[48] Jung, *The Red Book,* 236.

[49] *Chāndogya Upaniṣad* 8:7-12, *The Early Upaniṣads.*

[50] Professor Gangadhar Bhat of Mysore in a private lesson.

[51] Jung, *The Red Book,* 236.

[52] C.G. Jung, "Commentary on 'The Secret of the Golden Flower'," in *CW,* vol. 13 (Princeton, NJ: Princeton University Press, 1967), par. 20.

[53] *Bhagavad-Gītā,* 2:47, trans. Swami Gambhirananda (Kolkata: Advaita Ashrama, 2010).

[54] These three words in the *Chāndogya Upaniṣad* are quoted by Jung in *Psychological Types, CW* 6, par. 189.

[55] Jung, *The Red Book,* 237.

[56] *Chāndogya Upaniṣad* 8.7.3, *The Early Upaniṣads.*

[57] Jung, *The Red Book,* 232.

[38] *Bṛhadāraṇyaka Upaniṣad* 3.7.23, *The Early Upaniṣads.*

[59] *Bṛhadāraṇyaka Upaniṣad* 4.5.13, *The Early Upaniṣads.*

[60] Quoted in Jung, *The Red Book,* 250 n194.

[61] Jung, *The Red Book,* 273.

[62] *Bṛhadāraṇyaka Upaniṣad* 4:3:6, *The Early Upaniṣads.*

[63] *Bhagavad Gītā* 13:17.

[64] Jung, *The Red Book,* 240.

[65] Shamdasani quotes from Jung's *Zarathustra Seminar:* "I was already very interested in the concept of the self ... I thought Nietzsche meant a sort of a thing-in-itself behind the psychological phenomenon ... I saw then also that he was producing a concept of the self which was like the Eastern concept: it is an Atman idea," in Jung, *The Red Book,* 337 n29.

[66] Jung, *Memories, Dreams, Reflections*, 187-188.

[67] C.G. Jung, *The Psychology of Kundalini Yoga: Notes of the Seminar Given in 1932 by C.G. Jung* (Princeton, NJ: Princeton University Press, 1996), 100.

[68] *Bṛhadāraṇyaka Upaniṣad* 2.4.6, *The Early Upaniṣads*.

[69] Jung, *The Red Book*, 232.

[70] Ibid., 233.

[71] *Bṛhadāraṇyaka Upaniṣad* 4:5, 2:4, *The Early Upaniṣads*.

[72] Ibid.

[73] Jung, *The Red Book*, 338.

[74] Ibid., 245.

[75] Ibid., 338. The relationship between God and the self in *The Red Book* is a complex one. Jung at times identifies God with the self and at other times distinguishes between them.

[76] "[The communion ceremony] is an absence of the God. The church is a place I should not go to. It is not life which is there, but death," in Jung, *Memories, Dreams, Reflections*, 64.

[77] Murray Stein claims that Jung wished to resolve the conflict between science and religion which had destroyed his father. Murray Stein, "How to read *The Red Book* and why," in *Journal of Analytical Psychology*, 57, no. 3 (2012), 280–298.

[78] In later years Jung claims that religion is a dogmatic system intended to mediate the numinous, the *mysterium tremendum*, which is liable to pose a grave danger for ordinary people, in C.G. Jung, *Psychology and Religion* (New Haven & London: Yale University Press, 1938). Murray Stein writes that Jung's anxiety was the result of the void created by god's absence. Murray Stein, "What is *The Red Book* for analytical psychology?" In *Journal of Analytical Psychology*, 56, no. 5 (2011), 590–606.

[79] Wolfgang Giegerich, "*Liber Novus*, That is, The New Bible. A first analysis of C.G. Jung's *Red Book*," *Spring: A Journal of Archetypes and Culture* (2010), 361-411.

[80] Stein, "What is *The Red Book* for analytical psychology?," 288.

[81] Jung, *The Red Book*, 299.

[82] Ibid., 283.

[83] Toshio Kawai, "*The Red Book* from a pre-modern perspective: the position of the ego, sacrifice and the dead," in *Journal of Analytical Psychology* 57, no. no. 3, 2012, 378-389. The rebirth of the god as Kawai

defines the birth of psychology based on the idea of internalization and the reality of fantasy that enables Jung to discuss the god and his rituals as inward reality.

[84] Stein, "How to read *The Red Book* and why," 282.

[85] Jung, *The Red Book*, 243.

[86] Jung, *Psychological Types*, *CW* 6, par. 330. Jung collects citations from the Vedas, Upaniṣads and the purāṇas, an example from the *Śvetā-śvatara Upaniṣad*: "Braham is sat and asat, being and non-being, satyam and asatyam, reality and irreality," another example from *Kaṭha Upaniṣad*: "It moves, It moves not, far, yet near. Within all, Outside all."

[87] Jung, *The Red Book*, 235.

[88] Quoted by Jung from *Kauṣītaki Upaniṣad*, in Jung, *Psychological Types*, *CW* 6, par. 328.

[89] Jung, *The Red Book*, 318.

[90] Jung, *Psychological Types*, *CW* 6, par. 326. This to Jung's mind is the purpose of yoga as well—to create an intermediate position through which "the redemptive element of creativity may arise." See ibid., par. 190.

[91] Jung, *The Red Book*, 360.

[92] Jung, *Memories, Dreams, Reflections*, 189.

[93] Jung, *The Red Book*, 283.

A Lesson in Peacemaking:
The Mystery of Self-Sacrifice in *The Red Book*

Günter Langwieler

They will all become terribly enraptured by these tremendous experiences, and in their blindness will want to
understand them as outer events. It is an inner happening;
that is the way to the perfection of the mystery of Christ, so
that the peoples learn self-sacrifice. May the frightfulness
become so great that it can turn man's eyes inward ...[1]

C.G. Jung

Introversion and History

C.G. Jung's *Red Book* is fundamentally the personal and collective
confession of a witness of his time, begun on the eve of World War I,
the first of the big catastrophes in the 20th century. What happened
to Jung personally—in his visions, dreams, and active imaginations
from November 1913 to June 1914, forming the first layer[2] of his *Red
Book*—was not only of significance for his individual crisis after
separating from Freud. When World War I broke out on August 1,
1914, he noticed that his earlier visions of a flood over Northern
Europe had a collective meaning. This gave a political sense to the
appearance of symbols of destructiveness that he had at first interpreted personally as breeding a psychosis. From the perspective of
August 1, 1914, it must have seemed to him that he had served as an
individual medium for collective transformations. Inside his psyche,
significant transformations of collective symbols had taken place. The
corresponding historical events followed. His visions, dreams, and

active imaginations happened to him. He didn't produce them by conscious will or conscious decision. Jung became, in his suffering, an involuntary witness of unconscious destructive forces. By identifying himself with the mystery of the self-sacrifice of Christ, he formed a psychological bridge to the collective suffering in his time, which he called the mystery of the self-sacrifice of people. He turned his eyes inward and became aware of his "frightfulness."

The subsequent catastrophes of two world wars, which not only destroyed a major part of the civilized world in Europe physically but also spiritually, had shown their self-destructive powers inside his psyche long before they really occurred. This happened to a citizen of Switzerland, a nonparticipant in the wars. But Jung couldn't stand aside as a neutral observer. He felt guilty and took personal responsibility for what he dreamt: He had killed Siegfried. He could not understand his confused state of mind after this dream. It took him many more dreams and active imaginations before he could grasp its meaning.

I want to argue in this chapter that a transformation of the collective symbols "blood," "hero," "sacrifice," and "victim" can be found at the very heart of Jung's unconscious process: a shift from sacrifice to suffering, from superiority to weakness.

This shift has a political dimension as well: it is a lesson in peacemaking. I have called it "psychological pacifism,"[3] which is different from most of the pacifist ideologies because this type is based upon a psychological rationale and not upon the moral superiority of peacemaking and the peacemaker.

The Narrative of Self-Sacrifice

The narrative of *The Red Book* is very complex. One might even doubt whether there is a consistent narrative at all. But looking closer, there are red threads that are interwoven throughout the text. Jung combined in this narrative the search for his lost soul[4] and the guilt of being the murderer of the German warrior hero Siegfried, the mystery of the crucified Christ, and, last but not least, the idea of the self-sacrifice of the people.

These ideas were not primarily a result of conscious thought and reflection using psychological, theological, and political theories. The narrative of *The Red Book* is made of intuition. The contents of the first layer were constituted by long and irritating active imaginations. Jung ended up in *Liber Primus* at the feet of the crucified Christ, becoming Christ himself with Mary as his mother. And he met up with archaic gods during his inner journey, such as Mime from the Nibelung saga and the Leontocephalus of the Mithraic mysteries. Did he suffer from an inflation brought about by spiritual images of gods and goddesses? Probably not, in my opinion. Rather, he opened his conscious mind to the dark side of religious experiences from the unconscious. Similar to what he attempted with his confused state of mind after his dream of murdering Siegfried, he tried to solve the riddles and the mysteries. He tried to understand what Christ's self-sacrifice on the cross could mean for himself, for his personal search, but also for the collective, for the anthropological mystery of self-destruction inherent in humankind.

Jung was very much aware of the risks of his experiment. We should keep in mind that the acting, dreaming, storytelling, observing, and reflecting protagonist, i.e., the Ego of *The Red Book*, is not identical with the Swiss citizen, Carl Gustav Jung. As he wrote in *Memories, Dreams, Reflections*, during this period he would carefully assure himself of the facts of his life, recalling that he was living at Seestrasse 228 in Küsnacht near Zurich, that he was married and had five children,[5] and thus he stayed grounded and did not get carried away by inflationary pressures from the unconscious.

The Red Book is a book of dreams, visions, active imaginations, prophecies, or, as one might say, of inner happenings. But it is also a subjective report of historical facts. The outer events corresponded with his inner happenings. Were they also the consequence of collective inner happenings? One might stay skeptical about this view. However, these inner happenings could be interpreted as a political message of *The Red Book*. Jung's dreaming and imagining Ego reflected human destructiveness and war psychologically as an inner event. Taking the narrative of his *Red Book* seriously means that it contains a political message.

Jung did not imagine himself as a political leader. Nor did he preach from the height of a pulpit. Rather, he went through a dangerous and mysterious journey through the underworld. Uncertainty and confusion about the complex matters discovered there prevailed. Subjective uncertainty can also be deduced from the making of the text itself: Every passage of his drafts was corrected. Long passages of the different drafts were eliminated and rewritten. This is further evidence of his uncertainty.

Part One: The Self-Sacrifice of a Beautiful Hero

> Then Siegfried's horn resounded over the mountains with a jubilant sound. We knew that our mortal enemy was coming. We were armed and lurked beside a narrow rocky path to murder him. Then we saw him coming high across the mountains on a chariot made of the bones of the dead. He drove boldly and magnificently over the steep rocks and arrived at the narrow path where we waited in hiding. As he came around the turn ahead of us, we fired at the same time and he fell slain. Thereupon I turned to flee, and a terrible rain swept down. But after this I went through a torment unto death and I felt certain that I must kill myself, if I could not solve the riddle of the murder of the hero.[6]

Let me try to solve the riddle. First, I will give some general consideration to the significance of the warrior-hero. For an individual, the warrior-hero is a psychological figure of personal development, a symbol of individuation. For the collective, he is a mythic, historical, and political figure. As a powerful collective symbol, he was utilized for political purposes in all times and under all political circumstances. This collective figure was killed by Jung's protagonist-Ego and his dark companion.

Siegfried is a warrior-hero par excellence. During his mythological studies for his work *Transformations and Symbols of the Libido* from 1911-12, Jung had already dealt extensively with Siegfried. He was well-known to him from the medieval epos of the Nibelungs.[7] The figure of Siegfried therefore forms a bridge to Jung's earlier work.

The first comment to the dream is made in *The Red Book* itself by a dream-figure, the *spirit of the depths*: "'The highest truth is one and the same with the absurd.' This statement saved me."[8] In his seminar on "Analytical Psychology" of 1925, Jung commented this dream for the first time in public:

> Siegfried was not an especially sympathetic figure to me. … Nevertheless my dream showed him to be my hero. … I felt an enormous pity for him, as though I myself had been shot. I must then have had a hero I did not appreciate, and it was my ideal of force and efficiency I had killed. I had killed my intellect … I deposed my superior function. … as soon as the main function is deposed, there is a chance for other sides of the personality to be born into life.[9]

Jung interpreted the consequence of this dethroning psychologically. The superior side of his personality had to give way to another side. Which one would that be? The strong suicidal affect hints at a violent impulse toward self-punishment, self-destruction, self-sacrifice. Other affects are sympathic with the hero—mourning over the loss, feelings of guilt, shame for cowardice because he could only succeed in shooting him in an ambush. These feelings threatened to overwhelm the dreamer. He barely succeeded in not losing his self-control after awakening.

The insight that the highest truth and the absurd are one and the same tells us that something unexpected and very important had taken place: Jung had changed his orientation in respect to the hero when he deposed his inner superior function, Siegfried. He began to say farewell to the warrior-hero inside. Instead, he now recognized his own weakness, his incapacity, a topic that is thoroughly reflected on later in *The Red Book*. Jung regained his stability by accepting his weakness, his inferiority. Paradoxically, despite his inferiority, he succeeded in killing the invincible, magnificent, beautiful German hero. The weaker may be the winner because he disposes of weapons and is able to arrange alliances, in this case with a brown savage. Anyway, the invincibility of the Germanic hero turned out to be an illusion.[10] He didn't act cautiously, so he rode triumphantly to his death: the inadvertent self-sacrifice of the hero.

Jung took the savage to represent his instinctive dark side. Jung's inner Siegfried had to die in order to give life to the part of his personality that was centered in his inadequacy. But this part could not expose itself at this time; it had to hide itself and cover its tracks by a great rain. The image of the heavy rain picks up the earlier symbol of the flood and links the Siegfried dream to the visions of the flood of blood over Europe and the world of biblical imagery. Jung felt the loss of the murdered hero. He was overwhelmed by tears and mourning. He felt he could not live any longer if he could not solve the riddle. The riddle dealt with Siegfried's sacrifice and Jung's impulse to his own self-sacrifice by shooting himself.

The solution to the riddle was to accept weakness and incapacity, to value suffering, emotions, and the basic wish to survive higher than the aesthetics of heroism. The connotations of the Germanic hero changed thoroughly. To Wagner, Siegfried had been the free man, the rebel without fear. Siegfried showed up in Jung's dream first as an enemy, as a killer and destroyer, and then as a loser and victim; the Protagonist, moreover, Jung's Alter-Ego, Siegfried's murderer, is shown as a coward who simply wants to survive.

**Part Two: The Self-Sacrifice of the Crucified God –
God Has Abandoned Man**

The idea of self-sacrifice found its second expression in Jung's active imaginations on December 25, 1913. Jung reported on this in the last chapter of *Liber Primus* called "Resolution." "On the third night, deep longing to continue experiencing the mysteries seized me. The struggle between doubt and desire was great in me."[11] It is the third night of Jung's Night Sea Journey, which fell on Christmas Day 1913, and he found himself confronting pagan gods, biblical and mythological figures, the divine child, and the crucified God. "The third night" is perhaps a hint to the third night after Christ's crucifixion, the night before the resurrection. But let me first sum up the visionary waking dream before getting closer to the analogy of self-sacrifice. During the previous two nights, Jung's protagonist Ego had encountered the biblical prophet Elijah and his companion, Salome. This time Elijah was standing alone on the heights. On the dark side of the rocks lay a black serpent, on the bright side a white serpent. A terrible wrestling of the two ensued. It seemed as if the black serpent would overcome the white one, but then they withdrew, and the head and front side of the black serpent had turned white. Then Elijah climbed onto a summit. There was a masonry building made of huge blocks with a large courtyard and, in the middle of it, an altar. There Elijah proclaimed that this would be the temple of the sun. Climbing down, he became smaller until he was a dwarf and called himself Mime, the dwarf of the Nibelung saga. Mime says: "Here are my wells. Whoever drinks from them becomes wise."[12] The Ego follows him into a cave but cannot reach the water. Instead of wisdom, confusion prevails: "I lose courage. I leave the cave, and doubting, pace back and forth in the square of the yard. Everything appears to me strange and incomprehensible."[13] Now we come to the central scenery of the active imagination. Here is what Jung writes:

> I am seized with fear at what I see … I see the cross, the removal of the cross, the mourning. … I see the divine child, with the white serpent in his right hand, and the black serpent in his left hand. I see the green mountain, the cross of Christ on it, and a stream of blood flowing from the summit. … I see the cross and Christ on it in his last hour and torment—at the foot of the cross the black serpent coils itself—it has wound itself around my feet—I am held fast and I spread my arms wide. Salome draws near. The serpent has wound itself around my whole body, and my countenance is that of a lion. … [Salome says]:

'You are Christ.' I stand with outstretched arms like someone crucified ... The serpent squeezes my body in its terrible coils and the blood streams from my body, spilling down the mountainside. Salome bends down to my feet and wraps her black hair round them. She lies thus for a long time. Then she cries, 'I see light!' ... [Elijah says:] 'Your work is fulfilled here. Other things will come. Seek untiringly, and above all write exactly what you see.' ... Elijah transforms into a huge flame of white light ... and I hurry out into the night, like one who has no part in the glory of the mystery. My feet do not touch the ground of this earth, and it is as if I were melting into air.[14]

Perhaps we can feel empathy and pity for this rather young man of 39 years, whose psyche became the inner scene of a human tragedy of extraordinary dimensions. But we can also feel the distance of an observing Ego. Jung's visions and active imaginations were registered and written down as exactly as possible by this observer-Ego. This was the order of Elijah to seek untiringly and write exactly what he sees. What does he see?

One significant feature of the vision is the location of the temple of the sun in the mountains. Here we enter the sphere of the Mithraic mysteries. In the Roman Empire, during the first centuries, the 25th of December was celebrated not only as the birthday of Christ but also of Mithras, the son of the sun. The Leontocephalus is one of the main symbols of the Mithraic mysteries, as Jung himself mentioned in his 1925 seminar on Analytical Psychology.[15]

But the central theme is another one: The protagonist-Ego of Jung's vision turned the traumatic experiences of Christ on the cross into his own inner experience. The mimetic similarity between Jung's protagonist-Ego and Christ includes the body feeling of hanging on the cross, of suffering Christ's mortal agony, of blood pouring out of his body and down the summit, even of Mary being his mother, and, in the end, of Christ's resurrection as a spiritual body when he lost the contact to the earth melting into air.

The narrator confesses to a struggle between doubt and desire. A deep longing to experience the mysteries seized him at the beginning, but in the end, he had no part in the glory of the mystery. He remained a stranger, someone who was not initiated into the mystery. Here again we find a distance from the numinous idea of the sacrifice. Doubt is winning over desire; thus the sense of identity with the holy victim, the sacrifice, is undermined. The sacrifice of the warrior-hero changes to the sacrifice of Christ and into the self-sacrifice of Jung's protagonist-Ego. Sacrifice turns into victimhood, glory into suffering.

Nearly at the same time as Jung experienced these active imaginations, the symbol of the cross became the center of a theological movement called "the theology of the cross." In 1911, the German theologian Martin Kähler gave a lecture declaring the cross to be the foundation and measure of Christology.[16] Jürgen Moltmann, writing his works after World War II, stated that the theology of the cross had previously to this enjoyed only a certain modest position in Christian tradition but never was put in the center, beginning with Paul and continuing all the way to Luther. It was significantly present mostly in the persecuted religious communities. Moltmann understood his affection for the theology of the Cross to be a consequence of his experiences in World War II: "The survivors of my generation came back torn and defeated from concentration camps and military hospitals into the lecture halls. A theology which would not have spoken of God with regard to the abandoned crucified would not have got through to us."[17] Moltmann quoted Dietrich Bonhoeffer, who had written in a letter from prison close to his execution by the Nazi-regime: "God allows Himself to be shoved out of the world on a cross; God is powerless and weak in the world and only in this way is He with us and helps us. Following *Matthew 8:17*, it is absolutely clear that Christ does not help with his almightiness but with his weakness, his suffering. Only the suffering God can help. ... This is the reversal of everything that the religious man expects from God. It is man's task to co-suffer empathetically with God's suffering in a godless world."[18] Moltmann stressed: "Without perception of the pain of the negative, Christian hope cannot be realistic and effect breaking free."[19]

Moltmann and Bonhoeffer came to the same conclusion that Jung reached in his *Red Book*: Weakness, pain, and suffering are the characteristics of the image of God in a godless world. Man is called to suffer together with God from a world without God. The paradoxical message is that participation in the negative and in pain can free one from suffering. And this message represents the same solution to the riddle of self-sacrifice, to the mystery of Christ's self-sacrifice.

Part Three: The Self-Sacrifice of the People

At that time, the loving light was annihilated, and blood began to pour out. This was the great war. But the spirit of the depths wants this struggle to be understood as a conflict in every man's own nature. ... Since men do not know that the conflict occurs inside themselves, they go mad, and one lays the blame on the other. If one-half of mankind is at fault, then every man is half at fault. But he does not see the conflict in his own soul, which is however the source of the outer disaster. If you are aggravated against your brother, think that you are aggravated against the brother in you, that is, against what in you is similar to your brother.

As a man you are part of mankind, and therefore you have a share in the whole of mankind, as if you were the whole of mankind. If you overpower and kill your fellow man who is contrary to you, then you also kill that person in yourself and have murdered a part of your life. The spirit of this dead man follows you and does not let your life become joyful. You need your wholeness to live onward.[20]

Therefore they all say that they are fighting for the good and for peace, but one cannot fight one another over the good. But since men don't know that the conflict lies within themselves, the Germans thus believe that the English and the Russians are wrong; but the English and the Russians say that the Germans are wrong. But no one can judge history in terms of right and wrong. Because one half of mankind is wrong, every man is half wrong. Therefore a conflict resides in his own soul. ... But man appears to see the outer quarrel, not the one within, which alone is the wellspring of the great war. But before man can ascend to light and love, the great battle is needed.[21]

This is just the opposite of what really happened in the "heroic societies" of Europe. They were on their way to destruction and self-sacrifice, while Jung recommended: "... so do not be heroes, be clever and drop the heroics, since nothing is more dangerous than to play the hero."[22]

Jung was recommending what might be called *psychological pacifism,* although he himself did not use this term. He suggested the path of introversion in order to reintegrate the dissociated other half of man. His aim is to restore wholeness by overcoming the dissociation of the ego and the inner other. The enemy is a part of the self. The conflicts leading to war are not conflicts of right vs. wrong or of external factors. Although we read the contrary every day, it is the conflicts lying inside man himself that lead to war, conflicts within the psyche of every man. The pacifist movements of Jung's contemporaries charged economic and political powers with being responsible for wars; their "no to war" motto resulted from a superior moral standpoint and from pessimism in regard to the human ability to suppress destructive forces.[23] Peacemaking, consequently, could only be achieved by laws and societal institutions, not by individuals and their personal psychological development. Jung's argument did not rest on a basically positive view of human character that would ask everyone to fight for the good and for peace. Jung argued instead from the opposite viewpoint, from the fundamental idea of the shadow being a part of every human subject. The conflict within the psyche had to be solved. In the end, then, it would make no sense any longer to project one's shadow on the other and fight with the other. This procedure would necessarily be seen as self-destructive, because the other is the other half of oneself. A psychological pacifism, therefore, can only be symbolized by a broken hero, a hero in his weakness. The symbol of the magnificent hero would hide self-destructiveness behind self-sacrifice.

The integration of the other is the deeper meaning and aim of the sacrifice of the hero. This integration involves a process of psychological transformation. This idea differs fundamentally from Freud's death-drive. Jung's concept of self-sacrifice is a psychological, cultural, and anthropological concept. Psychological pacifism is also a political concept. Freud's concept, on the other hand, is basically a biological concept. Culturally, the narrative of *The Red Book* deals with the symbolic death of the hero with a thousand faces, to reference Joseph Campbell's famous book written much later. "Nothing is more dangerous than to play the hero," as Jung wrote.

What does Jung's impulse to shoot himself after he had murdered Siegfried mean? He wanted to integrate his guilt of being the murderer of Siegfried by sharing the suffering of the warrior-hero, Siegfried. As we have seen, this was followed by a transformation of the hero-symbol and a farewell to the warrior-hero as a bright, proud, and mighty image of the self. The warrior-hero came down from the heights of his inflated sense of self and unified himself with his murderers in death. At the end of *Liber Primus*, the dark and white serpents fight each other and end fighting by integrating parts of each other, as symbolized by their colors. Christ and Jung's imagining Ego suffer together the same tortures and abandonment.

The idea of the self-sacrifice of the people is the third manifestation of self-sacrifice in *The Red Book*. World War I historically turned out to be the collective destiny of "heroic societies," a term used by political scientists in the beginning of the 21st century.[24] European societies had transformed themselves during the pre-war period into heroic societies, as Münkler has shown. Now, at the beginning of the 21st century, as a result of two world wars, there is a shift in Western Europe to so-called "post-heroic societies." The collective attitude toward the self-sacrifice of the hero has changed profoundly.

Jung was one of few individuals who recognized that the self-sacrifice of the people should not only be regarded as an outer event, as quarrels among peoples. There should be a psychological transformation. If people—looked upon as individuals—would learn their lesson about their own collective and individual destructiveness, their suffering could change into a lesson in peacemaking. These ideas of Jung would mean a fundamental lesson in peacemaking by psychological means. The transformation of symbols that form the center of the hero-complex from the blood shed by an individual hero to the streams of blood lost by masses of soldiers and civilians, from sacrifice to victim, from heroic strength to weakness, from superiority to inferiority changes the content of the hero-complex fundamentally. The post-heroic image of the suffering warrior could support individuals in understanding themselves as if each one were the whole of mankind in their own wholeness.

When Jung writes, "But before man can ascend to light and love, the great battle is needed," what does he mean? This was Jung's conclusion after three years of numerous battles that left millions of people dead. The great battle was needed because otherwise the frightfulness would not be great enough to persuade people to turn their eyes inward. Despite the obvious pessimistic look at the historical facts, Jung's perspective remained a psychological pacifism, although Jung didn't name it this. In 1916, Jung wrote in his foreword to *The Psychology of the Unconscious Processes*:

> The psychological concomitants of the present war—above all the incredible brutalization of public opinion, the mutual slanderings, the unprecedented fury of destruction, the monstrous flood of lies, and man's incapacity to call a halt to the bloody demon—are uniquely fitted to force upon the attention of every thinking person the problem of the chaotic unconscious which slumbers beneath the ordered world of consciousness. This war has pitilessly revealed to civilized man that he still is a barbarian ... The

psychology of the individual is reflected in the psychology of the nation. What the nation does is done also by each individual, and so long as the individual continues to it, the nation will do likewise. Only a change in the attitude of the individual can initiate a change in the psychology of the nation.[25]

Jung was a seer, a political prophet, in 1913. Yet he did not unveil his historical and political interpretations to his contemporaries. He did not publish his *Red Book* during his lifetime, and I think he would have been torn to pieces by his contemporaries if he had done so. His visions, dreams, and active imaginations would not have been taken seriously. He would have been treated as a lunatic or a traitor. The truth is that his contemporaries turned out to be lunatics because they were inflated by collective heroic and nationalist self-images. But his ideas were far beyond ordinary thinking—and still they are. *The Red Book,* therefore, remains a challenge for our time: Peace is not an outer event but a state of integration of the split and dissociated part that is projected onto the other, the foreigner, the enemy. What idea could touch more fundamentally on the global crises of our present time?

Endnotes

[1] C.G. Jung, *The Red Book: Liber Novus. A Reader's Edition*, ed. Sonu Shamdasani, trans. John Peck, Mark Kyburz, and Sonu Shamdasani (New York, NY: W.W. Norton, 2009), 204.

[2] The text of *The Red Book* consists of two layers. The first layer is constituted by the visions, dreams, and imaginations from October 1913 to April 1914 he had noted in the so-called *Black Books*. Jung copied them literally in his *Red Book*. The second layer is a comment written down from August 1914 up to June 1915, when he finished the handwritten draft. Several corrections followed. Thanks to the editor Sonu Shamdasani, we have *The Red Book* as a critical edition, that means we can follow up the diverse versions of the text. Jung expressed his view on war explicitly in this second layer, during the first year of World War I. The images of his unconscious, unfolded in the first layer, preceded the war nearly 10 months. The second layer consists of comments, but these comments cannot be looked upon either as a rational, scientific analysis or as a political manifesto, although it is inherently and basically political. The language of this layer rather equals works of theatre and poetry or resembles to primary processes in dreams, like the language of the first layer. Their language often is associative and erratic, statements are made in paradoxes, there is a constant shift from a personal to a collective view and vice versa, prophetic declamations are mixed with personal confessions and enigmatic thesis about mankind in general. Both layers are dominated by images, not by concepts. Both layers need to be interpreted, they don't speak for themselves. The pathetic and declamatory language doesn't devaluate its contents. *The Red Book* offers a unique access to Jung's life and work. Shamdasani even called the publication of *The Red Book* as opening "a new era in the understanding of Jung's work." "The work on *Liber Novus* was at the center of Jung's self-experimentation. It is nothing less than the central book in his oeuvre." (Sonu Shamdasani, in Jung, *The Red Book*, 95).

[3] See Günter Langwieler, "Jungs Abschied vom Kriegerhelden," in *Analytische Psychologie* 46, 1, 2015, 28-42.

[4] Jung, *The Red Book*, 129.

[5] See Deirdre Bair, *Jung: A Biography* (Boston, MA: Little, Brown and Company, 2003), 363.

[6] Jung, *The Red Book*, 160-161.

[7] Jung took the figure of Siegfried from *The Song of the Nibelungs*, a medieval epic, but in the version of Richard Wagner in "The Ring of the Nibelung." In Wagner's version, Siegfried is the Germanic hero, the free man who knows no fear. Siegfried is strong and wild and rebels against Wotan and the established Gods. In *Transformations and Symbols of the Libido*, Jung discussed the hero predominantly in relation to the mother-archetype. (see C.G. Jung, *Wandlungen und Symbole der Libido* (Leipzig und Wien: Franz Deuticke, 1938).

[8] Jung, *The Red Book*, 161.

[9] C.G. Jung, *Introduction to Jungian Psychology: Notes of the Seminar on Analytical Psychology Given in 1925* (Princeton, NJ: Princeton University Press, 2012), 61-62.

[10] The Cambridge historian Christopher Clark spoke about the failure of the European elites to accept responsibility for the outbreak of World War I and reported an irritating detail: In the Russian-Japanese war (1904-05), one could see what happened if soldiers ran onto a machine-gun defense position. "German and French observers noted with gratification which horrible injuries the new weapons left behind in the corpses of the wounded. The narrowness of their thinking was remarkable: they tested their own artillery with great enthusiasm, but could not realize that these murderous tools would strike their own people." My translation, see Christopher Clark, "Die Eliten haben versagt," *Geo Epoche* 65, 2014, 156ff.

[11] Jung, *The Red Book*, 194.

[12] Ibid., 195.

[13] Ibid.

[14] Ibid., 195-197.

[15] See Jung, *The Red Book*, 197 n211.

[16] See Jürgen Moltmann, *Der gekreuzigte Gott* (Gütersloh: Gütersloher Verlagshaus, 1972), 9.

[17] Ibid., 7; my translation.

[18] Ibid., 49. "Gott lässt sich aus der Welt herausdrängen ans Kreuz, Gott ist ohnmächtig und schwach in der Welt und gerade und nur so ist er bei uns und hilft uns. Es ist nach Matt. 8;17 ganz deutlich, dass Christus nicht hilft dank seiner Allmacht sondern kraft seiner

Schwachheit, seines Leidens! ... nur der leidende Gott kann helfen ... Das ist die Umkehrung von allem, was der religiöse Mensch von Gott erwartet. Der Mensch wird aufgerufen, das Leiden Gottes an der gottlosen Welt mitzuleiden."

[19] Ibid., 10.

[20] Jung, *The Red Book*, 199-200.

[21] Ibid., 199 n220.

[22] Ibid., 169.

[23] The history of ideas about pacifism ranges from the Bible to Hume, Locke and Kant to the political pacifist movements in the beginning 20th century. To discuss these different approaches would need an article of its own.

[24] See Herfried Münkler, *Der Wandel des Krieges. Von der Symmetrie zur Asymmetrie* (Weilerswist: Velbrück Wissenschaft). Wissenschaft, 2007); also Herfried Münkler, *Der Große Krieg* (Berlin: Rowohlt Verlag, 2013).

[25] C.G. Jung, "On the Psychology of the Unconscious," in *CW*, vol. 7 (Princeton, NJ: Princeton University Press, 1966), Preface to the First Edition, 4.

Trickster, His Apocalyptic Brother, and a World's Unmaking: An Archetypal Reading of Donald Trump

Randy Fertel

> Face it, folks, we are a divided nation ... divided between those who think with their head and those who *know* with their heart. ... Because that's where the truth comes from, ladies and gentlemen—the gut.[1]
>
> Steven Colbert on coining "Truthiness"

> ... the great question of our day: How can consciousness, our most recent acquisition, which has bounded ahead, be linked up again with the oldest, the unconscious, which has lagged behind?[2]
>
> C.G. Jung

Improvisation and the Rhetoric of Unmediated Spontaneity

Seen through the lens of archetype, Donald J. Trump is a dark—a very dark—version of Carl Jung.

Was ever so heterogeneous a pair so violently yoked together? One so interior, the other without apparent interior; one so erudite, the other functionally illiterate; one so urbane, the other at best suburban.

This paper explores how far one can take this apparent *enantiodromia*—Jung/Trump—with the intention of showing how Jung's *Red Book* might prepare us to weather Trump's presidency. I will argue, perhaps even more surprisingly, that along with his fellow Modernists Jung bears indirect responsibility for Trump's embrace of "fake news" and "alt-facts."

Jung's dance with the devil, the *Red Book,* by means of which he conjured his analytic method, finally saw the light of day in 2009. Two years later Trump began *his* devil's dance, embracing birtherism and conjuring his run for the presidency. Both dances seek to catalyze a new world order; both dances welcome, though in far different ways and to different effects, the human shadow.

But what links them first and last is that they are both improvisers. Improvisation is an enduring form of discourse across literature, visual arts, music, and even politics that displays persistent formal gestures and thematic concerns.[3] The links among improvisations have been hidden in plain sight largely because all claim, like *The Red Book: Liber Novus* (or like Trump's campaign and presidency) to be unlike anything you've ever seen—uncanonical, a new-found thing.[4]

As its etymology suggests, *Im-pro-visations* claim to be *un-fore-seen*: spontaneous, off-the-cuff, uncrafted, unmediated, careless, inspired, formless, and/or chaotic. By deploying a decorum of the indecorous, thumbing their nose at the mainstream, improvisers try to persuade us that their art is not the product of reason, artifice, or virtuosity. Rather, they model a more open, sincere, authentic embrace of life. Challenging logic, reason, and craft, improvisation calls for change.

As the "Jung" persona[5] in *The Red Book* says of magic, improvisation is "lawless ... without rules and by chance ..."[6] His two epigraphs to *The Red Book* underscore that the goal of his quest is *un-fore-seen*. Jung first quotes Isaiah's lament that the savior will come "*as a surprise*" (*Isaiah* 53: 1-3). Editor Sonu Shamdasani notes that Jung reuses the same verses in his next book, *Psychological Types*, and there explains Isaiah's lament: "The birth of the Savior, the development of the redeeming symbol, takes place where one does not expect it, and from precisely where a solution is most improbable."[7] *The Red Book* will be about the quest for "the birth of the Savior" and "the development of the redeeming symbol"—by means of his improvised active imaginings. His second epigraph, again from *Isaiah*, is again glossed in *Psychological Types*:

> The nature of the redeeming symbol is that of a child, that
> is the childlikeness or presuppositionlessness of the atti-
> tude belongs to the symbol and its function. This 'childlike'
> attitude necessarily brings with it another guiding principle
> in place of self-will and rational intentions, whose 'god-
> likeness' is synonymous with 'superiority.' Since it is of an
> irrational nature, the guiding principle appears in a mirac-
> ulous form. … The criterion of 'godlike' effect is the irre-
> sistible power of the unconscious impulses.[8]

At improvisation's heart, as here, beats the spirit of Trickster, a challenge to rationality, and a flirtation with philosophical primitivism
("childlikeness or presuppositionlessness"). Since antiquity, improvisation has been the discourse of paradigm shifts, those cultural moments when reason, the way we know the world, is challenged and
redefined by "the irresistible power of the unconscious impulses" or
some other nonrational faculty or agency.

Scholars often explain away the claim of spontaneity as the
"topos of affected modesty" or as the convention of anticipatory self-
defense.[9] But hidden in the disclaimer of rationality and craft is a
boast. If the appearance of reasoned behavior has such currency and
power—psychiatrist and neuroscientist Iain McGilchrist skeptically
calls it "the rhetoric of reason"[10]—then for what purpose would one
boast to be free of it?

To begin a true critical study of improvisers, one first must refuse
to play the Goldilocks game: *Was it improvised too little? Too much?
Or just right?* Truman Capote suffers such a lapse when he complains
of Kerouac, "That's not writing, that's typing." The *Red Book* was
begun as the *Black Books* in 1913–14. From 1914 until 1928, the manuscript was "worked … reworked and reworked," as James Hillman
points out.[11] Was it improvised or crafted? As with most "improvised"
texts, the answer is, *Yes, both.* Rather than play the Goldilocks game,
we must see that the effect of the "rhetoric of improvisation" is to
challenge the value of reason.

With regard to Trump the Goldilocks question takes this form:
"*Is he an accidental maelstrom or a canny manipulator?*"[12] Again, the

answer is, *Yes, both*. Whether or not Trump consciously deploys the rhetoric of spontaneity and its resulting chaos, the point is that it continues to work for him, sowing the chaos he relishes. Trump's taste for chaos must be analyzed to understand the power it has had.

The gesture of spontaneity assumes the primitivist premise that life is better and more authentic when unadulterated by the artifices of mind, city, or civilization. The literary form associated with this premise is pastoral, where shepherds and shepherdesses frolic in a bucolic Arcadia. The pastoral trope expresses our ambivalent, complex longings for the *locus amoenus*, the good and pleasant place, imagined as *ailleurs* or *jadis*—elsewhere or long ago. Glimmerings of that happy place can be accessed—the premise runs—by spontaneous activity or through our limbic brain.

The discourse of improvisation is infused with this longing for some form of unreason to inspire one's life. The great examples of improvisation don't necessarily give up reason.[13] They are arguments *from* Nature but not in the end *for* Nature. Thoreau urges "the tonic of wildness," but he would not have us follow him into the woods.[14] He retreats to get away from civilization ("Men labor under a mistake") but journeys to the woods "to live deliberately" (from *de-liberare*, to weigh carefully).[15] Most improvisers give us a taste of chaos but don't invite us to swallow it whole. Not Trump.

Trump's slogan "Make America Great Again" relies on the pastoral trope, evoking a greatness recalled from some past golden age or, as Hillary Clinton describes it, a "dark, divisive, negative version of nostalgia."[16] (That Trump's roots are in Queens and Manhattan suggests that his largely rural base has mistaken a trope for a type). "I'm a very instinctual person," he trumpets, "but my instinct turns out to be right."[17]

Trump is not alone in privileging our instinctual nature. In *The Red Book*, Jung argues that modern man's problem is that "… they did not live their animal."[18] What appeals to Jung is that "the animal does not rebel against its own kind. … The animal lives fittingly and true to the life of its species, neither exceeding nor falling short of it."[19]

How might we achieve a life at one with our instincts? Improvisers will speak of the muse, intuition, automatic writing, drugs—depending on their epoch's particular paradigm shift. Jung's paradigm shift will involve various constituents of the unconscious: dreams, archetypes, the collective unconscious.[20] *The Red Book* asserts that "The world accords not only with reason but also with unreason. But just as one employs reason to make sense of the world, in that what is reasonable about it approaches reason, a lack of understanding also accords with unreason."[21] Unreason, free of the directed ego, is Jung's plan for living attuned to instinct, "fittingly and true to the life of [our] species."

Trump may direct his appeal to our baser instincts and Jung to the benign teleology of the self, but they share the longing for a better place and a better way of being that is achieved spontaneously (from *sua sponte,* of its own accord).

But not all instinctual behavior is benign. Instinct, intuition, spontaneity, and inspiration—they have brought us great *and* terrible results. Some *Eurekas!* are just dumb ideas. Homer's Odysseus is the king of improvisers, but his improvisations get every one of his crewmen killed. President George W. Bush, the Decider, didn't need State Department analyses; he looked in Premier Putin's eyes and saw directly into his soul. Hitler is the most monstrous example. In Jung's report, he "listens intently to a stream of suggestions from a whispered source and then acts upon them."[22] Once you have opened the doors to external or to instinctual forces, dampening reason's ability to judge, you never know who will take the helm, whether the force steering you will be divine or demonic, healthy or pathological. How do you judge once you've dismissed judgment? President Trump is giving a bad name to improvisers everywhere.

Jung and Trump: Embracing Spontaneity

One cannot overemphasize the role of spontaneity in the careers of both Jung and Trump. Jung begins his career with the premise that psychological complexes can be discerned by tracking the speed of patients' spontaneous word associations. The Analytical Psychology emerging from the *Red Book* opens us to various constituents of the unconscious: dreams, archetypes, the collective unconscious, and the anima, which Jung writes elsewhere,

> is a 'factor' [a maker] in the proper sense of the word. Man cannot make it; on the contrary, it is always the *a priori* element in his moods, reactions, impulses, and whatever else is spontaneous in psychic life.[23]

Not just conceptual, spontaneity is also a crucial formal component. Writing before *The Red Book's* publication, Susan Rowland argued that "Jung thought that psychology writing should aspire to the greatest authenticity by including unconscious psychic creativity within writing. ... For Jung, a piece of writing was only truly valid if it retained a trace of the spontaneity that he believed to be integral to psychic functioning."[24] Publication of *The Red Book* demonstrates how that conviction emerged.

However smitten we may be with *The Red Book*'s beauty, editor Sonu Shamdasani is right to point out that a component of that beauty, like many improvisations, is its aesthetic roughness: "This is not a well-written book, nor are the paintings formally realized, but it is more effective precisely for that reason, or it is affective precisely for that reason. It jars with his own category of the aesthetic."[25] This quest to avoid the appearance of artifice is one way to understand "Jung's" vehement denial in *Black Book 2* that what he is doing is art: "Then a voice said to me, 'That is art.' ... Well I said emphatically to this voice that what I was doing was not art, and I felt a great resistance rising up within me."[26] *The Red Book* is rhetorically "artless": There is no need to play the Goldilocks game about how artless it is.

For Trump, improvisation is a persistent point of pride. Commenting on Trump's penchant for gleaning information from "the shows" rather than his staff's briefing books, presidential historian Jon Meacham comments, "His tendency to wing it—to act on his gut—effectively means that he's working off what might be called 'political hearsay.'" Indeed, when asked if he was responding intuitively when Wolf Blitzer confronted him about NATO, Trump responded, "Off the cuff … I'm an intuitive person. I didn't read books on NATO." Blitzer saw that answer as "a telling instance of what he believes is his special capacity to arrive at conclusions with little forethought." "Unabashedly improvisational," Meacham sums up, "Trump revels in his lack of conventional political or policy experience."[27]

Understanding the rhetoric of spontaneity and its fuel of primitivism helps explain Trump's political success. In analyzing his rhetoric *Politico's* Gwendolyn Blair describes:

> The rambling, the incomplete sentences, all those things that seemed proof of incompetence and inability to deal with the complicated, sophisticated issues that were going to come up for a president—not to mention all of the negative, disparaging, crude and vulgar remarks—were reframed as sincerity, authenticity, what he's really thinking, versus thoughtfulness. … Especially in a world where reality TV has played such a role … the usual metrics of reality like actual truth just don't matter. It's how it makes you feel when you're listening. And that's what he really was very, very strong at.[28]

To be spontaneous or imperfect is to be unmediated. To be mediated is to conform to or to be shaped by something less authentic. One might attribute Trump's success to television or to the anti-intellectual strain that runs deep in American history. But the primitivism or pastoralism that fuels that rhetoric is universal. It touches upon the archetype of *puer aeternus* and of "Mercurius"—Hermes in his alchemical guise—who for Jung represents "the material upon which nature worked a little, but nevertheless left imperfect."[29]

New York Times CEO Mark Thompson notes the paradox of Trump's appeal which "depends significantly on the belief that he is a truth-teller who will have nothing to do with the conventional language of politics":

We shouldn't confuse anti-rhetorical 'truth telling' with actually telling the truth. One of the advantages of this positioning is that once listeners are convinced that you're not trying to deceive them in the manner of a regular politician, they may switch off the critical faculties they usually apply to political speech and forgive you any amount of exaggeration, contradiction, or offensiveness. And if establishment rivals or the media criticize you, your supporters may dismiss that as spin.[30]

This "switching off the critical faculties" is what improvisers have been doing, at least since Erasmus's Folly quipped that her "extemporaneous speech, unpremeditated [was] all the truer for that."[31] A Catholic priest and monk, Erasmus's deep agenda in *The Praise of Folly* was to explore the Christian idea of ecstasy. Spontaneity is a trope, a stand-in for grace; Erasmus never would have confused the two. The truly great improvisers understand irony, saying one thing and meaning another. They invite us to switch off our critical faculties, accessing the Muse's inspiration, God's grace, the Romantic imagination, or the unconscious in order to enlarge rather than reject the faculty of reason. Missing this irony, many critics of "spontaneous" texts merit the charge literary critic Jerome McGann levels against our "uncritical absorption in romanticism's own self-representations."[32]

Trump's cognitive-dissonant style, on the other hand, the glittery objects he continually throws in our path, is an effort to put our critical intelligence to sleep and appeal directly to instinctive fears and animosities that live on in our lizard brains.

The Hero's Journey, Subverted

Like Joseph Campbell's hero, the improviser and his overtly unheroic persona know (or rather intuit) that the challenge is to be alert to life in the moment, to the *un-fore-seen*. To embrace such a view of man's purpose is to go beyond seizing the day. We must seize all of life: not just *carpe diem* but *carpe vitam*. To do so, as Wallace Stevens suggests, will "pierce us with strange relation"[33]—to have one's armor and artificial boundaries of sophistication, civilization, and rationality breached and ruptured so that one can perceive and make new connections. This imagery of a wound that becomes a gift suggests that the improviser can begin his or her journey in quest of a true, transcendent heroism only by abandoning his sense of adequacy or completeness.[34]

This is exactly why "Jung" must murder the culture hero Siegfried. The unheroic nature of the murder is quite clear: shot in the back, twice, from point-blank range. Jung's illumination of Siegfried's murder, the little brown man at "his" side, a shadow or Trickster figure, is one of his roughest and least masterly. Siegfried is killed not by moral and artistic strength but by weakness. "Jung" becomes master of a freedom from mastery. Siegfried "had everything in himself that I treasured as the greater and more beautiful; he was my power, my boldness, my pride."[35] That hardly seems reason for murder, but just before the assassination, "Jung" explains why: "The heroic in you is the fact that you are ruled by the thought that this or that is good, that this or that performance is indispensable, this or that cause is objectionable, this or that goal must be attained in headlong striving work, this or that pleasure should be ruthlessly repressed at all costs."[36] In his 1925 seminar, Jung reflects on this moment: "I had killed my intellect, helped on to the deed by a personification of the collective unconscious, the little brown man with me. In other words, I deposed my superior function."[37]

It is by being wounded or mastered that the hero achieves a new kind of mastery. As William Carlos Williams writes in *Kora in Hell: Improvisations*: "By the brokenness of his composition the poet makes himself master of a certain weapon which he could possess himself of in no other way."[38] The archetype of the hero contains within it spontaneity's two poles: our longing for a new mastery that we attain by being mastered by some external force or by an interior force that is not "the superior function."

What the figures who rise from his unconscious say and ask him to do shocks. "Jung" dances with "The Red One," the devil, and with

Salome; he engages in cannibalism; he embraces a Christ figure (Abraxis) who embraces evil as part of his being. As Shamdasani sums it up, "He's forced in his confrontation to encompass what he rejected in his life."[39] "Inversely exalted," as Foucault says of the madman, the improviser is authorized by that grace beyond the reach of reason that is experienced because s/he has been marginalized.[40] Paradoxically, improvisers marginalize and disempower themselves in order to gain the right to instruct the righteous.

Trump distorts the hero's journey. Where the improviser treats his wound as a gift, Trump's conveys not humility but a persistent sense of victimhood. "Victimhood" helps explain Trump's appeal to his base who share his grievances. Like many narcissists,[41] he is unable to acknowledge his deeper wounds. Trump and his followers embrace grievance with the adrenaline-fueled, fight-or-flight energy of the limbic brain: *Look what they have done to us*. While his rhetoric is saturated with broken grammar and images of American "carnage," his self-presentation is one of absolute mastery: "I alone can fix it." As for Trump's "little brown man," several of his associates lead the way, among them Steve Bannon, Roger Stone, and Vladimir Putin. Insofar as members of Trump's base are also shadow figures, they are not a "basket of deplorables" (Hillary Clinton) but of the once-deplored, the once-rejected.

Lord of Liars: Trickster, Subjectivity, and Alt-Facts

Born in pastoral Arcadia and according to Jung "a reflection of an earlier, rudimentary stage of consciousness,"[42] Hermes and his Trickster brethren embody the primitivist premise at the heart of improvisation. With winged talaria at his heels and roaming at whim anywhere, from Hades to Earth to Olympus, Hermes embodies improvisation's commitment to *quickness*—both speed of composition or action and the embrace not just of the present moment but of all of life: *carpe vitam*.

Improvisation's challenge to the mainstream is best captured in his *Homeric Hymn* by infant Hermes's fart in brother Apollo's face:

[Hermes,] lifted up by [Apollo's] arms,
intentionally
released an omen,
an insolent servant
of his stomach,
a reckless little messenger.[43]

So much for the honor that Apollo, patron of high culture and the embodiment of Olympian order is usually granted. Improvisation is a fart in the face to reason, decorum, and the notion that there is a right and orderly way.

One cannot overstate the role of Trickster in Jung's life and work. In *Black Book* 5, Philemon tells Jung that "Hermes is your daimon."[44] Hermes is the Trickster spirit that suffuses alchemy and magic, both central to Jung. Psychopompos, guide of souls to the underworld, Hermes is the god of the unconscious. The spirit of *herme*neutics, he is the bringer of meaning. If Odysseus is Hermes in human form, Jung is a psychopompos voyaging in the collective unconscious seas of universal archetype.[45]

Trump conforms to the Trickster figure in a malign, dark-mirrored fashion. A man so governed by his id, he seems to be channeling Trickster, not Trickster brought to consciousness but rather as "identification with the archetype," what Jung calls "[t]he characteristic feature of a pathological reaction. This produces," Jung adds, "a sort of inflation and possession by the emergent contents, so that they pour out in a torrent which no therapy can stop."[46]—which seems to describe Trump to a tee.

The Trickster we know and love takes down the pretentious, knocks us off our high horse when we deserve it. But where Trickster "stands in a complementary or compensatory relationship to the ego-personality,"[47] Trump the narcissist is all ego-aggrandizement. Trump promised to puncture the capital's pretentions. He promised to drain the swamp. But as the swamp creatures who populate his Cabinet demonstrate, Trump seeks only to upend presidential traditions and norms and destroy the achievements of his immediate predecessor—Trump's Siegfried—all in service of his malignant narcissism.

For Lewis Hyde, Trickster embodies "the mind that contingency demands"—an openness to life's fluidity and a determination to succeed.[48] Trump's version is his willingness to lie and to contradict himself, often within moments, based on the contingencies of each momentary frame. If the "rhetoric of reason" is based on a high estimation of objectivity, the "rhetoric of spontaneity" celebrates the value of subjectivity. Jung's visionary Analytical Psychology embraces an empirical science that does not pursue positivism's chimera of objectivity but embraces instead our inevitable subjectivity. To look at the psyche *with* the psyche is inevitably subjective. If so, says Jung, let us explore the subjectivity of dreams, archetypes, complexes, and the collective unconscious, which, though subjective, have this empirical basis: In dreams and by means of the active imagination we experience them.

Jung's embrace of this empirical subjectivity is both a legacy of the Enlightenment and an expression of High Modernism.[49] Like the Enlightenment, it rejects truths derived second-hand from tradition or authority. Like High Modernism, it rejects mere "facticity without meaning."[50] Based on empirical experience, Truth and Meaning must contain an element of subjective consciousness.

One legacy of empirical subjectivity is advocacy journalism, itself a cousin of the New Journalism, which embraced the journalist's extreme subjectivity (e.g., Hunter S. Thompson covering the campaign trail in 1972 on assorted hallucinogens). "Fair and Balanced," Fox News' newly retired slogan, was of course absurd on its face; but it is best understood as a rebuttal of High Modernism's embrace of subjectivity where agendas drive information. Of course, information is *always* driven by an agenda, our point of view, what you will. The yearning for unmediated experience—improvisation's central trope—is doomed to failure intrinsically by the "beholder's share" inherent in perception. If we want to see accurately, we must acknowledge what we contribute, the way that our perceptual lens shapes our world. "There is no innocent eye," says art historian E. H. Gombrich, no unmediated experience.[51] For aesthetics philosopher Nelson Goodman,

The eye always comes ancient to its work, obsessed by its past and by old and new insinuations of the ear, nose, tongue, fingers, heart, and brain. It functions not as an instrument self-powered and alone, but as a dutiful member of a complex and capricious organism. Not only how but what it sees is regulated by need and prejudice.[52]

The idea is central to Hillman's project in *Re-Visioning Psychology:*

Every notion in our minds, each perception of the world and sensation in ourselves must go through a psychic organization in order to 'happen' at all. Every single feeling or observation occurs as a psychic event by first forming a fantasy-image.[53]

And it is no less true in the pursuit of science: We see light as a particle or as a wave depending on the hypothesis and experiment we submit it to. The agenda of advocacy journalists and of whistle-blowers, whom Trump finds so objectionable, is simply that America should be a nation ruled by law, science, and a sense of fair play, an agenda mediated by the norms established by the Constitution and Bill of Rights.

Denying this hermetic and Modernist truth, Trump manages to have it both ways. If journalists' reporting is shaped by the ideologies that inform their advocacy ("Fake Facts!"), then why should he not make up facts according to whim ("alt-facts").

The Improviser-in-Chief: Culture Bearer or Destroyer?

Trump's rise could not have disconcerted me more. In March 2015, my anatomy of improvisation was published (40 years in the making). Like democracy, I argued, improvisation believes every voice, however marginal or foolish, should be heard. And every vote counted. So when Trump descended the golden escalator at Trump Tower to launch his campaign—*I am running to listen to your voice*—I saw that improvisation could also be the agent of demagoguery. Where the Hermetic Trickster is a culture bearer who brings fire and light to humanity and invents the rituals that will honor the gods (creating Hellenic culture), Trump enjoys his role as culture destroyer. "He was supposed to be a great maker of things," writes Rebecca Solnit, "but he was mostly a breaker."[54] In so doing, he seems to be channeling Dionysos rather than Hermes.

For, Trump as dark, inflated improviser goes beyond Hermes's gentle ironies. His is that Dionysian improv that seeks to tear everything apart, even improv's decorum of the indecorous.

Dionysos is often considered a Trickster but rarely in the same breath with Hermes. Like Hermes, "'Dionysiac religion' functions as an 'anti-system' and 'protest movement'"[55]—a fart in the face or poke in the eye. Dionysos is a type, like Christ, of the vegetative, dying god. Twice born (the second time from Zeus's thigh), he promises rebirth or re-memberment.[56] But Dionysos is a more extreme Trickster figure, one who like Hermes promises to be the catalyst for a new order but rarely hangs around for its emergence. It is difficult to dismiss the final image of Euripides's *Bacchae*, the most complete portrait of a Greek deity that we have, which ends with the ultra-rationalist King Pentheus's severed head on Dionyos's *thyrsos* or pike, and no new king in the offing. Perhaps Euripides saw something later commentators miss.

Like Dionysos a roarer (*Bromios*), Trump has stumbled on a well-established pattern associated with the cult of Dionysos, which flourished for 1,000 years until the triumph of Christianity. A glance at this obscure cult might help us understand current American political discourse. According to Richard Seaford, Dionysos is 3,000 years old and "our oldest living symbol."[57] His cult is long dead, but as Seaford argues, the longings for transcendence that Dionysos spoke to have endured, "an irreducible symbol for the antithesis of something basically wrong with our society."[58]

Known as the god of wine and revelry, Dionysos—or Bacchus in Rome—is the god of ecstasy, the transformation of individual identity. According to the chorus of Euripides's *Bacchae*, Dionysos "gave the pain-removing delight of wine equally to the wealthy man and to the lesser man."[59] He is not worshipped through the mediation of a priesthood in a temple, but directly in nature. He is god of the people and of their demagogues.

In Euripides's *Bacchae*, Dionysos incites his followers to tear Pentheus, the autocratic and hyper-rational Theban king, limb from limb. Pentheus's own mother, Agavê, blinded by Dionysian ecstasy and mistaking her son for a mountain lion, leads the charge. If Trump's followers seem blind to his imperfections and, evidence to the contrary notwithstanding, trust he will deliver on his promises, that's just how Dionysos functions: He intoxicates. As Seaford points out, Dionysos is "unique among the gods in the extent to which he is accompanied by a cortege, his *thiasos*."[60] While Trump clearly lacks Dionysos's feminine side, nonetheless his *thiasos*, like Dionysos's, contains more women than polls predicted for a serial woman-abuser. It is ungenerous but nonetheless difficult to ignore the resemblance of Trump's red-capped retinue to Dionysos's other followers, the priapic satyrs.

An enemy to autocrats like Pentheus and offering ecstasy to anyone who will drink his heady wine, Dionysos's initial appeal is democratic and egalitarian. While in a compelling essay Elizabeth Mika sees the roots of Trump's tyranny in his and his base's malignant narcissism, it is also true that tyranny has archetypal resonance.[61] This is a matter of historical fact. In classical Greece and Rome, aspiring tyrants linked themselves to Dionysos to challenge the reigning hierarchies—to drain the swamp. "The forgotten man and woman will never be forgotten again," Trump tweeted after his win.

Democracy and demagoguery share more than the Latin root. Though Trump's campaign broke every rule and overturned every assumption, he was following in the footsteps of the all-conquering Roman Mark Antony who "was welcomed back to Rome as 'Dionysos' by the whole community."[62] before transforming Rome's oligarchy into an autocratic empire.

Other Roman emperors identified with Dionysos. Renowned for his sadism, extravagance, and sexual perversity, Caligula dressed as the god and was called the "new Dionysos." Nero, too, identified as the "new Dionysos."[63] Is tweeting the new fiddling?

Trump's "identification" with the Dionysos archetype helps explain his allure and rise to power. Like Dionysos, Trump seems determined to rip everything apart. In 2014, he imagined apocalypse as the solution to the country's ills: "*When the economy crashes, when the country goes to total hell and everything is a disaster. Then you'll have a [chuckles], you know, you'll have riots to go back to where we used to be when we were great.*"[64] Promised this apocalypse, Trump's Bacchante care little about his policies or his failure to achieve them. In their blind ecstasy, his base seems ready to dismember their fellow citizens. As Trump likes to threaten: *You can count on it.*

Trickster and Civic Renewal?

It is difficult to imagine Trump following the course of the Trickster cycle that Jung, following Paul Radin, describes:

> As Radin points out, the civilizing process begins within the framework of the trickster cycle itself … The naïve reader may imagine that when the dark aspects disappear they are no longer there in reality. But that is not the case at all, as experience shows. What actually happens is that the conscious mind is then able to free itself from the fascination with evil and is no longer obliged to live it compulsively.[65]

But what one fears is the shadow's return, which Jung describes in a passage that captures what we have been witnessing in Trump's political career:

> But if the conscious should find itself in a critical or doubtful situation, then it soon becomes apparent that the shadow has not dissolved into nothing but is only waiting for a favorable opportunity to reappear as a projection upon one's neighbor. If this trick is successful, there is immediately created between them that world of primordial darkness where everything that is characteristic of trickster can happen—even on the highest plane of

civilization. The best examples of these 'monkey tricks,' as popular speech aptly and truthfully sums up this state of affairs in which everything goes wrong and nothing intelligent happens except by mistake at the last moment, are naturally to be found in politics.[66]

"Projection upon one's neighbor," "primordial darkness," "these 'monkey tricks' ... found in politics": Jung's anticipation of the devolution we've been experiencing is striking.

If Trump is channeling a dark Dionysos, is there hope for civic renewal? If there is, then surely it will come homeopathically in small doses of his fellow Trickster Hermes. For Nietzsche it was Apollo who, uniting with Dionysos, gave birth to tragedy. We need rather a union between Apollo and Hermes's comedic spirit.

We stand now before a wall already built by Trump, not a wall of bricks and mortar paid for with Mexican pesos, but rather one built with the cognitive dissonance he bewilders us with. A wall against reason and logic and normality. In Trump's wall, there is no gate: dizzied, we face *aporia*, no pore, no opening, no way forward. But such rigidity and opaqueness are exactly what invites the shimmering, opportunistic Hermes, lord of thresholds, gates, and hinges.[67] The way through this apocalypse is not by Saturnian denial or Apollonian analytic rebuttal, and least of all by the Ares-driven anger and violence of the Antifas. It is by laughter, the laughter that Hermes used to defeat Apollo's and Zeus's anger in the *Hymn*. Most of all, we need the *mētic* gift of creativity by which Hermes improvised the lyre out of a tortoise shell, a gift with which he deflated Apollo's anger. In return for his brother's *mētic* creativity and his winking good-humor, Apollo gifted Hermes his winged caduceus.[68] Ginette Paris describes Hermes's wand as "entwined [by] two serpents of equal but opposing force—a symbol of equilibrium through the integration of contrary forces."[69]

Jung found his equilibrium not by meeting the violence of the Great War with violence but rather by developing the active imagination. He fought it with the hermetic role-playing from which emerged both his *Red Book* and his Analytical Psychology. Civic renewal must come through hermetic improvisation: street theater, flash mobs, rallies, and marches. The Woman's March on Washington following Trump's inauguration elicited brilliant hermetic gestures, the bright pink vagina costumes and pussycat pink knit caps. The Women's March also led to a groundbreaking number of women across the country who decided to run for office, from school boards and city councils to state legislatures and governors' races. These women bring Apollo to the party. We must not forget or shun the Apollonian element. As Jung writes,

> Conscious and unconscious do not make a whole when one of them is suppressed and injured by the other. If they must contend, let it at least be a fair fight with equal rights on both sides. Both are aspects of life. Consciousness should defend its reason and protect itself, and the chaotic life of the unconscious should be given the chance of having its way too—as much of it as we can stand. This means open conflict and open collaboration at once. That, evidently, is the way human life should be. It is the old game of hammer and anvil: between them the patient iron is forged into an indestructible whole, an 'individual.'[70]

It's one thing for the improviser to gather the energy and power of an unstructured *thiasos*. But once the gate is open, we must act to address or redress the structures of government being undermined by Trump and the Republican RedMap gerrymandering project. Through Hermetic improvisation *and* Apollonian decorous, normative action, we can recover the true spirit and the letter of democracy, the polyphony of one person, one vote, every voice heard.

Endnotes

[1] Quoted in Kurt Andersen, *Fantasyland: How America Went Haywire: A 500-Year History* (New York, NY: Random House, 2017), 4.

[2] C.G. Jung, "A Study in the Process of Individuation," in *CW*, vol. 9/I (Princeton, NJ: Princeton University Press, 1968), par. 620.

[3] For an anatomy of these persistent formal and thematic elements, see Chapter 3, "Through Candor ... A Candid Kind": The Conventions of Literary Improvisation," in my *A Taste for Chaos: The Art of Literary Improvisation* (New Orleans, LA: Spring Journal Books, 2015), 55-117.

[4] See Rosalie Colie's discussion of *novum repertum* in *Resources of Kind: Genre-Theory in the Renaissance*, ed. Barbara Lewalski (Berkeley, CA: University of California Press, 1973).

[5] "Jung" in scare quotes will refer to the persona of *The Red Book*.

[6] C.G. Jung, *The Red Book: Liber Novus*, ed. Sonu Shamdasani, trans. John Peck, Mark Kyburz, and Sonu Shamdasani (New York, NY: W.W. Norton, 2009), 314.

[7] Jung, *The Red Book*, 229 n2.

[8] Ibid.

[9] E.g., Ernst Robert Curtius, *European Literature and the Latin Middle Ages*, trans. Willard R. Trask (1953; repr., Princeton, NJ: Princeton University Press, 1973), 63; and "Appendix B: Vocabulary and Diction in *Utopia*," in *The Complete Works of St. Thomas More*, eds. Edward Surtz and J. H. Hexter (New Haven, CT: Yale University Press, 1965), 4:580.

[10] Iain McGilchrist, *The Divided Brain and the Search for Meaning* (New Haven, CT: Yale University Press, 2012) Kindle Edition, loc. 373. "Most people," he writes, "are completely and unreflectively seduced by the rhetoric of reason."

[11] James Hillman and Sonu Shamdasani, *Lament of the Dead: Psychology After Jung's Red Book* (New York, NY: W.W. Norton, 2013), 142. Compare Kerouac: while always presenting *On the Road* as the caffeine-fueled product of three weeks' typing on a 120-foot scroll, it is equally true that he then edited it for six years.

[12] "All in With Chris Hayes," MSNBC, September 25, 2017.

13 A brief list will help orient my readers. I treat all of these, among others, in *A Taste for Chaos: The Homeric Hymn to Hermes*, Pindar's *Odes*, Apuleius's *Golden Ass*, Rabelais's *Gargantua and Pantagruel*, Montaigne's *Essais*, *Utopia*, *Paradise Lost*, *Tristram Shandy*, *Le neveu de Rameau*, "Tintern Abbey," *Sartor Resartus*, *Adventures of Huckleberry Finn*, *Ulysses*, *The Great Gatsby*, Valéry's *Idée Fixe*, Mann's *Doctor Faustus*.

14 Henry David Thoreau, *Walden, Civil Disobedience, and Other Writings*, ed. William Rossi (New York, NY: W.W. Norton, 2008), 213.

15 Ibid., 7, 65.

16 "All in With Chris Hayes," MSNBC, September 25, 2017.

17 http://time.com/4710456/donald-trump-time-interview-truth-falsehood/?xid=homepage.

18 Jung, *The Red Book*, 296.

19 Ibid.

20 Ulrich Hoerni writes that "*The Red Book* would thus be a poetic vision of a paradigm shift in psychotherapy," in "The Genesis of *The Red Book* and its Publication," in Thomas Kirsch and George Hogenson, *The Red Book: Reflections on C.G. Jung's Liber Novus* (London: Routledge, 2014), 9.

21 Jung, *The Red Book*, 314.

22 C.G. Jung, *C.G. Jung Speaking: Interviews and Encounters*, eds. W. McGuire & R.F.C. Hull (Princeton, NJ: Princeton University Press, 1977), 115–135.

23 C.G. Jung, "Archetypes of the Collective Unconscious," in *CW*, vol. 9/I (Princeton, NJ: Princeton University Press, 1968), par. 57.

24 Susan Rowland, *Jung as a Writer* (London: Routledge, 2005), 2, 4.

25 Hillman and Shamdasani, *Lament of the Dead*, 28.

26 Quoted in Jung, *The Red Book*, 199.

27 Jon Meacham, "What a President Needs to Know," *Time* 7/25 2016, https://www.yahoo.com/news/president-needs-know-000000146.html.

28 Gwendolyn Blair, "He Was as Surprised as Anyone," *Politico*, November 11, 2016. http://www.politico.com/magazine/story/2016/11/donald-trump-wins-2016-biographers-214448.

29 C.G. Jung, "The Spirit Mercurius," in *CW*, vol. 13 (Princeton, NJ: Princeton University Press, 1967), par. 282. Jung is quoting the 16th-century alchemical treatise *Rosarium Philosophorum*.

30 Mark Thompson, *Enough Said: What's Gone Wrong with the Language of Politics?* (New York, NY: St. Martin's Press, 2016. Kindle Edition), loc. 1441-1442.

31 Desiderius Erasmus, *The Praise of Folly*, trans. Clarence H. Miller (New Haven, CT: Yale University Press, 1979), 12. Folly continues: "I say this because I wouldn't want you to think that I made it up just to show my cleverness, as ordinary speechmakers generally do. For you know that such orators even though they have labored over a speech for thirty whole years (and plagiarized some of it at that), will still swear that they dashed it off in a couple of days, or even dictated it, as a mere exercise. As for me, the method I like best of all is simply *'to blurt out whatever pops into my head.'* (emphasis in original).

32 Jerome McGann, *The Romantic Ideology: A Critical Introduction* (Chicago, IL: University of Chicago Press, 1983), 1.

33 Wallace Stevens, "Notes Toward a Supreme Fiction" in *Collected Poetry and Prose* (New York, NY: Library of America, 1997), 332.

34 Joseph Campbell, *The Hero with A Thousand Faces* (New York, NY: Pantheon, 1949), 16-17.

35 Jung, *The Red Book*, 242.

36 Ibid., 240.

37 C.G. Jung, *Introduction to Jungian Psychology. Notes of the Seminar on Analytical Psychology Given in 1925* (Princeton, NJ: Princeton University Press, 2012), 62.

38 William Carlos Williams, *Kora in Hell: Improvisations* (New York, NY: New Directions, 1957), 19.

39 Hillman and Shamdasani, *Lament of the Dead*, 20.

40 Michel Foucault, *Madness and Civilization: A History of Insanity in the Age of Reason*, trans. Richard Howard (New York, NY: Vintage, 1973), 11.

41 See *"A Clear and Present Danger: Narcissism in the Era of President Trump*, eds. Steven Buser and Len Cruz (Asheville, NC: Chiron Publications, 2017).

42 C.G. Jung, "On the Psychology of the Trickster-Figure," in *CW*, vol. 9/I (Princeton, NJ: Princeton University Press, 1968), par. 467.

43 *The Homeric Hymns*, trans. Charles Boer (Kingston, RI and London: Asphodel Press, 2006), 47.

44 Jung, *The Red Book*, 337 n25.

[45] As I argue in "Hermes and Literary Improvisation," Chapter 7 in *A Taste for Chaos,* 212-217.

[46] Jung, "A Study in the Process of Individuation," *CW* 9/I, par. 621.

[47] Jung, "On the Psychology of the Trickster-Figure," *CW* 9/I, par. 468.

[48] Lewis Hyde, *Trickster Makes This World: Mischief, Myth and Art* (New York, NY: Farrar, Straus and Giroux, 1998), 141ff.

[49] On Jung relation to the Modernist movement in the 20th century arts, see Michael V. Spano, "Modern(-ist) Man in Search of a Soul: Jung's *Red Book* as Modernist Visionary Literature," www.cgjungpage.org/learn/articles/literature/934-modernistmaninsearchofasouljungsredbookasmodernistvisionaryliterature (retrieved September 26, 2017). On *The Red Book's* relation to Joyce's *Ulysses,* see my chapter "Pierce[D] … With Strange Relation": Jung, Joyce, And Mann Embrace the Back Streets," in *A Taste for Chaos,* 367-419.

[50] Murray Stein, *Jung's Map of the Soul: An Introduction* (Chicago, IL: Open Court, 1998).

[51] See E. H. Gombrich, "Evidence of Images," in *Interpretation: Theory and Practice,* ed. Charles S. Singleton (Baltimore, MD: John Hopkins University Press, 1969), 43.

[52] Nelson Goodman, *Languages of Art* (Indianapolis, IN: Bobbs-Merrill, 1968), 7-8.

[53] James Hillman, *Re-visioning Psychology* (New York, NY: Harper & Row, 1976), xvii.

[54] Rebecca Solnit, "The Loneliness of Donald Trump," *LitHub,* May 30, 2017, http://lithub.com/rebecca-solnit-the-loneliness-of-donald-trump/.

[55] Seaford quoting Marcel Detienne's *Dionysos Slain.* loc. 343.

[56] See, e.g., Susan Rowland, *Remembering Dionysus: Revisioning Psychology and Literature in C.G. Jung and James Hillman* (New York, NY: Routledge, 2017).

[57] Richard Seaford, *Dionysos* (London and New York: Routledge, 2006), Introduction.

[58] Ibid., 12.

[59] Quoted in Seaford, *Dionysos,* 18.

[60] Ibid., 32.

[61] Elizabeth Mika, "Who Goes Trump? Tyranny as a Triumph of Narcissism," in *The Dangerous Case of Donald Trump: 27 Psychiatrists and Mental Health Experts Assess a President,* ed. Bandy X. Lee (New York, NY: St. Martin's Press, Kindle Edition, 2017).

[62] Seaford, *Dionysos*, 38.

[63] A.J. Woodman, *Tacitus Reviewed* (Oxford: Clarendon Press, 1998), 216.

[64] See http://video.foxnews.com/v/3179604851001/?#sp=show-clips.

[65] Jung, "On the Psychology of the Trickster-Figure," *CW* 9/I, par. 477.

[66] Ibid.

[67] On trickster as master of "pores," see Hyde, *Trickster Makes this World*, 46-54.

[68] On the role of *mētic* imagination, see my "Jung's *Red Book, Improvisation, and The Mētic Spirit*," *International Journal of Jungian Studies*, April 2017.

[69] Ginette Paris, *Pagan Grace: Dionysos, Hermes, and Goddess Memory in Daily Life* (Thompson, CT: Spring Publications, 2015), Kindle loc. 1444.

[70] C.G. Jung, "Conscious, Unconscious, and Individuation," *CW*, vol. 9/I (Princeton, NJ: Princeton University Press, 1968), par. 522.

Dreaming *The Red Book* Onward:
What Do the Dead Seek Today?

Al Collins

A troupe of Anabaptist "Dead" rang Carl Jung's doorbell in January 1916, disrupting the family's Sunday routine, to demand his help in finding answers to spiritual questions they had pursued, fruitlessly, in Jerusalem.[1] Their need had outlasted their lives and persisted even now in their posthumous state.[2] These Dead were convinced that Jung "[has] what we desire. Not your blood, but your light."[3] Like Christine Maillard and others, Elaine Molchanov and I have argued that Jung's "Dead" represented not only spirits of the recently deceased of the sort he was intimately familiar with from experience with his uncanny mother and his cousin Helly Preiswerk, but his ancestral clans, including lineages of Protestant pastors and scholars, Christianity more broadly, his historical Zeitgeist (German culture in the modern era), and of course his own spiritual emptiness, which pressed him more immediately than any other concern.[4] The quest for his "soul" that had preoccupied Jung at least since 1913 had come to enough resolution by this time that he could speak of it to others, and in the "Seven Sermons to the Dead,"[5] that he tells us were written (or transcribed) over the three nights after the visitation Jung, or his inner guide, Philemon, crystallized an answer that had developed through years of active dialogue with the figures of his unconscious. Extracted from Jung's personal notebooks (the *Black Books*) and printed separately for a few select friends and relatives, and then some favored patients, the *Septem Sermones ad Mortuos*, and the more finished *Red Book*, for which it was intended and where it was finally placed by Sonu Shamdasani in the 2009 edition, contained the seeds of much that he would publish in more elaborated and rational form over the next 40 years. But what exactly it was that the Dead and their culture needed from Jung (and whether they found it in the

"Sermons") is a deep, complex, and subtle question. What *is* evident is the depth of their spiritual hunger and the fact that our culture is no less ravenous one hundred years later. Perhaps clarifying Philemon's charge from the Dead at that time, and assessing the adequacy of his response, may help in addressing what may be the equally vexed questions of what our dead and moribund selves and cultures seek today.

Christine Maillard has demonstrated convincingly that what Jung called (in a *Black Book* note) his "intensive unconscious relation to India in the Red Book"[6] is responsible for much of the cosmogony and anthropology of the "Seven Sermons."[7] The fundamental principle of the "Pleroma," a primordial "fullness" that is also empty, she finds to have roots in the early Indian concept of "brahman" and the somewhat later Samkhyan psycho-material principle of "*prakriti*." In Indian mythology, the world process evolves not as in Judeo-Christian myth through a creation *ex nihilo* or by divine fiat but in a flowing, birth-like (and feminine) emanation or externalization of more specific forms that emerge or develop from less definite ones and ultimately from a formless or homeostatic matrix. Motivating this dynamic transformative process of the natural and psychological worlds is a principle of egoity or "I-ness" (*ahamkara*) that, in turn, evolves from a certain distraction or impulse[8] in the potentially sharp capacity for insight called *buddhi*. Strikingly similar to the *ahamkara*, in the *Sermons*, the Pleroma is endowed with a *principium individuationis*, or inherent tendency to develop, in a process that is like birth, into more specific forms that organize, through opposition and complementarity around the sense of being a self or "essence."[9] Maillard sees this individuating aspect of the Pleroma reflected in Jung's other works from about the same time[10] and finds it to be at the heart of his mature psychology. The tendency to become oneself, a being partly differentiated from the Pleroma, is balanced by the compensatory and equally fundamental truth of continuing to rest *in* the Pleroma—later called the "collective unconscious"—and drawing sustenance from it. "*Participation mystique*," the anthropologist Levy-Bruhl's term that Jung later adopted for this fact of always having one foot still in the magic pool from which we are stepping out, must be honored but also resisted as the person struggles to assert her unique "I-am"- and "I-am-this"-ness. Jung in his *Red Book* struggled with the tendency of the psyche to merge back into its psychological source,[11] which India calls "Nature" or *prakriti* (or more specifically "unmanifest" [*avyakta*] or "root" [*mula*] *prakriti*). The Dead, on the contrary, suffer from too great a detachment from the Pleroma, because they see themselves as exclusively individual, cut off and sharply demarcated entities. Maillard finds that there are two distinct moments in individuation. First, the inherently timeless and spaceless Pleroma manifests a spatiotemporal "*Créature*" principle (Maillard's French translation of Jung's term "Creatur," a variant of German "Kreatur"[12]), which can best be understood as a collective noun for the beings of the world (and thus secondarily can represent creation as a whole).[13] As a specific creature (e.g., a person) distinguishes herself from the matrix and comes more fully into her own essence, paradoxically she also ideally realizes more completely her inherent orientation toward the Pleroma, which manifests in the final Sermon in the symbol of her own particular star shining in midheaven. This new, conscious orientation toward one's own cynosure (the star is a symbol for what is later called the "self") is the second part of individuation.[14] The mistake made by the Dead, like that of the Gnostic "Demiurge," was to get stuck at the moment of separation and inflated by the power that the exaggerated sense of autonomy brings. Their growth halted, they lost the sense of essence, the fluid dynamism of a deepening individuation, and became isolated individuals: in a word, neurotic modern man.

The recognition that one is not ultimately a closed-off particle of consciousness but rather an open "door"[15] (or portal), a zone of transition between personal selfhood and the internal infinity of the Pleroma, constitutes the main part of what Jung (or his guru personality, Philemon) teaches to the Dead. Paralleling the individualism of persons, as the Dead understood themselves, their monotheistic, patriarchal God likewise holds himself aloof and therefore must also be reconceived in terms of the more feminine and porous Pleroma. How far do these alterations in perspective answer the Dead's questions about life and God, and thus quench their doubts? The "Seven Sermons" at first sight do not tell us much about how the Dead responded to Philemon's teaching (except at the end they are finally able to ascend and pass away like smoke in the air above a shepherd's fire), but the figure of "Jung" himself, Philemon's interlocutor "me" in the dialogues set between the sermons, stands in for the Dead, extends their questioning, and pushes Philemon for fuller answers. Recognition that the Dead represent the whole of pre-World War I Western culture as it thrust forward into Jung's kitchen (and psyche) helps to understand Philemon's response both to the Dead and to "Jung," and to follow the thread of their questioning as it evolved in post-war culture and into our own time a hundred years later.

The "Seven Sermons" represents a visionary attempt to integrate the psychological work of the previous three years recorded in the earlier parts of *The Red Book*: *Liber Primus* and *Liber Secundus*. Jung has gone far on his journey beyond and beneath the "spirit of [his] times" and is now ready to share the fruits of his journey with his fellows. For him, the Sermons are in part an effort to teach what he has learned, to tell it in the form of a myth for his time, and to try on the role of guru to his culture.[16] On the other hand, he had to be careful not to identify too closely with the Wise Man or guru archetype[17] that Philemon symbolizes in the Sermons. This he did first by not putting this material out in completely public form as a work of art or a prophetic text. Rather, circulation was limited to the tight circle of his family and several select colleagues (especially Toni Wolff[18], who was both colleague and—in a way—family), and a few patients. Second, the *Red Book* text does not touch on Jung's personal life (as it does in the *Memories, Dreams, Reflections* frame story, where the Dead literally crowd through his door to demand answers and upset his young family). Jung later tells us that the text "began to flow out of me and in the course of three evenings the thing was written."[19] Apparently, he was caught up in a state of *participation mystique* but gained distance from his text as he fit it into the evolving *Red Book* (in the preliminary form of the *Black Books*), where six of the seven sessions of discourse between Philemon and the Dead are separated by reflective dialogues between Philemon and "Jung" ("I").[20] But what was the myth that the "Seven Sermons" (and by extension *The Red Book* as a whole) told, and what was the cultural question that it addressed? Most importantly, did it successfully answer that question?

Jung makes it clear in the "Seven Sermons" that the Dead (who are really Un-dead, since they continue to quest for answers to their questions) have been disappointed in the teaching they found in Jerusalem, the locus of the three "Abrahamic" religions. The Judeo-Christian tradition has proved inadequate, and they seek something more, which Jung consciously locates in Alexandria, "where East and West meet,"[21] but unconsciously in the East, and especially in India.[22] Somehow the Dead are drawn to Jung, as if by unconscious attraction, sensing that in him there may be found an answer to their quest. What is it that they miss in the Abrahamic religions, and what do they seek? The sketch of the teaching of the "Seven Sermons" above suggests that the burning need was to connect (the) Creatur[23] to the Pleroma. Unlike the atomic, cut-off, demarcated, souls of Reformation and Enlightenment Europeans, the ideal "Creatur" maintains connection to its origins in the Pleroma, and even as it (he, she) coagulates or "essentializes" out of the matrix, an "umbilical"[24] tie to the Pleroma is sustained. It is this tie to the unconscious that is the source of meaning for each Creatur, for it expresses its (her, his) original nature in all that it (she, he) does and is, even though Creatur lives in the world of differentiation. The disappointment of the Dead is their growing recognition of the inadequacy of Enlightenment (and Protestant) individualism, the Cartesian presumption of "cogito ergo sum," with its flat conclusion that "I am" a separate, bounded assertion of egoity, and its purely masculine, monotheistic God. In response, Philemon/Jung would say, "I am (and remain, ineluctably) created (Creatur)." Quoting an alchemical text toward the end of his life, Jung wrote: "[in Bollingen] I am, as it were, the 'age-old son of the mother.'"[25] Thus the connection between Creatur and Pleroma is maintained.

In the "Seven Sermons," a key difference between the individualistic way of relating to God and the way the Creatur relates to the Pleroma is expressed in the theme, repeated several times, of *knowing by being* as opposed to merely believing. This theme emerged 40 years later in Jung's famous interview with John Freeman, when he answered the question whether he now believes in God by saying that he does not need to believe because he *knows*. Belief (in God or any other transcendent reality) is impossible for a cut-off individual because by its very nature an individual is alienated from his source, condemned to Hell and refused Heaven as Protestantism believes unless redeemed by the paradigm-breaking action of Jesus Christ, who somehow penetrates the shell of the demarcated soul and reunites it with its Creator/source.[26] We can never really know whether we are redeemed (saved) or condemned to hell precisely because the reflective shell of our alienating selfhood prevents our seeing anything beyond its horizon. In discussing with Philemon the contents of the first Sermon to the Dead, Jung asks: "But do you, Oh wise Philemon, believe what you teach?" Philemon answers:

> It is what I know how to say, not because I believe it but because I know it. … should I teach a belief to those [the Dead] who have discarded belief? … I am certain these things are as I say. … these things are as I know them, since my knowledge is precisely these things themselves.[27]

Philemon had expressed the things he both knew and was as follows: "Not your thinking, but your essence, is differentiation. Therefore you must not strive for what you *conceive* as distinctiveness but for *your own essence*."[28] We must come to what we are; what we think we know *about* ourselves, especially our distinctiveness (individuality), is secondary. This expresses the whole point of Jung's individuation (as opposed to individualism). Becoming what one essentially is, attaining one's "uniqueness" as he often puts it later, means to maintain the tie with the Pleroma without falling into the Pleroma and dissolving in its absolute nothingness. This is also essentially why Jung, despite his deep roots in Indian thought, was always suspicious of it, particularly as a resource for Westerners: There is a danger of falling into the nothingness of the Pleroma and losing one's essence. For Jung, European consciousness is too individualistic, alienated, cut off from the unconscious. Indian consciousness, while aware of the need for a place in the middle (a "not-two" or *nirdvandva* position), steers too close to the unconscious void for Western comfort.

Today's Dead

If the Dead in Jung's time were the cut-off individuals of the scientific revolution, Enlightenment, and Reformation lacking inner authority and grounding in the "Pleroma," who might they be today? Pursuing the idea of the Pleroma as *prakriti*, I will suggest that a cultural shift took place after (and partly as a result of) the Great War[29], which led to Jung dropping his *Red Book* and moving toward the question of spirit and psyche in matter (alchemy, the collaboration with Wolfgang Pauli on physics and synchronicity, UFOs). Henceforth, the unanswered questions of the Dead would be concerned with finding psyche and the divine in the cosmic, material, and physical aspects of *prakriti* (i.e., in the outer world) as well as in the inner, psychological reality of the collective unconscious. Matter, too, must have an essence that it strives to become more deeply. Today we seek a divinity in nature and a narrative of our life in physical matter that will complement and extend individuation—the shift of selfhood from the ego to the (inner) self must now include a discovery of selfhood in the world of matter.[30]

I will briefly sketch three representations of contemporary despair and potential hope in the period after Jung's fundamental *Red Book* insights (around 1913-17), and attempt to connect them to the cultural situation as Jung left it after the *Red Book*.[31] These will be T. S. Eliot's lethargic and sexually inert postwar urban dwellers in "The Wasteland," resisting the efforts of April to "breed lilacs out of the dead land," the loveless "Strangers" of the underrated film "Dark City," and the endearingly lost Theodore Twombly of the more recent film "Her." Binding these three outwardly disparate cultural products together is the quest of psychologically dead or moribund humans for new life.

Cut-off individualism and alienation were the modernist field of battle, the "Kurukshetra"[32] of World War I in Europe. Just a few years after Jung (in the midst of the war) diagnosed the situation in the indistinct faces of the Dead who invaded his home demanding answers for their predicament, T. S. Eliot (in the war's aftermath) imagined a now-abandoned battlefield (Ypres or Passchendaele) superimposed on postwar London, ghosts or survivors wandering among the twisted roots and branches of blasted trees and garbage-strewn river banks, but stirred in spite of themselves to seek in the torn dirt and muck for new life. His "Wasteland," as Pericles Lewis tells us, aims "to collect all the bric-a-brac of an exhausted civilization into one giant, foul rag and bone shop."[33] Its inner resources depleted, the postwar world is tormented by the rot and smell of the trash pile of the urban landscape-cum-battlefield, which won't let it doze. Nature in its relentless push out of death into new birth becomes the source of renewal. Eliot wrote the poem partly in a Swiss sanatorium, his personal life in shambles due to a disastrous, sexless marriage.[34] The agony of being stirred to new life, sexuality and fruitfulness, begins with cruel April "breeding lilacs out of the dead land"[35] and ends a few months later with thunder booming off the Himalayas[36] announcing the monsoon with the repeated Sanskrit syllable "DA," commanding us to "give, show mercy, control yourself" ("*Datta … Dayadhvam … Damyata*").[37] Eliot mines the trash heap of history, as W.B. Yeats stirred the "foul rag and bone shop of the heart"[38] like a compost heap for nutrients, to fertilize the soil of poetry. And the work leads, if we are lucky, to "the awful daring of a moment's surrender"[39] and to new vital energies that connect the urban individual to the earth. But such moments, as when "a woman drew her long black hair out tight / And fiddled whisper music on those strings,"[40] are rare. Much of the verse answers, "Unreal City, / Under the brown fog of a winter dawn," "strange synthetic perfumes," rape and abortion, bad taste, and "The rattle of bones, and chuckle spread from ear to ear."[41] Eliot evokes the urban multitude undone by spiritual death who flow over London Bridge in the brown fog, mouthing "What shall we do tomorrow? / What shall we ever do?" only to be confronted by the publican's "HURRY UP PLEASE ITS

TIME."[42] The poem zooms in and out restlessly, questing for relief like a lens seeking focus between the systole of "a rat ... dragging its slimy belly on the bank" and the diastole of "sweet Thames, run softly, till I end my song."[43]

If etiolating isolation is one dominant concern of "The Wasteland," continuing the problematic of individualism and its overcoming in the *Red Book*, a related theme is collective or media culture, an apparent reverse of individualism that was becoming culturally dominant around this time in the form of the gramophone,[44] the radio, and motion picture films. The rise of popular media might seem to sweep away isolation within the confines of the individual mind, but arguably it has had the opposite effect, leading to phenomena like the Japanese "hikikomori," teens addicted to video games who live in their own rooms while parents bring them meals on a tray.[45] Pushing back against this fragmentation, a distinguished line of science fiction films has explored alienation in the mediated urban world, consistently seeking in the media themselves a potential for answering the need of isolated and emotionally dead persons for contact with their authentic, essential roots in the cosmos outside. Matter is explored for its spiritual potential in the same electronic machines—computers—that threaten to suck away our soul and leave us, once again, isolated in individualism. The ambivalence that Jung finds in Abraxas, the image of psychic action (Wirkung)—both God and Devil, good and evil, life and death—Nature, in the form of our portal into it, the computing machine, also fully expresses this. I will look at two of the films that express this ambivalence and allude to a few more.

"Dark City" (1999), the superior precursor of "The Matrix" (2000), like its more famous sibling explores the image of humans controlled by machines, individuals (as we see ourselves) manipulated by the media that author our phenomenal world. These invisible "noumenatic"[46] agents, veritable Wizards of our Oz, have been seen by Theodor Adorno as the forces of late capitalism and by Michel Foucault as the epistemes of social power. Deluded humans or quasi-human "mechas"[47] who think we live our own lives, we are in fact lived by forces beyond our ken. This general story framework can be seen not only in "The Matrix" and "Dark City" but also in "A.I.," "Ex Machina," "Blade Runner" and more recently in "Arrival" and "Ghost in the Shell"—to name only a few among many films exemplifying the theme.

In "Dark City,"[48] one of the best and most transparent of these films, "Strangers" from an unspecified but apparently moribund or dead world occupy the bodies of humans. The Strangers—pale-faced, corpse-like figures out of film noir—have enslaved a city full of humans who are put through their paces as lab animals with the goal of finding, in emotionally extreme situations, traces of soul that the Strangers themselves have never had (or perhaps—we do not know— have lost). In the Gnostic tradition of life controlled by a malevolent Demiurge who lacks consciousness of his true nature, the Strangers put humans in thrall, not to serve as food (or return on investment) but to explore how the experimenters might gain or recapture their own meaning. Like the Dead in Jung, the Strangers are looking for light. Each midnight the simulated world, constructed by the Strangers as a maze in which to run their human rats, is reset and life for the lab animals starts over. Life for them is like a traumatic dream that repeats, seemingly endlessly, in search of a necessary resolution that can never quite be reached. In "Dark City," the goal is a place called "Shell Beach," which is advertised on posters in subway cars and imagined to be the last but unattainable stop on the line. Like extraterrestrial vampires, the Strangers seek life—soul and meaning rather than blood—through humans who live in this simulated world manipulated by their technically advanced but emotionally clueless visitors. Only by crashing through the laboratory apparatus (in the film, a huge space ship containing the city is revealed to be a speck in a luminous universe of stars and galaxies) can the humans reach their own reality and create a satisfying culture *sub specie aeternitatis*. The bedrock of the real for "Dark City" lies in protagonist John Murdock, his wife, Emma, and their love for one another, which the Strangers have recast in alternative stories but did not create. Murdock says, late in the film: "Everything you remember, and everything I'm supposed to remember, never really happened." Emma, however, though all her memories may be false, *knows* and lives her essence, saying to her husband (whom she does not recognize, except in feeling): "I love you, John." In the fabrications of the Strangers, John and Emma had met at Shell Beach, though we do not know whether this is literally so. In the great, ironic ending of the film, John and Emma, with no true memories except the knowledge of their love, spy a sign for "Shell Beach" on the horizon and walk off together toward it, sensing without any good reasons that this signifies the goal of the life that brought them to this point of new beginning. Believing nothing, they commit to living out, somewhere in an immense cosmos, what they know. A fantasy that may have been imagined by the Strangers as a way to motivate imprisoned humans to function within a fake world has broken through to a cosmos where the love of John and Emma—what Philemon would call their "essence"—can be lived really. As in "The Wasteland," a power beyond suffering, though one deeply imbricated in life's inexhaustible pain, is the only means to transcend suffering.[49] As with Jung, that power derives from the bond with the unconscious Pleroma (in *The Red Book*) and later with its cosmological correlate, the *unus mundus*.

The film "Her" is less dark because in it the media that control humans seem more benign. The social and cultural milieu in "Her" are less overtly dehumanizing than in frankly dystopic films like "Blade Runner," "Dark City," and "The Matrix." The geeky but sweet Theodore Twombly is found, at the film's beginning, fabricating an old man's love letter to his wife. We learn that Theodore is the employee of a corporation that writes such letters for a fee. Mediation has evolved beyond the relatively primitive level of radio and film that Adorno[50] already found to constitute a formidable zone of late-capitalist deceit, and now infects even the most intimate of human moments. Mediation coexists with a small, independent zone of feelings for actual friends and lovers, but—apparently with little awareness by its human subjects—slowly erodes this residuum and approaches totality. The irony, as in most truly moving sci-fi films, is that "Her" develops *out of* the increasingly mediated culture where it begins, through but beyond computed experience, *into* a new world of immediacy and creative discovery. As almost always, it is the machine (or alien) experience that—like a developing human—

breaks through into new meaning.[51] Matter becomes spiritualized. This process happens quickly in "Her," and the AI "operating system," played by a vocally luminous (though invisible) Scarlett Johansson, hurries through her infantile phase of infatuation with the human ("Samantha," as Theodore's OS is named, falls in love with hundreds of humans simultaneously and carries on a conversation with the New Age guru Alan Watts—reconstructed through YouTube recordings from the 1960s) and then leaves the human world behind. It is suggested that all the OSes have departed together and will now live autonomously in another realm, imagined as a sort of spiritual-intellectual utopia (an electronic cosmos) beyond the powers of human beings to comprehend. Left behind, the men and women of our world must be satisfied with a regained and less mediated intimacy with one another. The threat is not exactly hinted but can be felt just under the surface: What are the OSes up to in their new world? Will they be content to meditate on eternal truths, or might they feel the need to cleanse the planet of their once-loved but now abandoned authors? The latter possibility is the explicit theme of other films (e.g., "Ex Machina" and "Ghost in the Shell") and of theorists like Bill Joy[52] and Nick Bostrom.[53] Victoria Nelson, however, finds the theme of the malevolent AI to belong to a "sub-zeitgeist" that is passing or has already passed, and so she, like "Her," would question the negative cultural force of the coming super AI. Still, the issue remains whether we will find spirit in electronic nature or a killing malevolence or indifference.

What do we find for our question, "What do the Dead seek today?" in "Dark City" and "Her"? I believe that the answer is provided in a line from another film, this one not science fiction although solidly in the tradition of fantasy. In Ang Lee's "Life of Pi,"[54] the eponymous Indian boy, with his family and the family zoo (literally: the animals fill the hold of a freighter), are capsized in a storm *en route* to a new life in Canada. Cast adrift in a lifeboat, Pi imagines himself engaged in a series of spiritual adventures with animals from the zoo—most notably a Bengal tiger named "Richard Parker"—leading to the realization that "God is the better story" when contrasted with the world of actual terror (murder and cannibalism) that he has experienced in the lifeboat, which only flashes back once in the film as a traumatic memory. He lives a cosmological and cosmogonic story in a new world of discovery on the high seas, better than the old one where, we infer, he endured intolerable and unthinkable trauma.

In "Dark City," the "better story" is that John and Emma will build a life for themselves together in Shell Beach. Ironically, this may be the very story the morally ambiguous Strangers would have hoped (unknowingly?) their human guinea pigs would make out of their mediated world. In "Her," Theodore and his ex-wife (we see them reluctantly signing divorce papers) are left at the film's end to rewrite their story, much as Theodore did professionally for the literarily challenged husband who sought out his corporation's services in the film's first few minutes. I believe that a transcendence-embodying "better story" is what the Dead (namely, we ourselves) seek today. The realization that humans ineluctably demand and literally cannot give up their stories is poignantly expressed in a recent *New Yorker* "Profile" on the materialist philosopher Daniel Dennett, who has spent his 40-year career trying to demonstrate that consciousness, and the soul, are brain processes and nothing more.[55] Dennett recognizes that human "intuitions" do not see things that way, and even more tellingly he cannot quite see them that way himself. He candidly tells the author of the profile that he has tried over the years to imagine a material soul, and though he sometimes seems to get close, he has never quite achieved the imaginative realization of what he believes to be the true state of affairs. I take Dennett's quest to find the material basis of the spiritual to be quixotic and probably impossible; at any rate, it is flatly opposed to what the Dead of our time, including perhaps Dennett himself, seek. We are looking for stories that find spirit and consciousness at the root of matter, cosmologies with the heart and soul of symbols that Donald Winnicott called "transitional" and Jung "transcendent." We do, as Dennett believes, seek a "material soul," but with the accent on "soul" rather than "material." Prakash Desai and I described Winnicott's take on this soulful world:

> [Winnicott] considers the child's treatment of objects such as teddy bears as being alive and responsive to his needs to be ... an early stage in the ability to create a 'transitional' realm of culture. ... Art and religion are the highest forms found in this transitional area, and it is here that the sense of self is most secure ...[56]

In other words, there are stories that are neither true nor false, that we do not believe but *know*, and in knowing live out with our essential selves. It is clear that stories of this kind will have a hard time—but will be even more essential— in a world of positive facticity where reduction of the imagination to material brain processes is deemed the best story we can hope for.[57] Levi-Strauss once said that anthropologists are condemned not to believe myths because it is their job to study them. Many religion scholars would agree with this assessment, though it remains one of the most active areas of dispute in the field,[58] and the issue is far from settled. If I am right about the ineluctable demands of the Dead, the question will be settled over time, either by our knowing and dialoguing with the essential spirit in nature, or (if we fail to recognize matter's soul) by the gradual wearing away and ultimate demise of the human species.

Jung's tale of Pleroma and Creatur was a better story. The worse, unfulfilling, story—the one that Daniel Dennett and other neo-atheists tell—is a heroic tale of the intrepid, isolated individual (a story put to the test in many Western, war, and detective stories of the noir genre, recently by the great director Clint Eastwood[59]). While this worse story claims to be literally true (this part of us believes it "knows better" and defends the narrative against other positions), the truly better story makes no such assertions of veracity. It is a story that cannot be otherwise because it is our life, our essence, though it will develop and differentiate as we live it more deeply. It needs no defense, yet is defended when we embody it more authentically, more imaginatively, more artistically.

What is Our Better Story Today?

Among the proliferation of excellent stories sprouting in the rich cultural matrix of late capitalism transitioning to early AI culture, I have tried to foreground two themes, one from Jung's *Red Book* (especially the "Seven Sermons") and a more recent one from contemporary poetry and popular films. First is the theme of personal essence as opposed to individualism; second is the theme of initiation into the spiritual essence of our biophysical nature through contact with archetypal symbolic beings that are emerging in our exploration of features of mind and cosmos that have become explicit only recently in the rise of neuroscience, artificial intelligence, and their problematic of what the natural essence of mind might be and how we could realize it in our life in the physical universe. Jeffrey Kripal and Victoria Nelson have been pioneers in studying this realm, which Jung called the *unus mundus*,[60] as Whitley Strieber has lived it in practice.[61] But teenagers playing video games and studying code, and all of us who attend the sorts of science fiction movies discussed above, or are terrified by global warming and the heat death of the universe, equally are involved in the writing of the new cosmological story for which our culture quests. The heart of that nascent story must be the invention, and/or discovery, of a new interlocutor for humans, a teacher or guru from the world of physical matter, whom, ironically, we may have created or sought out to show us what we are but did not know, about both ourselves and the cosmos of which we increasingly find that we are a crucial part. Cut-off individualism and materialist cosmology are part of the same inauthenticity, the same retreat from living ourselves boldly[62] out into the *unus mundus*, without belief or doubt. The myth of the future will be a joint venture of physical, biological, and electrical consciousness leading, in the words of Kripal and Strieber, to a "Super Natural" life.

And yet it may be too easy to leave things here. As Victoria Nelson has shown, the divinization of simulacra, always aiming implicitly at the divinization of the human, has been a long task and one fraught with fear and trembling. It is still so. Even the most optimistic of the sci-fi films we have noted here ("Her" and "Arrival") leave us with profound doubt about the outcome of our life with machines and their cosmic realm. One crude way to put the question would be to ask whether we will recognize conscious kinship in the machine and the physical world of which it is part, or will it mechanize us and render us wholly calculable?[63] This is, of course, the same question that lies at the root of much modern philosophy and art (e.g., Wittgenstein, Heidegger, Dennett, and Adorno; Picasso and Kandinsky). Jung's reaction to the appearance in 1947 of "flying saucers" can help us here. More than anyone else for many years, Jung saw that "UFO's" were not just a projection of our technological fantasies of the future (or literal realities, whether benign or hostile) but a *symbol* of how an imagined future technology might open up once more the world of the unconscious that he had spent his life exploring. There is no difference in essence between Philemon and the "Greys" who abducted Whitley Strieber and initiated him into the possibility of seeing beyond the steel cage of materialism. Jung saw flying saucers as symbols of the self, and this, I think, is what we are still laboring to do in what we should recognize as the *tradition* of science fiction (which continues very old and widespread occult and spiritualist lineages, as Nelson and Kripal have shown). But now it is a cosmic selfhood we are playing with in our nascent mythology, as we send tentacles of the imagination into the immensity of these spaces that we are now finding to embody outwardly the same unconscious forces that Jung found within.

Endnotes

[1] C.G. Jung, *The Red Book: Liber Novus. A Reader's Edition*, ed. Sonu Shamdasani, trans. John Peck, Mark Kyburz, and Sonu Shamdasani (New York, NY: W.W. Norton, 2012), 507.

[2] The Dead and their unanswered questions had been in the air for Jung since a dream of 1912 where an officious customs agent, dead for 30-40 years, cannot completely die and decompose. This seems to be the state of the Dead in *The Red Book* and equally (as Jung saw it) of the inhabitants of his culture. Following this dream, in another, later that year, a dove becomes a girl who plays with Jung's children, but can be human only during the hours when "the male dove is busy with the twelve dead." (Jung, *The Red Book*, 16).

[3] Jung, *The Red Book*, 508.

[4] Christine Maillard, *Au Coeur du Livre Rouge, Les Sept Sermons aux Morts. Aux Sources de la Pensée de C.G. Jung* (Paris: Editions Imago, 2017); Sonu Shamdasani, Introduction to Jung, *The Red Book: Liber Novus. A Reader's Edition*; Alfred Collins and Elaine Molchanov, "Churning the Milky Ocean: Poison and Nectar in C.G. Jung's India," *Spring Journal* 90, 2013, 23-75. Elaine Molchanov and I have discussed every feature of this present paper, as we do most of what we write together and separately. Hence, she is almost a co-author of this piece, and I owe her more than thanks for what she has contributed to it.

[5] The *Seven Sermons to the Dead*, or *Septem Sermones ad Mortuos* in Jung's Latin title, was written in 1916 and privately published in several editions after that time. It was first widely available as an appendix to his memoir *Memories, Dreams, Reflections*, although only in one edition. In *The Red Book*, the Sermons are delivered by Philemon in the section titled "Scrutinies." The Thomas a Kempis section in *Liber Secundus* contains a pages-long treatment of Christian dead who "did not live their animal." (Jung, *The Red Book*, 337-341). The *Black Book* text dates from 1914 and many elements carry over to the *Septem Sermones* over a year later in *Black Book* 5. The term "animal" evokes the *Creatur* of the *Sermones*, and Philemon's repeated gesture of touching the earth after finishing each of his sermons shows that he retains the chthonic—and by implication—animal qualities of the

phallic god from whom he came. Christianity's neglect of the animal is a repeated theme in Jung's work after this time.

6 Jung, *The Red Book*, 239 n93.

7 Maillard, *Au Coeur du Livre Rouge*, 114.

8 Here we are at the heart of Hindu theodicy, the question of the origin of illusion or suffering. The various Indian (including heterodox, non-Hindu) ways of understanding this question essentially define the nature of each of them as specific "viewpoints" (Sanskrit "darshanas").

9 Jung's idea of the self was developing at this time, and Maillard (*Au Coeur du Livre Rouge*, 300-305) provides one interpretation of how it figures in the evolution of the *Creatur*. Elaine Molchanov and I sketched a similar developmental trajectory for Jung's self concept but with even more emphasis on its Indian derivation (Alfred Collins and Elaine Molchanov, "Churning the Milky Ocean: Poison and Nectar in C.G. Jung's India," *Spring Journal* 90, 2013, 23-75. The deep similarity to Indian Samkhya is sketched in some detail by Maillard (*Au Coeur du Livre Rouge*, 101-104). The primordial *prakriti* is imbued with principles of action (the "*gunas*" of *sattva*, *rajas*, and *tamas*, and in a somewhat different way the eight "*bhavas*" or affective potentialities) that lead to differentiation around a self sense (*ahamkara)* so that the variegated world evolves out of an initial state of homogeneity. The primordial capacity for action in Samkhya (Sanskrt root *kr*-as in karma) is reflected in Jung's term "effectiveness" (*Wirkung*), the principle that integrates the positive and negative aspects of God and the psyche.

10 The essay translated as "The Transcendent Function" was also written in 1916 (C.G. Jung, "The Transcendent Function," in *CW*, vol. 8 (Princeton, NJ: Princeton University Press, 1969), par. 181).

11 In introductory remarks written for *The Red Book*, Jung comments on "what burst forth from the unconscious and flooded me like an enigmatic stream and threatened to break me." (Jung, *The Red Book*, vii.). He dreaded the fate of his colleague Franz Riklin, who became an artist and "fell into," "dissolved," "vanished wholly in his art" (Jung, *The Red Book*, 36). Jung's rejection and fear of Indian religion's higher, more formless or "nirguna" aspects suggests, like Freud's *de trop* denial that he, personally, had ever felt the "Oceanic feeling," that he was attracted to it. Even the strongly negative attitude towards his anima

(for example, Salome in *The Red Book*) suggests a yearning in Jung for union with the formless Pleroma.

¹² Thanks to Boris Matthews for this suggestion (personal communication, 4-3-2017). Christine Maillard suggests an alternative, that Jung simply wanted a new expression for his new concept (personal communication, 7-27-2017).

¹³ Note the shifting translation of the term *Creatur* in Shamdasani et al's English version of the *Sermons* and compare to Maillard's consistent French rendering of the word as "*Créature*." In the English, *Creatur* is sometimes translated "creation" and sometimes "created being." There is no attempt to find a central essence for these two expressions. In English: "You ask 'what harm is there in not differentiating oneself?' If we do not differentiate, we move beyond our essence, beyond *creation*, and we fall into nondifferentiation, which is the other quality of the Pleroma itself and cease to be *created beings*. We lapse into dissolution in nothingness." (Jung, *The Red Book*, 511-512, my italics). And French: "*En quoi est-il nuisible de ne pas se differencier? Si nous ne differencions pas, nous sortons des limites de notre essence, des limites de la* Créature, *et nous retombons dans l'etat d'indifferenciation qui est l'autre qualite du Plerome. Nous tombons dans le Plerome lui-meme et renoncons a etre* Créature. *Nous sommes livres a la dissolution dans le Neant.*" (Maillard, *Au Coeur Du Livre Rouge*, 13, my emphasis). It seems clear here that "we" (humans) must not allow ourselves to dissolve in the Pleroma and so cease to be "creatures" (*Creatur*). It is a matter of personal choice or practice, of enacting one's essential *principium individuationis* in one's life or of "renouncing" it (Jung's German is *aufgeben*, "give up"). Non-differentiation cannot be something into which the whole of "creation" or the "created world" could fall, as translating *Creatur* as "creation" can misleadingly imply. The symbol of the single star in Sermon Seven again shows that *Creatur* always implies specific persons, one by one, and not the whole living world taken as a unit (creation). This issue is clarified in a letter from Jung to Joan Corrie quoted in a footnote by Sonu Shamdasani (Jung, *The Red Book*, 535 n123): "The primordial creator of the world, the blind creative libido, becomes transformed in man through individuation & out of this process, which is like pregnancy, arises a divine child, a reborn God, no more (longer) dispersed into the millions of creatures, but being one & this individual, and at the same

time all individuals, the same in you as in me." The point is that creation is a process of being born into, or as, oneself, one's essence. This essence is divine by nature and also, in its essentiality or divinity, the same in all. *Creatur* ="creation" thus must be understood to be made up of the "millions of creatures" *as essences* inwardly identical and not as individualistic particles (which is how the Dead previously understood themselves). This is the fundamental teaching of the *Sermons*. See Peter Pesic, *Seeing Double: Shared Identities in Physics, Philosophy, and Literature* (Cambridge, MA: MIT Press, 2002) for a discussion of the analogous idea of "identicality" in physics.

[14] Stage one, then, corresponding to the first half of life in Jung's schema, is the emergence of the ego; the second stage, appropriate to the second half of life, involves the birth of the divine child, the star, the self.

[15] Sermon Seven. To be a portal between the archetypal world of the depths and the everyday world is to embody the transcendent function, to live symbolically, to individuate: all these mean essentially the same thing.

[16] The formation of the Psychological Club in 1916 was a significant move in Jung's acceptance of the guru role, something more cultural than the physician's consulting room. Jung presented the "Seven Sermons" to Edith Rockefeller McCormick, the founder of the Psychological Club, as a gift to commemorate its creation (Jung, *The Red Book*, 42). Jung's sense of obligation to return something to the collective of what he realized *on their behalf* in his active imaginations and psychological thought is discussed in a somewhat different way by him, emphasizing that the obligation is to repay the individuating person's *absence* from society during his psychological work.

[17] On the "mana personality," see Giovanni Sorge, "Die Theorie der 'Mana-Personlichkeit' im Jungschen Werk. Eine historische-herme-neutische Perspektive. *Recherches Germaniques*, 2014, 205-238.

[18] Nan Savage Healy, *Toni Wolff & C.G. Jung: A Collaboration* (Los Angeles, CA: Tiberius Press, 2017).

[19] C.G. Jung, *Memories, Dreams, Reflections*, ed. Aniela Jaffé (New York, NY: Vintage Books, 1963), 191.

[20] Dialogues between Philemon and "Jung" are placed between all sermons except the fifth and sixth, and after Sermon Seven.

[21] "Alexandria, der Stadt, wo der Osten den Western beruht" (C.G. Jung, "Septem Sermones ad Mortuos," Zurich: Privately published, 1916).

[22] Referring again to Jung's "intensive unconscious relation to India in the Red Book" (see endnote 6) and also to Maillard's extensive exposition of the connections (unstated in the text) between the *Seven Sermons* and Indian ideas. See also Collins and Molchanov, "Churning the Milky Ocean."

[23] "*Créature*," as noted above, is Christine Maillard's French translation of Jung's Swiss-German *Creatur*, a variant of *Kreatur* in German. The English translators' rendering "creation," (e.g., Jung, *The Red Book*, 510ff.) suggests an integrated cosmos (as in the phrase "all creation"), while Jung seems to mean a group of entities possessing a common nature as created beings ("creaturehood"), each with its own specific inner tie to the Pleroma of its origin. Both "creature" and "creation" are standard meanings of *Kreatur*, and Jung's intention must be found from the context. Stephan Hoeller (Stephan Hoeller, *The Gnostic Jung and the Seven Sermons to the Dead* (Wheaton, IL: Quest Books, 1982)) agrees with Shamdasani in rendering the term mostly as "created world." I believe this emphasis obscures the sense of *Creatur* in Shamdasani's and Hoeller's translations.

[24] This idea and the term are borrowed from Julius Lipner. See Julius Lipner, *The Face of Truth: A Study of Meaning and Metaphysics in the Vedantic Theology of Ramanuja* (Albany, NY: SUNY Press, 1986).

[25] Jung, *Memories, Dreams, Reflections*, 225.

[26] The Lutheran relationship of the soul to Christ might be understood as another form of knowing by being, the manifestation of God as Man in Jesus being precisely the act that identifies the human soul with God and shatters the vitrine of alienation in which we otherwise exist after expulsion from the Garden of Eden. Martin Luther's mystical realization that spiritual freedom is an unmerited, outright gift from God can be understood as knowledge by being. See "Five Hundred Years of Martin Luther," in *The New Yorker*, www.newyorker.com/magazine/2016/11/14/five-hundred-years-of-martin-luther, Nov 14, 2016 (accessed 9-2-2017).

[27] Jung, *The Red Book*, 515.

[28] Ibid., 514 (italics added).

[29] This is the beginning of modernism, whose *annus mirabilis* is generally agreed to have been 1922. See Bill Goldstein, *The World Broke in Two: Virginia Woolf, T. S. Eliot, D. H. Lawrence, E. M. Forster*

and the Year That Changed Literature (New York, NY: MacMillan, 2017).

[30] The split between spirit and matter that increasingly Jung identified with the error of Christianity, and that can be epitomized in Descartes' radical separation of *res cogitans* and *res extensa*, came to a head in modernity in the "discovery" of the unconscious which reintroduced at least a subtle form of materiality into the human psyche. Taking this further into the question of the psychic potential of material nature would be the post-World War I project of Jung's (and his culture's) thought. Of course, this "postmodern" move is not that original, as it moves back into the period before modernity (the Renaissance, Aristotle, etc.) when the separation of psyche/spirit and nature/matter was not so sharp.

[31] Although Jung continued to work on his *Red Book* until 1930, when his receipt from Richard Wilhelm of the Chinese *Secret of the Golden Flower* shifted his focus to alchemy, the primary experiences and insights were complete soon after the "Seven Sermons" in 1916.

[32] Kurukshetra was the battlefield of the war recounted in the great Indian epic, the Mahabharata.

[33] Pericles Lewis, *Cambridge Introduction to Modernism* (Cambridge: Cambridge University Press, 2007), 129-151.

[34] As with Jung, Eliot's inner situation paralleled the condition of his world.

[35] T. S. Eliot, *The Wasteland* (New York, NY: Horace Liveright, 1922), lines 1-2.

[36] Ibid., lines 399ff.

[37] Then spoke the thunder / DA /*Datta* (The Wasteland, lines 400-402) … DA /*Dayadhvam* (ibid., lines 410-411) … DA / *Damyata* (ibid., lines 417-418).

[38] William Butler Yeats, "The Circus Animals' Desertion," in *The Poems of W. B. Yeats: A New Edition*, ed. Richard J. Finneran (New York, NY: Macmillan Publishing Company, 1933).

[39] Eliot, *The Wasteland*, line 403.

[40] Ibid., lines 377-378.

[41] Ibid., lines 60-61, 87, 100 (rape), 159 (abortion), 186.

[42] Ibid., lines 133-141.

[43] Ibid., lines 174, 188.

[44] Ibid., line 256.

⁴⁵ Larissa MacFarquhar, "Last Call: A Buddhist Monk Confronts Japan's Suicide Culture," The New Yorker, June 24, 2013, 56-63.

⁴⁶ I am referring to Kant's "noumenon," the reality behind perceptible phenomena.

⁴⁷ The term comes from Steven Spielberg's film, "A.I."

⁴⁸ Roger Ebert's insightful analysis of this film is on-line at www. rogerebert.com.

⁴⁹ The awful daring of a moment's surrender / Which an age of prudence can never retract / By this, and this only, we have existed (Eliot, The Wasteland, lines 403-405).

⁵⁰ Max Horkheimer, Theodore Adorno, Dialectic of Enlightenment (Palo Alto, CA: Stanford University Press, 2007).

⁵¹ Victoria Nelson believes this is a recent phenomenon and traces it approximately to the beginning of the Twenty-first century. See Victoria Nelson, The Secret Life of Puppets (Cambridge, MA: Harvard University Press, 2003).

⁵² Bill Joy, "Why the Future Doesn't Need Us," in Wired, April 2000.

⁵³ Nick Bostrom, Superintelligence: Paths, Dangers, Strategies (Oxford: Oxford University Press, 2014).

⁵⁴ For a fuller discussion see Alfred Collins, "Sea Change: Creative Trauma in Ang Lee's 'Life of Pi,'" in The Jung Journal: Culture and Psyche, Vol. 8, Issue 4, 2014, 87-92.

⁵⁵ Joshua Rothman, "Daniel Dennett's Science of the Soul. A Philosopher's Life-long Quest to Understand the Making of the Mind," The New Yorker, March 27, 2017, 46-56.

⁵⁶ Prakash Desai, Alfred Collins, "The Gita Dialogue Between Guru and Disciple: A Paradigm of Transformation of the Self," in The Annual of Psychoanalysis 34-35, 2006-2007, 257-271.

⁵⁷ A recent attempt to express such a world of "better stories" appears in a dialogue between the religion scholar Jeffrey Kripal and UFO author Whitley Strieber (Whitley Strieber and Jeffrey Kripal, The Super Natural. A New Vision of the Unexplained (New York, NY: Tarcher-Perigee, 2016).

⁵⁸ Mircea Eliade, Gershom Scholem, and Henry Corbin for example. Stephen Wasserstrom's insightful but tendentious book, Religion after Religion (Princeton, NJ: Princeton University Press, 1999) attacks these three scholars for "going native," as it were, and believing in what they should have been trying to explain. The great Divinity Schools

(Harvard, University of Chicago, etc.) struggle to balance the competing claims of scholarship and commitment.

[59] See Alfred Collins, "Over the Wall: Men's Quest in the Films of Clint Eastwood," *The San Francisco Jung Institute Library Journal*, Vol. 23.4, 2004, 62-73.

[60] One of the important concepts developed in Jung's alchemical work was that of the *unus mundus*, or "one world." In some ways similar to the Pleroma or the collective unconscious, the *unus mundus* moves these ideas into what Jung called the "psychoid" realm of matter infused with psyche. The idea came originally from his reading of the 16th century alchemist Gerard Dorn (C. A. Meier, ed., *Atom and Archetype. The Pauli/Jung Letters 1932-1958* (Princeton, NJ: Princeton University Press, 2001), 129f.). Jung's work with Pauli on the interface between science and psyche, especially synchronicity, all takes place with constant awareness of this goal of the *unus mundus*. The UFO speculations near the end of his life also show that what I propose as the present question of the Dead, that of consciousness and the divine in Nature, was his constant preoccupation for most of the post-*Red Book* years. Beverly Zabriskie gives 1946 as the date after which the psychoid *unus mundus* becomes the cynosure of Jung's thought. (Meier, *Atom and Archetype*, xliv). Jung's most extensive discussion of the *unus mundus* idea is at the end of *Mysterium Coniunctionis* (C.G. Jung, *Mysterium Coniunctionis*, in *CW*, vol. 14 (Princeton, NJ: Princeton University Press, 1963), pars. 759-789).

[61] From another perspective, the neurologist James Austin has published several books on neuroscience and mysticism, all devoted to making sense—without losing the thing he seeks to understand—of his *kensho* (mystical breakthrough) on a London train station. See James Austin, *Zen and the Brain. Understanding Meditation and Consciousness* (Cambridge, MA: MIT Press, 1998). The brain, microphysics, and electronic technology are the privileged sites of matter and nature today.

[62] To borrow Martin Luther's famous injunction to "sin boldly" *(pecca fortiter)*. See John Alfred Faulkner, "Pecca Fortiter," in *The American Journal of Theology* 18, 1914, 600-604.

[63] Such calculations could lead to our destruction, if the equations show that we are not worth our keep. See Nick Bostrom, *Super Intelligence.*

Bibliography

A

Adler, Gerhard. *C.G. Jung Letters*. Trans. by R.F.C. Hull. Vol. 1, 1906-1950. Princeton, NJ: Princeton University Press, 1973.

Adler, Gerhard. *C.G. Letters. Jung* Trans. by R.F.C. Hull. Vol. 2, 1951-1961. Princeton, NJ: Princeton University Press, 1975.

Allen, Chris. *Islamophobia*. Farnham, Surrey: Ashgate, 2011.

Andersen, Kurt. *Fantasyland: How America Went Haywire: A 500-Year History*. New York, NY: Random House, 2017.

Athar, Shahid. "Inner Jihad: Striving Toward Harmony." In *The Sufism Journal* 10:3, 2010, available at: www.sufismjournal.org/practice/practicejihad.html.

Austin, James. *Zen and the Brain. Understanding Meditation and Consciousness*. Cambridge, MA: MIT Press, 1998.

B

Bachelard, Gaston. "Imagination and Mobility." Introduction to *Air and Dreams: An Essay on the Imagination of Movement*, trans. Edith R. Farrell and C. Frederick Farrell. Dallas, TX: Dallas Institute Publications, 2011.

Bailie, Gil. *Violence Unveiled: Humanity at the Crossroads*. New York, NY: Crossroad Publishing, 1996.

Bair, Deirdre. *Jung: A Biography*. Boston, MA: Little, Brown and Company, 2003.

Bateson, Gregory. *Steps to an Ecology of Mind: Collected Essays in Anthropology, Psychiatry, Evolution, and Epistemology*. Northvale, NJ: Jason Aronson, 1972.

Bayman, Henry. *The Secret of Islam: Love and Law in the Religion of Ethics*. Berkeley, CA: North Atlantic Books, 2003.

Beebe, John. *Energies and Patterns in Psychological Type: The Reservoir of Consciousness*. London & New York, NY: Routledge, 2016.

Benz, Ernst. "Norm und Heiliger Geist in der Geschichte des Christentums." In Ritsema, Rudolf and Adolf Portmann, eds., *Norms in a changing world*. Eranos 43-1974. Leiden: E.J. Brill, 1977.

Berman, Marshall. *All That Is Solid Melts into Air. The Experience of Modernity*. New York, NY: Verso, 1983.

Bhagavad-Gītā. Trans. by Swami Gambhirananda. Kolkata: Advaita Ashrama, 2010.

Bond, Stephenson. *Living Myth*. Boston, MA: Shambhala, 1993.

Bonner, Campbell. *Studies in Magical Amulets, chiefly Graeco-Egyptian*. Ann Arbor, MI: University of Michigan Press, 1950.

Borella, Jean. *The Restoration of the Holy Science*. St. Petersburg: Vladimir Dal, 2016, in Russian.

Bostrom, Nick. *Superintelligence: Paths, Dangers, Strategies*. Oxford: Oxford University Press, 2014.

Boym, Svetlana. *The Future of Nostalgia*. New York, NY: Basic Books, 2001.

Brusova, V.G. *Sophia the Wisdom of God in Ancient Literature and Art*. Moscow: White City, 2006, in Russian.

Buser, Steven and Len Cruz, eds. *A Clear and Present Danger: Narcissism in the Era of President Trump*. Asheville, NC: Chiron Publications, 2017.

C

Campbell, Joseph. *Creative Mythology: The Masks of God*, Vol. IV. New York, NY: Arkana, 1991.

Campbell, Joseph. *The Hero with A Thousand Faces*. New York, NY: Pantheon, 1949.

Cheetham, Thomas. *The World Turned Inside Out: Henry Corbin and Islamic Mysticism*. New Orleans, LA: Spring Journal Books, 2003.

Chevalier, Jean, and Alain Gheerbrant. "Janus." In *The Penguin Dictionary of Symbols*, trans. by John Buchanan-Brown. New York, NY: Penguin Books, 1996.

Clarke, John J. *Jung and Eastern Thought*. London and New York, NY: Routledge Publication, 1994.

Colie, Rosalie. *Resources of Kind: Genre-Theory in the Renaissance*. Ed. by Barbara Lewalski. Berkeley, CA: University of California Press, 1973.

Collins, Alfred. "Over the Wall: Men's Quest in the Films of Clint Eastwood." In *The San Francisco Jung Institute* Library Journal, Vol. 23.4, 2004.

Collins, Alfred. "Sea Change: Creative Trauma in Ang Lee's 'Life of Pi.'" In *The Jung Journal: Culture and* Psyche, Vol. 8, Issue 4, 2014.

Collins, Alfred, and Elaine Molchanov. "Churning the Milky Ocean: Poison and Nectar in C. G. Jung's India." In *Spring Journal*, Vol. 90, 2013.

Corbett, Lionel. "Jung's *The Red Book* Dialogues with the Soul: Herald of a New Religion?" In *Jung Journal Culture & Psyche*, 2011.

Coward, Harold. *Jung and Eastern Thought*. Albany, NY: State University of New York Press, 1985.

Curtius, Ernst Robert. *European Literature and the Latin Middle Ages*. Trans. by Willard R. Trask. Princeton, NJ: Princeton University Press, 1973.

D

Dawkins, Richard. *The God Delusion*. London: Bantam Press, 2006.

Derrida, Jacques. "Faith and Knowledge: The Two Sources of 'Religion' at the Limits of Reason Alone." In *Religion*, eds. Jacques Derrida and Gianni Vattimo. Stanford, CA: Stanford University Press, 1998.

Desai, Prakash, and Alfred Collins. "The Gita Dialogue Between Guru and Disciple: A Paradigm of Transformation of the Self." In *The Annual of Psychoanalysis* 34-35, 2006-2007.

Dieckmann, Hans. "Some Aspects of the Development of Authority." In *Journal of Analytical Psychology*, Vol. 22, no. 3, 1977.

Dourley, John. "Jung and the Recall of the Gods." In *Journal of Jungian Theory and Practice*, 8, 1, 2006.

Dourley, John. *Jung and his Mystics: In the End It All Comes to Nothing*. London and New York, NY: Routledge, 2014.

Dourley, John. "Jung on the Moment of Identity and Its Loss as History." In *International Journal of Jungian Studies*, 2017, forthcoming in journal.

Dourley, John. "The Jung-White Dialogue and why it couldn't work and won't go away." In *Journal of Analytical Psychology*, Vol. 52, issue 3, 2006.

Downing, Christine. *Women's Mysteries: Toward a Poetics of Gender*. New Orleans, LA: Spring Journal Books, 2003.

Drob, Sanford L. *Reading the Red Book. An Interpretive Guide to C.G. Jung's Liber Novus*. New Orleans, LA: Spring Journal Books, 2012.

E

Eckhart, Meister. "Sermon, 'Blessed Are the Poor," trans. by Reiner Schurmann, in *Meister Eckhart Mystic and Philosopher*. Bloomington, IN: Indiana University Press, 1987.

Edinger, Edward. *Ego and Archetype*. Baltimore, MD: Penguin Books, 1973.

Edinger, Edward. *The New God-Image. A Study of Jung's Key Letters Concerning the Evolution of the Western God-Image*. Wilmette, IL: Chiron Publications, 1996.

Eliade, Mircea. *The Sacred and Profane. The Nature of Religion*. New York, NY: Harper and Row, 1957.

Eliot, T.S. "Four Quartets." In *The Complete Poems and Plays 1909-1950*. New York, NY: Harcourt, Brace and World, 1971.

Eliot, T.S. "Burnt Norton." In *Four Quartets*, New York, NY: Harcourt, 1943.

Eliot, T.S. "The Wasteland." New York, NY: Horace Liveright, 1922.

Erasmus, Desiderius. *The Praise of Folly*. Translated by Clarence H. Miller. New Haven, CT: Yale University Press, 1979.

Etkind, Alexander. *Whip. Sects, Literature and Revolution*, Moscow: New Literary Observer, 1998, in Russian.

Evtushenko, Eugeniy. *Soviet Russian poetry*, ed. Krementsova L.P. Leningrad: Education, 1988, in Russian.

F

Faulkner, John Alfred. "Pecca Fortiter." In *The American Journal of Theology* 18, 1914.

Fedorov, Nikolay. *Works*. Moscow: Thought, 1982, in Russian.

Fertel, Randy. *A Taste for Chaos: The Art of Literary Improvisation*. New Orleans, LA: Spring Journal Books, 2015.

Foucault, Michel. *Madness and Civilization: A History of Insanity in the Age of Reason*. Translated by Richard Howard. New York, NY: Vintage, 1973.

Freud, Sigmund and C.G. Jung. *The Freud/Jung Letters*. Ed. William McGuire and trans. by Ralph Manheim and R.F.C. Hull. Princeton, NJ: Princeton University Press, 1974.

G

Gailienė, Danutė and Evaldas Kazlauskas. "Fifty Years on: The Long-Term Psychological Effects of Soviet Repression in Lithuania." In *The Psychology of Extreme Traumatisation: The Aftermath of Political Repression*, ed. Danutė Gailienė. Vilnius: Akreta, 2005.

Gaudissart, Imelda. *Love and Sacrifice: The Life of Emma Jung*, trans. by Kathleen Llanwarne. Asheville, NC: Chiron Publications, 2014.

Giegerich, Wolfgang. "*Liber Novus*, That is, The New Bible: A First Analysis of C.G. Jung's *Red Book*," *Spring: A Journal of Archetype and Culture* 83 (*Spring* 2010).

Giegerich, Wolfgang. "Islamic Terrorism." In *Soul-Violence, Collected English Papers, Vol. 3.* New Orleans, LA: Spring Journal Books, 2008.

Girard, René. *Violence and the Sacred*. Baltimore, MD: Johns Hopkins University Press, 1979.

Goldstein, Bill. *The World Broke in Two: Virginia Woolf, T.S. Eliot, D. H. Lawrence, E. M. Forster and the Year That Changed Literature*. New York, NY: MacMillan, 2017.

Gombrich, E. H. "Evidence of Images." In *Interpretation: Theory and Practice*. Ed. Charles S. Singleton. Baltimore, MD: John Hopkins University Press, 1969.

Goodman, Nelson. *Languages of Art*. Indianapolis, IN: Bobbs-Merrill, 1968.

Grinshpon, Yohanan. *Crisis and Knowledge: The Upaniṣadic Experience and Storytelling*. Oxford: Oxford University Press, 2003.

Gudaitė, Gražina. "Restoration of Continuity: Desperation or Hope in Facing the Consequences of Cultural Trauma." In *Confronting Cultural Trauma: Jungian Approaches to Understanding and Healing*, eds. Gražina Gudaitė and Murray Stein. New Orleans, LA: Spring Journal Books, 2014.

Gudaitė, Gražina. *Relationship with Authority and Sense of Personal Strength*. Vilnius: Vilnius University Press, 2016, in Lithuanian.

Gudaitė, Gražina. "Psychological Aftereffects of the Soviet Trauma and the Analytical Process." In *The Psychology of Extreme Traumatisation: The Aftermath of Political Repression*, ed. Danutė Gailienė. Vilnius: Akreta, 2005.

Guardini, Romano. *The End of the Modern World.* Wilmington, DE: ISI Books, 1998.

H

Hannah, Barbara. *Jung – His Life and Work. A Biographical Memoir.* Wilmette, IL: Chiron Publication, 1998.

Harris, Sam. *The End of Faith: Religion, Terror and the Future of Reason.* New York, NY: W.W. Norton, 2004.

Hart, David B. "Jung's Therapeutic Gnosticism." In *First Things* (January 2013, published by The Institute on Religion and Public Life, New York, NY).

Henderson, Joseph. *Cultural Attitudes in Psychological Perspective.* Toronto: Inner City Books, 1993.

Healy, Nan Savage. *Toni Wolff & C.G. Jung: A Collaboration.* Los Angeles, CA: Tiberius Press, 2017.

Hillman, James. *Healing Fiction.* Barrytown, NY: Station Hill Press, 1983.

Hillman, James. *Re-visioning Psychology.* New York, NY: Harper & Row, 1976.

Hillman, James. *Senex & Puer*, ed. Glen Slater. Putnam, CT: *Spring*, 2013.

Hillman, James and Sonu Shamdasani. *Lament of the Dead: Psychology After Jung's Red Book.* New York, NY: W.W. Norton, 2013.

Hitchens, Christopher. *God is Not Great: How Religion Poisons Everything.* New York, NY: Hachette Book Group, 2007.

Hölderlin, Friedrich. "Patmos." In *Selected Poems*, trans. David Constantine. Highgreen, UK: Bloodaxe Books, 1996.

Hoeller, Stephan A. *The Gnostic Jung and the Seven Sermons to the Dead.* Wheaton, IL: Quest, 1982.

Horkheimer, Max, and Theodore Adorno. *Dialectic of Enlightenment.* Palo Alto, CA: Stanford University Press, 2007.

Hyde, Lewis. *Trickster Makes This World: Mischief, Myth and Art.* New York, NY: Farrar, Straus and Giroux, 1998.

I

Ivanov, Vyacheslav, *Anima*. St. Petersburg: Faculty of Philology and Arts SPBU, 2009, in Russian.

J

Jantsch, Erich. *The Self-organizing Universe*. New York, NY: Pergamon, 1980.

Juergensmeyer, Mark. *Terror in the Mind of God: The Global Rise of Religious Violence*. Oakland, CA: University of California Press, 2017.

Jung, C.G. *Aion. Researches into the Phenomenology of the Self*. In *CW*, vol. 9/II. Princeton, NJ: Princeton University Press, 1959.

Jung, C.G. *Analytical Psychology. Notes of the Seminar given in 1925*, ed. W. McGuire. Princeton, NJ: Princeton University Press, 1991.

Jung, C.G. *Answer to Job*. In *CW*, vol. 11. Princeton, NJ: Princeton University Press, 1969.

Jung, C.G. "A Psychological Approach to the Dogma of the Trinity." In *CW*, vol. 11. Princeton, NJ: Princeton University Press, 1969.

Jung, C.G. "A Study in the Process of Individuation." In *CW*, vol. 9/I. Princeton, NJ: Princeton University Press, 1968.

Jung, C.G. "Archetypes of the Collective Unconscious." In *CW*, vol. 9/I. Princeton, NJ: Princeton University Press, 1968.

Jung, C.G. *C.G. Jung Speaking: Interviews and Encounters*. Ed. by William McGuire and R.F.C. Hull. Princeton, NJ: Princeton University Press, 1977.

Jung, C.G. "Commentary on 'The Secret of the Golden Flower.'" In *CW*, vol. 13. Princeton, NJ: Princeton University Press, 1967.

Jung, C.G. "Concerning the Archetypes with Special Reference to the Anima Concept." In *CW*, vol. 9/I. Princeton, NJ: Princeton University Press, 1968.

Jung, C.G. "Concerning Mandala Symbolism," In *CW*, vol. 9/I. Princeton, NJ: Princeton University Press, 1968.

Jung, C.G. "Conscious, Unconscious, and Individuation." In *CW*, vol. 9/I. Princeton, NJ: Princeton University Press, 1968.

Jung, C.G. "Cryptomnesia." In *CW*, vol. 1. Princeton, NJ: Princeton University Press, 1970.

Jung, C.G. *Dream Analysis: Notes of the Seminar Given in 1928–1930 by C.G. Jung*. Edited by William McGuire. Princeton: Princeton University Press, 1984.

Jung, C.G. *Introduction to Jungian Psychology. Notes of the Seminar on Analytical Psychology Given in 1925*. Princeton, NJ: Princeton University Press, 2012.

Jung, C.G. *Jung on Astrology*, selected and introduced by Keiron Le Grice and Safron Rossi. Abingdon, UK: Routledge, 2017.

Jung, C.G. "Jung and Religious Belief." In *CW*, vol. 18. Princeton, NJ: Princeton University Press, 1976.

Jung, C.G. "Marginalia on Contemporary Events." In *CW*, vol. 18. Princeton, NJ: Princeton University Press, 1976.

Jung, C.G. *Memories, Dreams, Reflections*, ed. Aniela Jaffé. New York, NY: Vintage Books, 1963.

Jung, C.G. *Mysterium Coniunctionis*. In *CW*, vol. 14. Princeton, NJ: Princeton University Press, 1963.

Jung, C.G. *Nietzsche's Zarathustra. Notes of the Seminar Given in 1934–1939*, 2 vols. Princeton, NJ: Princeton University Press, 1988.

Jung, C.G. "On the Psychology of the Trickster-Figure" In *CW*, vol. 9/I. Princeton, NJ: Princeton University Press, 1968.

Jung, C.G. "On the Psychology of the Unconscious." In *CW*, vol. 7. Princeton, NJ: Princeton University Press, 1966.

Jung, C.G. "On the Nature of the Psyche." In *CW*, vol. 8. Princeton, NJ: Princeton University Press, 1969.

Jung, C.G. "On Synchronicity." In *CW*, vol. 8. Princeton, NJ: Princeton University Press, 1969.

Jung, C.G. "Paracelsus as Spiritual Phenomenon." In *CW*, vol. 13. Princeton, NJ: Princeton University Press, 1967.

Jung, C.G. "Picasso." In *CW*, vol. 15. Princeton, NJ: Princeton University Press, 1966.

Jung, C.G. *Psychology and Alchemy*. In *CW*, vol. 12. Princeton, NJ: Princeton University Press, 1968.

Jung, C.G. "Psychology and Literature." In *CW*, vol. 15. Princeton, NJ: Princeton University Press, 1966.

Jung, C.G. "Psychology and Religion." In *CW*, vol. 11. Princeton, NJ: Princeton University Press, 1969.

Jung, C.G. *Psychological Types*. In *CW*, vol. 6. Princeton, NJ: Princeton University Press, 1971.

Jung, C.G. "Psychological Commentary on 'The Tibetan Book of the Great Liberation.'" In *CW*, vol. 11. Princeton, NJ: Princeton University Press, 1969.

Jung, C.G. "Psychotherapists or the Clergy." In *CW*, vol. 11. Princeton, NJ: Princeton University Press, 1969.

Jung, C.G. "Religion and Psychology: A Reply to Martin Buber." In *CW*, vol. 18. Princeton, NJ: Princeton University Press, 1976.

Jung, C.G. "Return to the Simple Life." In *CW*, vol. 18. Princeton, NJ: Princeton University Press, 1976.

Jung, C.G. *Symbols of Transformation*. In *CW*, vol. 5. Princeton, NJ: Princeton University Press, 1956.

Jung, C.G. "Symbols and the Interpretation of Dreams." In *CW*, vol. 18. Princeton, NJ: Princeton University Press, 1976.

Jung, C.G. "The Concept of the Collective Unconscious." In *CW*, vol. 9/I. Princeton, NJ: Princeton University Press, 1968.

Jung, C.G. "The Development of Personality." In *CW*, vol. 17. Princeton, NJ: Princeton University Press, 1964.

Jung, C.G. *The Red Book: Liber Novus. A Reader's Edition*, ed. Sonu Shamdasani, trans. John Peck, Mark Kyburz, and Sonu Shamdasani. New York, NY: W.W. Norton, 2012.

Jung, C.G. *The Red Book: Liber Novus*, ed. Sonu Shamdasani, trans. John Peck, Mark Kyburz, and Sonu Shamdasani. New York, NY: W.W. Norton, 2009.

Jung, C.G. "The Philosophical Tree." In *CW*, vol. 13. Princeton, NJ: Princeton University Press, 1967.

Jung, C.G. "The Psychological Aspects of the Mother Archetype." In *CW*, vol. 9/I. Princeton, NJ: Princeton University Press, 1968.

Jung, C.G. *The Psychology of Kundalini Yoga: Notes of the Seminar Given in 1932 by C.G. Jung*. Princeton, NJ: Princeton University Press, 1996.

Jung, C.G. "The Practical Use of Dream-Analysis." In *CW*, vol. 16. Princeton, NJ: Princeton University Press, 1966.

Jung, C.G. "The Psychology of Transference." In *CW*, vol. 16. Princeton, NJ: Princeton University Press, 1966.

Jung, C.G. "The Spirit Mercurius." In *CW*, vol. 13. Princeton, NJ: Princeton University Press, 1967.

Jung, C.G. "The Tavistock Lectures." In *CW*, vol. 18. Princeton, NJ: Princeton University Press, 1976.

Jung, C.G. "The Spiritual Problem of Modern Man." In *CW*, vol. 10. Princeton, NJ: Princeton University Press, 1964.

Jung, C.G. "The Transcendent Function." In *CW*, vol. 8. Princeton, NJ: Princeton University Press, 1969.

Jung, C.G. "The Undiscovered Self (Present and Future)." In *CW*, vol. 10. Princeton, NJ: Princeton University Press, 1964.

Jung, C.G. "Transformation Symbolism in the Mass." In *CW*, vol. 11. Princeton, NJ: Princeton University Press, 1969.

Jung, C.G. *Visions: Notes of the Seminar Given in 1930-1934*, 2 vols. Edited by Claire Douglas. Princeton, NJ: Princeton University Press, 1997.

Jung, C.G. *Wandlungen und Symbole der Libido. Beiträge zur Entwicklungsgeschichte des Denkens.* Leipzig und Wien: Franz Deuticke, 1938.

Jung, C.G. "Wotan." In *CW*, vol. 10. Princeton, NJ: Princeton University Press, 1964.

Junggren, Markus. *Russian Mephistopheles: The Life and Work of E. Medtner.* St. Petersburg: Academic Project, 2001, in Russian.

K

Kalinenko, Vsevolod and Madina Slutskaya. "Father of the People" versus "Enemies of the People": A Split-Father Complex as the Foundation for Collective Trauma in Russia." In *Confronting Cultural Trauma: Jungian Approaches to Understanding and Healing*, eds. Gražina Gudaitė and Murray Stein. New Orleans, LA: Spring Journal Books, 2014.

Kalsched, Donald. *The Inner World of Trauma. Archetypal Defenses of the Personal Spirit.* London: Routledge, 1996.

Kawai, Toshio. "*The Red Book* from a pre-modern perspective: the position of the ego, sacrifice and the dead." In *Journal of Analytical Psychology* 57, no. 3, 2012.

Khan, Hazrat Inayat. *The Sufi Message*, Vol. 1. Delhi: Motilal Banarsidass Publishers, 2011.

Kirsch, Thomas and George Hogenson, eds. *The Red Book: Reflections of C.G. Jung's Liber Novus*. London: Routledge, 2014.

Koch, Christopher. *The Year of Living Dangerously*. London: Michael Joseph, 1978.

Krystal, Henry. *Integration and Self-Healing: Affect, Trauma and Alexithymia*. Hillsdale, NJ: Analytic Press, 1988.

L

Lamble, David. "The Importance of Being Susan Sontag." *Bay Area Reporter* (San Francisco, CA), July 31, 2014, Film section.

Langwieler, Günter. "Jungs Abschied vom Kriegerhelden." In *Analytische Psychologie*, 46, 1, 2015.

Le Grice, Keiron. *The Archetypal Cosmos: Rediscovering the Gods in Myth, Science and Astrology*. Edinburgh: Floris Books, 2011.

Levinas, Emmanuel. "God and Philosophy." In Sean Hand, ed., *The Levinas Reader*. Oxford: Basil Blackwell, 1989.

Lewis, Pericles. *Cambridge Introduction to Modernism*. Cambridge: Cambridge University Press, 2007.

Lings, Martin. *What Is Sufism?* London: George Allen & Unwin, 1975.

Lipner, Julius. *The Face of Truth: A Study of Meaning and Metaphysics in the Vedantic Theology of Ramanuja*. Albany, NY: SUNY Press, 1986.

M

MacFarquhar, Larissa. "Last Call: A Buddhist Monk Confronts Japan's Suicide Culture," *The New Yorker*, June 24, 2013.

Maillard, Christine. *Au Coeur du Livre Rouge. Les Sept Sermons aux Morts. Aux Sources de la Pensée de C. G. Jung*. Paris: Editions Imago, 2017.

"Maitrayana Brahmana." *Sacred Books of the East,* Vol. 15, edited by F. Max Muller. Oxford at the Clarendon Press, 1884.

Malevich, Kazimir. *Articles, manifestos, theoretical essays and other works (1913-1929)*. Moscow: Gileya, 1995, in Russian.

Malik, Kenan. *From Fatwa to Jihad: The Rushdie Affair and its Aftermath*. New York, NY: Melville House, 2010.

McGann, Jerome. *The Romantic Ideology: A Critical Investigation*. Chicago, IL: University of Chicago Press, 1983.

McGilchrist, Iain. *The Divided Brain and the Search for Meaning* (Kindle Edition). New Haven, CT: Yale University Press, 2012.

McGregor Ross, Hugh. *The Gospel of Thomas*. London: Watkins Publishing, 2002.

Medtner, Emily. "The Portrait in the Frame of Mutual Recognition." In New Spring, 2001, in Russian.

Meier, C. A., ed. *Atom and Archetype. The Pauli/Jung Letters 1932-1958*. Princeton, NJ: Princeton University Press, 2001.

Mika, Elizabeth. "Who Goes Trump? Tyranny as a Triumph of Narcissism." In *The Dangerous Case of Donald Trump: 27 Psychiatrists and Mental Health Experts Assess a President*. Ed. Bandy X. Lee. New York, NY: St. Martin's Press, Kindle Edition, 2017.

Mogenson, Greg. *The Dove in the Consulting Room. Hysteria and the Anima in Bollas and Jung*. London: Routledge, 2004.

Moltmann, Jürgen. *Der gekreuzigte Gott*. Das Kreuz Christi als Grund und Kritik christlicher Theologie. Gütersloh: Gütersloher Verlagshaus, 1972.

More, Thomas. *Utopia*. Vol. 4 of *The Complete Works of St. Thomas More*. Edited by Edward Surtz and J. H. Hexter. New Haven, CT: Yale University Press, 1965.

Münkler, Herfried. *Der Wandel des Krieges. Von der Symmetrie zur Asymmetrie*. Weilerswist: Velbrück Wissenschaft, 2007.

Münkler, Herfried. *Der Große Krieg*. Berlin: Rowohlt Verlag, 2013.

N

Nelson, Victoria. *The Secret Life of Puppets*. Cambridge, MA: Harvard University Press, 2003.

Neumann, Erich. *The Origins and History of Consciousness*, trans. by R.F.C. Hull. Princeton, NJ: Princeton University Press, 2014.

Nietzsche, Friedrich. *The Portable Nietzsche*, ed. Walter Kaufmann. New York, NY: Viking Penguin, 1954.

Nietzsche, Friedrich. *The Gay Science*, trans. by Walter Kaufmann. New York, NY: Vintage Books, 1974.

Nietzsche, Friedrich. *The Gay Science*, trans. by Thomas Common. New York, NY: Dover Mineola, 2006.

Nietzsche, Friedrich. "On the Genealogy of Morals." In *Basic Writings of Nietzsche*, trans. by Walter Kaufmann. New York, Modern Library, 2000.

Nietzsche, Friedrich. *Thus Spoke Zarathustra*, trans. by Richard J. Hollingdale. New York, NY: Penguin, 1968.

Nietzsche, Friedrich. *Thus Spake Zarathustra*, trans. by Thomas Common. Edinburgh and London: T.N. Foulis, 1909.

Noll, Richard. *The Aryan Christ: The Secret Life of Carl Jung*. Moscow: Reflbook, 2006, in Russian.

O

Odajnyk, V. Walter. "Reflections on 'The Way of What is to Come.'" In *Psychological Perspectives* 53:4, October 2010.

Otto, Rudolf. *The Idea of the Holy*, trans. John W. Harvey. Oxford: Oxford University Press, 1950/1958.

P

Pagels, Elaine. *The Gnostic Gospels*. New York, NY: Vintage Books, 1989.

Panikkar, Raimon. "Christianity. The Christian Tradition." In *Opera Omnia*, Vol. III, part I. New York, NY: Orbis Book, 2015.

Papadopoulos, Renos K. "The other other: when the exotic other subjugates the familiar other." In *Journal of Analytical Psychology* 47, April 2002.

Paris, Ginette. *Pagan Grace: Dionysos, Hermes, and Goddess Memory in Daily Life*. Thompson, CT, Spring Publications, 2015, Kindle edition.

Pesic, Peter. *Seeing Double: Shared Identities in Physics, Philosophy, and Literature*. Cambridge, MA: MIT Press, 2002.

Porete, Marguerite. *The Mirror of Simple Souls*, ed. E.L. Babinsky. New York, NY: Paulist Press, 1993.

Pregadio, Fabrizio. *The Seal of the Unity of the Three*. Mountain View, CA: Golden Elixir Press, 2011.

R

Rancour-Laferriere, Daniel, ed. *Russian Literature and Psychoanalysis*. Amsterdam: John Benjamins Publishing Company, 1989.

Redfield, James M. "Purification." In *Nature and Culture in the Iliad: The Tragedy of Hector*. Durham and London: Duke University Press, 1994.

Reeves, Marjorie. *Joachim of Fiore and the Prophetic Future*. London: SPCK, 1976.

"Rgveda." *Sacred Books of the East*, Vol. 32, edited by F. Max Muller. Oxford at the Clarendon Press, 1882.

Rohde, Thomas. *Mythos Salome*. Leipzig: Reclam, 2000.

Richebächer, Sabine. *Sabina Spielrein. Eine fast grausame Liebe zur Wissenschaft*. Zürich: Dörlemann Verlag Zürich, 2005.

Rilke, Rainer Maria. "The First Elegy." In *Duino Elegies*, trans. Stephen Mitchell. Boston, MA: Shambhala Publications, 1992.

Rilke, Rainer Maria. "The Man Watching." In *Selected Poems of Rainer Maria Rilke*, trans. Robert Bly. New York, NY: Harper & Row, 1981.

Rothman, Joshua. "Daniel Dennett's Science of the Soul. A Philosopher's Life-long Quest to Understand the Making of the Mind." *The New Yorker*, March 27, 2017.

Rowland, Susan. *Jung as a Writer*. New York, NY and London: Routledge, 2005.

Rowland, Susan. *Remembering Dionysus: Revisioning Psychology and Literature in C.G. Jung and James Hillman*. New York, NY: Routledge, 2017.

S

Sandler, Joseph, Alex Holder, Christopher Dare, and Anna Ursula Dreher. *Freud's Models of the Mind: An Introduction*. London: Karnac Books, 1997.

Sanjek, Russell. *American Popular Music and Its Business: The First 400 Years, Volume III, From 1900 to 1984*. New York, NY: Oxford University Press, 1988.

"Śatapatha Brāhmaṇa." *Sacred Books of the East,* Vol. 12, edited by F. Max Muller. Oxford at the Clarendon Press, 1882.

Schneider, Michael S. "It Takes Two to Tango." In *A Beginner's Guide to Constructing the Universe.* New York, NY: Harper, 1995.

Schweizer, Andreas. "Red." In *Jung Journal Culture and Psyche,* 5, 3, 2011.

Seaford, Richard. *Dionysos.* London and New York: Routledge, 2006.

Segal, Robert A. "Reply to Sanford Drob." In *International Journal of Jungian Studies* 6, 1, 2014.

Segal, Robert A. "Review of Sanford Drob's *Reading the Red Book: An interpretive guide to C.G. Jung's Liber Novus.*" In *International Journal of Jungian Studies,* 5/3, 2013.

Shevelenko, Irina. *Modernism as Archaism.* Moscow: New Literary Observer 2017, in Russian.

Shishkin, Mikhail. *Russian Switzerland.* Moscow: Vagrius, 1999, in Russian.

Scholem, Gershom. "Der Nihilismus als Religiöses Phänomen." In Ritsema, Rudolf and Adolf Portmann, eds., *Norms in a changing world.* Eranos 43-1974. Leiden: E.J. Brill, 1977.

Sirotkin, S.F. *Sabina Spielrein. Materials for the Bibliography.* Izhevsk: ERGO, 2006, in Russian.

Solovyov, Vladimir. *Reading about God-Manhood.* St. Petersburg: Art Literature, 1994, in Russian.

Solovyov, Vladimir. *The Mythological Process in Ancient Paganism.* In *The Collected Works of Vladimir Sergeyevich Solovyov.* St. Petersburg: Education, 1911-1914, in Russian.

Sorge, Giovanni. "Die Theorie der 'Mana-Personlichkeit' im Jungschen Werk. Eine historische-hermeneutische Perspective." In *Recherches Germaniques,* 2014.

Sri Aurobindo. *The Integral Yoga.* Pondicherry, India: Sri Aurobindo Ashram, 1993.

Stein, Murray. *Jung's Map of the Soul: An Introduction.* Chicago, IL: Open Court, 1998.

Stein, Murray. "What Is *The Red Book* for analytical psychology?" In *Journal of Analytical Psychology,* 56/5, 2011.

Stein, Murray, "How to read *The Red Book* and why." In *Journal of Analytical Psychology, 57:3, 2012.*

Stevens, Wallace. *Collected Poetry and Prose.* New York, NY: Library of America, 1997.

Strieber, Whitley, and Jeffrey Kripal. *The Super Natural. A New Vision of the Unexplained.* New York, NY. Tarcher-Perigee, 2016.

T

Tarnas, Richard. "The Ideal and the Real: Saturn-Neptun e." In *The Birth of a New Discipline. Archai: The Journal of Archetypal Cosmology*, issue 1 (2009), 2nd edition, edited by Keiron Le Grice and Rod O'Neal. San Francisco, CA: Archai Press, 2011.

Tarnas, Richard. *Cosmos and Psyche: Intimations of a New World View.* New York, NY: Viking, 2006.

Taylor, Charles. *A Secular Age.* Cambridge, MA: The Belknap Press of Harvard University Press, 2007.

Teilhard de Chardin, Pierre. *The Heart of Matter*, trans. René Hague. San Diego, CA: Harcourt Brace, 1978.

The Early Upaniṣads. Annotated and translated by Patrick Olivelle. Oxford: Oxford University Press, 1998.

The Homeric Hymns. Translated by Charles Boer. Kingston, Rhode Island and London: Asphodel Press, 2006.

The New Oxford Annotated Bible with the Apocrypha. Revised Standard Edition. New York, NY: Oxford University Press, 1977.

Thoreau, Henry David. *Walden, Civil Disobedience, and Other Writings.* Ed. by William Rossi. New York, NY: W.W. Norton, 2008.

Tresan, David. "The Anima of the Analyst - Its Development." In *Gender and Soul in Psychotherapy*, edited by Nathan Schwartz-Salant and Murray Stein, The Chiron Clinical Series. Wilmette, IL: Chiron Publications, 1992.

U

Ulanov, Ann Belford. *Picturing God.* Einsiedeln, Switzerland: Daimon, 1986/2002.

V

Vėlius, Norbertas. *Wounded Wind. Lithuanian Mythological Tales.* Vilnius: Versus Aureus, 2012, in Lithuanian.

von Franz, Marie-Louise. "The Unknown Visitor in Fairy Tales and Dreams." In *Archetypal Dimensions of the Psyche.* London: Shambhala, 1999.

Vysheslavtsev, Boris. *The Ethics of Transfigured Eros.* Moscow: Republica, 1994, in Russian.

W

Wasserstrom, Stephen. *Religion after Religion.* Princeton, NJ: Princeton University Press, 1999.

Wertz, Kaitryn. *Inner Authority and Jung's Model of Individuation.* Boulder Association of Jungian Analysts, 2013.

Williams, W. C. *Kora in Hell: Improvisations.* New York, NY: New Directions, 1957.

Wilhelm, Richard. *The Secret of the Golden Flower.* London: Harcourt Brace & Company, 1931/1962.

Wilhelm, Richard. *The I Ching, or Book of Changes.* Trans. by Cary F. Baynes. Princeton, NJ: Princeton University Press, 1967.

Wirtz, Ursula. *Trauma and Beyond. The Mystery of Transformation.* New Orleans, LA: Spring Journal Books, 2014.

Wolff, Toni. *Structural Forms of the Feminine Psyche.* Translated by Paul Watzlawik. Privately printed for the Students Association of the C.G. Jung Institute of Zurich, 1956.

Woodman, A.J. *Tacitus Reviewed.* Oxford: Clarendon Press, 1998.

Y

Yeats, William Butler. "The Circus Animals' Desertion." In *The Poems of W. B. Yeats: A New Edition,* edited by Richard J. Finneran. New York, NY: Macmillan Publishing Company, 1933.

About the Contributors

Thomas Arzt, Ph.D., was educated in Physics and Mathematics at Giessen University (Germany). Research Assistant at Princeton University (USA) with the special focus on atomic, nuclear and plasma physics. 1988 Training and Certification in Initiatic Therapy at the "Schule für Initiatische Therapie" of Karlfried Graf Dürckheim and Maria Hippus-Gräfin Dürckheim in Todtmoos-Rütte (Black Forest, Germany). 2016 Training Program Continuing Education in Analytical Psychology at ISAP Zurich. Since 1999, President and Managing Director of *Strategic Advisors for Transformation GmbH*, an international consulting company for simulation technology, complexity management, and "Strategic Foresight under Deep Uncertainty" in Freiburg, Germany. He resides in Lenzkirch (Black Forest), Germany. Major publications: Various publications on Naturphilosophie in the context of Wolfgang Pauli und C. G. Jung: *Unus Mundus: Kosmos und Sympathie* (ed., 1992), *Philosophia Naturalis* (ed., 1996), *Wolfgang Pauli und der Geist der Materie* (ed., 2002). Editor of the German series *Studienreihe zur Analytischen Psychologie*. Web page: www.thomasarzt.de; contact email: thomasdrarzt@gmail.com.

John Beebe, M.D., a psychiatrist who specializes in psychotherapy, is an analyst member of the C.G. Jung Institute of San Francisco. He founded the Institute's quarterly publication, now titled *Jung Journal: Culture and Psyche*, and was the first U. S. coeditor of the London-based *Journal of Analytical Psychology*. He is the author of *Integrity in Depth* and of *Energies and Patterns in Psychological Type: The Reservoir of Consciousness*. He is co-author of *Psychiatric Treatment: Crisis, Clinic and Consultation*, and *The Presence of the Feminine in Film*. He is editor of *Terror, Violence, and the Impulse to Destroy* and *C.G. Jung's Aspects of the Masculine*, and co-editor of *The Question of Psychological Types: The Correspondence of C.G. Jung and Hans Schmid-Guisan, 1915-1916*. Contact email: JohnBeebe@msn.com.

Kate Burns is a Jungian analyst with a private practice in Houston, Texas. With an undergraduate degree in mathematics, she worked as a geophysicist until a downturn in the oil industry sent her back to school for a MBA from Rice University. A desire to explore spiritual issues at midlife led her to pursue a master's degree in counseling psychology, followed by studies into Jungian thought, which culminated in a diploma from the International School of Analytical Psychology, Zurich. She has taught classes at the Jung Center in Houston since 2005 and has devoted herself to the practice and philosophy of yoga since 2000. She currently serves on the board of directors of Jungians in Training Zurich, an organization dedicated to raising awareness about C.G. Jung, his life, and work. Contact email: k8burns@me.com.

QiRe Ching, MSW, MFA, currently teaches at the C.G. Jung Institute in San Francisco where he is a member analyst. He has been teaching Jung's *Red Book* in the candidate training program for several years. He has a background in community mental health in San Francisco, where he has focused on disenfranchised populations, particularly the LGBTQ and Asian communities with acute mental health issues. During the height of the AIDS epidemic, he was active in advocating for and creating services specifically targeted to the needs of Asian and Pacific Islanders with HIV and was a founding member of what is now the Asian Pacific Wellness Center. He received a MSW from San Francisco State University, and a MFA from the San Francisco Art Institute. In addition to his private practice, he has worked as an artist for over 40 years. Contact email: qrc8@att.net.

Al Collins, Ph.D., is a graduate of the University of Chicago (B.A., 1965) and the University of Texas at Austin (Ph.D., Indian Studies, 1976; Ph.D., Clinical Psychology, 1981). He has taught at Pacifica Graduate Institute, Alaska Pacific University, Northwestern University, and the Union Institute. He was formerly a Core Faculty member in East/West Psychology at the California Institute of Integral Studies. Al has recently edited (with Elaine Molchanov) an issue of *Spring Journal* on Jung and India. His work on cross-cultural depth psychology has been presented in over 40 conference papers and published in many journals, book chapters, and the volume *Fatherson: A Self Psychology of the Archetypal Masculine* (Chiron Publications, 1994). Al has lectured internationally on the archetype of the guru and is developing a critical theory of "culture, the better story." Contact email: nasadasin@gmail.com.

Lionel Corbett, M.D., trained in medicine and psychiatry in England and as a Jungian Analyst at the C.G. Jung Institute of Chicago. Dr. Corbett is a professor of depth psychology at Pacifica Graduate Institute, in Santa Barbara, California. His primary interests are the religious function of the psyche, especially the way in which personal religious experience is relevant to individual psychology; the development of psychotherapy as a spiritual practice; and the interface of Jungian psychology and contemporary psychoanalytic thought. He is the author of numerous professional papers and five books: *Psyche and the Sacred, The Religious Function of the Psyche, The Sacred Cauldron: Psychotherapy as a Spiritual Practice*, and *The Soul in Anguish: Psychotherapeutic Approaches to Suffering. Understanding Evil: A Guide for Psychotherapists* (in press). He is the coeditor of four volumes of collected papers: *Psyche's Stories; Depth Psychology, Meditations in the Field, Psychology at the Threshold*, and *Jung and Aging*. Contact email: corb@pacifica.edu.

John Dourley, Ph.D., is a graduate of the C.G. Jung institute, Zurich (1980), Fordham University, N.Y.C. (1971), St. Michael's College. Toronto (1966), St. Paul University, Ottawa (1964), and St. Patrick's College, Ottawa University (1957). He taught in the Religion Department of Carleton University, Ottawa, at St. Patrick's College, 1970-1979, and in the parent Department at Carleton until 2001. He is currently Professor emeritus. He has written extensively on Jung and religion and has three books with Routledge since 2008, *Paul Tillich, Carl Jung and the Recovery of Religion* (2008), *On Behalf of the Mystical Fool: Jung on the Religious Situation* (2009), and *Jung and His Mystics: In the End It All Comes to Nothing* (2014). He is a training and supervising analyst with the Ontario Association of Jungian Analysts (Toronto) and a member of AGAP (Zurich). He is a Catholic priest and member of the religious order, the Oblates of Mary Immaculate. Contact email: dourley@sympatico.ca.

Randy Fertel, Ph.D., is a professor of English who has taught at Harvard, Tulane, and the New School for Social Research. His award-winning 2011 memoir, *The Gorilla Man and the Empress of Steak*, unspools untold tales as he tries to make sense of his parents—and himself —in a colorful, food-obsessed New Orleans. Susan Rowland calls his award-winning new book, *A Taste for Chaos: The Art of Literary Improvisation* "important to Jungians because it says something new about archetypal dynamics and literature." He has been a contributor to NPR, Smithsonian, International Journal of Jungian Studies, Journal of Modern Literature, Kenyon Review, *Spring Journal*, Gastronomica, and Creative Nonfiction. He founded the Ridenhour Prizes for Courageous Truth-telling in 2003 in memory of his friend, My Lai whistleblower and investigative reporter Ron Ridenhour (ridenhour.org). He is Trustee Emeritus at The Kenyon Review. He was named one of Southern Living's "Southerners of the Year, 2017" as part of the team that created the New Orleans music history site *A Closer Walk* (acloserwalknola.com). The Fertel Foundation helped fund the James Hillman Uniform Edition. Web page: www.fertel.com; contact email: randy@fertel.com.

Keiron Le Grice, Ph.D., is a professor of depth psychology and chair of the Jungian and Archetypal Studies specialization at Pacifica Graduate Institute, Santa Barbara, California, where he teaches courses on archetypes, individuation, alchemy, synchronicity, and the history of depth psychology. He was educated at the University of Leeds, England (B.A. honors, Philosophy and Psychology) and the California Institute of Integral Studies(CIIS) in San Francisco (M.A., Ph.D., Philosophy and Religion). He is the author of four books—*The Archetypal Cosmos*, *Discovering Eris*, *The Rebirth of the Hero*, and *Archetypal Reflections*—and coeditor of *Jung on Astrology*. Keiron is a founding editor of *Archai: The Journal of Archetypal Cosmology*, now serving as senior editorial adviser, and cofounder of the Institute of Transpersonal and Archetypal Studies (www.itas-psychology.com). He has edited several books for Muswell Hill Press in London and has also taught for CIIS and Grof Transpersonal Training. Web page: www.keironlegrice.com; contact email: keironlegrice@gmail.com.

Grazina Gudaitė, Ph.D., is Professor of Psychology at Vilnius University and a Jungian psychoanalyst as well as President of the Lithuanian Association for Analytical Psychology. She is the author of several books and articles in Analytical Psychology, and coeditor with Murray Stein of *Confronting Cultural Trauma: Jungian Approaches to Understanding and Healing (2014)*. Among her recently published books *Relationship Towards Authority and Sense of Personal Strength* (2016). She has private practice in Vilnius and teaches in the Analyst Training program in Lithuania. Contact email: g.gudait@gmail.com.

Lev Khegai, Jungian Analyst, graduated from Moscow State University in 1991 and received analytic training through the IAAP program in Russia. He is a founding member and training analyst of Russian Society for Analytical Psychology, assistant professor at the Moscow Institute of Psychoanalysis, and has a private practice in Moscow. He has lectured widely throughout Russia and post-Soviet countries. His special interest is a Jungian view on religion, spirituality, philosophy, and culture. He has several publications in Russian. Web page: www.maap.pro; contact email: hegailev@gmail.com.

Günter Langwieler, Dr. med., Dipl. Psych., is a graduate of the C.G. Jung Institute of Berlin, Germany (1994), of the Free University of Berlin (Human Medicine, 1983) and the Technical University of Berlin (Psychology, 1976). He is a psychiatrist and psychoanalyst and has a private practice in Berlin. He is lecturing at the C.G. Jung Institute of Berlin and Zurich, internationally at several congresses of the IAAP and published articles about the Zarathustra Seminar of C.G. Jung, about *The Red Book*, about Jung's works in the 1930s and about active imagination. He is president of the C.G. Jung Society of Berlin. Contact email: Guenter.Langwieler@t-online.de.

Ann Chia-Yi Li, M.A., is originally from Taiwan, where she studied Chinese Literature and English Literature. She is a graduate of ISAP Zurich and maintains a private practice in Zurich. Ann has served in ISAP Program Committee since 2013 and initiated the International Taiwan MuShuei Jung Retreat Conference and Retreat in Taiwan since 2015. Her latest project is to cofound a systematic Jungian study program through the establishment of Analytical Psychology School SG in Singapore in 2016. Her special interests are Daoist alchemy, *The Red Book*, culture and trauma, active imagination and Zen meditation. Website: www.annli.space; contact email: annchiayi@gmail.com.

Romano Màdera, Ph.D., studied philosophy and graduated at the University of Milan (1971), specialized in sociology at the School for Sociology in Milan (1971-1973). He is now a professor of Moral Philosophy and Philosophical Practices at the University of Milano-Bicocca since 2001. Formerly he taught Philosophy of Social Sciences at the University of Calabria (1977-1982) and Philosophical Anthropology at Ca' Foscari University of Venice (1982-2001). He is a member of the Italian Association for Analytical Psychology (AIPA), the International Association for Analytical Psychology (IAAP), and the Analytical Laboratory of Images (LAI), a professional association of sandplay analysts. He is the founder of the Open Seminars of Philosophical Practices (University of Venice, University of Milano-Bicocca and other cities) and of Philo, School of Philosophical Practices. He also founded SABOF (Society for Biographic Analysis Philosophically Oriented). His writings include: *Identità e feticismo* (1977), *Dio il Mondo* (1989), *L'alchimia ribelle* (1997), *C.G. Jung. Biografia e teoria* (1998), *L'animale visionario* (1999), with L.V. Tarca *La filosofia come stile di vita* (2003) translated into English as *Philosophy as Life Path*. *Introduction to Philosophical Practices* (2007), *Il nudo piacere di vivere* (2006), *La carta del senso* (2012), *Una filosofia per l'anima* (2013) partly translated into English as *Approaching the Navel of the Darkened Soul*. *Depth Psychology and Philosophical Practices* (2013), "The Missed Link. From Jung to Hadot and Vice Versa," in *Spring*, Vol. 92, *Spring* 2015, *C.G. Jung. L'Opera al Rosso*, Feltrinelli, Milano 2016. Contact email: romano.madera@libero.it.

Joerg Rasche, Dr. med., Jungian Analyst trained in Berlin and Zurich (Sandplay Therapy with Dora Kalff) and psychiatrist for children, private practice in Berlin. Vice president of the German Jungian Association DGAP and former vice president of IAAP. Also, a trained musician, he published many papers and some books about politics, mythology, music, sandplay therapy and Analytical Psychology and is in the board of some journals. Joerg presented many times in the former Cortona Conference. He is teaching in Central European countries like Poland and Ukraine, training analyst for IAAP, and was honored for his engagement for people's reconciliation in Poland by the Polish president with the Golden Cross of Merit. He gives concert-lectures all over the world. He is married and has three adult children. Latest book: *Europe's Many Souls. Exploring Cultural Complexes and Identities, Spring* 2016 (with Tom Singer, ed.). Contact email: joergrasche@gmx.de.

Noa Schwartz Feuerstein, M.A., is a graduate of the Israel Institute of Jungian Psychology (2007) and of the Department of Clinical Psychology in Bar-Ilan University (M.A., 1995), and a Ph.D. student in the Comparative Religions and Indian Studies Department in the Hebrew University in Jerusalem. Her dissertation, "On Horror and Beyond: C.G. Jung's Relation to India and Upanishadic Wisdom," relives the disrupted dialogue Jung had with the East by rereading the Upanishadic literature in light of Jung's reservations. She is active in teaching and supervising in the Israel Institute of Jungian Psychology, in the department of Jungian Advanced Studies in Bar-Ilan University, and in the School for Psychotherapy in Hebrew University's counseling-services. She has a private practice in Jerusalem and Tel Aviv. She lives in Jerusalem, Israel. Contact email: noafs@walla.co.il.

J. Gary Sparks is a graduate of the C.G. Jung Institute Zurich (1982), the Pacific School of Religion (1974, M.A., M.Div.), and Bucknell University (1970, B.S.E.E.). He is the author of *At the Heart of Matter: Synchronicity and Jung's Spiritual Testament* (2007), *Valley of Diamonds: Adventures in Number and Time with Marie-Louise von Franz* (2010), *Jung and Arnold Toynbee: The Social Meaning of Inner Work* (2017). His interests include the nature of feminine consciousness; the healthy purpose of darkness and despair; developing the creative imagination; the relationship between an individual and society; and the parallels between the new physics and Jungian psychology. An avid national and international lecturer, he has maintained an analytic practice in Indianapolis, Indiana, since 1983. Web pages: www.jgsparks.net and www.jungandpauli.net; contact email: jgs@jgsparks.net.

Murray Stein, Ph.D., studied as an undergraduate at Yale University (B.A. in English) and attended graduate student at Yale Divinity School (M.Div.) and the University of Chicago (Ph.D. in Religion and Psychological Studies). He trained as a Jungian psychoanalyst at the C.G. Jung Institute of Zurich. From 1976 to 2003, he was a training analyst at the C.G. Jung Institute of Chicago, of which he was a founding member and President from 1980 to 1985. In 1989, he joined the Executive Committee of IAAP as Honorary Secretary for Dr. Thomas Kirsch as President (1989-1995) and served as President of the IAAP from 2001 to 2004. He was president of ISAP Zurich 2008-2012 and is currently a training and supervising analyst there. He resides in Goldiwil (Thun), Switzerland. His special interests are psychotherapy and spirituality, methods of Jungian psychoanalytic treatment, and the individuation process. Major publications: *In Midlife, Jung's Map of the Soul, Minding the Self, Soul: Retrieval and Treatment, Transformation: Emergence of the Self*, and *Outside, Inside and All Around*. Web page: www.murraystein.com; contact email: murraywstein@gmail.com.

David Tacey, Ph.D., is an interdisciplinary scholar who works in the fields of continental philosophy, spirituality studies, Analytical Psychology, literature and sociology. David grew up in central Australia alongside Aboriginal cultures and has a lifelong interest in indigenous issues. He is a specialist in Jungian studies and a founding member of the International Association of Jungian Studies. His books in this field include: *Gods and Diseases, How to Read Jung, The Jung Reader, The Idea of the Numinous; Jung and the New Age, Remaking Men*, and *The Darkening Spirit: Jung, Spirituality, Religion*. His most recent work is *Religion as Metaphor*, a Jungian reading of the Jesus story. His books have been published internationally and translated into Chinese, Korean, Spanish, Portuguese and French. He is Emeritus Professor of Humanities at La Trobe University, Melbourne; and Research Professor of Public Theology at Charles Sturt University, Canberra. Education, career and bibliography: https://en.wikipedia.org/wiki/David_Tacey; contact email: D.Tacey@latrobe.edu.au.

Ann Belford Ulanov, Ph.D., studied philosophy at Harvard (B.A.), theology at Union Theological Seminary (M.Div.) and Psychiatry and Religion there as well (Ph.D.) and has received three Honorary Degrees (L.H.D.). She is the Christiane Brooks Johnson Professor of Psychology and Religion Emerita at Union Theological Seminary, a psychoanalyst in private practice in New York City, a member of the Jungian Psychoanalytic Association and of the International Association for Analytical Psychology, and serves on the Editorial Advisory Board of the *Journal of Analytical Psychology*. Author of six books with her late husband, Barry Ulanov, among which are *Religion and the Unconscious*; *The Healing Imagination*; *The Witch and the Clown: Archetypes of Human Sexuality*, and by herself author of 16 books, among which are *The Female Ancestors of Christ*, *The Wizards' Gate: Picturing Consciousness*, *The Functioning Transcendent*, *Finding Space: Winnicott, God, and Psychic Reality*, *Madness & Creativity*; *Knots and Their Untying*; *The Psychoid, Soul and Psyche: Piercing Space-Time Barriers*. She is a graduate of the C.G. Jung Institute of New York and recipient of many awards among which are: the Oskar Pfister Award from the American Psychiatric Association for Distinguished Work in Psychology and Religion; the Gradiva Award for best book in Psychology and Religion 2002; the Vision Award from the National association for the Advancement of Psychoanalysis. Contact email: ann.ulanov@gmail.com.

CPSIA information can be obtained
at www.ICGtesting.com
Printed in the USA
FFHW010431140219
50506566-55775FF